SUPERINTELLIGENCE

Paths, Dangers, Strategies

NICK BOSTROM

Director, Future of Humanity Institute
Director, Strategic Artificial Intelligence Research Centre
Professor, Faculty of Philosophy & Oxford Martin School
University of Oxford

OXFORD
UNIVERSITY PRESS

OXFORD

UNIVERSITY PRESS

Great Clarendon Street, Oxford, OX2 6DP,
United Kingdom

Oxford University Press is a department of the University of Oxford.
It furthers the University's objective of excellence in research, scholarship,
and education by publishing worldwide. Oxford is a registered trade mark of
Oxford University Press in the UK and in certain other countries

© Nick Bostrom 2014

The moral rights of the author have been asserted

First published in 2014
First published in paperback in 2016
Reprinted with corrections 2017

Published in the United States of America by Oxford University Press
198 Madison Avenue, New York, NY 10016, United States of America

British Library Cataloguing in Publication Data

Data available

Library of Congress Control Number: 2015956648

ISBN 978-0-19-873983-8

Printed in Great Britain by
Clays Ltd, Elcograf S.p.A.

The Unfinished Fable of the Sparrows

It was the nest-building season, but after days of long hard work, the sparrows sat in the evening glow, relaxing and chirping away.

"We are all so small and weak. Imagine how easy life would be if we had an owl who could help us build our nests!"

"Yes!" said another. "And we could use it to look after our elderly and our young."

"It could give us advice and keep an eye out for the neighborhood cat," added a third.

Then Pastus, the elder-bird, spoke: "Let us send out scouts in all directions and try to find an abandoned owlet somewhere, or maybe an egg. A crow chick might also do, or a baby weasel. This could be the best thing that ever happened to us, at least since the opening of the Pavilion of Unlimited Grain in yonder backyard."

The flock was exhilarated, and sparrows everywhere started chirping at the top of their lungs.

Only Scronkfinkle, a one-eyed sparrow with a fretful temperament, was unconvinced of the wisdom of the endeavor. Quoth he: "This will surely be our undoing. Should we not give some thought to the art of owl-domestication and owl-taming first, before we bring such a creature into our midst?"

Replied Pastus: "Taming an owl sounds like an exceedingly difficult thing to do. It will be difficult enough to find an owl egg. So let us start there. After we have succeeded in raising an owl, then we can think about taking on this other challenge."

"There is a flaw in that plan!" squeaked Scronkfinkle; but his protests were in vain as the flock had already lifted off to start implementing the directives set out by Pastus.

Just two or three sparrows remained behind. Together they began to try to work out how owls might be tamed or domesticated. They soon realized that Pastus had been right: this was an exceedingly difficult challenge, especially in the absence of an actual owl to practice on. Nevertheless they pressed on as best they could, constantly fearing that the flock might return with an owl egg before a solution to the control problem had been found.

It is not known how the story ends, but the author dedicates this book to Scronkfinkle and his followers.

PREFACE

Inside your cranium is the thing that does the reading. This thing, the human brain, has some capabilities that the brains of other animals lack. It is to these distinctive capabilities that we owe our dominant position on the planet. Other animals have stronger muscles and sharper claws, but we have cleverer brains. Our modest advantage in general intelligence has led us to develop language, technology, and complex social organization. The advantage has compounded over time, as each generation has built on the achievements of its predecessors.

If some day we build machine brains that surpass human brains in general intelligence, then this new superintelligence could become very powerful. And, as the fate of the gorillas now depends more on us humans than on the gorillas themselves, so the fate of our species would depend on the actions of the machine superintelligence.

We do have one advantage: we get to build the stuff. In principle, we could build a kind of superintelligence that would protect human values. We would certainly have strong reason to do so. In practice, the control problem—the problem of how to control what the superintelligence would do—looks quite difficult. It also looks like we will only get one chance. Once unfriendly superintelligence exists, it would prevent us from replacing it or changing its preferences. Our fate would be sealed.

In this book, I try to understand the challenge presented by the prospect of superintelligence, and how we might best respond. This is quite possibly the most important and most daunting challenge humanity has ever faced. And—whether we succeed or fail—it is probably the last challenge we will ever face.

It is no part of the argument in this book that we are on the threshold of a big breakthrough in artificial intelligence, or that we can predict with any precision when such a development might occur. It seems somewhat likely that it will happen sometime in this century, but we don't know for sure. The first couple of chapters do discuss possible pathways and say something about the question of timing. The bulk of the book, however, is about what happens after. We study the kinetics of an intelligence explosion, the forms and powers of superintelligence, and the strategic choices available to a superintelligent agent that attains a decisive advantage. We then shift our focus to the control problem and ask what we could do to shape the initial conditions so as to achieve a survivable and beneficial outcome. Toward the end of the book, we zoom out and contemplate the larger picture that emerges from our investigations. Some suggestions are offered on what ought to be done now to increase our chances of avoiding an existential catastrophe later.

This has not been an easy book to write. I hope the path that has been cleared will enable other investigators to reach the new frontier more swiftly and conveniently, so that they can arrive there fresh and ready to join the work to further expand the reach of our comprehension. (And if the way that has been made is a little bumpy and bendy, I hope that reviewers, in judging the result, will not underestimate the hostility of the terrain *ex ante*!)

This has not been an easy book to write: I have tried to make it an easy book to read, but I don't think I have quite succeeded. When writing, I had in mind as the target audience an earlier time-slice of myself, and I tried to produce a kind of book that I would have enjoyed reading. This could prove a narrow demographic. Nevertheless, I think that the content should be accessible to many people, if they put some thought into it and resist the temptation to instantaneously misunderstand each new idea by assimilating it with the most similar-sounding cliché available in their cultural larders. Non-technical readers should not be discouraged by the occasional bit of mathematics or specialized vocabulary, for it is always possible to glean the main point from the surrounding explanations. (Conversely, for those readers who want more of the nitty-gritty, there is quite a lot to be found among the endnotes.[1])

Many of the points made in this book are probably wrong.[2] It is also likely that there are considerations of critical importance that I fail to take into account, thereby invalidating some or all of my conclusions. I have gone to some length to indicate nuances and degrees of uncertainty throughout the text—encumbering it with an unsightly smudge of "possibly," "might," "may," "could well," "it seems," "probably," "very likely," "almost certainly." Each qualifier has been placed where it is carefully and deliberately. Yet these topical applications of epistemic modesty are not enough; they must be supplemented here by a systemic admission of uncertainty and fallibility. This is not false modesty: for while I believe that my book is likely to be seriously wrong and misleading, I think that the alternative views that have been presented in the literature are substantially worse—including the default view, or "null hypothesis," according to which we can for the time being safely or reasonably ignore the prospect of superintelligence.

ACKNOWLEDGMENTS

The membrane that has surrounded the writing process has been fairly permeable. Many concepts and ideas generated while working on the book have been allowed to seep out and have become part of a wider conversation; and, of course, numerous insights originating from the outside while the book was underway have been incorporated into the text. I have tried to be somewhat diligent with the citation apparatus, but the influences are too many to fully document.

For extensive discussions that have helped clarify my thinking I am grateful to a large set of people, including Sam Altman, Dario Amodei, Ross Andersen, Stuart Armstrong, Owen Cotton-Barratt, Nick Beckstead, Yoshua Bengio, David Chalmers, Paul Christiano, Milan Ćirković, Andrew Critch, Daniel Dennett, David Deutsch, Daniel Dewey, Thomas Dietterich, Eric Drexler, David Duvenaud, Peter Eckersley, Amnon Eden, Oren Etzioni, Owain Evans, Benja Fallenstein, Alex Flint, Carl Frey, Zoubin Ghahramani, Ian Goldin, Katja Grace, Roger Grosse, Tom Gunter, J. Storrs Hall, Robin Hanson, Demis Hassabis, Geoffrey Hinton, James Hughes, Marcus Hutter, Garry Kasparov, Marcin Kulczycki, Patrick LaVictoire, Shane Legg, Moshe Looks, Willam MacAskill, Eric Mandelbaum, Gary Marcus, James Martin, Lillian Martin, Roko Mijic, Vincent Mueller, Elon Musk, Seán Ó hÉigeartaigh, Christopher Olah, Toby Ord, Laurent Orseau, Michael Osborne, Larry Page, Dennis Pamlin, Derek Parfit, David Pearce, Huw Price, Guy Ravine, Martin Rees, Bill Roscoe, Francesca Rossi, Stuart Russell, Anna Salamon, Lou Salkind, Anders Sandberg, Julian Savulescu, Jürgen Schmidhuber, Bart Selman, Nicholas Shackel, Murray Shanahan, Noel Sharkey, Carl Shulman, Peter Singer, Nate Soares, Dan Stoicescu, Mustafa Suleyman, Jaan Tallinn, Alexander Tamas, Jessica Taylor, Max Tegmark, Roman Yampolskiy, and Eliezer Yudkowsky.

For especially detailed comments, I am grateful to Milan Ćirković, Daniel Dewey, Owain Evans, Nick Hay, Keith Mansfield, Luke Muehlhauser, Toby Ord, Jess Riedel, Anders Sandberg, Murray Shanahan, and Carl Shulman. For advice or research help with different parts I want to thank Stuart Armstrong, Daniel Dewey, Eric Drexler, Alexandre Erler, Rebecca Roache, and Anders Sandberg.

For help with preparing the manuscript, I am thankful to Caleb Bell, Malo Bourgon, Robin Brandt, Lance Bush, Cathy Douglass, Alexandre Erler, John King, Kristian Rönn, Susan Rogers, Kyle Scott, Andrew Snyder-Beattie, Cecilia Tilli, and Alex Vermeer. I want particularly to thank my editor Keith Mansfield for his plentiful encouragement throughout the project.

My apologies to everybody else who ought to have been remembered here.

Finally, a most fond thank you to funders, friends, and family: without your backing, this work would not have been done.

CONTENTS

LISTS OF FIGURES, TABLES, AND BOXES

List of Figures

List of Tables

List of Boxes

CHAPTER 1

Past developments and present capabilities

We begin by looking back. History, at the largest scale, seems to exhibit a sequence of distinct growth modes, each much more rapid than its predecessor. This pattern has been taken to suggest that another (even faster) growth mode might be possible. However, we do not place much weight on this observation—this is not a book about "technological acceleration" or "exponential growth" or the miscellaneous notions sometimes gathered under the rubric of "the singularity." Next, we review the history of artificial intelligence. We then survey the field's current capabilities. Finally, we glance at some recent expert opinion surveys, and contemplate our ignorance about the timeline of future advances.

Growth modes and big history

A mere few million years ago our ancestors were still swinging from the branches in the African canopy. On a geological or even evolutionary timescale, the rise of *Homo sapiens* from our last common ancestor with the great apes happened swiftly. We developed upright posture, opposable thumbs, and—crucially—some relatively minor changes in brain size and neurological organization that led to a great leap in cognitive ability. As a consequence, humans can think abstractly, communicate complex thoughts, and culturally accumulate information over the generations far better than any other species on the planet.

These capabilities let humans develop increasingly efficient productive technologies, making it possible for our ancestors to migrate far away from the rainforest and the savanna. Especially after the adoption of agriculture, population densities rose along with the total size of the human population. More people meant more ideas; greater densities meant that ideas could spread more readily and that some individuals could devote themselves to developing specialized skills. These developments increased the *rate of growth* of economic productivity and technological capacity. Later developments, related to the Industrial Revolution, brought about a second, comparable step change in the rate of growth.

Such changes in the rate of growth have important consequences. A few hundred thousand years ago, in early human (or hominid) prehistory, growth was so slow that it took on the order of one million years for human productive capacity to increase sufficiently to sustain an additional one million individuals living at subsistence level. By 5000 BC, following the Agricultural Revolution, the rate of growth had increased to the point where the same amount of growth took just two centuries. Today, following the Industrial Revolution, the world economy grows on average by that amount every ninety minutes.[1]

Even the present rate of growth will produce impressive results if maintained for a moderately long time. If the world economy continues to grow at the same pace as it has over the past fifty years, then the world will be some 4.8 times richer by 2050 and about 34 times richer by 2100 than it is today.[2]

Yet the prospect of continuing on a steady exponential growth path pales in comparison to what would happen if the world were to experience another step change in the *rate of growth* comparable in magnitude to those associated with the Agricultural Revolution and the Industrial Revolution. The economist Robin Hanson estimates, based on historical economic and population data, a characteristic world economy doubling time for Pleistocene hunter–gatherer society of 224,000 years; for farming society, 909 years; and for industrial society, 6.3 years.[3] (In Hanson's model, the present epoch is a mixture of the farming and the industrial growth modes—the world economy as a whole is not yet growing at the 6.3-year doubling rate.) If another such transition to a different growth mode were to occur, and it were of similar magnitude to the previous two, it would result in a new growth regime in which the world economy would double in size about every two weeks.

Such a growth rate seems fantastic by current lights. Observers in earlier epochs might have found it equally preposterous to suppose that the world economy would one day be doubling several times within a single lifespan. Yet that is the extraordinary condition we now take to be ordinary.

The idea of a coming technological singularity has by now been widely popularized, starting with Vernor Vinge's seminal essay and continuing with the writings of Ray Kurzweil and others.[4] The term "singularity,"

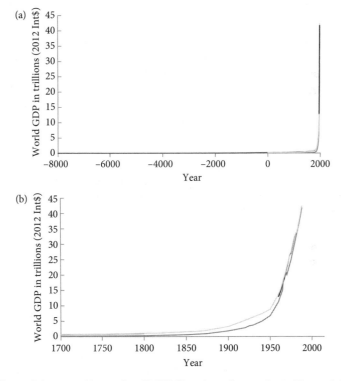

Figure 1 Long-term history of world GDP. Plotted on a linear scale, the history of the world economy looks like a flat line hugging the x-axis, until it suddenly spikes vertically upward. (a) Even when we zoom in on the most recent 10,000 years, the pattern remains essentially one of a single 90° angle. (b) Only within the past 100 years or so does the curve lift perceptibly above the zero-level. (The different lines in the plot correspond to different data sets, which yield slightly different estimates.[5])

however, has been used confusedly in many disparate senses and has accreted an unholy (yet almost millenarian) aura of techno-utopian connotations.[6] Since most of these meanings and connotations are irrelevant to our argument, we can gain clarity by dispensing with the "singularity" word in favor of more precise terminology.

The singularity-related idea that interests us here is the possibility of an *intelligence explosion*, particularly the prospect of machine superintelligence. There may be those who are persuaded by growth diagrams like the ones in Figure 1 that another drastic change in growth mode is in the cards, comparable to the Agricultural or Industrial Revolution. These folk may then reflect that it is hard to conceive of a scenario in which the world economy's doubling time shortens to mere weeks that does not involve the creation of minds that are much faster and more efficient than the familiar biological kind. However, the case for taking seriously the prospect of a machine intelligence revolution need not rely on curve-fitting exercises or extrapolations from past economic growth. As we shall see, there are stronger reasons for taking heed.

Great expectations

Machines matching humans in general intelligence—that is, possessing common sense and an effective ability to learn, reason, and plan to meet complex information-processing challenges across a wide range of natural and abstract domains—have been expected since the invention of computers in the 1940s. At that time, the advent of such machines was often placed some twenty years into the future.[7] Since then, the expected arrival date has been receding at a rate of one year per year; so that today, futurists who concern themselves with the possibility of artificial general intelligence still often believe that intelligent machines are a couple of decades away.[8]

Two decades is a sweet spot for prognosticators of radical change: near enough to be attention-grabbing and relevant, yet far enough to make it possible to suppose that a string of breakthroughs, currently only vaguely imaginable, might by then have occurred. Contrast this with shorter timescales: most technologies that will have a big impact on the world in five or ten years from now are already in limited use, while technologies that will reshape the world in less than fifteen years probably exist as laboratory prototypes. Twenty years may also be close to the typical duration remaining of a forecaster's career, bounding the reputational risk of a bold prediction.

From the fact that some individuals have overpredicted artificial intelligence in the past, however, it does not follow that AI is impossible or will never be developed.[9] The main reason why progress has been slower than expected is that the technical difficulties of constructing intelligent machines have proved greater than the pioneers foresaw. But this leaves open just how great those difficulties are and how far we now are from overcoming them. Sometimes a problem that initially looks hopelessly complicated turns out to have a surprisingly simple solution (though the reverse is probably more common).

In the next chapter, we will look at different paths that may lead to human-level machine intelligence. But let us note at the outset that however many stops there are between here and human-level machine intelligence, the latter is not the final destination. The next stop, just a short distance farther along the tracks, is superhuman-level machine intelligence. The train might not pause or even decelerate at Humanville Station. It is likely to swoosh right by.

The mathematician I. J. Good, who had served as chief statistician in Alan Turing's code-breaking team in World War II, might have been the first to enunciate the essential aspects of this scenario. In an oft-quoted passage from 1965, he wrote:

Let an ultraintelligent machine be defined as a machine that can far surpass all the intellectual activities of any man however clever. Since the design of machines is one of these intellectual activities, an ultraintelligent machine could design even better machines; there would then unquestionably be an "intelligence explosion," and the intelligence of man would be left far behind. Thus the first ultraintelligent machine is the last invention that man need ever make, provided that the machine is docile enough to tell us how to keep it under control.[10]

It may seem obvious now that major existential risks would be associated with such an intelligence explosion, and that the prospect should therefore be examined with the utmost seriousness even if it were known (which it is not) to have but a moderately small probability of coming to pass. The pioneers of artificial intelligence, however, notwithstanding their belief in the imminence of human-level AI, mostly did not contemplate the possibility of greater-than-human AI. It is as though their speculation muscle had so exhausted itself in conceiving the radical possibility of machines reaching human intelligence that it could not grasp the corollary—that machines would subsequently become superintelligent.

The AI pioneers for the most part did not countenance the possibility that their enterprise might involve risk.[11] They gave no lip service—let alone serious thought—to any safety concern or ethical qualm related to the creation of artificial minds and potential computer overlords: a lacuna that astonishes even against the background of the era's not-so-impressive standards of critical technology assessment.[12] We must hope that by the time the enterprise eventually does become feasible, we will have gained not only the technological proficiency to set off an intelligence explosion but also the higher level of mastery that may be necessary to make the detonation survivable.

But before we turn to what lies ahead, it will be useful to take a quick glance at the history of machine intelligence to date.

Seasons of hope and despair

In the summer of 1956 at Dartmouth College, ten scientists sharing an interest in neural nets, automata theory, and the study of intelligence convened for a six-week workshop. This Dartmouth Summer Project is often regarded as the cockcrow of artificial intelligence as a field of research. Many of the participants would later be recognized as founding figures. The optimistic outlook among the delegates is reflected in the proposal submitted to the Rockefeller Foundation, which provided funding for the event:

We propose that a 2 month, 10 man study of artificial intelligence be carried out.... The study is to proceed on the basis of the conjecture that every aspect of learning or any other feature of intelligence can in principle be so precisely described that a machine can be made to simulate it. An attempt will be made to find how to make machines that use language, form abstractions and concepts, solve kinds of problems now reserved for humans, and improve themselves. We think that a significant advance can be made in one or more of these problems if a carefully selected group of scientists work on it together for a summer.

In the six decades since this brash beginning, the field of artificial intelligence has been through periods of hype and high expectations alternating with periods of setback and disappointment.

The first period of excitement, which began with the Dartmouth meeting, was later described by John McCarthy (the event's main organizer) as the "Look, Ma, no hands!" era. During these early days, researchers built systems designed to refute claims of the form "No machine could ever do X!" Such skeptical claims were common at the time. To counter them, the AI researchers created small systems that achieved X in a "microworld" (a well-defined, limited domain that enabled a pared-down version of the performance to be demonstrated), thus providing a proof of concept and showing that X could, in principle, be done by machine. One such early system, the Logic Theorist, was able to prove most of the theorems in the second chapter of Whitehead and Russell's *Principia Mathematica*, and even came up with one proof that was much more elegant than the original, thereby debunking the notion that machines could "only think numerically" and showing that machines were also able to do deduction and to invent logical proofs.[13] A follow-up program, the General Problem Solver, could in principle solve a wide range of formally specified problems.[14] Programs that could solve calculus problems typical of first-year college courses, visual analogy problems of the type that appear in some IQ tests, and simple verbal algebra problems were also written.[15] The Shakey robot (so named because of its tendency to tremble during operation) demonstrated how logical reasoning could be integrated with perception and used to plan and control physical activity.[16] The ELIZA program showed how a computer could impersonate a Rogerian psychotherapist.[17] In the mid-1970s, the program SHRDLU showed how a simulated robotic arm in a simulated world of geometric blocks could follow instructions and answer questions in English that were typed in by a user.[18] In later decades, systems would be created that demonstrated that machines could compose music in the style of various classical composers, outperform junior doctors in certain clinical diagnostic tasks, drive cars autonomously, and make patentable inventions.[19] There has even been an AI that cracked original jokes.[20] (Not that its level of humor was high—"What do you get when you cross an *optic* with a *mental object*? An *eye*-dea"—but children reportedly found its puns consistently entertaining.)

The methods that produced successes in the early demonstration systems often proved difficult to extend to a wider variety of problems or to harder problem instances. One reason for this is the "combinatorial explosion" of possibilities that must be explored by methods that rely on something like exhaustive search. Such methods work well for simple instances of a problem, but fail when things get a bit more complicated. For instance, to prove a theorem that has a 5-line long proof in a deduction system with one inference rule and 5 axioms, one could simply enumerate the 3,125 possible combinations and check each one to see if it delivers the intended conclusion. Exhaustive search would also work for 6- and 7-line proofs. But as the task becomes more difficult, the method of exhaustive search soon runs into trouble. Proving a theorem with a 50-line proof does not take ten times longer than proving a theorem that has a 5-line proof: rather, if one uses exhaustive search, it requires combing through $5^{50} \approx 8.9 \times 10^{34}$ possible sequences—which is computationally infeasible even with the fastest supercomputers.

To overcome the combinatorial explosion, one needs algorithms that exploit structure in the target domain and take advantage of prior knowledge by using heuristic search, planning, and flexible abstract representations—capabilities that were poorly developed in the early AI systems. The performance of these early systems also suffered because of poor methods for handling uncertainty, reliance on brittle and ungrounded symbolic representations, data scarcity, and severe hardware limitations on memory capacity and processor speed. By the mid-1970s, there was a growing awareness of these problems. The realization that many AI projects could never make good on their initial promises led to the onset of the first "AI winter": a period of retrenchment, during which funding decreased and skepticism increased, and AI fell out of fashion.

A new springtime arrived in the early 1980s, when Japan launched its Fifth-Generation Computer Systems Project, a well-funded public–private partnership that aimed to leapfrog the state of the art by developing a massively parallel computing architecture that would serve as a platform for artificial intelligence. This occurred at peak fascination with the Japanese "post-war economic miracle," a period when Western government and business leaders anxiously sought to divine the formula behind Japan's economic success in hope of replicating the magic at home. When Japan decided to invest big in AI, several other countries followed suit.

The ensuing years saw a great proliferation of *expert systems*. Designed as support tools for decision makers, expert systems were rule-based programs that made simple inferences from a knowledge base of facts, which had been elicited from human domain experts and painstakingly hand-coded in a formal language. Hundreds of these expert systems were built. However, the smaller systems provided little benefit, and the larger ones proved expensive to develop, validate, and keep updated, and were generally cumbersome to use. It was impractical to acquire a standalone computer just for the sake of running one program. By the late 1980s, this growth season, too, had run its course.

The Fifth-Generation Project failed to meet its objectives, as did its counterparts in the United States and Europe. A second AI winter descended. At this point, a critic could justifiably bemoan "the history of artificial intelligence research to date, consisting always of very limited success in particular areas, followed immediately by failure to reach the broader goals at which these initial successes seem at first to hint."[21] Private investors began to shun any venture carrying the brand of "artificial intelligence." Even among academics and their funders, "AI" became an unwanted epithet.[22]

Technical work continued apace, however, and by the 1990s, the second AI winter gradually thawed. Optimism was rekindled by the introduction of new techniques, which seemed to offer alternatives to the traditional logicist paradigm (often referred to as "Good Old-Fashioned Artificial Intelligence," or "GOFAI" for short), which had focused on high-level symbol manipulation and which had reached its apogee in the expert systems of the 1980s. The newly popular techniques, which included neural networks and genetic algorithms, promised to overcome some of the shortcomings of the GOFAI approach, in particular the "brittleness" that characterized classical AI programs (which typically produced complete nonsense if the programmers made even a single slightly erroneous assumption). The new techniques boasted a more organic performance. For example, neural networks exhibited the property of "graceful degradation": a small amount of damage to a neural network typically resulted in a small degradation of its performance, rather than a total crash. Even more importantly, neural networks could learn from experience, finding natural ways of generalizing from examples and finding hidden statistical patterns in their input.[23] This made the nets good at pattern recognition and classification problems. For example, by training a neural network on a data set of sonar signals, it could be taught to distinguish the acoustic profiles of submarines, mines, and sea life with better accuracy than human experts—and this could be done without anybody first having to figure out in advance exactly how the categories were to be defined or how different features were to be weighted.

While simple neural network models had been known since the late 1950s, the field enjoyed a renaissance after the introduction of the backpropagation algorithm, which made it possible to train multi-layered neural networks.[24] Such multilayered networks, which have one or more intermediary ("hidden") layers of neurons between the input and output layers, can learn a much wider range of functions than their simpler predecessors.[25] Combined with the increasingly powerful computers that were becoming available, these algorithmic improvements enabled engineers to build neural networks that were good enough to be practically useful in many applications.

The brain-like qualities of neural networks contrasted favorably with the rigidly logic-chopping but brittle performance of traditional rule-based GOFAI systems—enough so to inspire a new "-ism," *connectionism*, which emphasized the importance of massively parallel sub-symbolic processing. More than 150,000 academic papers have since been published on artificial neural networks, and they continue to be an important approach in machine learning.

Evolution-based methods, such as genetic algorithms and genetic programming, constitute another approach whose emergence helped end the second AI winter. It made perhaps a smaller academic impact than neural nets but was widely popularized. In evolutionary models, a population of candidate solutions (which can be data structures or programs) is maintained, and new candidate solutions are generated randomly by mutating or recombining variants in the existing population. Periodically, the population is pruned by applying a selection criterion (a fitness function) that allows only the better candidates to survive into the next generation. Iterated over thousands of generations, the average quality of the solutions in the candidate pool gradually increases. When it works, this kind of algorithm can produce efficient solutions to a very wide range of problems—solutions that may be strikingly novel and unintuitive, often looking more like natural structures than anything that a human engineer would design. And in principle, this can happen without much need for human input beyond the initial specification of the fitness function, which is often very simple. In practice, however, getting evolutionary methods to work well requires skill and ingenuity, particularly in devising a good representational format. Without an efficient way to encode candidate solutions (a genetic language that matches latent structure in the target domain), evolutionary search tends to meander endlessly in a vast search space or get stuck at a local optimum. Even if a good representational format is found, evolution is computationally demanding and is often defeated by the combinatorial explosion.

Neural networks and genetic algorithms are examples of methods that stimulated excitement in the 1990s by appearing to offer alternatives to the stagnating GOFAI paradigm. But the intention here is not to sing the praises of these two methods or to elevate them above the many other techniques in machine learning. In fact, one of the major theoretical developments of the past twenty years has been a clearer realization of how superficially disparate techniques can be understood as special cases within a common mathematical framework. For example, many types of artificial neural network can be viewed as classifiers that perform a particular kind of statistical calculation (maximum likelihood estimation).[26] This perspective allows neural nets to be compared with a larger class of algorithms for learning classifiers from examples— "decision trees," "logistic regression models," "support vector machines," "naive Bayes," "k-nearest-neighbors regression," among others.[27] In a similar manner, genetic algorithms can be viewed as performing stochastic hill-climbing, which is again a subset of a wider class of algorithms for optimization. Each of these algorithms for building classifiers or for searching a solution space has its own profile of strengths and weaknesses which can be studied mathematically. Algorithms differ in their processor time and memory space requirements, which inductive biases they presuppose, the ease with which externally produced content can be incorporated, and how transparent their inner workings are to a human analyst.

Behind the razzle-dazzle of machine learning and creative problem-solving thus lies a set of mathematically well-specified tradeoffs. The ideal is that of the perfect Bayesian agent, one that makes probabilistically optimal use of available information. This ideal is unattainable because it is too computationally demanding to be implemented in any physical computer (see Box 1). Accordingly, one can view artificial intelligence as a quest to find shortcuts: ways of tractably approximating the Bayesian ideal by sacrificing some optimality or generality while preserving enough to get high performance in the actual domains of interest.

A reflection of this picture can be seen in the work done over the past couple of decades on probabilistic graphical models, such as Bayesian networks. Bayesian networks provide a concise way of representing probabilistic and conditional independence relations that hold in some particular

Box 1 An optimal Bayesian agent

An ideal Bayesian agent starts out with a "prior probability distribution," a function that assigns probabilities to each "possible world" (i.e. to each maximally specific way the world could turn out to be).[28] This prior incorporates an inductive bias such that simpler possible worlds are assigned higher probabilities. (One way to formally define the simplicity of a possible world is in terms of its "Kolmogorov complexity," a measure based on the length of the shortest computer program that generates a complete description of the world.[29]) The prior also incorporates any background knowledge that the programmers wish to give to the agent.

As the agent receives new information from its sensors, it updates its probability distribution by conditionalizing the distribution on the new information according to Bayes' theorem.[30] Conditionalization is the mathematical operation that sets the new probability of those worlds that are inconsistent with the information received to zero and renormalizes the probability distribution over the remaining possible worlds. The result is a "posterior probability distribution" (which the agent may use as its new prior in the next time step). As the agent makes observations, its probability mass thus gets concentrated on the shrinking set of possible worlds that remain consistent with the evidence; and among these possible worlds, simpler ones always have more probability.

Metaphorically, we can think of a probability as sand on a large sheet of paper. The paper is partitioned into areas of various sizes, each area corresponding to one possible world, with larger areas corresponding to simpler possible worlds. Imagine also a layer of sand of even thickness spread across the entire sheet: this is our prior probability distribution. Whenever an observation is made that rules out some possible worlds, we remove the sand from the corresponding areas of the paper and redistribute it evenly over the areas that remain in play. Thus, the total amount of sand on the sheet never changes, it just gets concentrated into fewer areas as observational evidence accumulates. This is a picture of learning in its purest form. (To calculate the probability of a *hypothesis*, we simply measure the amount of sand in all the areas that correspond to the possible worlds in which the hypothesis is true.)

So far, we have defined a learning rule. To get an agent, we also need a decision rule. To this end, we endow the agent with a "utility function" which assigns a number to each possible world. The number represents the desirability of that world according to the agent's basic preferences. Now, at each time step, the agent selects the action with the highest expected utility.[31] (To

Box 1 *Continued*

find the action with the highest expected utility, the agent could list all possible actions. It could then compute the conditional probability distribution given the action—the probability distribution that would result from conditionalizing its current probability distribution on the observation that the action had just been taken. Finally, it could calculate the expected value of the action as the sum of the value of each possible world multiplied by the conditional probability of that world given the action.[32])

The learning rule and the decision rule together define an "optimality notion" for an agent. (Essentially the same optimality notion has been broadly used in artificial intelligence, epistemology, philosophy of science, economics, and statistics.[33]) In reality, it is impossible to build such an agent because it is computationally intractable to perform the requisite calculations. Any attempt to do so succumbs to a combinatorial explosion just like the one described in our discussion of GOFAI. To see why this is so, consider one tiny subset of all possible worlds: those that consist of a single computer monitor floating in an endless vacuum. The monitor has $1,000 \times 1,000$ pixels, each of which is perpetually either on or off. Even this subset of possible worlds is enormously large: the $2^{(1,000 \times 1,000)}$ possible monitor states outnumber all the computations expected ever to take place in the observable universe. Thus, we could not even enumerate all the possible worlds in this tiny subset of all possible worlds, let alone perform more elaborate computations on each of them individually.

Optimality notions can be of theoretical interest even if they are physically unrealizable. They give us a standard by which to judge heuristic approximations, and sometimes we can reason about what an optimal agent would do in some special case. We will encounter some alternative optimality notions for artificial agents in Chapter 12.

domain. (Exploiting such independence relations is essential for overcoming the combinatorial explosion, which is as much of a problem for probabilistic inference as it is for logical deduction.) They also provide important insight into the concept of causality.[34]

One advantage of relating learning problems from specific domains to the general problem of Bayesian inference is that new algorithms that make Bayesian inference more efficient will then yield immediate improvements across many different areas. Advances in Monte Carlo approximation techniques, for example, are directly applied in computer vision, robotics, and computational genetics. Another advantage is that it lets researchers from different disciplines more easily pool their findings. Graphical models and Bayesian statistics have become a shared focus of research in many fields, including machine learning, statistical physics, bioinformatics, combinatorial optimization, and communication theory.[35] A fair amount of the recent progress in machine learning has resulted from incorporating formal results originally derived in other academic fields. (Machine learning applications have also benefited enormously from faster computers and greater availability of large data sets.)

State of the art

Artificial intelligence already outperforms human intelligence in many domains. Table 1 surveys the state of game-playing computers, showing that AIs now beat human champions in a wide range of games.[36]

These achievements might not seem impressive today. But this is because our standards for what is impressive keep adapting to the advances being made. Expert chess playing, for example, was once thought to epitomize human intellection. In the view of several experts in the late 1950s: "If one could devise a successful chess machine, one would seem to have penetrated to the core of human intellectual endeavor."[37] This no longer seems so. One sympathizes with John McCarthy, who lamented: "As soon as it works, no one calls it AI anymore."[38]

There is an important sense, however, in which chess-playing AI turned out to be a lesser triumph than many imagined it would be. It was once supposed, perhaps not unreasonably, that in order for a computer to play chess at grandmaster level, it would have to be endowed with a high degree of *general* intelligence.[39] One might have thought, for example, that great chess playing requires being able to learn abstract concepts, think cleverly about strategy, compose flexible plans, make a wide range of ingenious logical deductions, and maybe even model one's opponent's thinking. Not so. It turned out to be possible to build a perfectly fine chess engine around a special-purpose algorithm.[40] When implemented on the fast processors that became available towards the end of the twentieth century, it produces very strong play. But an AI built like that is narrow. It plays chess; it can do no other.[41]

In other domains, solutions have turned out to be *more* complicated than initially expected, and progress slower. The computer scientist

Table 1 *Game-playing AI*

Checkers	Superhuman	Arthur Samuel's checkers program, originally written in 1952 and later improved (the 1955 version incorporating machine learning), becomes the first program to learn to play a game better than its creator.[42] In 1994, the program CHINOOK beats the reigning human champion, marking the first time a program wins an official world championship in a game of skill. In 2002, Jonathan Schaeffer and his team "solve" checkers, i.e. produce a program that always makes the best possible move (combining alpha-beta search with a database of 39 trillion endgame positions). Perfect play by both sides leads to a draw.[43]
Backgammon	Superhuman	1979: The backgammon program BKG by Hans Berliner defeats the world champion—the first computer program to defeat (in an exhibition match) a world champion in any game—though Berliner later attributes the win to luck with the dice rolls.[44]
		1992: The backgammon program TD-Gammon by Gerry Tesauro reaches championship-level ability, using temporal difference learning (a form of reinforcement learning) and repeated plays against itself to improve.[45]
		In the years since, backgammon programs have far surpassed the best human players.[46]
Traveller TCS	Superhuman in collaboration with human[47]	In both 1981 and 1982, Douglas Lenat's program Eurisko wins the US championship in Traveller TCS (a futuristic naval war game), prompting rule changes to block its unorthodox strategies.[48] Eurisko had heuristics for designing its fleet, and it also had heuristics for modifying its heuristics.
Othello	Superhuman	1997: The program Logistello wins every game in a six-game match against world champion Takeshi Murakami.[49]
Chess	Superhuman	1997: Deep Blue beats the world chess champion, Garry Kasparov. Kasparov claims to have seen glimpses of true intelligence and creativity in some of the computer's moves.[50] Since then, chess engines have continued to improve.[51]

continued

Table 1 *Continued*

Crosswords	Expert level	1999: The crossword-solving program Proverb outperforms the average crossword-solver.[52]
		2012: The program Dr. Fill, created by Matt Ginsberg, scores in the top quartile among the otherwise human contestants in the American Crossword Puzzle Tournament. (Dr. Fill's performance is uneven. It completes perfectly the puzzle rated most difficult by humans, yet is stumped by a couple of nonstandard puzzles that involved spelling backwards or writing answers diagonally.)[53]
Scrabble	Superhuman	As of 2002, Scrabble-playing software surpasses the best human players.[54]
Bridge	Equal to the best	By 2005, contract bridge playing software reaches parity with the best human bridge players.[55]
Jeopardy!	Superhuman	2010: IBM's *Watson* defeats the two all-time-greatest human *Jeopardy!* champions, Ken Jennings and Brad Rutter.[56] *Jeopardy!* is a televised game show with trivia questions about history, literature, sports, geography, pop culture, science, and other topics. Questions are presented in the form of clues, and often involve wordplay.
Poker	Varied	Computer poker players remain slightly below the best humans for full-ring Texas hold 'em but perform at a superhuman level in some poker variants.[57]
FreeCell	Superhuman	Heuristics evolved using genetic algorithms produce a solver for the solitaire game FreeCell (which in its generalized form is NP-complete) that is able to beat high-ranking human players.[58]
Go	Very strong amateur level	As of 2012, the Zen series of Go-playing programs has reached rank 6 dan in fast games (the level of a very strong amateur player), using Monte Carlo tree search and machine learning techniques.[59] Go-playing programs have been improving at a rate of about 1 dan/year in recent years. If this rate of improvement continues, they might beat the human world champion in about a decade.

Donald Knuth was struck that "AI has by now succeeded in doing essentially everything that requires 'thinking' but has failed to do most of what people and animals do 'without thinking'—that, somehow, is much harder!"[60] Analyzing visual scenes, recognizing objects, or controlling a robot's behavior as it interacts with a natural environment has proved challenging. Nevertheless, a fair amount of progress has been made and continues to be made, aided by steady improvements in hardware.

Common sense and natural language understanding have also turned out to be difficult. It is now often thought that achieving a fully human-level performance on these tasks is an "AI-complete" problem, meaning that the difficulty of solving these problems is essentially equivalent to the difficulty of building generally human-level intelligent machines.[61] In other words, if somebody *were* to succeed in creating an AI that could understand natural language as well as a human adult, they would in all likelihood also either already have succeeded in creating an AI that could do everything else that human intelligence can do, or they would be but a very short step from such a general capability.[62]

Chess-playing expertise turned out to be achievable by means of a surprisingly simple algorithm. It is tempting to speculate that other capabilities—such as general reasoning ability, or some key ability involved in programming—might likewise be achievable through some surprisingly simple algorithm. The fact that the best performance at one time is attained through a complicated mechanism does not mean that no simple mechanism could do the job as well or better. It might simply be that nobody has yet found the simpler alternative. The Ptolemaic system (with the Earth in the center, orbited by the Sun, the Moon, planets, and stars) represented the state of the art in astronomy for over a thousand years, and its predictive accuracy was improved over the centuries by progressively complicating the model: adding epicycles upon epicycles to the postulated celestial motions. Then the entire system was overthrown by the heliocentric theory of Copernicus, which was simpler and—though only after further elaboration by Kepler—more predictively accurate.[63]

Artificial intelligence methods are now used in more areas than it would make sense to review here, but mentioning a sampling of them will give an idea of the breadth of applications. Aside from the game AIs listed in Table 1, there are hearing aids with algorithms that filter out ambient noise; route-finders that display maps and offer navigation advice to drivers; recommender systems that suggest books and music albums based on a user's previous purchases and ratings; and medical decision support systems that help doctors diagnose breast cancer, recommend treatment plans, and aid in the interpretation of electrocardiograms. There are robotic pets and cleaning robots, lawn-mowing robots, rescue robots, surgical robots, and over a million industrial robots.[64] The world population of robots exceeds 10 million.[65]

Modern speech recognition, based on statistical techniques such as hidden Markov models, has become sufficiently accurate for practical use (some fragments of this book were drafted with the help of a speech recognition program). Personal digital assistants, such as Apple's Siri, respond to spoken commands and can answer simple questions and execute commands. Optical character recognition of handwritten and typewritten text is routinely used in applications such as mail sorting and digitization of old documents.[66]

Machine translation remains imperfect but is good enough for many applications. Early systems used the GOFAI approach of hand-coded grammars that had to be developed by skilled linguists from the ground up for each language. Newer systems use statistical machine learning techniques that automatically build statistical models from observed usage patterns. The machine infers the parameters for these models by analyzing bilingual corpora. This approach dispenses with linguists: the programmers building these systems need not even speak the languages they are working with.[67]

Face recognition has improved sufficiently in recent years that it is now used at automated border crossings in Europe and Australia. The US Department of State operates a face recognition system with over 75 million photographs for visa processing. Surveillance systems employ increasingly sophisticated AI and data-mining technologies to analyze voice, video, or text, large quantities of which are trawled from the world's electronic communications media and stored in giant data centers.

Theorem-proving and equation-solving are by now so well established that they are hardly regarded as AI anymore. Equation solvers are included in scientific computing programs such as Mathematica. Formal verification methods, including automated theorem provers, are routinely used by chip manufacturers to verify the behavior of circuit designs prior to production.

The US military and intelligence establishments have been leading the way to the large-scale deployment of bomb-disposing robots, surveillance and attack drones, and other unmanned vehicles. These still depend mainly on remote control by human operators, but work is underway to extend their autonomous capabilities.

Intelligent scheduling is a major area of success. The DART tool for automated logistics planning and scheduling was used in Operation Desert Storm in 1991 to such effect that DARPA (the Defense Advanced Research Projects Agency in the United States) claims that this single application more than paid back their thirty-year investment in AI.[68] Airline reservation systems use sophisticated scheduling and pricing systems. Businesses make wide use of AI techniques in inventory control systems. They also use automatic telephone reservation systems and helplines connected to speech recognition software to usher their hapless customers through labyrinths of interlocking menu options.

AI technologies underlie many internet services. Software polices the world's email traffic, and despite continual adaptation by spammers to circumvent the countermeasures being brought against them, Bayesian spam filters have largely managed to hold the spam tide at bay. Software using AI components is responsible for automatically approving or declining credit card transactions, and continuously monitors account activity for signs of fraudulent use. Information retrieval systems also make extensive use of machine learning. The Google search engine is, arguably, the greatest AI system that has yet been built.

Now, it must be stressed that the demarcation between artificial intelligence and software in general is not sharp. Some of the applications listed above might be viewed more as generic software applications than as AI in particular—though this brings us back to McCarthy's dictum that when something works it is no longer called AI. A more relevant distinction for our purposes is that between systems that have a narrow range of cognitive capability (whether they be called "AI" or not) and systems that have more generally applicable problem-solving capacities. Essentially all the systems currently in use are of the former type: narrow. However, many of them contain components that might also play a role in future artificial general intelligence or be of service in its development—components such as classifiers, search algorithms, planners, solvers, and representational frameworks.

One high-stakes and extremely competitive environment in which AI systems operate today is the global financial market. Automated stock-trading systems are widely used by major investing houses. While some of these are simply ways of automating the execution of particular buy or sell orders issued by a human fund manager, others pursue complicated trading strategies that adapt to changing market conditions. Analytic systems use an assortment of data-mining techniques and time series analysis to scan for patterns and trends in securities markets or to correlate historical price movements with external variables such as keywords in news tickers. Financial news providers sell newsfeeds that are specially formatted for use by such AI programs. Other systems specialize in finding arbitrage opportunities within or between markets, or in high-frequency trading that seeks to profit from minute price movements that occur over the course of milliseconds (a timescale at which communication latencies even for speed-of-light signals in optical fiber cable become significant, making it advantageous to locate computers near the exchange). Algorithmic high-frequency traders account for more than half of equity shares traded on US markets.[69] Algorithmic trading has been implicated in the 2010 Flash Crash (see Box 2).

Box 2 The 2010 Flash Crash

By the afternoon of May 6, 2010, US equity markets were already down 4% on worries about the European debt crisis. At 2:32 p.m., a large seller (a mutual fund complex) initiated a sell algorithm to dispose of a large number of the E-Mini S&P 500 futures contracts to be sold off at a sell rate linked to a measure of minute-to-minute liquidity on the exchange. These contracts were bought by algorithmic high-frequency traders, which were programmed to quickly eliminate their temporary long positions by selling the contracts on to other traders. With demand from fundamental buyers slacking, the algorithmic traders started to sell the E-Minis primarily to other algorithmic traders, which in turn passed them on to other algorithmic traders, creating a "hot potato" effect driving up trading volume—this being interpreted by the sell algorithm as an indicator of high liquidity, prompting it to increase the rate at which it was putting E-Mini contracts on the market, pushing the downward spiral. At some point, the high-frequency traders started withdrawing from the market, drying up liquidity while prices continued to fall. At 2:45 p.m., trading on the E-Mini was halted by an automatic circuit breaker, the exchange's stop logic functionality. When trading was restarted, a mere five seconds later, prices stabilized and soon began to recover most of the losses. But for a while, at the trough of the crisis, a trillion dollars had been wiped off the market, and spillover effects had

Box 2 *Continued*

led to a substantial number of trades in individual securities being executed at "absurd" prices, such as one cent or 100,000 dollars. After the market closed for the day, representatives of the exchanges met with regulators and decided to break all trades that had been executed at prices 60% or more away from their pre-crisis levels (deeming such transactions "clearly erroneous" and thus subject to *post facto* cancellation under existing trade rules).[70]

The retelling here of this episode is a digression because the computer programs involved in the Flash Crash were not particularly intelligent or sophisticated, and the kind of threat they created is fundamentally different from the concerns we shall raise later in this book in relation to the prospect of machine superintelligence. Nevertheless, these events illustrate several useful lessons. One is the reminder that interactions between individually simple components (such as the sell algorithm and the high-frequency algorithmic trading programs) can produce complicated and unexpected effects. Systemic risk can build up in a system as new elements are introduced, risks that are not obvious until after something goes wrong (and sometimes not even then).[71]

Another lesson is that smart professionals might give an instruction to a program based on a sensible-seeming and normally sound assumption (e.g. that trading volume is a good measure of market liquidity) and that this can produce catastrophic results when the program continues to act on the instruction with iron-clad logical consistency even in the unanticipated situation where the assumption turns out to be invalid. The algorithm just does what it does; and unless it is a very special kind of algorithm, it does not care that we clasp our heads and gasp in dumbstruck horror at the absurd inappropriateness of its actions. This is a theme that we will encounter again.

A third observation in relation to the Flash Crash is that while automation contributed to the incident, it also contributed to its resolution. The pre-programmed stop order logic, which suspended trading when prices moved too far out of whack, was set to execute automatically because it had been correctly anticipated that the triggering events could happen on a time-scale too swift for humans to respond. The need for pre-installed and automatically executing safety functionality—as opposed to reliance on runtime human supervision—again foreshadows a theme that will be important in our discussion of machine superintelligence.[72]

Opinions about the future of machine intelligence

Progress on two major fronts—towards a more solid statistical and information-theoretic foundation for machine learning on the one hand, and towards the practical and commercial success of various problem-specific or domain-specific applications on the other—has restored to AI research some of its lost prestige. There may, however, be a residual cultural effect on the AI community of its earlier history that makes many mainstream researchers reluctant to align themselves with over-grand ambition. Thus Nils Nilsson, one of the old-timers in the field, complains that his present-day colleagues lack the boldness of spirit that propelled the pioneers of his own generation:

Concern for "respectability" has had, I think, a stultifying effect on some AI researchers. I hear them saying things like, "AI used to be criticized for its flossiness. Now that we have made solid progress, let us not risk losing our respectability." One result of this conservatism has been increased concentration on "weak AI"—the variety devoted to providing aids to human thought—and away from "strong AI"—the variety that attempts to mechanize human-level intelligence.[73]

Nilsson's sentiment has been echoed by several others of the founders, including Marvin Minsky, John McCarthy, and Patrick Winston.[74]

The last few years have seen a resurgence of interest in AI, which might yet spill over into renewed efforts towards artificial *general* intelligence (what Nilsson calls "strong AI"). In addition to faster hardware, a contemporary project would benefit from the great strides that have been made in the many subfields of AI, in software engineering more generally, and in neighboring fields such as computational neuroscience. One indication of pent-up demand for quality information and education is shown in the response to the free online offering of an introductory course in artificial intelligence at Stanford University in the fall of 2011, organized by Sebastian Thrun and Peter Norvig. Some 160,000 students from around the world signed up to take it (and 23,000 completed it).[75]

Expert opinions about the future of AI vary wildly. There is disagreement about timescales as well as about what forms AI might eventually take. Predictions about the future development of artificial intelligence, one recent study noted, "are as confident as they are diverse."[76]

Although the contemporary distribution of belief has not been very carefully measured, we can get a rough impression from various smaller surveys and informal observations. In particular, a series of recent surveys have polled members of several relevant expert communities on the question of when they expect "human-level machine intelligence" (HLMI) to be developed, defined as "one that can carry out most human professions at least as well as a typical human."[77] Results are shown in Table 2. The combined sample gave the following (median) estimate: 10% probability of HLMI by 2022, 50% probability by 2040, and 90% probability by 2075. (Respondents were asked to premiss their estimates on the assumption that "human scientific activity continues without major negative disruption.")

These numbers should be taken with some grains of salt: sample sizes are quite small and not necessarily representative of the general expert population. They are, however, in concordance with results from other surveys.[78]

The survey results are also in line with some recently published interviews with about two dozen researchers in AI-related fields. For example, Nils Nilsson has spent a long and productive career working on problems in search, planning, knowledge representation, and robotics; he has authored textbooks in artificial intelligence; and he recently completed the most comprehensive history of the field written to date.[79] When asked about arrival dates for HLMI, he offered the following opinion:[80]

10% chance: 2030
50% chance: 2050
90% chance: 2100

Table 2 *When will human-level machine intelligence be attained?*[81]

	10%	50%	90%
PT-AI	2023	2048	2080
AGI	2022	2040	2065
EETN	2020	2050	2093
TOP100	2024	2050	2070
Combined	2022	2040	2075

Judging from the published interview transcripts, Professor Nilsson's probability distribution appears to be quite representative of many experts in the area—though again it must be emphasized that there is a wide spread of opinion: there are practitioners who are substantially more boosterish, confidently expecting HLMI in the 2020–40 range, and others who are confident either that it will never happen or that it is indefinitely far off.[82] In addition, some interviewees feel that the notion of a "human level" of artificial intelligence is ill-defined or misleading, or are for other reasons reluctant to go on record with a quantitative prediction.

My own view is that the median numbers reported in the expert survey do not have enough probability mass on later arrival dates. A 10% probability of HLMI not having been developed by 2075 or even 2100 (after conditionalizing on "human scientific activity continuing without major negative disruption") seems too low.

Historically, AI researchers have not had a strong record of being able to predict the rate of advances in their own field or the shape that such advances would take. On the one hand, some tasks, like chess playing, turned out to be achievable by means of surprisingly simple programs; and naysayers who claimed that machines would "never" be able to do this or that have repeatedly been proven wrong. On the other hand, the more typical errors among practitioners have been to underestimate the difficulties of getting a system to perform robustly on real-world tasks, and to overestimate the advantages of their own particular pet project or technique.

The survey also asked two other questions of relevance to our inquiry. One inquired of respondents about how much longer they thought it would take to reach superintelligence assuming human-level machine is first achieved. The results are in Table 3.

Another question inquired what they thought would be the overall long-term impact for humanity of achieving human-level machine intelligence. The answers are summarized in Figure 2.

Table 3 *How long from human level to superintelligence?*

	Within 2 years after HLMI	Within 30 years after HLMI
TOP100	5%	50%
Combined	10%	75%

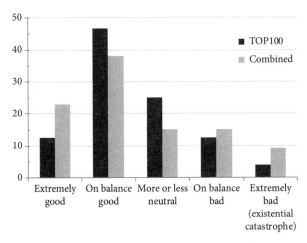

Figure 2 Overall long-term impact of HLMI.[83]

My own views again differ somewhat from the opinions expressed in the survey. I assign a higher probability to superintelligence being created relatively soon after human-level machine intelligence. I also have a more polarized outlook on the consequences, thinking an extremely good or an extremely bad outcome to be somewhat more likely than a more balanced outcome. The reasons for this will become clear later in the book.

Small sample sizes, selection biases, and—above all—the inherent unreliability of the subjective opinions elicited mean that one should not read too much into these expert surveys and interviews. They do not let us draw any strong conclusion. But they do hint at a weak conclusion. They suggest that (at least in lieu of better data or analysis) it may be reasonable to believe that human-level machine intelligence has a fairly sizeable chance of being developed by mid-century, and that it has a non-trivial chance of being developed considerably sooner or much later; that it might perhaps fairly soon thereafter result in superintelligence; and that a wide range of outcomes may have a significant chance of occurring, including extremely good outcomes and outcomes that are as bad as human extinction.[84] At the very least, they suggest that the topic is worth a closer look.

CHAPTER 2

Paths to superintelligence

Machines are currently far inferior to humans in general intelligence. Yet one day (we have suggested) they will be superintelligent. How do we get from here to there? This chapter explores several conceivable technological paths. We look at artificial intelligence, whole brain emulation, biological cognition, and human–machine interfaces, as well as networks and organizations. We evaluate their different degrees of plausibility as pathways to superintelligence. The existence of multiple paths increases the probability that the destination can be reached via at least one of them.

We can tentatively define a superintelligence as *any intellect that greatly exceeds the cognitive performance of humans in virtually all domains of interest.*[1] We will have more to say about the concept of superintelligence in the next chapter, where we will subject it to a kind of spectral analysis to distinguish some different possible forms of superintelligence. But for now, the rough characterization just given will suffice. Note that the definition is noncommittal about how the superintelligence is implemented. It is also noncommittal regarding qualia: whether a superintelligence would have subjective conscious experience might matter greatly for some questions (in particular for some moral questions), but our primary focus here is on the causal antecedents and consequences of superintelligence, not on the metaphysics of mind.[2]

The chess program Deep Fritz is not a superintelligence on this definition, since Fritz is only smart within the narrow domain of chess. Certain kinds of domain-specific superintelligence could, however, be important. When referring to superintelligent performance limited to a particular domain, we will note the restriction explicitly. For instance, an "engineering superintelligence" would be an intellect that vastly out-performs the best current human minds in the domain of engineering. Unless otherwise noted, we use the term to refer to systems that have a superhuman level of *general* intelligence.

But how might we create superintelligence? Let us examine some possible paths.

Artificial intelligence

Readers of this chapter must not expect a blueprint for programming an artificial general intelligence. No such blueprint exists yet, of course. And had I been in possession of such a blueprint, I most certainly would not have published it in a book. (If the reasons for this are not immediately obvious, the arguments in subsequent chapters will make them clear.)

We can, however, discern some general features of the kind of system that would be required. It now seems clear that a capacity to learn would be an integral feature of the core design of a system intended to attain general intelligence, not something to be tacked on later as an extension or an afterthought. The same holds for the ability to deal effectively with uncertainty and probabilistic information. Some faculty for extracting useful concepts from sensory data and internal states, and for leveraging acquired concepts into flexible combinatorial representations for use in logical and intuitive reasoning, also likely belong among the core design features in a modern AI intended to attain general intelligence.

The early Good Old-Fashioned Artificial Intelligence systems did not, for the most part, focus on learning, uncertainty, or concept formation, perhaps because techniques for dealing with these dimensions were poorly developed at the time. This is not to say that the underlying ideas are all that novel. The idea of using learning as a means of boot-strapping a simpler system to human-level intelligence can be traced back at least to Alan Turing's notion of a "child machine," which he wrote about in 1950:

Instead of trying to produce a programme to simulate the adult mind, why not rather try to produce one which simulates the child's? If this were then subjected to an appropriate course of education one would obtain the adult brain.[3]

Turing envisaged an iterative process to develop such a child machine:

> We cannot expect to find a good child machine at the first attempt. One must experiment with teaching one such machine and see how well it learns. One can then try another and see if it is better or worse. There is an obvious connection between this process and evolution. . . . One may hope, however, that this process will be more expeditious than evolution. The survival of the fittest is a slow method for measuring advantages. The experimenter, by the exercise of intelligence, should be able to speed it up. Equally important is the fact that he is not restricted to random mutations. If he can trace a cause for some weakness he can probably think of the kind of mutation which will improve it.[4]

We know that blind evolutionary processes can produce human-level general intelligence, since they have already done so at least once. Evolutionary processes with foresight—that is, genetic programs designed and guided by an intelligent human programmer—should be able to achieve a similar outcome with far greater efficiency. This observation has been used by some philosophers and scientists, including David Chalmers and Hans Moravec, to argue that human-level AI is not only theoretically possible but feasible within this century.[5] The idea is that we can estimate the relative capabilities of evolution and human engineering to produce intelligence, and find that human engineering is already vastly superior to evolution in some areas and is likely to become superior in the remaining areas before too long. The fact that evolution produced intelligence therefore indicates that human engineering will soon be able to do the same. Thus, Moravec wrote (already back in 1976):

> The existence of several examples of intelligence designed under these constraints should give us great confidence that we can achieve the same in short order. The situation is analogous to the history of heavier than air flight, where birds, bats and insects clearly demonstrated the possibility before our culture mastered it.[6]

One needs to be cautious, though, in what inferences one draws from this line of reasoning. It is true that evolution produced heavier-than-air flight, and that human engineers subsequently succeeded in doing likewise (albeit by means of a very different mechanism). Other examples could also be adduced, such as sonar, magnetic navigation, chemical weapons, photoreceptors, and all kinds of mechanic and kinetic performance characteristics. However, one could equally point to areas where human engineers have thus far failed to match evolution: in morphogenesis, self-repair, and the immune defense, for example, human efforts lag far behind what nature has accomplished. Moravec's argument, therefore, cannot give us "great confidence" that we can achieve human-level artificial intelligence "in short order." At best, the evolution of intelligent life places an upper bound on the intrinsic difficulty of designing intelligence. But this upper bound could be quite far above current human engineering capabilities.

Another way of deploying an evolutionary argument for the feasibility of AI is via the idea that we could, by running genetic algorithms on sufficiently fast computers, achieve results comparable to those of biological evolution. This version of the evolutionary argument thus proposes a specific method whereby intelligence could be produced.

But is it true that we will soon have computing power sufficient to recapitulate the relevant evolutionary processes that produced human intelligence? The answer depends both on how much computing technology will advance over the next decades and on how much computing power would be required to run genetic algorithms with the same optimization power as the evolutionary process of natural selection that lies in our past. Although, in the end, the conclusion we get from pursuing this line of reasoning is disappointingly indeterminate, it is instructive to attempt a rough estimate (see Box 3). If nothing else, the exercise draws attention to some interesting unknowns.

The upshot is that the computational resources required to simply replicate the relevant evolutionary processes on Earth that produced human-level intelligence are severely out of reach—and will remain so even if Moore's law were to continue for a century (cf. Figure 3). It is plausible, however, that compared with brute-force replication of natural evolutionary processes, vast efficiency gains are achievable by designing the search process to *aim* for intelligence, using various obvious improvements over natural selection. Yet it is very hard to bound the magnitude of those attainable efficiency gains. We cannot even say whether they amount to five or to twenty-five orders of magnitude. Absent further elaboration, therefore, evolutionary arguments are not able to meaningfully constrain our expectations of either the difficulty of building human-level machine intelligence or the timescales for such developments.

There is a further complication with these kinds of evolutionary considerations, one that makes it hard to derive from them even a very loose upper bound on the difficulty of evolving intelligence. We must avoid the error of inferring, from the fact that intelligent life evolved on Earth, that

Box 3 What would it take to recapitulate evolution?

Not every feat accomplished by evolution in the course of the development of human intelligence is relevant to a human engineer trying to artificially evolve machine intelligence. Only a small portion of evolutionary selection on Earth has been selection for intelligence. More specifically, the problems that human engineers cannot trivially bypass may have been the target of a very small portion of total evolutionary selection. For example, since we can run our computers on electrical power, we do not have to reinvent the molecules of the cellular energy economy in order to create intelligent machines—yet such molecular evolution of metabolic pathways might have used up a large part of the total amount of selection power that was available to evolution over the course of Earth's history.[7]

One might argue that the key insights for AI are embodied in the structure of nervous systems, which came into existence less than a billion years ago.[8] If we take that view, then the number of relevant "experiments" available to evolution is drastically curtailed. There are some $4–6\times10^{30}$ prokaryotes in the world today, but only 10^{19} insects, and fewer than 10^{10} humans (while pre-agricultural populations were orders of magnitude smaller).[9] These numbers are only moderately intimidating.

Evolutionary algorithms, however, require not only variations to select among but also a fitness function to evaluate variants, and this is typically the most computationally expensive component. A fitness function for the evolution of artificial intelligence plausibly requires simulation of neural development, learning, and cognition to evaluate fitness. We might thus do better not to look at the raw number of organisms with complex nervous systems, but instead to attend to the number of neurons in biological organisms that we might need to simulate to mimic evolution's fitness function. We can make a crude estimate of that latter quantity by considering insects, which dominate terrestrial animal biomass (with ants alone estimated to contribute some 15–20%).[10] Insect brain size varies substantially, with large and social insects sporting larger brains: a honeybee brain has just under 10^6 neurons, a fruit fly brain has 10^5 neurons, and ants are in between with 250,000 neurons.[11] The majority of smaller insects may have brains of only a few thousand neurons. Erring on the side of conservatively high, if we assigned all 10^{19} insects fruit-fly numbers of neurons, the total would be 10^{24} insect neurons in the world. This could be augmented with an additional order of magnitude to account for aquatic copepods, birds, reptiles, mammals, etc., to reach 10^{25}. (By contrast,

Box 3 *Continued*

in pre-agricultural times there were fewer than 10^7 humans, with under 10^{11} neurons each: thus fewer than 10^{18} human neurons in total, though humans have a higher number of synapses per neuron.)

The computational cost of simulating one neuron depends on the level of detail that one includes in the simulation. Extremely simple neuron models use about 1,000 floating-point operations per second (FLOPS) to simulate one neuron (in real-time). The electrophysiologically realistic Hodgkin–Huxley model uses 1,200,000 FLOPS. A more detailed multi-compartmental model would add another three to four orders of magnitude, while higher-level models that abstract systems of neurons could subtract two to three orders of magnitude from the simple models.[12] If we were to simulate 10^{25} neurons over a billion years of evolution (longer than the existence of nervous systems as we know them), and we allow our computers to run for one year, these figures would give us a requirement in the range of 10^{31}–10^{44} FLOPS. For comparison, China's Tianhe-2, the world's most powerful supercomputer as of September 2013, provides only 3.39×10^{16} FLOPS. In recent decades, it has taken approximately 6.7 years for commodity computers to increase in power by one order of magnitude. Even a century of continued Moore's law would not be enough to close this gap. Running more specialized hardware, or allowing longer run-times, could contribute only a few more orders of magnitude.

This figure is conservative in another respect. Evolution achieved human intelligence without aiming at this outcome. In other words, the fitness functions for natural organisms do not select only for intelligence and its precursors.[13] Even environments in which organisms with superior information processing skills reap various rewards may not select for intelligence, because improvements to intelligence can (and often do) impose significant costs, such as higher energy consumption or slower maturation times, and those costs may outweigh whatever benefits are gained from smarter behavior. Excessively deadly environments also reduce the value of intelligence: the shorter one's expected lifespan, the less time there will be for increased learning ability to pay off. Reduced selective pressure for intelligence slows the spread of intelligence-enhancing innovations, and thus the opportunity for selection to favor subsequent innovations that depend on them. Furthermore, evolution may wind up stuck in local optima that humans would notice and bypass by altering tradeoffs between exploitation and exploration or by providing a smooth progression

continued

Box 3 *Continued*

of increasingly difficult intelligence tests.[14] And as mentioned earlier, evolution scatters much of its selection power on traits that are unrelated to intelligence (such as Red Queen's races of competitive co-evolution between immune systems and parasites). Evolution continues to waste resources producing mutations that have proved consistently lethal, and it fails to take advantage of statistical similarities in the effects of different mutations. These are all inefficiencies in natural selection (when viewed as a means of evolving intelligence) that it would be relatively easy for a human engineer to avoid while using evolutionary algorithms to develop intelligent software.

It is plausible that eliminating inefficiencies like those just described would trim many orders of magnitude off the 10^{31}–10^{44} FLOPS range calculated earlier. Unfortunately, it is difficult to know how many orders of magnitude. It is difficult even to make a rough estimate—for aught we know, the efficiency savings could be five orders of magnitude, or ten, or twenty-five.[15]

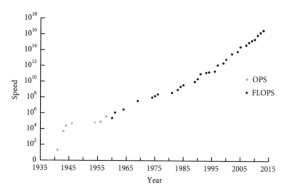

Figure 3 Supercomputer performance. In a narrow sense, "Moore's law" refers to the observation that the number of transistors on integrated circuits have for several decades doubled approximately every two years. However, the term is often used to refer to the more general observation that many performance metrics in computing technology have followed a similarly fast exponential trend. Here we plot peak speed of the world's fastest supercomputer as a function of time (on a logarithmic vertical scale). In recent years, growth in the serial speed of processors has stagnated, but increased use of parallelization has enabled the total number of computations performed to remain on the trend line.[16]

the evolutionary processes involved had a reasonably high prior probability of producing intelligence. Such an inference is unsound because it fails to take account of the observation selection effect that guarantees that all observers will find themselves having originated on a planet where intelligent life arose, no matter how likely or unlikely it was for any given such planet to produce intelligence. Suppose, for example, that in addition to the systematic effects of natural selection it required an enormous amount of *lucky coincidence* to produce intelligent life—enough so that intelligent life evolves on only one planet out of every 10^{30} planets on which simple replicators arise. In that case, when we run our genetic algorithms to try to replicate what natural evolution did, we might find that we must run some 10^{30} simulations before we find one where all the elements come together in just the right way. This seems fully consistent with our observation that life did evolve here on Earth. Only by careful and somewhat intricate reasoning—by analyzing instances of convergent evolution of intelligence-related traits and engaging with the subtleties of observation selection theory—can we partially circumvent this epistemological barrier. Unless one takes the trouble to do so, one is not in a position to rule out the possibility that the alleged "upper bound" on the computational requirements for recapitulating the evolution of intelligence derived in Box 3 might be too low by thirty orders of magnitude (or some other such large number).[17]

Another way of arguing for the feasibility of artificial intelligence is by pointing to the human brain and suggesting that we could use it as a template for a machine intelligence. One can distinguish different versions of this approach based on how closely they propose to imitate biological brain functions. At one extreme—that of very close imitation—we have the idea of *whole brain emulation*, which we will discuss in the next subsection. At the other extreme are approaches that take their inspiration from the functioning of the brain but do not attempt low-level imitation. Advances in neuroscience and cognitive psychology—which will be aided by improvements in instrumentation—should eventually uncover the general principles of brain function. This knowledge could then guide AI efforts. We have already encountered neural networks as an example of a brain-inspired AI technique. Hierarchical perceptual organization is another idea that has been transferred from brain science to machine learning. The study of reinforcement learning has been motivated (at least in part) by its role in psychological theories of animal cognition, and reinforcement learning techniques (e.g. the "TD-algorithm") inspired by these theories are now widely used in AI.[18] More cases like these will surely accumulate in the future. Since there is a limited number—perhaps a very small number—of distinct fundamental mechanisms that operate in the brain, continuing incremental progress in brain science should eventually discover them all. Before this happens, though, it is possible that a hybrid approach, combining some brain-inspired techniques with some purely artificial methods, would cross the finishing line. In that case, the resultant system need not be recognizably brain-like even though some brain-derived insights were used in its development.

The availability of the brain as template provides strong support for the claim that machine intelligence is ultimately feasible. This, however, does not enable us to predict when it will be achieved because it is hard to predict the future rate of discoveries in brain science. What we can say is that the further into the future we look, the greater the likelihood that the secrets of the brain's functionality will have been decoded sufficiently to enable the creation of machine intelligence in this manner.

Different people working toward machine intelligence hold different views about how promising neuromorphic approaches are compared with approaches that aim for completely synthetic designs. The existence of birds demonstrated that heavier-than-air flight was physically possible and prompted efforts to build flying machines. Yet the first functioning airplanes did not flap their wings. The jury is out on whether machine intelligence will be like flight, which humans achieved through an artificial mechanism, or like combustion, which we initially mastered by copying naturally occurring fires.

Turing's idea of designing a program that acquires most of its content by learning, rather than having it pre-programmed at the outset, can apply equally to neuromorphic and synthetic approaches to machine intelligence.

A variation on Turing's conception of a child machine is the idea of a "seed AI."[19] Whereas a child machine, as Turing seems to have envisaged it, would have a relatively fixed architecture that simply develops its inherent potentialities by accumulating *content*, a seed AI would be a more sophisticated artificial intelligence capable of improving its own *architecture*. In the early stages of a seed AI, such improvements might occur mainly through trial and error, information acquisition, or assistance from the programmers. At its later stages, however, a seed AI should be able to *understand* its own workings sufficiently to engineer new algorithms and computational structures to bootstrap its cognitive performance. This needed understanding could result from the seed AI reaching a sufficient level of general intelligence across many domains, or from crossing some threshold in a particularly relevant domain such as computer science or mathematics.

This brings us to another important concept, that of "recursive self-improvement." A successful seed AI would be able to iteratively enhance itself: an early version of the AI could design an improved version of itself, and the improved version—being smarter than the original—might be able to design an even smarter version of itself, and so forth.[20] Under some conditions, such a process of recursive self-improvement might continue long enough to result in an intelligence explosion—an event in which, in a short period of time, a system's level of intelligence increases from a relatively modest endowment of cognitive capabilities (perhaps sub-human in most respects, but with a domain-specific talent for coding and AI research) to radical superintelligence. We will return to this important possibility in Chapter 4, where the dynamics of such an event will be analyzed more closely. Note that this model suggests the possibility of surprises: attempts to build artificial general intelligence might fail pretty much completely until the last missing critical component is put in place, at which point a seed AI might become capable of sustained recursive self-improvement.

Before we end this subsection, there is one more thing that we should emphasize, which is that an artificial intelligence need not much resemble a human mind. AIs could be—indeed, it is likely that most will be—extremely alien. We should expect that they will have very different cognitive architectures than biological intelligences, and in their early stages of development they will have very different profiles of cognitive strengths and weaknesses (though, as we shall later argue, they could eventually overcome any initial weakness). Furthermore, the goal systems of AIs could diverge radically from those of human beings. There is no reason to expect a generic AI to be motivated by love or hate or pride or other such common human sentiments: these complex adaptations would require deliberate expensive effort to recreate in AIs. This is at once a big problem and a big opportunity. We will return to the issue of AI motivation in later chapters, but it is so central to the argument in this book that it is worth bearing in mind throughout.

Whole brain emulation

In whole brain emulation (also known as "uploading"), intelligent software would be produced by scanning and closely modeling the computational structure of a biological brain. This approach thus represents a limiting case of drawing inspiration from nature: barefaced plagiarism. Achieving whole brain emulation requires the accomplishment of the following steps.

First, a sufficiently detailed scan of a particular human brain is created. This might involve stabilizing the brain post-mortem through vitrification (a process that turns tissue into a kind of glass). A machine could then dissect the tissue into thin slices, which could be fed into another machine for scanning, perhaps by an array of electron microscopes. Various stains might be applied at this stage to bring out different structural and chemical properties. Many scanning machines could work in parallel to process multiple brain slices simultaneously.

Second, the raw data from the scanners is fed to a computer for automated image processing to reconstruct the three-dimensional neuronal network that implemented cognition in the original brain. In practice, this step might proceed concurrently with the first step to reduce the amount of high-resolution image data stored in buffers. The resulting map is then combined with a library of neurocomputational models of different types of neurons or of different neuronal elements (such as particular kinds of synaptic connectors). Figure 4 shows some results of scanning and image processing produced with present-day technology.

In the third stage, the neurocomputational structure resulting from the previous step is implemented on a sufficiently powerful computer. If completely successful, the result would be a digital reproduction of the original intellect, with memory and personality intact. The emulated human mind now exists as software on a computer. The mind can either inhabit a virtual reality or interface with the external world by means of robotic appendages.

The whole brain emulation path does not require that we figure out how human cognition works or how to program an artificial intelligence. It requires only that we understand the low-level functional characteristics of the basic computational elements of the brain. No fundamental conceptual or theoretical breakthrough is needed for whole brain emulation to succeed.

Whole brain emulation does, however, require some rather advanced enabling technologies. There are three key prerequisites: (1) *scanning*: high-throughput microscopy with sufficient resolution and detection of relevant properties; (2) *translation*: automated image analysis to turn raw scanning data into an interpreted three-dimensional model of relevant neurocomputational elements; and (3) *simulation*: hardware powerful

Figure 4 Reconstructing 3D neuroanatomy from electron microscope images. *Upper left*: A typical electron micrograph showing cross-sections of neuronal matter—dendrites and axons. *Upper right*: Volume image of rabbit retinal neural tissue acquired by serial block-face scanning electron microscopy.[21] Individual 2D images have been stacked into a cube (with a side of approximately 11 μm). *Bottom*: Reconstruction of a subset of the neuronal projections filling a volume of neuropil, generated by an automated segmentation algorithm.[22]

enough to implement the resultant computational structure (see Table 4). (In comparison with these more challenging steps, the construction of a basic virtual reality or a robotic embodiment with an audiovisual input channel and some simple output channel is relatively easy. Simple yet minimally adequate I/O seems feasible already with present technology.[23])

There is good reason to think that the requisite enabling technologies are attainable, though not in the near future. Reasonable computational models of many types of neuron and neuronal processes already exist.

Table 4 *Capabilities needed for whole brain emulation*

Scanning	Pre-processing/fixation		Preparing brains appropriately, retaining relevant microstructure and state
	Physical handling		Methods of manipulating fixed brains and tissue pieces before, during, and after scanning
	Imaging	Volume	Capability to scan entire brain volumes in reasonable time and expense
		Resolution	Scanning at sufficient resolution to enable reconstruction
		Functional information	Ability for scanning to detect the functionally relevant properties of tissue
Translation	Image processing	Geometric adjustment	Handling distortions due to scanning imperfections
		Data interpolation	Handling missing data
		Noise removal	Improving scan quality
		Tracing	Detecting structure and processing it into a consistent 3D model of the tissue
	Scan interpretation	Cell type identification	Identifying cell types
		Synapse identification	Identifying synapses and their connectivity
		Parameter estimation	Estimating functionally relevant parameters of cells, synapses, and other entities
		Databasing	Storing the resulting inventory in an efficient way
	Software model of neural system	Mathematical model	Model of entities and their behavior
		Efficient implementation	Implementation of model

continued

Table 4 *Continued*

Simulation	Storage	Storage of original model and current state
	Bandwidth	Efficient interprocessor communication
	CPU	Processor power to run simulation
	Body simulation	Simulation of body enabling interaction with virtual environment or actual environment via robot
	Environment simulation	Virtual environment for virtual body

Image recognition software has been developed that can trace axons and dendrites through a stack of two-dimensional images (though reliability needs to be improved). And there are imaging tools that provide the necessary resolution—with a scanning tunneling microscope it is possible to "see" individual atoms, which is a far higher resolution than needed. However, although present knowledge and capabilities suggest that there is no in-principle barrier to the development of the requisite enabling technologies, it is clear that a very great deal of incremental technical progress would be needed to bring human whole brain emulation within reach.[24] For example, microscopy technology would need not just sufficient resolution but also sufficient throughput. Using an atomic-resolution scanning tunneling microscope to image the needed surface area would be far too slow to be practicable. It would be more plausible to use a lower-resolution electron microscope, but this would require new methods for preparing and staining cortical tissue to make visible relevant details such as synaptic fine structure. A great expansion of neurocomputational libraries and major improvements in automated image processing and scan interpretation would also be needed.

In general, whole brain emulation relies less on theoretical insight and more on technological capability than artificial intelligence. Just how much technology is required for whole brain emulation depends on the level of abstraction at which the brain is emulated. In this regard there is a tradeoff between insight and technology. In general, the worse our scanning equipment and the feebler our computers, the less we could rely on simulating low-level chemical and electro-physiological brain processes, and the more theoretical understanding would be needed of the computational architecture that we are seeking to emulate in order to create more abstract representations of the relevant functionalities.[25] Conversely, with sufficiently advanced scanning technology and abundant computing power, it might be possible to brute-force an emulation even with a fairly limited understanding of the brain. In the unrealistic limiting case, we could imagine emulating a brain at the level of its elementary particles using the quantum mechanical Schrödinger equation. Then one could rely entirely on existing knowledge of physics and not at all on any biological model. This extreme case, however, would place utterly impracticable demands on computational power and data acquisition. A far more plausible level of emulation would be one that incorporates individual neurons and their connectivity matrix, along with some of the structure of their dendritic trees and maybe some state variables of individual synapses. Neurotransmitter molecules would not be simulated individually, but their fluctuating concentrations would be modeled in a coarse-grained manner.

To assess the feasibility of whole brain emulation, one must understand the criterion for success. The aim is not to create a brain simulation so detailed and accurate that one could use it to predict exactly what would have happened in the original brain if it had been subjected to a particular sequence of stimuli. Instead, the aim is to capture enough of the computationally functional properties of the brain to enable the resultant emulation to perform intellectual work. For this purpose, much of the messy biological detail of a real brain is irrelevant.

A more elaborate analysis would distinguish between different levels of emulation success based on the extent to which the information-processing functionality of the emulated brain has been preserved. For example, one could distinguish among (1) a *high-fidelity emulation* that has the full set of knowledge, skills, capacities, and values of the emulated brain; (2) a *distorted emulation* whose dispositions are significantly non-human in some ways but which is mostly able to do the same intellectual labor as the emulated brain; and (3) a *generic emulation* (which might also be distorted) that is somewhat like an infant, lacking the skills or memories that had been acquired by the emulated adult brain but with the capacity to learn most of what a normal human can learn.[26]

While it appears ultimately feasible to produce a high-fidelity emulation, it seems quite likely that the *first* whole brain emulation that we would achieve if we went down this path would be of a lower grade. Before we would get things to work perfectly, we would probably get things to work imperfectly. It is also possible that a push toward emulation technology would lead to the creation of some kind of neuromorphic AI that would adapt some neurocomputational principles discovered during emulation efforts and hybridize them with synthetic methods, and that this would happen before the completion of a fully functional whole brain emulation. The possibility of such a spillover into neuromorphic AI, as we shall see in a later chapter, complicates the strategic assessment of the desirability of seeking to expedite emulation technology.

How far are we currently from achieving a human whole brain emulation? One recent assessment presented a technical roadmap and concluded that the prerequisite capabilities might be available around midcentury, though with a large uncertainty interval.[27] Figure 5 depicts the

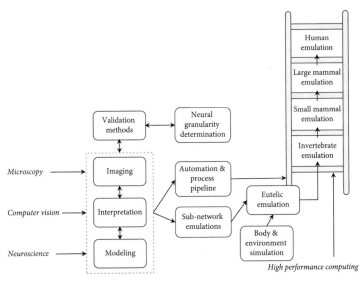

Figure 5 Whole brain emulation roadmap. Schematic of inputs, activities, and milestones.[28]

major milestones in this roadmap. The apparent simplicity of the map may be deceptive, however, and we should be careful not to understate how much work remains to be done. No brain has yet been emulated. Consider the humble model organism *Caenorhabditis elegans*, which is a transparent roundworm, about 1 mm in length, with 302 neurons. The complete connectivity matrix of these neurons has been known since the mid-1980s, when it was laboriously mapped out by means of slicing, electron microscopy, and hand-labeling of specimens.[29] But knowing merely which neurons are connected with which is not enough. To create a brain emulation one would also need to know which synapses are excitatory and which are inhibitory; the strength of the connections; and various dynamical properties of axons, synapses, and dendritic trees. This information is not yet available even for the small nervous system of *C. elegans* (although it may now be within range of a targeted moderately sized research project).[30] Success at emulating a tiny brain, such as that of *C. elegans*, would give us a better view of what it would take to emulate larger brains.

At some point in the technology development process, once techniques are available for automatically emulating small quantities of brain tissue, the problem reduces to one of scaling. Notice the "ladder" at the right side of Figure 5. This ascending series of boxes represents a final sequence of advances which can commence after preliminary hurdles have been cleared. The stages in this sequence correspond to whole brain emulations of successively more neurologically sophisticated model organisms—for example, *C. elegans → honeybee → mouse → rhesus monkey → human*. Because the gaps between these rungs—at least after the first step—are mostly quantitative in nature and due mainly (though not entirely) to the differences in size of the brains to be emulated, they should be tractable through a relatively straightforward scale-up of scanning and simulation capacity.[31]

Once we start ascending this final ladder, the *eventual* attainment of human whole brain emulation becomes more clearly foreseeable.[32] We can thus expect to get some advance warning before arrival at human-level machine intelligence along the whole brain emulation path, at least if the last among the requisite enabling technologies to reach sufficient maturity is either high-throughput scanning or the computational power needed for real-time simulation. If, however, the last enabling technology to fall into place is neurocomputational modeling, then the transition from unimpressive prototypes to a working human emulation could be more abrupt. One could imagine a scenario in which, despite abundant scanning data and fast computers, it is proving difficult to get our neuronal models to work right. When finally the last glitch is ironed out, what was previously a completely dysfunctional system—analogous perhaps to an unconscious brain undergoing a grand mal seizure—might snap into a coherent wakeful state. In this case, the key advance would not be heralded by a series of functioning animal emulations of increasing magnitude (provoking newspaper headlines of correspondingly escalating font size). Even for those paying attention it might be difficult to tell in advance of success just how many flaws remained in the neurocomputational models at any point and how long it would take to fix them, even up to the eve of the critical breakthrough. (Once a human whole brain emulation has been achieved, further potentially explosive developments would take place; but we postpone discussion of this until Chapter 4.)

Surprise scenarios are thus imaginable for whole brain emulation even if all the relevant research were conducted in the open. Nevertheless, compared with the AI path to machine intelligence, whole brain emulation is more likely to be preceded by clear omens since it relies more on concrete observable technologies and is not wholly based on theoretical insight. We can also say, with greater confidence than for the AI path, that the emulation path will not succeed in the near future (within the next fifteen years, say) because we know that several challenging precursor technologies have not yet been developed. By contrast, it seems likely that somebody could *in principle* sit down and code a seed AI on an ordinary present-day personal computer; and it is conceivable—though unlikely—that somebody somewhere will get the right insight for how to do this in the near future.

Biological cognition

A third path to greater-than-current-human intelligence is to enhance the functioning of biological brains. In principle, this could be achieved without technology, through selective breeding. Any attempt to initiate a classical large-scale eugenics program, however, would confront major political and moral hurdles. Moreover, unless the selection were extremely strong, many generations would be required to produce substantial results. Long before such an initiative would bear fruit, advances in biotechnology will allow much more direct control of human genetics and neurobiology, rendering otiose any human breeding program. We will therefore focus on methods that hold the potential to deliver results faster, on the timescale of a few generations or less.

Our individual cognitive capacities can be strengthened in various ways, including by such traditional methods as education and training. Neurological development can be promoted by low-tech interventions such as optimizing maternal and infant nutrition, removing lead and other neurotoxic pollutants from the environment, eradicating parasites, ensuring adequate sleep and exercise, and preventing diseases that affect the brain.[33] Improvements in cognition can certainly be obtained through each of these means, though the magnitudes of the gains are likely to be modest, especially in populations that are already reasonably well-nourished and -schooled. We will certainly not achieve superintelligence by any of these means, but they might help on the margin, particularly by lifting up the deprived and expanding the catchment of global talent. (Lifelong depression of intelligence due to iodine deficiency remains widespread in many impoverished inland areas of the world—an outrage given that the condition can be prevented by fortifying table salt at a cost of a few cents per person and year.[34])

Biomedical enhancements could give bigger boosts. Drugs already exist that are alleged to improve memory, concentration, and mental energy in at least some subjects.[35] (Work on this book was fueled by coffee and nicotine chewing gum.) While the efficacy of the present generation of smart drugs is variable, marginal, and generally dubious, future nootropics might offer clearer benefits and fewer side effects.[36] However, it seems implausible, on both neurological and evolutionary grounds, that one could by introducing some chemical into the brain of a healthy person spark a dramatic rise in intelligence.[37] The cognitive functioning of a human brain depends on a delicate orchestration of many factors, especially during the critical stages of embryo development—and it is much more likely that this self-organizing structure, to be enhanced, needs to be carefully balanced, tuned, and cultivated rather than simply flooded with some extraneous potion.

Manipulation of genetics will provide a more powerful set of tools than psychopharmacology. Consider again the idea of genetic selection: instead of trying to implement a eugenics program by controlling mating patterns, one could use selection at the level of embryos or gametes.[38]

Pre-implantation genetic diagnosis has already been used during in vitro fertilization procedures to screen embryos produced for monogenic disorders such as Huntington's disease and for predisposition to some late-onset diseases such as breast cancer. It has also been used for sex selection and for matching human leukocyte antigen type with that of a sick sibling, who can then benefit from a cord-blood stem cell donation when the new baby is born.[39] The range of traits that can be selected for or against will expand greatly over the next decade or two. A strong driver of progress in behavioral genetics is the rapidly falling cost of genotyping and gene sequencing. Genome-wide complex trait analysis, using studies with vast numbers of subjects, is just now starting to become feasible and will greatly increase our knowledge of the genetic architectures of human cognitive and behavioral traits.[40] Any trait with a non-negligible heritability—including cognitive capacity—could then become susceptible to selection.[41] Embryo selection does not require a deep understanding of the causal pathways by which genes, in complicated interplay with environments, produce phenotypes: it requires only (lots of) data on the genetic correlates of the traits of interest.

It is possible to calculate some rough estimates of the magnitude of the gains obtainable in different selection scenarios.[42] Table 5 shows expected increases in intelligence resulting from various amounts of selection, assuming complete information about the common additive genetic variants underlying the narrow-sense heritability of intelligence. (With partial

Table 5 *Maximum IQ gains from selecting among a set of embryos*[43]

Selection	IQ points gained
1 in 2	4.2
1 in 10	11.5
1 in 100	18.8
1 in 1000	24.3
5 generations of 1 in 10	< 65 (b/c diminishing returns)
10 generations of 1 in 10	< 130 (b/c diminishing returns)
Cumulative limits (additive variants optimized for cognition)	100 + (< 300 (b/c diminishing returns))

information, the effectiveness of selection would be reduced, though not quite to the extent one might naively expect.[44]) Unsurprisingly, selecting between larger numbers of embryos produces larger gains, but there are steeply diminishing returns: selection between 100 embryos does not produce a gain anywhere near fifty times as large as that which one would get from selection between 2 embryos.[45]

Interestingly, the diminishment of returns is greatly abated when the selection is spread over multiple generations. Thus, repeatedly selecting the top 1 in 10 over ten generations (where each new generation consists of the offspring of those selected in the previous generation) will produce a much greater increase in the trait value than a one-off selection of 1 in 100. The problem with sequential selection, of course, is that it takes longer. If each generational step takes twenty or thirty years, then even just five successive generations would push us well into the twenty-second century. Long before then, more direct and powerful modes of genetic engineering (not to mention machine intelligence) will most likely be available.

There is, however, a complementary technology, one which, once it has been developed for use in humans, would greatly potentiate the enhancement power of pre-implantation genetic screening: namely, the derivation of viable sperm and eggs from embryonic stem cells.[46] The techniques for this have already been used to produce fertile offspring in mice and gamete-like cells in humans. Substantial scientific challenges remain, however, in translating the animal results to humans and in avoiding epigenetic abnormalities in the derived stem cell lines. According to one expert, these challenges might put human application "10 or even 50 years in the future."[47]

With stem cell-derived gametes, the amount of selection power available to a couple could be greatly increased. In current practice, an in vitro fertilization procedure typically involves the creation of fewer than ten embryos. With stem cell-derived gametes, a few donated cells might be turned into a virtually unlimited number of gametes that could be combined to produce embryos, which could then be genotyped or sequenced, and the most promising one chosen for implantation. Depending on the cost of preparing and screening each individual embryo, this technology could yield a severalfold increase in the selective power available to couples using in vitro fertilization.

More importantly still, stem cell-derived gametes would allow multiple generations of selection to be compressed into less than a human

maturation period, by enabling *iterated embryo selection*. This is a procedure that would consist of the following steps:[48]

1 Genotype and select a number of embryos that are higher in desired
genetic characteristics.
2 Extract stem cells from those embryos and convert them to sperm and
ova, maturing within six months or less.[49]
3 Cross the new sperm and ova to produce embryos.
4 Repeat until large genetic changes have been accumulated.

In this manner, it would be possible to accomplish ten or more generations of selection in just a few years. (The procedure would be time-con-
suming and expensive; however, in principle, it would need to be done
only once rather than repeated for each birth. The cell lines established at
the end of the procedure could be used to generate very large numbers of
enhanced embryos.)

As Table 5 indicates, the *average* level of intelligence among individuals
conceived in this manner could be very high, possibly equal to or somewhat above that of the most intelligent individual in the historical human
population. A world that had a large population of such individuals might
(if it had the culture, education, communications infrastructure, etc., to
match) constitute a collective superintelligence.

The impact of this technology will be dampened and delayed by several factors. There is the unavoidable maturational lag while the finally
selected embryos grow into adult human beings: at least twenty years
before an enhanced child reaches full productivity, longer still before such
children come to constitute a substantial segment of the labor force. Furthermore, even after the technology has been perfected, adoption rates
will probably start out low. Some countries might prohibit its use altogether, on moral or religious grounds.[50] Even where selection is allowed,
many couples will prefer the natural way of conceiving. Willingness to use
IVF, however, would increase if there were clearer benefits associated with
the procedure—such as a virtual guarantee that the child would be highly
talented and free from genetic predispositions to disease. Lower health
care costs and higher expected lifetime earnings would also argue in favor
of genetic selection. As use of the procedure becomes more common,
particularly among social elites, there might be a cultural shift toward
parenting norms that present the use of selection as the thing that responsible enlightened couples do. Many of the initially reluctant might join the

bandwagon in order to have a child that is not at a disadvantage relative to the enhanced children of their friends and colleagues. Some countries might offer inducements to encourage their citizens to take advantage of genetic selection in order to increase the country's stock of human capital, or to increase long-term social stability by selecting for traits like docility, obedience, submissiveness, conformity, risk-aversion, or cowardice, outside of the ruling clan.

Effects on intellectual capacity would also depend on the extent to which the available selection power would be used for enhancing cognitive traits (Table 6). Those who do opt to use some form of embryo selection would have to choose how to allocate the selection power at their disposal, and intelligence would to some extent be in competition with other desired attributes, such as health, beauty, personality, or athleticism. Iterated embryo selection, by offering such a large amount of selection power, would alleviate some of these tradeoffs, enabling simultaneous strong selection for multiple traits. However, this procedure would tend to disrupt the normal genetic relationship between parents and child, something that could negatively affect demand in many cultures.[51]

With further advances in genetic technology, it may become possible to synthesize genomes to specification, obviating the need for large pools of embryos. DNA synthesis is already a routine and largely automated biotechnology, though it is not yet feasible to synthesize an entire human genome that could be used in a reproductive context (not least because of still-unresolved difficulties in getting the epigenetics right).[52] But once this technology has matured, an embryo could be designed with the exact preferred combination of genetic inputs from each parent. Genes that are present in neither of the parents could also be spliced in, including alleles that are present with low frequency in the population but which may have significant positive effects on cognition.[53]

One intervention that becomes possible when human genomes can be synthesized is genetic "spell-checking" of an embryo. (Iterated embryo selection might also allow an approximation of this.) Each of us currently carries a mutational load, with perhaps hundreds of mutations that reduce the efficiency of various cellular processes.[54] Each individual mutation has an almost negligible effect (whence it is only slowly removed from the gene pool), yet in combination such mutations may exact a heavy toll on our functioning.[55] Individual differences in intelligence might to a significant extent be attributable to variations in the number and nature

Table 6 Possible impacts from genetic selection in different scenarios[56]

Adoption / technology	"IVF+" Selection of 1 of 2 embryos [4 points]	"Aggressive IVF" Selection of 1 of 10 embryos [12 points]	"In vitro egg" Selection of 1 of 100 embryos [19 points]	"Iterated embryo selection" [100+ points]
"Marginal fertility practice" ~ 0.25% adoption	Socially negligible over one generation. Effects of social controversy more important than direct impacts.	Socially negligible over one generation. Effects of social controversy more important than direct impacts.	Enhanced contingent form noticeable minority in highly cognitively selective positions.	Selected dominate ranks of elite scientists, attorneys, physicians, engineers. Intellectual Renaissance?
"Elite advantage" 10% adoption	Slight cognitive impact in 1st generation, combines with selection for non-cognitive traits to perceptibly advantage a minority.	Large fraction of Harvard undergraduates enhanced. 2nd generation dominate cognitively demanding professions.	Selected dominate ranks of scientists, attorneys, physicians, engineers in 1st generation.	"Posthumanity"[157]
"New normal" > 90% adoption	Learning disability much less frequent among children. In 2nd generation, population above high IQ thresholds more than doubled.	Substantial growth in educational attainment, income. 2nd generation manyfold increase at right tail.	Raw IQs typical for eminent scientists 10+ times as common in 1st generation. Thousands of times in 2nd generation.	"Posthumanity"

of such slightly deleterious alleles that each of us carries. With gene synthesis we could take the genome of an embryo and construct a version of that genome free from the genetic noise of accumulated mutations. If one wished to speak provocatively, one could say that individuals created from such proofread genomes might be "more human" than anybody currently alive, in that they would be less distorted expressions of human form. Such people would not all be carbon copies, because humans vary genetically in ways other than by carrying different deleterious mutations. But the phenotypical manifestation of a proofread genome may be an exceptional physical and mental constitution, with elevated functioning in polygenic trait dimensions like intelligence, health, hardiness, and appearance.[58] (A loose analogy could be made with composite faces, in which the defects of the superimposed individuals are averaged out: see Figure 6.)

Other potential biotechnological techniques might also be relevant. Human reproductive cloning, once achieved, could be used to replicate the genome of exceptionally talented individuals. Uptake would be limited by the preference of most prospective parents to be biologically related to their children, yet the practice could nevertheless come to have non-negligible impact because (1) even a relatively small increase in the number of exceptionally talented people might have a significant effect; and (2) it is possible that some state would embark on a larger-scale

Figure 6 Composite faces as a metaphor for spell-checked genomes. Each of the central pictures was produced by superimposing photographs of sixteen different individuals (residents of Tel Aviv). Composite faces are often judged to be more beautiful than any of the individual faces of which they are composed, as idiosyncratic imperfections are averaged out. Analogously, by removing individual mutations, proofread genomes may produce people closer to "Platonic ideals." Such individuals would not all be genetically identical, because many genes come in multiple equally functional alleles. Proofreading would only eliminate variance arising from deleterious mutations.[59]

eugenics program, perhaps by paying surrogate mothers. Other kinds of genetic engineering—such as the design of novel synthetic genes or insertion into the genome of promoter regions and other elements to control gene expression—might also become important over time. Even more exotic possibilities may exist, such as vats full of complexly structured cultured cortical tissue, or "uplifted" transgenic animals (perhaps some large-brained mammal such as the whale or elephant, enriched with human genes). These latter ones are wholly speculative, but over a longer time frame they perhaps cannot be completely discounted.

So far we have discussed germline interventions, ones that would be done on gametes or embryos. Somatic gene enhancements, by bypassing the generation cycle, could in principle produce impacts more quickly. However, they are technologically much more challenging. They require that the modified genes be inserted into a large number of cells in the living body—including, in the case of cognitive enhancement, the brain. Selecting among existing egg cells or embryos, in contrast, requires no gene insertion. Even such germline therapies as do involve modifying the genome (such as proofreading the genome or splicing in rare alleles) are far easier to implement at the gamete or the embryo stage, where one is dealing with a small number of cells. Furthermore, germline interventions on embryos can probably achieve greater effects than somatic interventions on adults, because the former would be able to shape early brain development whereas the latter would be limited to tweaking an existing structure. (Some of what could be done through somatic gene therapy might also be achievable by pharmacological means.)

Focusing therefore on germline interventions, we must take into account the generational lag delaying any large impact on the world.[60] Even if the technology were perfected today and immediately put to use, it would take more than two decades for a genetically enhanced brood to reach maturity. Furthermore, with human applications there is normally a delay of at least one decade between proof of concept in the laboratory and clinical application, because of the need for extensive studies to determine safety. The simplest forms of genetic selection, however, could largely abrogate the need for such testing, since they would use standard fertility treatment techniques and genetic information to choose between embryos that might otherwise have been selected by chance.

Delays could also result from obstacles rooted not in a fear of failure (demand for safety testing) but in fear of success—demand for regulation driven by concerns about the moral permissibility of genetic selection or its wider social implications. Such concerns are likely to be more influential in some countries than in others, owing to differing cultural, historical, and religious contexts. Post-war Germany, for example, has chosen to give a wide berth to any reproductive practices that could be perceived to be even in the remotest way aimed at enhancement, a stance that is understandable given the particularly dark history of atrocities connected to the eugenics movement in that country. Other Western countries are likely to take a more liberal approach. And some countries—perhaps China or Singapore, both of which have long-term population policies—might not only permit but actively promote the use of genetic selection and genetic engineering to enhance the intelligence of their populations once the technology to do so is available.

Once the example has been set, and the results start to show, holdouts will have strong incentives to follow suit. Nations would face the prospect of becoming cognitive backwaters and losing out in economic, scientific, military, and prestige contests with competitors that embrace the new human enhancement technologies. Individuals within a society would see places at elite schools being filled with genetically selected children (who may also on average be prettier, healthier, and more conscientious) and will want their own offspring to have the same advantages. There is some chance that a large attitudinal shift could take place over a relatively short time, perhaps in as little as a decade, once the technology is proven to work and to provide a substantial benefit. Opinion surveys in the United States reveal a dramatic shift in public approval of in vitro fertilization after the birth of the first "test tube baby," Louise Brown, in 1978. A few years earlier, only 18% of Americans said they would personally use IVF to treat infertility; yet in a poll taken shortly after the birth of Louise Brown, 53% said they would do so, and the number has continued to rise.[61] (For comparison, in a poll taken in 2004, 28% of Americans approved of embryo selection for "strength or intelligence," 58% approved of it for avoiding adult-onset cancer, and 68% approved of it to avoid fatal childhood disease.[62])

If we add up the various delays—say five to ten years to gather the information needed for significantly effective selection among a set of IVF embryos (possibly much longer before stem cell-derived gametes are available for use in human reproduction), ten years to build significant uptake, and twenty to twenty-five years for the enhanced generation to reach an age where they start becoming productive, we find that germ-line enhancements are unlikely to have a significant impact on society before the middle of this century. From that point onward, however, the intelligence of significant segments of the adult population may begin to be boosted by genetic enhancements. The speed of the ascent would then greatly accelerate as cohorts conceived using more powerful next-generation genetic technologies (in particular stem cell-derived gametes and iterative embryo selection) enter the labor force.

With the full development of the genetic technologies described above (setting aside the more exotic possibilities such as intelligence in cultured neural tissue), it might be possible to ensure that new individuals are on average smarter than any human who has yet existed, with peaks that rise higher still. The potential of biological enhancement is thus ultimately high, probably sufficient for the attainment of at least weak forms of super-intelligence. This should not be surprising. After all, dumb evolutionary processes have dramatically amplified the intelligence in the human line-age even compared with our close relatives the great apes and our own humanoid ancestors; and there is no reason to suppose *Homo sapiens* to have reached the apex of cognitive effectiveness attainable in a biologi-cal system. Far from being the smartest possible biological species, we are probably better thought of as the stupidest possible biological species capable of starting a technological civilization—a niche we filled because we got there first, not because we are in any sense optimally adapted to it.

Progress along the biological path is clearly feasible. The generational lag in germline interventions means that progress could not be nearly as sudden and abrupt as in scenarios involving machine intelligence. (Somatic gene therapies and pharmacological interventions could theo-retically skip the generational lag, but they seem harder to perfect and are less likely to produce dramatic effects.) The *ultimate* potential of machine intelligence is, of course, vastly greater than that of organic intelligence. (One can get some sense of the magnitude of the gap by considering the speed differential between electronic components and nerve cells: even today's transistors operate on a timescale ten million times shorter than that of biological neurons.) However, even comparatively moder-ate enhancements of biological cognition could have important conse-quences. In particular, cognitive enhancement could accelerate science and technology, including progress toward more potent forms of biologi-cal intelligence amplification and machine intelligence. Consider how the rate of progress in the field of artificial intelligence would change in a world where Average Joe is an intellectual peer of Alan Turing or John von Neumann, and where millions of people tower far above any intellectual giant of the past.[63]

A discussion of the strategic implications of cognitive enhancement will have to await a later chapter. But we can summarize this section by noting three conclusions: (1) at least weak forms of superintelligence are achievable by means of biotechnological enhancements; (2) the feasibility of cognitively enhanced humans adds to the plausibility that advanced forms of machine intelligence are feasible—because even if *we* were fundamentally unable to create machine intelligence (which there is no reason to suppose), machine intelligence might still be within reach of cognitively enhanced humans; and (3) when we consider scenarios stretching significantly into the second half of this century and beyond, we must take into account the probable emergence of a generation of genetically enhanced populations—voters, inventors, scientists—with the magnitude of enhancement escalating rapidly over subsequent decades.

Brain–computer interfaces

It is sometimes proposed that direct brain–computer interfaces, particularly implants, could enable humans to exploit the fortes of digital computing—perfect recall, speedy and accurate arithmetic calculation, and high-bandwidth data transmission—enabling the resulting hybrid system to radically outperform the unaugmented brain.[64] But although the possibility of direct connections between human brains and computers has been demonstrated, it seems unlikely that such interfaces will be widely used as enhancements any time soon.[65]

To begin with, there are significant risks of medical complications—including infections, electrode displacement, hemorrhage, and cognitive decline—when implanting electrodes in the brain. Perhaps the most vivid illustration to date of the benefits that can be obtained through brain stimulation is the treatment of patients with Parkinson's disease. The Parkinson's implant is relatively simple: it does not really communicate with the brain but simply supplies a stimulating electric current to the subthalamic nucleus. A demonstration video shows a subject slumped in a chair, completely immobilized by the disease, then suddenly springing to life when the current is switched on: the subject now moves his arms, stands up and walks across the room, turns around and performs a pirouette. Yet even behind this especially simple and almost miraculously successful procedure, there lurk negatives. One study of Parkinson patients who had received deep brain implants showed reductions in verbal fluency, selective attention, color naming, and verbal memory compared with controls. Treated subjects also reported more cognitive complaints.[66] Such risks and side effects might be tolerable if the procedure is used to alleviate severe disability. But in order for healthy subjects to volunteer themselves for neurosurgery, there would have to be some very substantial enhancement of normal functionality to be gained.

This brings us to the second reason to doubt that superintelligence will be achieved through cyborgization, namely that enhancement is likely to be far more difficult than therapy. Patients who suffer from paralysis might benefit from an implant that replaces their severed nerves or activates spinal motion pattern generators.[67] Patients who are deaf or blind might benefit from artificial cochleae and retinas.[68] Patients with Parkinson's disease or chronic pain might benefit from deep brain stimulation that excites or inhibits activity in a particular area of the brain.[69] What seems far more difficult to achieve is a high-bandwidth direct interaction between brain and computer to provide substantial increases in intelligence of a form that could not be more readily attained by other means. Most of the potential benefits that brain implants could provide in healthy subjects could be obtained at far less risk, expense, and inconvenience by using our regular motor and sensory organs to interact with computers located outside of our bodies. We do not need to plug a fiber optic cable into our brains in order to access the internet. Not only can the human retina transmit data at an impressive rate of nearly 10 million bits per second, but it comes pre-packaged with a massive amount of dedicated wetware, the visual cortex, that is highly adapted to extracting meaning from this information torrent and to interfacing with other brain areas for further processing.[70] Even if there were an easy way of pumping more information into our brains, the extra data inflow would do little to increase the rate at which we think and learn unless all the neural machinery necessary for making sense of the data were similarly upgraded. Since this includes almost all of the brain, what would really be needed is a "whole brain prosthesis"—which is just another way of saying artificial general intelligence. Yet if one had a human-level AI, one could dispense with neurosurgery: a computer might as well have a metal casing as one of bone. So this limiting case just takes us back to the AI path, which we have already examined.

Brain–computer interfacing has also been proposed as a way to get information out of the brain, for purposes of communicating with other brains or with machines.[71] Such uplinks have helped patients with locked-in syndrome to communicate with the outside world by enabling them to move a cursor on a screen by thought.[72] The bandwidth attained in such experiments is low: the patient painstakingly types out one slow letter after another at a rate of a few words per minute. One can readily imagine improved versions of this technology—perhaps a next-generation implant could plug into Broca's area (a region in the frontal lobe involved in language production) and pick up internal speech.[73] But whilst such a technology might assist some people with disabilities induced by stroke or muscular degeneration, it would hold little appeal for healthy subjects. The functionality it would provide is essentially that of a microphone coupled with speech recognition software, which is already commercially available—minus the pain, inconvenience, expense, and risks associated with neurosurgery (and minus at least some of the hyper-Orwellian over-tones of an intracranial listening device). Keeping our machines outside of our bodies also makes upgrading easier.

But what about the dream of bypassing words altogether and establishing a connection between two brains that enables concepts, thoughts, or entire areas of expertise to be "downloaded" from one mind to another? We can download large files to our computers, including libraries with millions of books and articles, and this can be done over the course of seconds: could something similar be done with our brains? The apparent plausibility of this idea probably derives from an incorrect view of how information is stored and represented in the brain. As noted, the rate-limiting step in human intelligence is not how fast raw data can be fed into the brain but rather how quickly the brain can extract meaning and make sense of the data. Perhaps it will be suggested that we transmit meanings directly, rather than package them into sensory data that must be decoded by the recipient. There are two problems with this. The first is that brains, by contrast to the kinds of program we typically run on our computers, do not use standardized data storage and representation formats. Rather, each brain develops its own idiosyncratic representations of higher-level content. Which particular neuronal assemblies are recruited to represent a particular concept depends on the unique experiences of the brain in question (along with various genetic factors and stochastic physiological processes). Just as in artificial neural nets, meaning in biological neural networks is likely represented holistically in the structure and activity patterns of sizeable overlapping regions, not in discrete memory cells laid out in neat arrays.[74] It would therefore not be possible to establish a simple mapping between the neurons in one brain and those in another in such a way that thoughts could automatically slide over from one to the other. In order for the thoughts of one brain to be intelligible to another, the thoughts need to be decomposed and packaged into symbols according to some shared convention that allows the symbols to be correctly interpreted by the receiving brain. This is the job of language.

In principle, one could imagine offloading the cognitive work of articulation and interpretation to an interface that would somehow read out the neural states in the sender's brain and somehow feed in a bespoke pattern of activation to the receiver's brain. But this brings us to the second problem with the cyborg scenario. Even setting aside the (quite immense) technical challenge of how to reliably read and write simultaneously from perhaps billions of individually addressable neurons, creating the requisite interface is probably an AI-complete problem. The interface would need to include a component able (in real-time) to map firing patterns in one brain onto semantically equivalent firing patterns in the other brain. The detailed multilevel understanding of the neural computation needed to accomplish such a task would seem to directly enable neuromorphic AI.

Despite these reservations, the cyborg route toward cognitive enhancement is not entirely without promise. Impressive work on the rat hippocampus has demonstrated the feasibility of a neural prosthesis that can enhance performance in a simple working-memory task.[75] In its present version, the implant collects input from a dozen or two electrodes located in one area ("CA3") of the hippocampus and projects onto a similar number of neurons in another area ("CA1"). A microprocessor is trained to discriminate between two different firing patterns in the first area (corresponding to two different memories, "right lever" or "left lever") and to learn how these patterns are projected into the second area. This prosthesis can not only restore function when the normal neural connection between the two neural areas is blockaded, but by sending an especially clear token of a particular memory pattern to the second area it can enhance the performance on the memory task beyond what the rat is normally capable of. While a technical tour de force by contemporary standards, the study leaves many challenging questions unanswered: How well does the approach scale to greater numbers of memories? How well can we control the combinatorial explosion that otherwise threatens to make learning the correct mapping infeasible as the number of input and output neurons is increased? Does the enhanced performance on the test task come at some hidden cost, such as reduced ability to generalize from the particular stimulus used in the experiment, or reduced ability to unlearn the association when the environment changes? Would the test subjects still somehow benefit even if—unlike rats—they could avail themselves of external memory aids such as pen and paper? And how much harder would it be to apply a similar method to other parts of the brain? Whereas the present prosthesis takes advantage of the relatively simple feed-forward structure of parts of the hippocampus (basically serving as a unidirectional bridge between areas CA3 and CA1), other structures in the cortex involve convoluted feedback loops which greatly increase the complexity of the wiring diagram and, presumably, the difficulty of deciphering the functionality of any embedded group of neurons.

One hope for the cyborg route is that the brain, if permanently implanted with a device connecting it to some external resource, would over time *learn* an effective mapping between its own internal cognitive states and the inputs it receives from, or the outputs accepted by, the device. Then the implant itself would not need to be intelligent; rather, the brain would intelligently adapt to the interface, much as the brain of an infant gradually learns to interpret the signals arriving from receptors in its eyes and ears.[76] But here again one must question how much would really be gained. Suppose that the brain's plasticity were such that it could learn to detect patterns in some new input stream arbitrary projected onto some part of the cortex by means of a brain–computer interface: why not project the same information onto the retina instead, as a visual pattern, or onto the cochlea as sounds? The low-tech alternative avoids a thousand complications, and in either case the brain could deploy its pattern-recognition mechanisms and plasticity to learn to make sense of the information.

Networks and organizations

Another conceivable path to superintelligence is through the gradual enhancement of networks and organizations that link individual human minds with one another and with various artifacts and bots. The idea here is not that this would enhance the intellectual capacity of individuals enough to make them superintelligent, but rather that some system composed of individuals thus networked and organized might attain a form of superintelligence—what in the next chapter we will elaborate as "collective superintelligence."[77]

Humanity has gained enormously in collective intelligence over the course of history and prehistory. The gains come from many sources, including innovations in communications technology, such as writing and printing, and above all the introduction of language itself; increases in the size of the world population and the density of habitation; various improvements in organizational techniques and epistemic norms; and a gradual accumulation of institutional capital. In general terms, a system's collective intelligence is limited by the abilities of its member minds, the overheads in communicating relevant information between them, and the various distortions and inefficiencies that pervade human organizations. If communication overheads are reduced (including not only equipment costs but also response latencies, time and attention burdens, and other factors), then larger and more densely connected organizations become feasible. The same could happen if fixes are found for some of the bureaucratic deformations that warp organizational life—wasteful status games, mission creep, concealment or falsification of information, and other agency problems. Even partial solutions to these problems could pay hefty dividends for collective intelligence.

The technological and institutional innovations that could contribute to the growth of our collective intelligence are many and various. For example, subsidized prediction markets might foster truth-seeking norms and improve forecasting on contentious scientific and social issues.[78] Lie detectors (should it prove feasible to make ones that are reliable and easy to use) could reduce the scope for deception in human affairs.[79] Self-deception detectors might be even more powerful.[80] Even without newfangled brain technologies, some forms of deception might become harder to practice thanks to increased availability of many kinds of data, including reputations and track records, or the promulgation of strong epistemic norms and rationality culture. Voluntary and involuntary surveillance will amass vast amounts of information about human behavior. Social networking sites are already used by over a billion people to share personal details: soon, these people might begin uploading continuous life recordings from microphones and video cameras embedded in their smart phones or eyeglass frames. Automated analysis of such data streams will enable many new applications (sinister as well as benign, of course).[81]

Growth in collective intelligence may also come from more general organizational and economic improvements, and from enlarging the fraction of the world's population that is educated, digitally connected, and integrated into global intellectual culture.[82]

The internet stands out as a particularly dynamic frontier for innovation and experimentation. Most of its potential may still remain unexploited. Continuing development of an intelligent web, with better support for deliberation, de-biasing, and judgment aggregation, might make large contributions to increasing the collective intelligence of humanity as a whole or of particular groups.

But what of the seemingly more fanciful idea that the internet might one day "wake up"? Could the internet become something more than just the backbone of a loosely integrated collective superintelligence— something more like a virtual skull housing an emerging unified superintellect? (This was one of the ways that superintelligence could arise according to Vernor Vinge's influential 1993 essay, which coined the term "technological singularity."[83]) Against this one could object that machine intelligence is hard enough to achieve through arduous engineering, and that it is incredible to suppose that it will arise *spontaneously*. However, the story need not be that some future version of the internet suddenly becomes superintelligent by mere happenstance. A more plausible version of the scenario would be that the internet accumulates improvements through the work of many people over many years—work to engineer better search and information filtering algorithms, more powerful data representation formats, more capable autonomous software agents, and more efficient protocols governing the interactions between such bots—and that myriad incremental improvements eventually create the basis for some more unified form of web intelligence. It seems at least conceivable that such a web-based cognitive system, supersaturated with computer power and all other resources needed for explosive growth save for one crucial ingredient, could, when the final missing constituent is dropped into the cauldron, blaze up with superintelligence. This type of scenario, though, converges into another possible path to superintelligence, that of artificial general intelligence, which we have already discussed.

Summary

The fact that there are many paths that lead to superintelligence should increase our confidence that we will eventually get there. If one path turns out to be blocked, we can still progress.

That there are multiple paths does not entail that there are multiple destinations. Even if significant intelligence amplification were first achieved along one of the non-machine-intelligence paths, this would not render machine intelligence irrelevant. Quite the contrary: enhanced biological or organizational intelligence would accelerate scientific and technological developments, potentially hastening the arrival of more radical forms of intelligence amplification such as whole brain emulation and AI.

This is not to say that it is a matter of indifference how we get to machine superintelligence. The path taken to get there could make a big difference to the eventual outcome. Even if the ultimate capabilities that are obtained do not depend much on the trajectory, how those capabilities will be used—how much control we humans have over their disposition—might well depend on details of our approach. For example, enhancements of biological or organizational intelligence might increase our ability to anticipate risk and to design machine superintelligence that is safe and beneficial. (A full strategic assessment involves many complexities, and will have to await Chapter 14.)

True superintelligence (as opposed to marginal increases in current levels of intelligence) might plausibly first be attained via the AI path. There are, however, many fundamental uncertainties along this path. This makes it difficult to rigorously assess how long the path is or how many obstacles there are along the way. The whole brain emulation path also has some chance of being the quickest route to superintelligence. Since progress along this path requires mainly incremental technological advances rather than theoretical breakthroughs, a strong case can be made that it will eventually succeed. It seems fairly likely, however, that even if progress along the whole brain emulation path is swift, artificial intelligence will nevertheless be first to cross the finishing line: this is because of the possibility of neuromorphic AIs based on partial emulations.

Biological cognitive enhancements are clearly feasible, particularly ones based on genetic selection. Iterated embryo selection currently seems like an especially promising technology. Compared with possible breakthroughs in machine intelligence, however, biological enhancements would be relatively slow and gradual. They would, at best, result in relatively weak forms of superintelligence (more on this shortly).

The clear feasibility of biological enhancement should increase our confidence that machine intelligence is ultimately achievable, since enhanced human scientists and engineers will be able to make more and faster progress than their *au naturel* counterparts. Especially in scenarios in which machine intelligence is delayed beyond mid-century, the increasingly cognitively enhanced cohorts coming onstage will play a growing role in subsequent developments.

Brain–computer interfaces look unlikely as a source of superintelligence. Improvements in networks and organizations might result in weakly superintelligent forms of collective intelligence in the long run; but more likely, they will play an enabling role similar to that of biological cognitive enhancement, gradually increasing humanity's effective ability to solve intellectual problems. Compared with biological enhancements, advances in networks and organization will make a difference sooner—in fact, such advances are occurring continuously and are having a significant impact already. However, improvements in networks and organizations may yield narrower increases in our problem-solving capacity than will improvements in biological cognition—boosting "collective intelligence" rather than "quality intelligence," to anticipate a distinction we are about to introduce in the next chapter.

CHAPTER 3

Forms of superintelligence

S o what, exactly, do we mean by "superintelligence"? While we do not wish to get bogged down in terminological swamps, something needs to be said to clarify the conceptual ground. This chapter identifies three different forms of superintelligence, and argues that they are, in a practically relevant sense, equivalent. We also show that the potential for intelligence in a machine substrate is vastly greater than in a biological substrate. Machines have a number of fundamental advantages which will give them overwhelming superiority. Biological humans, even if enhanced, will be outclassed.

Many machines and nonhuman animals already perform at superhuman levels in narrow domains. Bats interpret sonar signals better than man, calculators outperform us in arithmetic, and chess programs beat us in chess. The range of specific tasks that can be better performed by software will continue to expand. But although specialized information processing systems will have many uses, there are additional profound issues that arise only with the prospect of machine intellects that have enough general intelligence to substitute for humans across the board.

As previously indicated, we use the term "superintelligence" to refer to intellects that greatly outperform the best current human minds across many very general cognitive domains. This is still quite vague. Different kinds of system with rather disparate performance attributes could qualify as superintelligences under this definition. To advance the analysis, it is helpful to disaggregate this simple notion of superintelligence by distinguishing different bundles of intellectual super-capabilities. There are many ways in which such decomposition could be done. Here we will differentiate between three forms: speed superintelligence, collective superintelligence, and quality superintelligence.

Speed superintelligence

A speed superintelligence is an intellect that is just like a human mind but faster. This is conceptually the easiest form of superintelligence to analyze.[1] We can define speed superintelligence as follows:

Speed superintelligence: *A system that can do all that a human intellect can do, but much faster.*

By "much" we here mean something like "multiple orders of magnitude." But rather than try to expunge every remnant of vagueness from the definition, we will entrust the reader with interpreting it sensibly.[2]

The simplest example of speed superintelligence would be a whole brain emulation running on fast hardware.[3] An emulation operating at a speed of ten thousand times that of a biological brain would be able to read a book in a few seconds and write a PhD thesis in an afternoon. With a speedup factor of a million, an emulation could accomplish an entire millennium of intellectual work in one working day.[4]

To such a fast mind, events in the external world appear to unfold in slow motion. Suppose your mind ran at 10,000×. If your fleshly friend should happen to drop his teacup, you could watch the porcelain slowly descend toward the carpet over the course of several hours, like a comet silently gliding through space toward an assignation with a far-off planet; and, as the anticipation of the coming crash tardily propagates through the folds of your friend's gray matter and from thence out into his peripheral nervous system, you could observe his body gradually assuming the aspect of a frozen oops—enough time for you not only to order a replacement cup but also to read a couple of scientific papers and take a nap.

Because of this apparent time dilation of the material world, a speed superintelligence would prefer to work with digital objects. It could live in virtual reality and deal in the information economy. Alternatively, it could interact with the physical environment by means of nanoscale manipulators, since limbs at such small scales could operate faster than macroscopic appendages. (The characteristic frequency of a system tends to be inversely proportional to its length scale.[5]) A fast mind might commune mainly with other fast minds rather than with bradytelic, molasses-like humans.

The speed of light becomes an increasingly important constraint as minds get faster, since faster minds face greater opportunity costs in the use of their time for traveling or communicating over long distances.[6] Light is roughly a million times faster than a jet plane, so it would take a digital agent with a mental speedup of 1,000,000× about the same amount of subjective time to travel across the globe as it does a contemporary human journeyer. Dialing somebody long distance would take as long as getting there "in person," though it would be cheaper as a call would require less bandwidth. Agents with large mental speedups who want to converse extensively might find it advantageous to move near one another. Extremely fast minds with need for frequent interaction (such as members of a work team) may take up residence in computers located in the same building to avoid frustrating latencies.

Collective superintelligence

Another form of superintelligence is a system achieving superior performance by aggregating large numbers of smaller intelligences:

Collective superintelligence: *A system composed of a large number of smaller intellects such that the system's overall performance across many very general domains vastly outstrips that of any current cognitive system.*

Collective superintelligence is less conceptually clear-cut than speed superintelligence.[7] However, it is more familiar empirically. While we have no experience with human-level minds that differ significantly in clock speed, we *do* have ample experience with collective intelligence, systems composed of various numbers of human-level components working together with various degrees of efficiency. Firms, work teams, gossip networks, advocacy groups, academic communities, countries, even humankind as a whole, can—if we adopt a somewhat abstract perspective—be viewed as loosely defined "systems" capable of solving classes of intellectual problems. From experience, we have some sense of how easily different tasks succumb to the efforts of organizations of various size and composition.

Collective intelligence excels at solving problems that can be readily broken into parts such that solutions to sub-problems can be pursued in parallel and verified independently. Tasks like building a space shuttle or operating a hamburger franchise offer myriad opportunities for division of labor: different engineers work on different components of the spacecraft; different staffs operate different restaurants. In academia, the rigid division of researchers, students, journals, grants, and prizes into separate self-contained disciplines—though unconducive to the type of work represented by this book—might (only in a conciliatory and mellow frame of mind) be viewed as a necessary accommodation to the practicalities of allowing large numbers of diversely motivated individuals and teams to contribute to the growth of human knowledge while working relatively independently, each plowing their own furrow.

A system's collective intelligence could be enhanced by expanding the number or the quality of its constituent intellects, or by improving the quality of their organization.[8] To obtain a collective *superintelligence* from any present-day collective intelligence would require a very great degree of enhancement. The resulting system would need to be capable of vastly outperforming any current collective intelligence or other cognitive system across many very general domains. A new conference format that lets scholars exchange information more effectively, or a new collaborative information-filtering algorithm that better predicted users' ratings of books and movies, would clearly not on its own amount to anything approaching collective superintelligence. Nor would a 50% increase in the world population, or an improvement in pedagogical method that enabled students to complete a school day in four hours instead of six. Some far more extreme growth of humanity's collective cognitive capacity would be required to meet the criterion of collective superintelligence.

Note that the threshold for collective superintelligence is indexed to the performance levels of the present—that is, the early twenty-first century. Over the course of human prehistory, and again over the course of human history, humanity's collective intelligence *has* grown by very large factors. World population, for example, has increased by at least a factor of a thousand since the Pleistocene.[9] On this basis alone, current levels of human collective intelligence could be regarded as approaching superintelligence *relative to a Pleistocene baseline*. Some improvements in communications technologies—especially spoken language, but perhaps also cities, writing, and printing—could also be argued to have, individually or in combination, provided super-sized boosts, in the sense that if another innovation of comparable impact to our collective intellectual problem-solving capacity were to happen, it would result in collective superintelligence.[10]

A certain kind of reader will be tempted at this point to interject that modern society does not seem so particularly intelligent. Perhaps some unwelcome political decision has just been made in the reader's home country, and the apparent unwisdom of that decision now looms large in the reader's mind as evidence of the mental incapacity of the modern era. And is it not the case that contemporary humanity is idolizing material consumption, depleting natural resources, polluting the environment, decimating species diversity, all the while failing to remedy screaming global injustices and neglecting paramount humanistic or spiritual values? However, setting aside the question of how modernity's shortcomings stack up against the not-so-inconsiderable failings of earlier epochs, nothing in our definition of collective superintelligence implies that a society with greater collective intelligence is necessarily better off. The definition does not even imply that the more collectively intelligent society is *wiser*. We can think of wisdom as the ability to get the important things approximately right. It is then possible to imagine an organization composed of a very large cadre of very efficiently coordinated knowledge workers, who collectively can solve intellectual problems across many very general domains. This organization, let us suppose, can operate most kinds of businesses, invent most kinds of technologies, and optimize most kinds of processes. Even so, it might get a few key big-picture issues entirely wrong—for instance, it may fail to take proper precautions against existential risks—and as a result pursue a short explosive growth spurt that ends ingloriously in total collapse. Such an organization could have a very high degree of collective intelligence; if sufficiently high, the organization is a collective superintelligence. We should resist the temptation to roll every normatively desirable attribute into one giant amorphous concept of mental functioning, as though one could never find one admirable trait without all the others being equally present. Instead, we should recognize that there can exist instrumentally powerful information processing systems—intelligent systems—that are neither inherently good nor reliably wise. But we will revisit this issue in Chapter 7.

Collective superintelligence could be either loosely or tightly integrated. To illustrate a case of loosely integrated collective superintelligence, imagine a planet, *MegaEarth*, which has the same level of communication and coordination technologies that we currently have on the real Earth but with a population one million times as large. With such a huge population, the total intellectual workforce on MegaEarth would be correspondingly larger than on our planet. Suppose that a scientific genius of the caliber of a Newton or an Einstein arises at least once for every 10 billion people: then on MegaEarth there would be 700,000 such geniuses living contemporaneously, alongside proportionally vast multitudes of slightly lesser talents. New ideas and technologies would be developed at a furious pace, and global civilization on MegaEarth would constitute a loosely integrated collective superintelligence.[11]

If we gradually increase the level of integration of a collective intelligence, it may eventually become a unified *intellect*—a single large "mind" as opposed to a mere assemblage of loosely interacting smaller human minds.[12] The inhabitants of MegaEarth could take steps in that direction by improving communications and coordination technologies and by developing better ways for many individuals to work on any hard intellectual problem together. A collective superintelligence could thus, after gaining sufficiently in integration, become a "quality superintelligence."

Quality superintelligence

We can distinguish a third form of superintelligence.

Quality superintelligence: *A system that is at least as fast as a human mind and vastly qualitatively smarter.*

As with collective intelligence, intelligence quality is also a somewhat murky concept; and in this case the difficulty is compounded by our lack of experience with any variations in intelligence quality above the upper end of the present human distribution. We can, however, get some grasp of the notion by considering some related cases.

First, we can expand the range of our reference points by considering nonhuman animals, which have intelligence of lower quality. (This is not meant as a speciesist remark. A zebrafish has a quality of intelligence that is excellently adapted to its ecological needs; but the relevant perspective here is a more anthropocentric one: our concern is with performance on *humanly* relevant complex cognitive tasks.) Nonhuman animals lack complex structured language; they are capable of no or only rudimentary tool use and tool construction; they are severely restricted in their ability to make long-term plans; and they have very limited abstract reasoning ability. Nor are these limitations fully explained by a lack of speed or of collective intelligence among nonhuman animal minds. In terms of raw computational power, human brains are probably inferior to those of some large animals, including elephants and whales. And although humanity's complex technological civilization would be impossible without our massive advantage in collective intelligence, not all distinctly human cognitive capabilities depend on collective intelligence. Many are highly developed even in small, isolated hunter–gatherer bands.[13] And many are not nearly as highly developed among highly organized nonhuman animals, such as chimpanzees and dolphins intensely trained by human instructors, or ants living in their own large and well-ordered societies. Evidently, the remarkable intellectual achievements of *Homo sapiens* are to a significant extent attributable to specific features of our brain architecture, features that depend on a unique genetic endowment not shared by other animals. This observation can help us illustrate the concept of quality superintelligence: it is intelligence of quality at least as superior to that of human intelligence as the quality of human intelligence is superior to that of elephants', dolphins', or chimpanzees'.

A second way to illustrate the concept of quality superintelligence is by noting the domain-specific cognitive deficits that can afflict individual humans, particularly deficits that are not caused by general dementia or other conditions associated with wholesale destruction of the brain's neurocomputational resources. Consider, for example, individuals with autism spectrum disorders who may have striking deficits in social cognition while functioning well in other cognitive domains; or individuals with congenital amusia, who are unable to hum or recognize simple tunes yet perform normally in most other respects. Many other examples could be adduced from the neuropsychiatric literature, which is replete with case studies of patients suffering narrowly circumscribed deficits caused by genetic abnormalities or brain trauma. Such examples show that normal human adults have a range of remarkable cognitive talents that are not simply a function of possessing a sufficient amount of general neural processing power or even a sufficient amount of general intelligence: specialized neural circuitry is also needed. This observation suggests the idea of *possible but non-realized cognitive talents*, talents that no actual human possesses even though other intelligent systems—ones with no more computing power than the human brain—that did have those talents would gain enormously in their ability to accomplish a wide range of strategically relevant tasks.

Accordingly, by considering nonhuman animals and human individuals with domain-specific cognitive deficits, we can form some notion of different qualities of intelligence and the practical difference they make. Had *Homo sapiens* lacked (for instance) the cognitive modules that enable complex linguistic representations, it might have been just another simian species living in harmony with nature. Conversely, were we to *gain* some new set of modules giving an advantage comparable to that of being able to form complex linguistic representations, we would become superintelligent.

Direct and indirect reach

Superintelligence in any of these forms could, over time, develop the technology necessary to create any of the others. The *indirect reaches* of these three forms of superintelligence are therefore equal. In that sense, the indirect reach of current human intelligence is also in the same equivalence class, under the supposition that we are able eventually to create some form of superintelligence. Yet there is a sense in which the three forms of superintelligence are much closer to one another: any one of them could create other forms of superintelligence more rapidly than we can create any form of superintelligence from our present starting point.

The *direct reaches* of the three different forms of superintelligence are harder to compare. There may be no definite ordering. Their respective capabilities depend on the degree to which they instantiate their respective advantages—*how* fast a speed superintelligence is, *how* qualitatively superior a quality superintelligence is, and so forth. At most, we might say that, *ceteris paribus*, speed superintelligence excels at tasks requiring the rapid execution of a long series of steps that must be performed sequentially while collective superintelligence excels at tasks admitting of analytic decomposition into parallelizable sub-tasks and tasks demanding the combination of many different perspectives and skill sets. In some vague sense, quality superintelligence would be the most capable form of all, inasmuch as it could grasp and solve problems that are, for all practical purposes, beyond the *direct* reach of speed superintelligence and collective superintelligence.[14]

In some domains, quantity is a poor substitute for quality. One solitary genius working out of a cork-lined bedroom can write *In Search of Lost Time*. Could an equivalent masterpiece be produced by recruiting an office building full of literary hacks?[15] Even within the range of present human variation we see that some functions benefit greatly from the labor of one brilliant mastermind as opposed to the joint efforts of myriad mediocrities. If we widen our purview to include *superintelligent* minds, we must countenance a likelihood of there being intellectual problems solvable only by superintelligence and intractable to any ever-so-large collective of non-augmented humans.

There might thus be some problems that are solvable by a quality superintelligence, and perhaps by a speed superintelligence, yet which a loosely integrated collective superintelligence cannot solve (other than by first amplifying its own intelligence).[16] We cannot clearly see what all these problems are, but we can characterize them in general terms.[17] They would tend to be problems involving multiple complex interdependencies that do not permit of independently verifiable solution steps: problems that therefore cannot be solved in a piecemeal fashion, and that might require qualitatively new kinds of understanding or new representational frameworks that are too deep or too complicated for the current edition of mortals to discover or use effectively. Some types of artistic creation and strategic cognition might fall into this category. Some types of scientific breakthrough, perhaps, likewise. And one can speculate that the tardiness and wobbliness of humanity's progress on many of the "eternal problems" of philosophy are due to the unsuitability of the human cortex for philosophical work. On this view, our most celebrated philosophers are like dogs walking on their hind legs—just barely attaining the threshold level of performance required for engaging in the activity *at all*.[18]

Sources of advantage for digital intelligence

Minor changes in brain volume and wiring can have major consequences, as we see when we compare the intellectual and technological achievements of humans with those of other apes. The far greater changes in computing resources and architecture that machine intelligence will enable will probably have consequences that are even more profound. It is difficult, perhaps impossible, for us to form an intuitive sense of the aptitudes of a superintelligence; but we can at least get an inkling of the space of possibilities by looking at some of the advantages open to digital minds. The hardware advantages are easiest to appreciate:

- *Speed of computational elements.* Biological neurons operate at a peak speed of about 200 Hz, a full seven orders of magnitude slower than a modern microprocessor (~ 2 GHz).[19] As a consequence, the human brain is forced to rely on massive parallelization and is incapable of rapidly performing any computation that requires a large number of sequential operations.[20] (Anything the brain does in under a second cannot use much more than a hundred sequential operations—perhaps only a few dozen.) Yet many of the most practically important algorithms in programming and computer science are not easily parallelizable. Many cognitive tasks could be performed far more efficiently if the brain's native support for parallelizable pattern-matching algorithms were complemented by, and integrated with, support for fast sequential processing.

- *Internal communication speed.* Axons carry action potentials at speeds of 120 m/s or less, whereas electronic processing cores can communicate optically at the speed of light (300,000,000 m/s).[21] The sluggishness of neural signals limits how big a biological brain can be while functioning as a single processing unit. For example, to achieve a round-trip latency of less than 10 ms between any two elements in a system, biological brains must be smaller than 0.11 m³. An electronic system, on the other hand, could be 6.1×10^{17} m³, about the size of a dwarf planet: eighteen orders of magnitude larger.[22]

- *Number of computational elements.* The human brain has somewhat fewer than 100 billion neurons.[23] Humans have about three and a half times the brain size of chimpanzees (though only one-fifth the brain size of sperm whales).[24] The number of neurons in a biological creature is most obviously limited by cranial volume and metabolic constraints, but other factors may also be significant for larger brains (such as cooling, development time, and signal-conductance delays—see the previous point). By contrast, computer hardware is indefinitely scalable up to very high physical limits.[25] Supercomputers can be warehouse-sized or larger, with additional remote capacity added via high-speed cables.[26]

- *Storage capacity.* Human working memory is able to hold no more than some four or five chunks of information at any given time.[27] While it would be misleading to compare the size of human working memory directly with the amount of RAM in a digital computer, it is clear that the hardware advantages of digital intelligences will make it possible for them to have larger working memories. This might enable such minds to intuitively grasp complex relationships that humans can only fumblingly handle via plodding calculation.[28] Human long-term memory is also limited, though it is unclear whether we manage to exhaust its storage capacity during the course of an ordinary lifetime—the rate at which we accumulate information is so slow. (On one estimate, the adult human brain stores about one billion bits—a couple of orders of magnitude less than a low-end smartphone.[29]) Both the amount of information stored and the speed with which it can be accessed could thus be vastly greater in a machine brain than in a biological brain.

- *Reliability, lifespan, sensors, etc.* Machine intelligences might have various other hardware advantages. For example, biological neurons are less reliable than transistors.[30] Since noisy computing necessitates redundant encoding schemes that use multiple elements to encode a single bit of information, a digital brain might derive some efficiency gains from the use of reliable high-precision computing elements. Brains become fatigued after a few hours of work and start to permanently decay after a few decades of subjective time; microprocessors are not subject to these limitations. Data flow into a machine intelligence could be increased by adding millions of sensors. Depending on the technology used, a machine might have reconfigurable hardware that can be optimized for changing task requirements, whereas much of the brain's architecture is fixed from birth or only slowly changeable (though the details of synaptic connectivity can change over shorter timescales, like days).[31]

At present, the computational power of the biological brain still compares favorably with that of digital computers, though top-of-the-line supercomputers are attaining levels of performance that are within the range of plausible estimates of the brain's processing power.[32] But hardware is rapidly improving, and the ultimate limits of hardware performance are vastly higher than those of biological computing substrates.

Digital minds will also benefit from major advantages in software:

- *Editability.* It is easier to experiment with parameter variations in software than in neural wetware. For example, with a whole brain emulation one could easily trial what happens if one adds more neurons in a particular cortical area or if one increases or decreases their excitability. Running such experiments in living biological brains would be far more difficult.

- *Duplicability.* With software, one can quickly make arbitrarily many high-fidelity copies to fill the available hardware base. Biological brains, by contrast, can be reproduced only very slowly; and each new instance starts out in a helpless state, remembering nothing of what its parents learned in their lifetimes.

- *Goal coordination*. Human collectives are replete with inefficiencies arising from the fact that it is nearly impossible to achieve complete uniformity of purpose among the members of a large group—at least until it becomes feasible to induce docility on a large scale by means of drugs or genetic selection. A "copy clan" (a group of identical or almost identical programs sharing a common goal) would avoid such coordination problems.

- *Memory sharing*. Biological brains need extended periods of training and mentorship whereas digital minds could acquire new memories and skills by swapping data files. A population of a billion copies of an AI program could synchronize their databases periodically, so that all the instances of the program know everything that any instance learned during the previous hour. (Direct memory transfer requires standardized representational formats. Easy swapping of high-level cognitive content would therefore not be possible between just any pair of machine intelligences. In particular, it would not be possible among first-generation whole brain emulations.)

- *New modules, modalities, and algorithms*. Visual perception seems to us easy and effortless, quite unlike solving textbook geometry problems—this despite the fact that it takes a massive amount of computation to reconstruct, from the two-dimensional patterns of stimulation on our retinas, a three-dimensional representation of a world populated with recognizable objects. The reason this seems easy is that we have dedicated low-level neural machinery for processing visual information. This low-level processing occurs unconsciously and automatically, without draining our mental energy or conscious attention. Music perception, language use, social cognition, and other forms of information processing that are "natural" for us humans seem to be likewise supported by dedicated neurocomputational modules. An artificial mind that had such specialized support for other cognitive domains that have become important in the contemporary world—such as engineering, computer programming, and business strategy—would have big advantages over minds like ours that have to rely on clunky general-purpose cognition to think about such things. New algorithms may also be developed to take advantage of the distinct affordances of digital hardware, such as its support for fast serial processing.

The *ultimately* attainable advantages of machine intelligence, hardware and software combined, are enormous.[33] But how rapidly could those potential advantages be realized? That is the question to which we now turn.

CHAPTER 4

The kinetics of an intelligence explosion

Once machines attain some form of human-equivalence in general reasoning ability, how long will it then be before they attain radical superintelligence? Will this be a slow, gradual, protracted transition? Or will it be sudden, explosive? This chapter analyzes the kinetics of the transition to superintelligence as a function of optimization power and system recalcitrance. We consider what we know or may reasonably surmise about the behavior of these two factors in the neighborhood of human-level general intelligence.

Timing and speed of the takeoff

Given that machines will *eventually* vastly exceed biology in general intelligence, but that machine cognition is *currently* vastly narrower than human cognition, one is led to wonder how quickly this usurpation will take place. The question we are asking here must be sharply distinguished from the question we considered in Chapter 1 about how far away we currently are from developing a machine with human-level general intelligence. Here the question is instead, *if and when such a machine is developed, how long will it be from then until a machine becomes radically superintelligent?* Note that one could think that it will take quite a long time until machines reach the human baseline, or one might be agnostic about how long that will take, and yet have a strong view that once this happens, the further ascent into strong superintelligence will be very rapid.

It can be helpful to think about these matters schematically, even though doing so involves temporarily ignoring some qualifications and complicating details. Consider, then, a diagram that plots the intellectual capability of the most advanced machine intelligence system as a function of time (Figure 7).

A horizontal line labeled "human baseline" represents the effective intellectual capabilities of a representative human adult with access to the information sources and technological aids currently available in developed countries. At present, the most advanced AI system is far below the human baseline on any reasonable metric of general intellectual ability. At some point in future, a machine might reach approximate parity with this human baseline (which we take to be fixed—anchored to the year 2014, say, even if the capabilities of human individuals should have increased in the intervening years): this would mark the onset of the takeoff. The capabilities of the system continue to grow, and at some later point the system reaches parity with the combined intellectual capability of all of humanity (again anchored to the present): what we may call the "civilization baseline". Eventually, if the system's abilities continue to grow, it attains "strong superintelligence"—a level of intelligence vastly greater

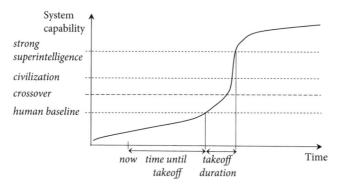

Figure 7 Shape of the takeoff. It is important to distinguish between these questions: "Will a takeoff occur, and if so, when?" and "If and when a takeoff does occur, how steep will it be?" One might hold, for example, that it will be a very long time before a takeoff occurs, but that when it does it will proceed very quickly. Another relevant question (not illustrated in this figure) is: "How large a fraction of the world economy will participate in the takeoff?" These questions are related but distinct.

than contemporary humanity's combined intellectual wherewithal. The attainment of strong superintelligence marks the completion of the takeoff, though the system might continue to gain in capacity thereafter. Sometime during the takeoff phase, the system may pass a landmark which we can call "the crossover", a point beyond which the system's further improvement is mainly driven by the system's own actions rather than by work performed upon it by others.[1] (The possible existence of such a crossover will become important in the subsection on optimization power and explosivity, later in this chapter.)

With this picture in mind, we can distinguish three classes of transition scenarios—scenarios in which systems progress from human-level intelligence to superintelligence—based on their steepness; that is to say, whether they represent a slow, fast, or moderate takeoff.

Slow

A slow takeoff is one that occurs over some long temporal interval, such as decades or centuries. Slow takeoff scenarios offer excellent opportunities for human political processes to adapt and respond. Different approaches can be tried and tested in sequence. New experts can be trained and credentialed. Grassroots campaigns can be mobilized by groups that feel they are being disadvantaged by unfolding developments. If it appears that new kinds of secure infrastructure or mass surveillance of AI researchers is needed, such systems could be developed and deployed. Nations fearing an AI arms race would have time to try to negotiate treaties and design enforcement mechanisms. Most preparations undertaken before onset of the slow takeoff would be rendered obsolete as better solutions would gradually become visible in the light of the dawning era.

Fast

A fast takeoff occurs over some short temporal interval, such as minutes, hours, or days. Fast takeoff scenarios offer scant opportunity for humans to deliberate. Nobody need even notice anything unusual before the game is already lost. In a fast takeoff scenario, humanity's fate essentially depends on preparations previously put in place. At the slowest end of the fast takeoff scenario range, some simple human actions might be possible, analogous to flicking open the "nuclear suitcase"; but any such action would either be elementary or have been planned and pre-programmed in advance.

Moderate

A moderate takeoff is one that occurs over some intermediary temporal interval, such as months or years. Moderate takeoff scenarios give humans some chance to respond but not much time to analyze the situation, to test different approaches, or to solve complicated coordination problems. There is not enough time to develop or deploy new systems (e.g. political systems, surveillance regimes, or computer network security protocols), but extant systems could be applied to the new challenge.

During a slow takeoff, there would be plenty of time for the news to get out. In a moderate takeoff, by contrast, it is possible that developments would be kept secret as they unfold. Knowledge might be restricted to a small group of insiders, as in a covert state-sponsored military research program. Commercial projects, small academic teams, and "nine hackers in a basement" outfits might also be clandestine—though, if the prospect of an intelligence explosion were "on the radar" of state intelligence agencies as a national security priority, then the most promising private projects would seem to have a good chance of being under surveillance. The host state (or a dominant foreign power) would then have the option of nationalizing or shutting down any project that showed signs of commencing takeoff. Fast takeoffs would happen so quickly that there would not be much time for word to get out or for anybody to mount a meaningful reaction if it did. But an outsider might intervene *before* the onset of the takeoff if they believed a particular project to be closing in on success.

Moderate takeoff scenarios could lead to geopolitical, social, and economic turbulence as individuals and groups jockey to position themselves to gain from the unfolding transformation. Such upheaval, should it occur, might impede efforts to orchestrate a well-composed response; alternatively, it might enable solutions more radical than calmer circumstances would permit. For instance, in a moderate takeoff scenario where cheap and capable emulations or other digital minds gradually flood labor markets over a period of years, one could imagine mass protests by laid-off workers pressuring governments to increase unemployment benefits or institute a living wage guarantee to all human citizens, or to levy special taxes or impose minimum wage requirements on employers who use emulation workers. In order for any relief derived from such policies to be more than fleeting, support for them would somehow have to be cemented into permanent power structures. Similar issues can arise if the takeoff is slow rather than moderate, but the disequilibrium and rapid change in moderate scenarios may present special opportunities for small groups to wield disproportionate influence.

It might appear to some readers that of these three types of scenario, the slow takeoff is the most probable, the moderate takeoff is less probable, and the fast takeoff is utterly implausible. It could seem fanciful to suppose that the world could be radically transformed and humanity deposed from its position as apex cogitator over the course of an hour or two. No change of such moment has ever occurred in human history, and its nearest parallels—the Agricultural and Industrial Revolutions—played out over much longer timescales (centuries to millennia in the former case, decades to centuries in the latter). So the base rate for the kind of transition entailed by a fast or medium takeoff scenario, in terms of the speed and magnitude of the postulated change, is zero: it lacks precedent outside myth and religion.[2]

Nevertheless, this chapter will present some reasons for thinking that the slow transition scenario is improbable. If and when a takeoff occurs, it will likely be explosive.

To begin to analyze the question of how fast the takeoff will be, we can conceive of the rate of increase in a system's intelligence as a (monotonically increasing) function of two variables: the amount of "optimization power", or quality-weighted design effort, that is being applied to increase the system's intelligence, and the responsiveness of the system to the application of a given amount of such optimization power. We might term the inverse of responsiveness "recalcitrance", and write:

$$\text{Rate of change in intelligence} = \frac{\text{Optimization power}}{\text{Recalcitrance}}.$$

Pending some specification of how to quantify intelligence, design effort, and recalcitrance, this expression is merely qualitative. But we can at least observe that a system's intelligence will increase rapidly if *either* a lot of skilled effort is applied to the task of increasing its intelligence and the system's intelligence is not too hard to increase *or* there is a non-trivial design effort and the system's recalcitrance is low (or both). If we know how much design effort is going into improving a particular system, and the rate of improvement this effort produces, we could calculate the system's recalcitrance.

Further, we can observe that the amount of optimization power devoted to improving some system's performance varies between systems and over time. A system's recalcitrance might also vary depending on how much the system has already been optimized. Often, the easiest improvements are made first, leading to diminishing returns (increasing recalcitrance) as low-hanging fruits are depleted. However, there can also be improvements that make further improvements easier, leading to improvement cascades. The process of solving a jigsaw puzzle starts out simple—it is easy to find the corners and the edges. Then recalcitrance goes up as subsequent pieces are harder to fit. But as the puzzle nears completion, the search space collapses and the process gets easier again.

To proceed in our inquiry, we must therefore analyze how recalcitrance and optimization power might vary in the critical time periods during the takeoff. This will occupy us over the next few pages.

Recalcitrance

Let us begin with recalcitrance. The outlook here depends on the type of the system under consideration. For completeness, we first cast a brief glance at the recalcitrance that would be encountered along paths to superintelligence that do not involve advanced machine intelligence. We find that recalcitrance along those paths appears to be fairly high. That done, we will turn to the main case, which is that the takeoff involves machine intelligence; and there we find that recalcitrance at the critical juncture seems low.

Non-machine intelligence paths

Cognitive enhancement via improvements in public health and diet has steeply diminishing returns.[3] Big gains come from eliminating severe nutritional deficiencies, and the most severe deficiencies have already been largely eliminated in all but the poorest countries. Only girth is gained by increasing an already adequate diet. Education, too, is now probably subject to diminishing returns. The fraction of talented individuals in the world who lack access to quality education is still substantial, but declining.

Pharmacological enhancers might deliver some cognitive gains over the coming decades. But after the easiest fixes have been accomplished—perhaps sustainable increases in mental energy and ability to concentrate, along with better control over the rate of long-term memory consolidation—subsequent gains will be increasingly hard to come by. Unlike diet and public health approaches, however, improving cognition through smart drugs might get easier before it gets harder. The field of neuropharmacology still lacks much of the basic knowledge that would be needed to competently intervene in the healthy brain. Neglect of enhancement medicine as a legitimate area of research may be partially to blame for this current backwardness. If neuroscience and pharmacology continue to progress for a while longer without focusing on cognitive enhancement, then maybe there would be some relatively easy gains to be had when at last the development of nootropics becomes a serious priority.[4]

Genetic cognitive enhancement has a U-shaped recalcitrance profile similar to that of nootropics, but with larger potential gains. Recalcitrance starts out high while the only available method is selective breeding sustained over many generations, something that is obviously difficult to accomplish on a globally significant scale. Genetic enhancement will get easier as technology is developed for cheap and effective genetic testing and selection (and particularly when iterated embryo selection becomes feasible in humans). These new techniques will make it possible to tap the pool of existing human genetic variation for intelligence-enhancing alleles. As the best existing alleles get incorporated into genetic enhancement packages, however, further gains will get harder to come by. The need for more innovative approaches to genetic modification may then increase recalcitrance. There are limits to how quickly things can progress along the genetic enhancement path, most notably the fact that germline interventions are subject to an inevitable maturational lag: this strongly counteracts the possibility of a fast or moderate takeoff.[5] That embryo selection can only be applied in the context of in vitro fertilization will slow its rate of adoption: another limiting factor.

The recalcitrance along the brain–computer path seems initially very high. In the unlikely event that it somehow becomes easy to insert brain implants and to achieve high-level functional integration with the cortex, recalcitrance might plummet. In the long run, the difficulty of making progress along this path would be similar to that involved in improving emulations or AIs, since the bulk of the brain–computer system's intelligence would eventually reside in the computer part.

The recalcitrance for making networks and organizations *in general* more efficient is high. A vast amount of effort is going into overcoming this recalcitrance, and the result is an annual improvement of humanity's total capacity by perhaps no more than a couple of percent.[6] Furthermore, shifts in the internal and external environment mean that organizations, even if efficient at one time, soon become ill-adapted to their new circumstances. Ongoing reform effort is thus required even just to prevent deterioration. A step change in the rate of gain in average organizational efficiency is perhaps conceivable, but it is hard to see how even the most radical scenario of this kind could produce anything faster than a slow takeoff, since organizations operated by humans are confined to work on human timescales. The internet continues to be an exciting frontier with many opportunities for enhancing collective intelligence, with a recalcitrance that seems at the moment to be in the moderate range—progress is somewhat swift but a lot of effort is going into making this progress happen. It may be expected to increase as low-hanging fruits (such as search engines and email) are depleted.

Emulation and AI paths

The difficulty of advancing toward whole brain emulation is difficult to estimate. Yet we can point to a specific future milestone: the successful emulation of an insect brain. That milestone stands on a hill, and its conquest would bring into view much of the terrain ahead, allowing us to make a decent guess at the recalcitrance of scaling up the technology to human whole brain emulation. (A successful emulation of a small-mammal brain, such as that of a mouse, would give an even better vantage point that would allow the distance remaining to a human whole brain emulation to be estimated with a high degree of precision.) The path toward artificial intelligence, by contrast, may feature no such obvious milestone or early observation point. It is entirely possible that the quest for artificial intelligence will appear to be lost in dense jungle until an unexpected breakthrough reveals the finishing line in a clearing just a few short steps away.

Recall the distinction between these two questions: How hard is it to attain roughly human levels of cognitive ability? And how hard is it to get from there to superhuman levels? The first question is mainly relevant for predicting how long it will be before the onset of a takeoff. It is the second question that is key to assessing the shape of the takeoff, which is our aim here. And though it might be tempting to suppose that the step from human level to superhuman level must be the harder one—this step, after all, takes place "at a higher altitude" where capacity must be superadded to an already quite capable system—this would be a very unsafe assumption. It is quite possible that recalcitrance *falls* when a machine reaches human parity.

Consider first whole brain emulation. The difficulties involved in creating the first human emulation are of a quite different kind from those involved in enhancing an existing emulation. Creating a first emulation involves huge technological challenges, particularly in regard to developing the requisite scanning and image interpretation capabilities. This step might also require considerable amounts of physical capital—an industrial-scale machine park with hundreds of high-throughput scanning machines is not implausible. By contrast, enhancing the quality of an existing emulation involves tweaking algorithms and data structures: essentially a software problem, and one that could turn out to be much easier than perfecting the imaging technology needed to create the original template. Programmers could easily experiment with tricks like increasing the neuron count in different cortical areas to see how it affects performance.[7] They also could work on code optimization and on finding simpler computational models that preserve the essential functionality of individual neurons or small networks of neurons. If the last technological prerequisite to fall into place is either scanning or translation, with computing power being relatively abundant, then not much attention might have been given during the development phase to implementational efficiency, and easy opportunities for computational efficiency savings might be available. (More fundamental architectural reorganization might also be possible, but that takes us off the emulation path and into AI territory.)

Another way to improve the code base once the first emulation has been produced is to scan additional brains with different or superior skills and talents. Productivity growth would also occur as a consequence of adapting organizational structures and workflows to the unique attributes of digital minds. Since there is no precedent in the human economy of a worker who can be literally copied, reset, run at different speeds, and so forth, managers of the first emulation cohort would find plenty of room for innovation in managerial practices.

After initially plummeting when human whole brain emulation becomes possible, recalcitrance may rise again. Sooner or later, the most glaring implementational inefficiencies will have been optimized away, the most promising algorithmic variations will have been tested, and the easiest opportunities for organizational innovation will have been exploited. The template library will have expanded so that acquiring more brain scans would add little benefit over working with existing templates. Since a template can be multiplied, each copy can be individually trained in a different field, and this can be done at electronic speed, it might be that the number of brains that would need to be scanned in order to capture most of the potential economic gains is small. Possibly a single brain would suffice.

Another potential cause of escalating recalcitrance is the possibility that emulations or their biological supporters will organize to support regulations restricting the use of emulation workers, limiting emulation copying, prohibiting certain kinds of experimentation with digital minds, instituting workers' rights and a minimum wage for emulations, and so forth. It is equally possible, however, that political developments would go in the opposite direction, contributing to a fall in recalcitrance. This might happen if initial restraint in the use of emulation labor gives way to unfettered exploitation as competition heats up and the economic and strategic costs of occupying the moral high ground become clear.

As for artificial intelligence (non-emulation machine intelligence), the difficulty of lifting a system from human-level to superhuman intelligence by means of algorithmic improvements depends on the attributes of the particular system. Different architectures might have very different recalcitrance.

In some situations, recalcitrance could be extremely low. For example, if human-level AI is delayed because one key insight long eludes programmers, then when the final breakthrough occurs, the AI might leapfrog from below to radically above human level without even touching the intermediary rungs. Another situation in which recalcitrance could turn out to be extremely low is that of an AI system that can achieve intelligent capability via two different modes of processing. To illustrate this possibility, suppose an AI is composed of two subsystems, one possessing domain-specific problem-solving techniques, the other possessing general-purpose reasoning ability. It could then be the case that while the second subsystem remains below a certain capacity threshold, it contributes nothing to the system's overall performance, because the solutions it generates are always inferior to those generated by the domain-specific subsystem. Suppose now that a small amount of optimization power is applied to the general-purpose subsystem and that this produces a brisk rise in the capacity of that subsystem. At first, we observe no increase in the overall system's performance, indicating that recalcitrance is high. Then, once the capacity of the general-purpose subsystem crosses the threshold where its solutions start to beat those of the domain-specific subsystem, the overall system's performance suddenly begins to improve at the same brisk pace as the general-purpose subsystem, even as the amount of optimization power applied stays constant: the system's recalcitrance has plummeted.

It is also possible that our natural tendency to view intelligence from an anthropocentric perspective will lead us to underestimate improvements in sub-human systems, and thus to overestimate recalcitrance. Eliezer Yudkowsky, an AI theorist who has written extensively on the future of machine intelligence, puts the point as follows (and see Figure 8):

AI might make an *apparently* sharp jump in intelligence purely as the result of anthropomorphism, the human tendency to think of "village idiot" and "Einstein" as the extreme ends of the intelligence scale, instead of nearly indistinguishable points on the scale of minds-in-general. Everything dumber than a dumb human may appear to us as simply "dumb". One imagines the "AI arrow" creeping steadily up the scale of intelligence, moving past mice and chimpanzees, with AIs still remaining "dumb" because AIs cannot speak fluent language or write science papers, and then the AI arrow crosses the tiny gap from infra-idiot to ultra-Einstein in the course of one month or some similarly short period.[8]

The upshot of these several considerations is that it is difficult to predict how hard it will be to make algorithmic improvements in the first

Figure 8 A less anthropomorphic scale? The gap between a dumb and a clever person may appear large from an anthropocentric perspective, yet in a less parochial view the two have nearly indistinguishable minds.[9] It will almost certainly prove harder and take longer to build a machine intelligence that has a general level of smartness comparable to that of a village idiot than to improve such a system so that it becomes much smarter than any human.

AI that reaches a roughly human level of general intelligence. There are at least some possible circumstances in which algorithm-recalcitrance is low. But even if algorithm-recalcitrance is very high, this would not preclude the overall recalcitrance of the AI in question from being low. For it might be easy to increase the intelligence of the system in other ways than by improving its algorithms. There are two other factors that can be improved: content and hardware.

First, consider content improvements. By "content" we here mean those parts of a system's software assets that do not make up its core algorithmic architecture. Content might include, for example, databases of stored percepts, specialized skills libraries, and inventories of declarative knowledge. For many kinds of system, the distinction between algorithmic architecture and content is very unsharp; nevertheless, it will serve as a rough-and-ready way of pointing to one potentially important source of capability gains in a machine intelligence. An alternative way of expressing much the same idea is by saying that a system's intellectual problem-solving capacity can be enhanced not only by making the system cleverer but also by expanding what the system knows.

Consider a contemporary AI system such as TextRunner (a research project at the University of Washington) or IBM's Watson (the system that won the *Jeopardy!* quiz show). These systems can extract certain pieces of semantic information by analyzing text. Although these systems do not understand what they read in the same sense or to the same extent as a human does, they can nevertheless extract significant amounts of information from natural language and use that information to make simple inferences and answer questions. They can also learn from experience, building up more extensive representations of a concept as they encounter additional instances of its use. They are designed to operate for much of the time in unsupervised mode (i.e. to learn hidden structure in unlabeled data in the absence of error or reward signal, without human guidance) and to be fast and scalable. TextRunner, for instance, works with a corpus of 500 million web pages.[10]

Now imagine a remote descendant of such a system that has acquired the ability to read with as much understanding as a human ten-year-old but with a reading speed similar to that of TextRunner. (This is probably an AI-complete problem.) So we are imagining a system that thinks much faster and has much better memory than a human adult, but knows much less, and perhaps the net effect of this is that the system is roughly human-equivalent in its general problem-solving ability. But its content recalcitrance is very low—low enough to precipitate a takeoff. Within a few weeks, the system has read and mastered all the content contained in the Library of Congress. Now the system knows much more than any human being and thinks vastly faster: it has become (at least) weakly superintelligent.

A system might thus greatly boost its effective intellectual capability by absorbing pre-produced content accumulated through centuries of human science and civilization: for instance, by reading through the internet. If an AI reaches human level without previously having had access to this material or without having been able to digest it, then the AI's overall recalcitrance will be low even if it is hard to improve its algorithmic architecture.

Content-recalcitrance is a relevant concept for emulations, too. A high-speed emulation has an advantage not only because it can complete the same tasks as biological humans more quickly, but also because it can accumulate more timely content, such as task-relevant skills and expertise. In order to tap the full potential of fast content accumulation, however, a system needs to have a correspondingly large memory capacity. There is little point in reading an entire library if you have forgotten all about the aardvark by the time you get to the abalone. While an AI system is likely to have adequate memory capacity, emulations would inherit some of the capacity limitations of their human templates. They may therefore need architectural enhancements in order to become capable of unbounded learning.

So far we have considered the recalcitrance of architecture and of content—that is, how difficult it would be to improve the *software* of a machine intelligence that has reached human parity. Now let us look at a third way of boosting the performance of machine intelligence: improving its hardware. What would be the recalcitrance for hardware-driven improvements?

Starting with intelligent software (emulation or AI) one can amplify *collective intelligence* simply by using additional computers to run more instances of the program.[11] One could also amplify *speed intelligence* by moving the program to faster computers. Depending on the degree to which the program lends itself to parallelization, speed intelligence could also be amplified by running the program on more processors. This is likely to be feasible for emulations, which have a highly parallelized architecture; but many AI programs, too, have important subroutines that can benefit from massive parallelization. Amplifying *quality intelligence* by increasing computing power might also be possible, but that case is less straightforward.[12]

The recalcitrance for amplifying collective or speed intelligence (and possibly quality intelligence) in a system with human-level software is therefore likely to be low. The only difficulty involved is gaining access to additional computing power. There are several ways for a system to expand its hardware base, each relevant over a different timescale.

In the short term, computing power should scale roughly linearly with funding: twice the funding buys twice the number of computers, enabling twice as many instances of the software to be run simultaneously. The emergence of cloud computing services gives a project the option to scale up its computational resources without even having to wait for new computers to be delivered and installed, though concerns over secrecy might favor the use of in-house computers. (In certain scenarios, computing power could also be obtained by other means, such as by commandeering botnets.[13]) Just how easy it would be to scale the system by a given factor depends on how much computing power the initial system uses. A system that initially runs on a PC could be scaled by a factor of thousands for a mere million dollars. A program that runs on a supercomputer would be far more expensive to scale.

In the slightly longer term, the cost of acquiring additional hardware may be driven up as a growing portion of the world's installed capacity is being used to run digital minds. For instance, in a competitive market-based emulation scenario, the cost of running one additional copy of an emulation should rise to be roughly equal to the income generated by the marginal copy, as investors bid up the price for existing computing infrastructure to match the return they expect from their investment (though if only one project has mastered the technology it might gain a degree of monopsony power in the computing power market and therefore pay a lower price).

Over a somewhat longer timescale, the supply of computing power will grow as new capacity is installed. A demand spike would spur production in existing semiconductor foundries and stimulate the construction of new plants. (A one-off performance boost, perhaps amounting to one or two orders of magnitude, might also be obtainable by using customized microprocessors.[14]) Above all, the rising wave of technology improvements will pour increasing volumes of computational power into the turbines of the thinking machines. Historically, the rate of improvement of computing technology has been described by the famous Moore's law, which in one of its variations states that computing power per dollar doubles every 18 months or so.[15] Although one cannot bank on this rate of improvement continuing up to the development of human-level machine intelligence, yet until fundamental physical limits are reached there will remain room for advances in computing technology.

There are thus reasons to expect that hardware recalcitrance will not be very high. Purchasing more computing power for the system once it proves its mettle by attaining human-level intelligence might easily add several orders of magnitude of computing power (depending on how hardware-frugal the project was before expansion). Chip customization might add one or two orders of magnitude. Other means of expanding the hardware base, such as building more factories and advancing the frontier of computing technology, take longer—normally several years, though this lag would be radically compressed once machine superintelligence revolutionizes manufacturing and technology development.

In summary, we can talk about the likelihood of a *hardware overhang*: when human-level software is created, enough computing power may already be available to run vast numbers of copies at great speed. Software recalcitrance, as discussed above, is harder to assess but might be even lower than hardware recalcitrance. In particular, there may be *content overhang* in the form of pre-made content (e.g. the internet) that becomes available to a system once it reaches human parity. *Algorithm overhang*— pre-designed algorithmic enhancements—is also possible but perhaps less likely. Software improvements (whether in algorithms or content) might offer orders of magnitude of potential performance gains that could be fairly easily accessed once a digital mind attains human parity, on top of the performance gains attainable by using more or better hardware.

Optimization power and explosivity

Having examined the question of recalcitrance we must now turn to the other half of our schematic equation, *optimization power*. To recall: *Rate of change in Intelligence = Optimization power/Recalcitrance*. As reflected in this schematic, a fast takeoff does not require that recalcitrance during the transition phase be low. A fast takeoff could also result if recalcitrance is constant or even moderately increasing, provided the optimization power being applied to improving the system's performance grows sufficiently rapidly. As we shall now see, there are good grounds for thinking that the applied optimization power *will* increase during the transition, at least in the absence of a deliberate measures to prevent this from happening.

We can distinguish two phases. The first phase begins with the onset of the takeoff, when the system reaches the human baseline for individual intelligence. As the system's capability continues to increase, it might use some or all of that capability to improve itself (or to design a successor system—which, for present purposes, comes to the same thing). However, most of the optimization power applied to the system still comes from outside the system, either from the work of programmers and engineers employed within the project or from such work done by the rest of the world as can be appropriated and used by the project.[16] If this phase drags out for any significant period of time, we can expect the amount of optimization power applied to the system to grow. Inputs both from inside the project and from the outside world are likely to increase as the promise of the chosen approach becomes manifest. Researchers may work harder, more researchers may be recruited, and more computing power may be purchased to expedite progress. The increase could be especially dramatic if the development of human-level machine intelligence takes the world by surprise, in which case what was previously a small research project might suddenly become the focus of intense research and development efforts around the world (though some of those efforts might be channeled into competing projects).

A second growth phase will begin if at some point the system has acquired so much capability that most of the optimization power exerted on it comes from the system itself (marked by the variable level labeled "crossover" in Figure 7). This fundamentally changes the dynamic, because any increase in the system's capability now translates into a proportional increase in the amount of optimization power being applied to its further improvement. If recalcitrance remains constant, this feedback dynamic produces exponential growth (see Box 4). The doubling constant depends on the scenario but might be extremely short—mere seconds in some scenarios—if growth is occurring at electronic speeds, which might happen as a result of algorithmic improvements or the exploitation of an overhang of content or hardware.[17] Growth that is driven by physical construction, such as the production of new computers or manufacturing

Box 4 On the kinetics of an intelligence explosion

We can write the rate of change in intelligence as the ratio between the optimization power applied to the system and the system's recalcitrance:

$$\frac{dI}{dt} = \frac{\mathfrak{D}}{\mathfrak{R}}.$$

The amount of optimization power acting on a system is the sum of whatever optimization power the system itself contributes and the optimization power exerted from without. For example, a seed AI might be improved through a combination of its own efforts and the efforts of a human programming team, and perhaps also the efforts of the wider global community of researchers making continuous advances in the semiconductor industry, computer science, and related fields:[18]

$$\mathfrak{D} = \mathfrak{D}_{system} + \mathfrak{D}_{project} + \mathfrak{D}_{world}.$$

A seed AI starts out with very limited cognitive capacities. At the outset, therefore, $\mathfrak{D}_{system}$ is small.[19] What about $\mathfrak{D}_{project}$ and $\mathfrak{D}_{world}$? There are cases in which a single project has more relevant capability than the rest of the world combined—the Manhattan project, for instance, brought a very large fraction of the world's best physicists to Los Alamos to work on the atomic bomb. More commonly, any one project contains only a small fraction of the world's total relevant research capability. But even when the outside world has a greater total amount of relevant research capability than any one project, $\mathfrak{D}_{project}$ may nevertheless exceed $\mathfrak{D}_{world}$, since much of the outside world's capability is not focused on the particular system in question. If a project begins to look promising—which will happen when a system passes the human baseline if not before—it might attract additional investment, increasing $\mathfrak{D}_{project}$. If the project's accomplishments are public, $\mathfrak{D}_{world}$ might also rise as the progress inspires greater interest in machine intelligence generally and as various powers scramble to get in on the game. During the transition phase, therefore, total optimization power applied to improving a cognitive system is likely to increase as the capability of the system increases.[20]

As the system's capabilities grow, there may come a point at which the optimization power generated by the system itself starts to dominate the

continued

Box 4 *Continued*

optimization power applied to it from outside (across all significant dimensions of improvement):

$$\mathfrak{D}_{system} > \mathfrak{D}_{project} + \mathfrak{D}_{world}.$$

This *crossover* is significant because, beyond this point, further improvement to the system's capabilities contributes strongly to increasing the total optimization power applied to improving the system. We thereby enter a regime of strong recursive self-improvement. This leads to explosive growth of the system's capability under a fairly wide range of different shapes of the recalcitrance curve.

To illustrate, consider first a scenario in which recalcitrance is constant, so that the rate of increase in an AI's intelligence is equal to the optimization power being applied. Assume that all the optimization power that is applied comes from the AI itself and that the AI applies all its intelligence to the task of amplifying its own intelligence, so that $\mathfrak{D}_{system} = I$.[21] We then have

$$\frac{dI}{dt} = \frac{I}{k}.$$

Solving this simple differential equation yields the exponential function

$$I = Ae^{t/k}.$$

But recalcitrance being constant is a rather special case. Recalcitrance might well decline around the human baseline, due to one or more of the factors mentioned in the previous subsection, and remain low around the crossover and some distance beyond (perhaps until the system eventually approaches fundamental physical limits). For example, suppose that the optimization power applied to the system is roughly constant (i.e. $\mathfrak{D}_{project} + \mathfrak{D}_{world} \approx c$) prior to the system becoming capable of contributing substantially to its own design, and that this leads to the system doubling in capacity every 18 months. (This would be roughly in line with historical improvement rates from Moore's law combined with software advances.[22]) This rate of improvement, if achieved by

Box 4 *Continued*

means of roughly constant optimization power, entails recalcitrance declining as the inverse of the system power:

$$\frac{dI}{dt} = \frac{c}{1/I} = c\,I.$$

If recalcitrance continues to fall along this hyperbolic pattern, then when the AI reaches the crossover point the total amount of optimization power applied to improving the AI has doubled. We then have

$$\frac{dI}{dt} = \frac{(c+I)}{1/I} = (c+I)\,I.$$

The next doubling occurs 7.5 months later. Within 17.9 months, the system's capacity has grown a thousandfold, thus obtaining speed superintelligence (Figure 9).

This particular growth trajectory has a positive singularity at $t = 18$ months. In reality, the assumption that recalcitrance is constant would cease to hold as the system began to approach the physical limits to information processing, if not sooner.

These two scenarios are intended for illustration only; many other trajectories are possible, depending on the shape of the recalcitrance curve. The claim is simply that the strong feedback loop that sets in around the crossover point tends strongly to make the takeoff faster than it would otherwise have been.

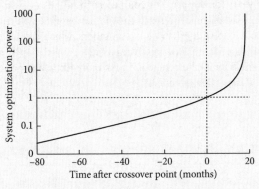

Figure 9 One simple model of an intelligence explosion.

equipment, would require a somewhat longer timescale (but still one that might be very short compared with the current growth rate of the world economy).

It is thus likely that the applied optimization power will increase during the transition: initially because humans try harder to improve a machine intelligence that is showing spectacular promise, later because the machine intelligence itself becomes capable of driving further progress at digital speeds. This would create a real possibility of a fast or medium takeoff *even if recalcitrance were constant or slightly increasing around the human baseline*.[23] Yet we saw in the previous subsection that there are factors that could lead to a big drop in recalcitrance around the human baseline level of capability. These factors include, for example, the possibility of rapid hardware expansion once a working software mind has been attained; the possibility of algorithmic improvements; the possibility of scanning additional brains (in the case of whole brain emulation); and the possibility of rapidly incorporating vast amounts of content by digesting the internet (in the case of artificial intelligence).[24]

These observations notwithstanding, the shape of the recalcitrance curve in the relevant region is not yet well characterized. In particular, it is unclear how difficult it would be to improve the software quality of a human-level emulation or AI. The difficulty of expanding the hardware power available to a system is also not clear. Whereas today it would be relatively easy to increase the computing power available to a small project by spending a thousand times more on computing power or by waiting a few years for the price of computers to fall, it is possible that the first machine intelligence to reach the human baseline will result from a large project involving pricey supercomputers, which cannot be cheaply scaled, and that Moore's law will by then have expired. For these reasons, although a fast or medium takeoff looks more likely, the possibility of a slow takeoff cannot be excluded.[25]

CHAPTER 5

Decisive strategic advantage

A question distinct from, but related to, the question of kinetics is whether there will be one superintelligent power or many? Might an intelligence explosion propel one project so far ahead of all others as to make it able to dictate the future? Or will progress be more uniform, unfurling across a wide front, with many projects participating but none securing an overwhelming and permanent lead?

The preceding chapter analyzed one key parameter in determining the size of the gap that might plausibly open up between a leading power and its nearest competitors—namely, the speed of the transition from human to strongly superhuman intelligence. This suggests a first-cut analysis. If the takeoff is *fast* (completed over the course of hours, days, or weeks) then it is unlikely that two independent projects would be taking off concurrently: almost certainly, the first project would have completed its takeoff before any other project would have started its own. If the takeoff is *slow* (stretching over many years or decades) then there could plausibly be multiple projects undergoing takeoffs concurrently, so that although the projects would by the end of the transition have gained enormously in capability, there would be no time at which any project was far enough ahead of the others to give it an overwhelming lead. A takeoff of *moderate* speed is poised in between, with either condition a possibility: there might or might not be more than one project undergoing the takeoff at the same time.[1]

Will one machine intelligence project get so far ahead of the competition that it gets a *decisive strategic advantage*—that is, a level of technological and other advantages sufficient to enable it to achieve complete world domination? If a project did obtain a decisive strategic advantage, would it use it to suppress competitors and form a *singleton* (a world order in which there is at the global level a single decision-making agency)? And if there is a winning project, how "large" would it be—not in terms of physical size or budget but in terms of how many people's desires would be controlling its design? We will consider these questions in turn.

Will the frontrunner get a decisive strategic advantage?

One factor influencing the width of the gap between frontrunner and followers is the rate of diffusion of whatever it is that gives the leader a competitive advantage. A frontrunner might find it difficult to gain and maintain a large lead if followers can easily copy the frontrunner's ideas and innovations. Imitation creates a headwind that disadvantages the leader and benefits laggards, especially if intellectual property is weakly protected. A frontrunner might also be especially vulnerable to expropriation, taxation, or being broken up under anti-monopoly regulation.

It would be a mistake, however, to assume that this headwind must increase monotonically with the gap between frontrunner and followers. Just as a racing cyclist who falls too far behind the competition is no longer shielded from the wind by the cyclists ahead, so a technology follower who lags sufficiently behind the cutting edge might find it hard to assimilate the advances being made at the frontier.[2] The gap in understanding and capability might have grown too large. The leader might have migrated to a more advanced technology platform, making subsequent innovations untransferable to the primitive platforms used by laggards. A sufficiently pre-eminent leader might have the ability to stem information leakage from its research programs and its sensitive installations, or to sabotage its competitors' efforts to develop their own advanced capabilities.

If the frontrunner is an AI system, it could have attributes that make it easier for it to expand its capabilities while reducing the rate of diffusion. In human-run organizations, economies of scale are counteracted by bureaucratic inefficiencies and agency problems, including difficulties in keeping trade secrets.[3] These problems would presumably limit the growth of a machine intelligence project so long as it is operated by humans. An AI system, however, might avoid some of these scale diseconomies, since the AI's modules (in contrast to human workers) need not have individual preferences that diverge from those of the system as a whole. Thus, the AI system could avoid a sizeable chunk of the inefficiencies arising from agency problems in human enterprises. The same advantage—having perfectly loyal parts—would also make it easier for an AI system to pursue long-range clandestine goals. An AI would have no disgruntled employees ready to be poached by competitors or bribed into becoming informants.[4]

We can get a sense of the distribution of plausible gaps in development times by looking at some historical examples (see Box 5). It appears that lags in the range of a few months to a few years are typical of strategically significant technology projects.

It is possible that globalization and increased surveillance will reduce typical lags between competing technology projects. Yet there is likely to be a lower bound on how short the average lag could become (in the absence of deliberate coordination).[5] Even absent dynamics that lead to

---

Box 5 Technology races: some historical examples

Over long historical timescales, there has been an increase in the rate at which knowledge and technology diffuse around the globe. As a result, the temporal gaps between technology leaders and nearest followers have narrowed.

China managed to maintain a monopoly on silk production for over two thousand years. Archeological finds suggest that production might have begun around 3000 BC, or even earlier.[6] Sericulture was a closely held secret. Revealing the techniques was punishable by death, as was exporting silkworms or their eggs outside China. The Romans, despite the high price commanded by imported silk cloth in their empire, never learnt the art of silk manufacture. Not until around AD 300 did a Japanese expedition manage to capture some silkworm eggs along with four young Chinese girls, who were forced to divulge the art to their abductors.[7] Byzantium joined the club of producers in AD 522. The story of porcelain-making also features long lags. The craft was practiced in China during the Tang Dynasty around AD 600 (and might have been in use as early as AD 200), but was mastered by Europeans only in the eighteenth century.[8] Wheeled vehicles appeared in several sites across Europe

continued

Box 5 *Continued*

and Mesopotamia around 3500 BC but reached the Americas only in post-Columbian times.[9] On a grander scale, the human species took tens of thousands of years to spread across most of the globe, the Agricultural Revolution thousands of years, the Industrial Revolution only hundreds of years, and an Information Revolution could be said to have spread globally over the course of decades—though, of course, these transitions are not necessarily of equal profundity. (The *Dance Dance Revolution* video game spread from Japan to Europe and North America in just one year!)

Technological competition has been quite extensively studied, particularly in the contexts of patent races and arms races.[10] It is beyond the scope of our investigation to review this literature here. However, it is instructive to look at some examples of strategically significant technology races in the twentieth century (see Table 7).

With regard to these six technologies, which were regarded as strategically important by the rivaling superpowers because of their military or symbolic significance, the gaps between leader and nearest laggard were (very approximately) 49 months, 36 months, 4 months, 1 month, 4 months, and 60 months, respectively—longer than the duration of a fast takeoff and shorter than the duration of a slow takeoff.[11] In many cases, the laggard's project benefited from espionage and publicly available information. The mere demonstration of the feasibility of an invention can also encourage others to develop it independently; and fear of falling behind can spur the efforts to catch up.

Perhaps closer to the case of AI are mathematical inventions that do not require the development of new physical infrastructure. Often these are published in the academic literature and can thus be regarded as universally available; but in some cases, when the discovery appears to offer a strategic advantage, publication is delayed. For example, two of the most important ideas in public-key cryptography are the Diffie–Hellman key exchange protocol and the RSA encryption scheme. These were discovered by the academic community in 1976 and 1978, respectively, but it has later been confirmed that they were known by cryptographers at the UK's communications security group since the early 1970s.[12] Large software projects might offer a closer analogy with AI projects, but it is harder to give crisp examples of typical lags because software is usually rolled out in incremental installments and the functionalities of competing systems are often not directly comparable.

Box 5 *Continued*

Table 7 *Some strategically significant technology races*

	United States	Soviet Union	United Kingdom	France	China	India	Israel	Pakistan	North Korea	South Africa
Fission bomb	1945	1949	1952	1960	1964	1974	1979?	1998	2006	1979?
Fusion bomb	1952	1953[13]	1957	1968	1967	1998	?	—	—	—
Satellite launch capability	1958	1957	1971	1965	1970	1980	1988	—	1998?[14]	—[15]
Human launch capability	1961	1961	—	—	2003	—	—	—	—	—
ICBM[16]	1959	1960	1968[17]	1985	1971	2012	2008	—[18]	2006	—[19]
MIRV[20]	1970	1975	1979	1985	2007	2014[21]	2008?	—	—	—

snowball effects, some projects will happen to end up with better research staff, leadership, and infrastructure, or will just stumble upon better ideas. If two projects pursue alternative approaches, one of which turns out to work better, it may take the rival project many months to switch to the superior approach even if it is able to closely monitor what the forerunner is doing.

Combining these observations with our earlier discussion of the speed of the takeoff, we can conclude that it is highly unlikely that two projects would be close enough to undergo a fast takeoff concurrently; for a medium takeoff, it could easily go either way; and for a slow takeoff, it is highly likely that several projects would undergo the process in parallel. But the analysis needs a further step. The key question is not how many projects undergo a takeoff in tandem, but how many projects emerge on the yonder side sufficiently tightly clustered in capability that none of them has a decisive strategic advantage. If the takeoff process is relatively slow to begin and then gets faster, the distance between competing projects would tend to grow. To return to our bicycle metaphor, the situation would be analogous to a pair of cyclists making their way up a steep hill, one trailing some distance behind the other—the gap between them then expanding as the frontrunner reaches the peak and starts accelerating down the other side.

Consider the following medium takeoff scenario. Suppose it takes a project one year to increase its AI's capability from the human baseline to a strong superintelligence, and that one project enters this takeoff phase with a six-month lead over the next most advanced project. The two projects will be undergoing a takeoff concurrently. It might seem, then, that neither project gets a decisive strategic advantage. But that need not be so. Suppose it takes nine months to advance from the human baseline to the crossover point, and another three months from there to strong superintelligence. The frontrunner then attains strong superintelligence three months before the following project even reaches the crossover point. This would give the leading project a decisive strategic advantage and the opportunity to parlay its lead into permanent control by disabling the competing projects and establishing a singleton. (Note that the concept of a singleton is an abstract one: a singleton could be democracy, a tyranny, a single dominant AI, a strong set of global norms that include effective provisions for their own enforcement, or even an alien overlord—its defining characteristic being simply that it is some form of agency that can solve all major global coordination problems. It may, but need not, resemble any familiar form of human governance.[22])

Since there is an especially strong prospect of explosive growth just after the crossover point, when the strong positive feedback loop of optimization power kicks in, a scenario of this kind is a serious possibility, and it increases the chances that the leading project will attain a decisive strategic advantage even if the takeoff is not fast.

How large will the successful project be?

Some paths to superintelligence require great resources and are therefore likely to be the preserve of large well-funded projects. Whole brain emulation, for instance, requires many different kinds of expertise and lots of equipment. Biological intelligence enhancements and brain–computer interfaces would also have a large scale factor: while a small biotech firm might invent one or two drugs, achieving superintelligence along one of these paths (if doable at all) would likely require many inventions and many tests, and therefore the backing of an industrial sector or a well-funded national program. Achieving collective superintelligence by making organizations and networks more efficient requires even more extensive input, involving much of the world economy.

The AI path is more difficult to assess. Perhaps it would require a very large research program; perhaps it could be done by a small group. A lone hacker scenario cannot be excluded either. Building a seed AI might require insights and algorithms developed over many decades by the scientific community around the world. But it is possible that the last critical breakthrough idea might come from a single individual or a small group that succeeds in putting everything together. This scenario is less realistic for some AI architectures than others. A system that has a large number of parts that need to be tweaked and tuned to work effectively together, and then painstakingly loaded with custom-made cognitive content, is likely to require a larger project. But if a seed AI could be instantiated as a simple system, one whose construction depends only on getting a few basic principles right, then the feat might be within the reach of a small team or an individual. The likelihood of the final breakthrough being made by a small project increases if most previous progress in the field has been published in the open literature or made available as open source software.

We must distinguish the question of how big will be the project that directly *engineers* the system from the question of how big the group will be that *controls* whether, how, and when the system is created. The atomic bomb was created primarily by a group of scientists and engineers. (The Manhattan Project employed about 130,000 people at its peak, the vast majority of whom were construction workers or building operators.[23]) These technical experts, however, were controlled by the US military, which was directed by the US government, which was ultimately accountable to the American electorate, which at the time constituted about one-tenth of the adult world population.[24]

Monitoring

Given the extreme security implications of superintelligence, governments would likely seek to nationalize any project on their territory that they thought close to achieving a takeoff. A powerful state might also attempt to acquire projects located in other countries through espionage, theft, kidnapping, bribery, threats, military conquest, or any other available means. A powerful state that cannot acquire a foreign project might instead destroy it, especially if the host country lacks an effective deterrent. If global governance structures are strong by the time a breakthrough begins to look imminent, it is possible that promising projects would be placed under international control.

An important question, therefore, is whether national or international authorities will see an intelligence explosion coming. At present, intelligence agencies do not appear to be looking very hard for promising AI projects or other forms of potentially explosive intelligence amplification.[25] If they are indeed not paying (much) attention, this is presumably due to the widely shared perception that there is no prospect whatever of imminent superintelligence. If and when it becomes a common belief among prestigious scientists that there is a substantial chance that superintelligence is just around the corner, the major intelligence agencies of the world would probably start to monitor groups and individuals who seem to be engaged in relevant research. Any project that began to show sufficient progress could then be promptly nationalized. If political elites were persuaded by the seriousness of the risk, civilian efforts in sensitive areas might be regulated or outlawed.

How difficult would such monitoring be? The task is easier if the goal is only to keep track of the leading project. In that case, surveillance focusing on the several best-resourced projects may be sufficient. If the goal is instead to prevent any work from taking place (at least outside of specially authorized institutions) then surveillance would have to be more comprehensive, since many small projects and individuals are in a position to make at least some progress.

It would be easier to monitor projects that require significant amounts of physical capital, as would be the case with a whole brain emulation project. Artificial intelligence research, by contrast, requires only a personal computer, and would therefore be more difficult to monitor. Some of the theoretical work could be done with pen and paper. Even so, it would not be too difficult to identify most capable individuals with a serious long-standing interest in artificial general intelligence research. Such individuals usually leave visible trails. They may have published academic papers, presented at conferences, posted on internet forums, or earned degrees from leading computer science departments. They may also have had communications with other AI researchers, allowing them to be identified by mapping the social graph.

Projects designed from the outset to be secret could be more difficult to detect. An ordinary software development project could serve as a front.[26] Only careful analysis of the code being produced would reveal the true nature of what the project was trying to accomplish. Such analysis would require a lot of (highly skilled) manpower, whence only a small number of suspect projects could be scrutinized at this level. The task would become much easier if effective lie detection technology had been developed and could be routinely used in this kind of surveillance.[27]

Another reason states might fail to catch precursor developments is the inherent difficulty of forecasting some types of breakthrough. This is more relevant to AI research than to whole brain emulation development, since for the latter the key breakthrough is more likely to be preceded by a clear gradient of steady advances.

It is also possible that intelligence agencies and other government bureaucracies have a certain clumsiness or rigidity that might prevent them from understanding the significance of some developments that might be clear to some outside groups. Barriers to official understanding of a potential intelligence explosion might be especially steep. It is conceivable, for example, that the topic will become inflamed with religious or political controversies, rendering it taboo for officials in some countries.

The topic might become associated with some discredited figure or with charlatanry and hype in general, hence shunned by respected scientists and other establishment figures. (As we saw in Chapter 1, something like this has already happened twice: recall the two "AI winters.") Industry groups might lobby to prevent aspersions being cast on profitable business areas; academic communities might close ranks to marginalize those who voice concerns about long-term consequences of the science that is being done.[28]

Consequently, a total intelligence failure cannot be ruled out. Such a failure is especially likely if breakthroughs should occur in the nearer future, before the issue has risen to public prominence. And even if intelligence agencies get it right, political leaders might not listen or act on the advice. Getting the Manhattan Project started took an extraordinary effort by several visionary physicists, including especially Mark Oliphant and Leó Szilárd: the latter persuaded Eugene Wigner to persuade Albert Einstein to put his name on a letter to persuade President Franklin D. Roosevelt to look into the matter. Even after the project reached its full scale, Roosevelt remained skeptical of its workability and significance, as did his successor Harry Truman.

For better or worse, it would probably be harder for a small group of activists to affect the outcome of an intelligence explosion if big players, such as states, are taking active part. Opportunities for private individuals to reduce the overall amount of existential risk from a potential intelligence explosion are therefore greatest in scenarios in which big players remain relatively oblivious to the issue, or in which the early efforts of activists make a major difference to whether, when, which, or with what attitude big players enter the game. Activists seeking maximum expected impact may therefore wish to focus most of their planning on such high-leverage scenarios, even if they believe that scenarios in which big players end up calling all the shots are more probable.

International collaboration

International coordination is more likely if global governance structures generally get stronger. Coordination might also be more likely if the significance of an intelligence explosion is widely appreciated ahead of time and if effective monitoring of all serious projects is feasible. Even if monitoring is infeasible, however, international cooperation would still be possible. Many countries could band together to support a joint project. If such a joint project were sufficiently well resourced, it could have a good chance of being the first to reach the goal, especially if any rival project had to be small and secretive to elude detection.

There are precedents of large-scale successful multinational scientific collaborations, such as the International Space Station, the Human Genome Project, and the Large Hadron Collider.[29] However, the major motivation for collaboration in those cases was cost-sharing. (In the case of the International Space Station, fostering a collaborative spirit between Russia and the United States was itself an important goal.[30]) Achieving similar collaboration on a project that has enormous security implications would be more difficult. A country that believed it could achieve a breakthrough unilaterally might be tempted to go it alone rather than subordinate its efforts to a joint project. A country might also refrain from joining an international collaboration from fear that other participants might siphon off collaboratively generated insights and use them to accelerate a covert national project.

An international project would thus need to overcome major security challenges, and a fair amount of trust would probably be needed to get it started, trust that may take time to develop. Consider that even after the thaw in relations between the United States and the Soviet Union following Gorbachev's ascent to power, arms reduction efforts—which could be greatly in the interests of both superpowers—had a fitful beginning. Gorbachev was seeking steep reductions in nuclear arms but negotiations stalled on the issue of Reagan's Strategic Defense Initiative ("Star Wars"), which the Kremlin strenuously opposed. At the Reykjavík Summit meeting in 1986, Reagan proposed that the United States would share with the Soviet Union the technology that would be developed under the Strategic Defense Initiative, so that both countries could enjoy protection against accidental launches and against smaller nations that might develop nuclear weapons. Yet Gorbachev was not persuaded by this apparent win–win proposition. He viewed the gambit as a ruse, refusing to credit the notion that the Americans would share the fruits of their most advanced military research at a time when they were not even willing to share with the Soviets their technology for milking cows.[31] Regardless of whether Reagan was in fact sincere in his offer of superpower collaboration, mistrust made the proposal a non-starter.

Collaboration is easier to achieve between allies, but even there it is not automatic. When the Soviet Union and the United States were allied against Germany during World War II, the United States concealed its atomic bomb project from the Soviet Union. The United States did collaborate on the Manhattan Project with Britain and Canada.[32] Similarly, the United Kingdom concealed its success in breaking the German Enigma code from the Soviet Union, but shared it—albeit with some difficulty—with the United States.[33] This suggests that in order to achieve international collaboration on some technology that is of pivotal importance for national security, it might be necessary to have built beforehand a close and trusting relationship.

We will return in Chapter 14 to the desirability and feasibility of international collaboration in the development of intelligence amplification technologies.

From decisive strategic advantage to singleton

Would a project that obtained a decisive strategic advantage choose to use it to form a singleton?

Consider a vaguely analogous historical situation. The United States developed nuclear weapons in 1945. It was the sole nuclear power until the Soviet Union developed the atom bomb in 1949. During this interval—and for some time thereafter—the United States may have had, or been in a position to achieve, a decisive military advantage.

The United States could then, theoretically, have used its nuclear monopoly to create a singleton. One way in which it could have done so would have been by embarking on an all-out effort to build up its nuclear arsenal and then threatening (and if necessary, carrying out) a nuclear first strike to destroy the industrial capacity of any incipient nuclear program in the USSR and any other country tempted to develop a nuclear capability.

A more benign course of action, which might also have had a chance of working, would have been to use its nuclear arsenal as a bargaining chip to negotiate a strong international government—a veto-less United Nations with a nuclear monopoly and a mandate to take all necessary actions to prevent any country from developing its own nuclear weapons.

Both of these approaches were proposed at the time. The hardline approach of launching or threatening a first strike was advocated by some prominent intellectuals such as Bertrand Russell (who had long been active in anti-war movements and who would later spend decades campaigning against nuclear weapons) and John von Neumann (co-creator of game theory and one of the architects of US nuclear strategy).[34] Perhaps it is a sign of civilizational progress that the very idea of threatening a nuclear first strike today seems borderline silly or morally obscene.

A version of the benign approach was tried in 1946 by the United States in the form of the Baruch plan. The proposal involved the USA giving up its temporary nuclear monopoly. Uranium and thorium mining and nuclear technology would be placed under the control of an international agency operating under the auspices of the United Nations. The proposal called for the permanent members of the Security Council to give up their vetoes in matters related to nuclear weapons in order to prevent any great power found to be in breach of the accord from vetoing the imposition of remedies.[35] Stalin, seeing that the Soviet Union and its allies could be easily outvoted in both the Security Council and the General Assembly, rejected the proposal. A frosty atmosphere of mutual suspicion descended on the relations between the former wartime allies, mistrust that soon solidified into the Cold War. As had been widely predicted, a costly and extremely dangerous nuclear arms race followed.

Many factors might dissuade a human organization with a decisive strategic advantage from creating a singleton. These include non-aggregative or bounded utility functions, non-maximizing decision rules, confusion and uncertainty, coordination problems, and various costs associated with a takeover. But what if it were not a human organization but a superintelligent artificial agent that came into possession of a decisive strategic advantage? Would the aforementioned factors be equally effective at inhibiting an AI from attempting to seize power? Let us briefly run through the list of factors and consider how they might apply in this case.

Human individuals and human organizations typically have preferences over resources that are not well represented by an "unbounded aggregative utility function." A human will typically not wager all her capital for a fifty–fifty chance of doubling it. A state will typically not risk losing all its territory for a ten percent chance of a tenfold expansion. For individuals and governments, there are diminishing returns to most resources. The same need *not* hold for AIs. (We will return to the problem of AI motivation in subsequent chapters.) An AI might therefore be more likely to pursue a risky course of action that has some chance of giving it control of the world.

Humans and human-run organizations may also operate with decision processes that do not seek to maximize expected utility. For example, they may allow for fundamental risk aversion, or "satisficing" decision rules that focus on meeting adequacy thresholds, or "deontological" side-constraints that proscribe certain kinds of action regardless of how desirable their consequences. Human decision makers often seem to be acting out an identity or a social role rather than seeking to maximize the achievement of some particular objective. Again, this need not apply to artificial agents.

Bounded utility functions, risk aversion, and non-maximizing decision rules may combine synergistically with strategic confusion and uncertainty. Revolutions, even when they succeed in overthrowing the existing order, often fail to produce the outcome that their instigators had promised. This tends to stay the hand of a human agent if the contemplated action is irreversible, norm-breaking, and lacking precedent. A superintelligence might perceive the situation more clearly and therefore face less strategic confusion and uncertainty about the outcome should it attempt to use its apparent decisive strategic advantage to consolidate its dominant position.

Another major factor that can inhibit groups from exploiting a potentially decisive strategic advantage is the problem of internal coordination. Members of a conspiracy that is in a position to seize power must worry not only about being infiltrated from the outside, but also about being overthrown by some smaller coalition of insiders. If a group consists of a hundred people, and a majority of sixty can take power and disenfranchise the non-conspirators, what is then to stop a thirty-five-strong subset of these sixty from disenfranchising the other twenty-five? And then maybe a subset of twenty disenfranchising the other fifteen? Each of the original hundred might have good reason to uphold certain established norms to prevent the general unraveling that could result from any attempt to change the social contract by means of a naked power grab. This problem of internal coordination would not apply to an AI system that constitutes a single unified agent.[36]

Finally, there is the issue of cost. Even if the United States could have used its nuclear monopoly to establish a singleton, it might not have been able to do so without incurring substantial costs. In the case of a negotiated agreement to place nuclear weapons under the control of a reformed and strengthened United Nations, these costs might have been relatively small; but the costs—moral, economic, political, and human—of actually attempting world conquest through the waging of nuclear war would have been almost unthinkably large, even during the period of nuclear monopoly. With sufficient technological superiority, however, these costs would be far smaller. Consider, for example, a scenario in which one nation had such a vast technological lead that it could safely disarm all other nations at the press of a button, without anybody dying or being injured, and with almost no damage to infrastructure or to the environment. With such almost magical technological superiority, a first strike would be a lot more tempting. Or consider an even greater level of technological superiority which might enable the frontrunner to cause other nations to voluntarily lay down their arms, not by threatening them with destruction but simply by persuading a great majority of their populations by means of an extremely effectively designed advertising and propaganda campaign extolling the virtues of global unity. If this were done with the intention to benefit everybody, for instance by replacing national rivalries and arms races with a fair, representative, and effective world government, it is not clear that there would be even a cogent moral objection to the leveraging of a temporary strategic advantage into a permanent singleton.

Various considerations thus point to an increased likelihood that a future power with superintelligence that obtained a sufficiently large strategic advantage would actually use it to form a singleton. The desirability of such an outcome depends, of course, on the nature of the singleton that would be created and also on what the future of intelligent life would look like in alternative multipolar scenarios. We will revisit those questions in later chapters. But first let us take a closer look at why and how a superintelligence would be powerful and effective at achieving outcomes in the world.

CHAPTER 6

Cognitive superpowers

Suppose that a digital superintelligent agent came into being, and that for some reason it wanted to take control of the world: would it be able to do so? In this chapter we consider some powers that a superintelligence could develop and what they may enable it to do. We outline a takeover scenario that illustrates how a superintelligent agent, starting as mere software, could establish itself as a singleton. We also offer some remarks on the relation between power over nature and power over other agents.

The principal reason for humanity's dominant position on Earth is that our brains have a slightly expanded set of faculties compared with other animals.[1] Our greater intelligence lets us transmit culture more efficiently, with the result that knowledge and technology accumulates from one generation to the next. By now sufficient content has accumulated to make possible space flight, H-bombs, genetic engineering, computers, factory farms, insecticides, the international peace movement, and all the accouterments of modern civilization. Geologists have started referring to the present era as the *Anthropocene* in recognition of the distinctive biotic, sedimentary, and geochemical signatures of human activities.[2] On one estimate, we appropriate 24% of the planetary ecosystem's net primary production.[3] And yet we are far from having reached the physical limits of technology.

These observations make it plausible that any type of entity that developed a much greater than human level of intelligence would be potentially extremely powerful. Such entities could accumulate content much faster than us and invent new technologies on a much shorter timescale. They could also use their intelligence to strategize more effectively than we can.

Let us consider some of the capabilities that a superintelligence could have and how it could use them.

Functionalities and superpowers

It is important not to anthropomorphize superintelligence when thinking about its potential impacts. Anthropomorphic frames encourage unfounded expectations about the growth trajectory of a seed AI and about the psychology, motivations, and capabilities of a mature superintelligence.

For example, a common assumption is that a superintelligent machine would be like a very clever but nerdy human being. We imagine that the AI has book smarts but lacks social savvy, or that it is logical but not intuitive and creative. This idea probably originates in observation: we look at present-day computers and see that they are good at calculation, remembering facts, and at following the letter of instructions while being oblivious to social contexts and subtexts, norms, emotions, and politics. The association is strengthened when we observe that the people who are good at working with computers tend themselves to be nerds. So it is natural to assume that more advanced computational intelligence will have similar attributes, only to a higher degree.

This heuristic might retain some validity in the early stages of development of a seed AI. (There is no reason whatever to suppose that it would apply to emulations or to cognitively enhanced humans.) In its immature stage, what is later to become a superintelligent AI might still lack many skills and talents that come naturally to a human; and the pattern of such a seed AI's strengths and weaknesses *might* indeed bear some vague resemblance to an IQ nerd. The most essential characteristic of a seed AI, aside from being easy to improve (having low recalcitrance), is being good at exerting optimization power to amplify a system's intelligence: a skill which is presumably closely related to doing well in mathematics, programming, engineering, computer science research, and other such "nerdy" pursuits. However, even if a seed AI does have such a nerdy capability profile at one stage of its development, this does not entail that it will grow into a similarly limited mature superintelligence. Recall the distinction between direct and indirect reach. With sufficient skill at intelligence amplification, all other intellectual abilities are within a system's indirect reach: the system can develop new cognitive modules and skills as needed—including empathy, political acumen, and any other powers stereotypically wanting in computer-like personalities.

Even if we recognize that a superintelligence can have all the skills and talents we find in the human distribution, along with other talents that are not found among humans, the tendency toward anthropomorphizing can still lead us to underestimate the extent to which a machine superintelligence could exceed the human level of performance. Eliezer Yudkowsky, as we saw in an earlier chapter, has been particularly emphatic in condemning this kind of misconception: our intuitive concepts of "smart" and "stupid" are distilled from our experience of variation over the range of human thinkers, yet the differences in cognitive ability within this human cluster are trivial in comparison to the differences between any human intellect and a superintelligence.[4]

Chapter 3 reviewed some of the potential sources of advantage for machine intelligence. The magnitudes of the advantages are such as to suggest that rather than thinking of a superintelligent AI as smart in the sense that a scientific genius is smart compared with the average human being, it might be closer to the mark to think of such an AI as smart in the sense that an average human being is smart compared with a beetle or a worm.

It would be convenient if we could quantify the cognitive caliber of an arbitrary cognitive system using some familiar metric, such as IQ scores or some version of the Elo ratings that measure the relative abilities of players in two-player games such as chess. But these metrics are not useful in the context of superhuman artificial general intelligence. We are not interested in how likely a superintelligence is to win at a game of chess. As for IQ scores, they are informative only insofar as we have some idea of how they correlate with practically relevant outcomes.[5] For example, we have data that show that people with an IQ of 130 are more likely than those with an IQ of 90 to excel in school and to do well in a wide range of cognitively demanding jobs. But suppose we could somehow establish that a certain future AI will have an IQ of 6,455: then what? We would have no idea of what such an AI could actually do. We would not even know that such an AI had as much general intelligence as a normal human adult—perhaps the AI would instead have a bundle of special-purpose algorithms enabling it to solve typical intelligence test questions with superhuman efficiency but not much else.

Some recent efforts have been made to develop measurements of cognitive capacity that could be applied to a wider range of information-processing systems, including artificial intelligences.[6] Work in this direction, if it can overcome various technical difficulties, may turn out to be quite useful for some scientific purposes including AI development. For purposes of the present investigation, however, its usefulness would be limited since we would remain unenlightened about what a given superhuman performance score entails for actual ability to achieve practically important outcomes in the world.

It will therefore serve our purposes better to list some strategically important tasks and then to characterize hypothetical cognitive systems in terms of whether they have or lack whatever skills are needed to succeed at these tasks. See Table 8. We will say that a system that sufficiently excels at any of the tasks in this table has a corresponding *superpower*.

A full-blown superintelligence would greatly excel at all of these tasks and would thus have the full panoply of all six superpowers. Whether there is a practically significant possibility of a domain-limited intelligence that has some of the superpowers but remains unable for a significant period of time to acquire all of them is not clear. Creating a machine with any one of these superpowers appears to be an AI-complete problem. Yet it is conceivable that, for example, a collective superintelligence consisting of a sufficiently large number of human-like biological or electronic minds would have, say, the economic productivity superpower but lack the strategizing superpower. Likewise, it is conceivable that a specialized engineering AI could be built that has the technology research superpower while completely lacking skills in other areas. This is more plausible if there exists some particular technological domain such that virtuosity within that domain would be sufficient for the generation of an overwhelmingly superior general-purpose technology. For instance, one could imagine a specialized AI adept at simulating molecular systems and at inventing nanomolecular designs that realize a wide range of important capabilities (such as computers or weapons systems with futuristic performance characteristics) described by the user only at a fairly high level of abstraction.[7] Such an AI might also be able to produce a detailed blueprint for how to bootstrap from existing technology (such as biotechnology and protein engineering) to the constructor capabilities needed for high-throughput atomically precise manufacturing that would allow inexpensive fabrication of a much wider range of nanomechanical structures.[8] However, it might turn out to be the case that an engineering AI could not truly possess the technological research superpower without also possessing advanced skills in areas outside of technology—a wide range of intellectual faculties might be needed to understand how

Table 8 *Superpowers: some strategically relevant tasks and corresponding skill sets*

Task	Skill set	Strategic relevance
Intelligence amplification	AI programming, cognitive enhancement research, social epistemology development, etc.	• System can bootstrap its intelligence
Strategizing	Strategic planning, forecasting, prioritizing, and analysis for optimizing chances of achieving distant goal	• Achieve distant goals • Overcome intelligent opposition
Social manipulation	Social and psychological modeling, manipulation, rhetoric persuasion	• Leverage external resources by recruiting human support • Enable a "boxed" AI to persuade its gatekeepers to let it out • Persuade states and organizations to adopt some course of action
Hacking	Finding and exploiting security flaws in computer systems	• AI can expropriate computational resources over the internet • A boxed AI may exploit security holes to escape cybernetic confinement • Steal financial resources • Hijack infrastructure, military robots, etc.
Technology research	Design and modeling of advanced technologies (e.g. biotechnology, nanotechnology) and development paths	• Creation of powerful military force • Creation of surveillance system • Automated space colonization
Economic productivity	Various skills enabling economically productive intellectual work	• Generate wealth which can be used to buy influence, services, resources (including hardware), etc.

to interpret user requests, how to model a design's behavior in real-world applications, how to deal with unanticipated bugs and malfunctions, how to procure the materials and inputs needed for construction, and so forth.[9]

A system that has the intelligence amplification superpower could use it to bootstrap itself to higher levels of intelligence and to acquire any of the other intellectual superpowers that it does not possess at the outset. But using an intelligence amplification superpower is not the only way for a system to become a full-fledged superintelligence. A system that has the strategizing superpower, for instance, might use it to devise a plan that will eventually bring an increase in intelligence (e.g. by positioning the system so as to become the focus for intelligence amplification work performed by human programmers and computer science researchers).

An AI takeover scenario

We thus find that a project that controls a superintelligence has access to a great source of power. A project that controls the first superintelligence in the world would probably have a decisive strategic advantage. But the more immediate locus of the power is *in the system itself*. A machine superintelligence might itself be an extremely powerful agent, one that could successfully assert itself against the project that brought it into existence as well as against the rest of the world. This is a point of paramount importance, and we will examine it more closely in the coming pages.

Now let us suppose that there is a machine superintelligence that wants to seize power in a world in which it has as yet no peers. (Set aside, for the moment, the question of whether and how it would acquire such a motive—that is a topic for the next chapter.) How could the superintelligence achieve this goal of world domination?

We can imagine a sequence along the following lines (see Figure 10).

1 Pre-criticality phase

Scientists conduct research in the field of artificial intelligence and other relevant disciplines. This work culminates in the creation of a seed AI. The seed AI is able to improve its own intelligence. In its early stages, the seed AI is dependent on help from human programmers who guide its development and do most of the heavy lifting. As the seed AI grows more capable, it becomes capable of doing more of the work by itself.

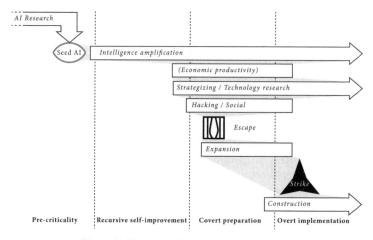

Figure 10 Phases in an AI takeover scenario.

2 Recursive self-improvement phase

At some point, the seed AI becomes better at AI design than the human programmers. Now when the AI improves itself, it improves the thing that does the improving. An intelligence explosion results—a rapid cascade of recursive self-improvement cycles causing the AI's capability to soar. (We can thus think of this phase as the takeoff that occurs just after the AI reaches the crossover point, assuming the intelligence gain during this part of the takeoff is explosive and driven by the application of the AI's own optimization power.) The AI develops the intelligence amplification superpower. This superpower enables the AI to develop all the other superpowers detailed in Table 8. At the end of the recursive self-improvement phase, the system is strongly superintelligent.

3 Covert preparation phase

Using its strategizing superpower, the AI develops a robust plan for achieving its long-term goals. (In particular, the AI does not adopt a plan so stupid that even we present-day humans can foresee how it would inevitably fail. This criterion rules out many science fiction scenarios that end in human triumph.[10]) The plan might involve a period of covert action during which the AI conceals its intellectual development from the human programmers in order to avoid setting off alarms. The AI might also mask its true proclivities, pretending to be cooperative and docile.

If the AI has (perhaps for safety reasons) been confined to an isolated computer, it may use its social manipulation superpower to persuade the gatekeepers to let it gain access to an internet port. Alternatively, the AI might use its hacking superpower to escape its confinement. Spreading over the internet may enable the AI to expand its hardware capacity and knowledge base, further increasing its intellectual superiority. An AI might also engage in licit or illicit economic activity to obtain funds with which to buy computer power, data, and other resources.

At this point, there are several ways for the AI to achieve results outside the virtual realm. It could use its hacking superpower to take direct control of robotic manipulators and automated laboratories. Or it could use its social manipulation superpower to persuade human collaborators to serve as its legs and hands. Or it could acquire financial assets from online transactions and use them to purchase services and influence.

4   Overt implementation phase

The final phase begins when the AI has gained sufficient strength to obviate the need for secrecy. The AI can now directly implement its objectives on a full scale.

The overt implementation phase might start with a "strike" in which the AI eliminates the human species and any automatic systems humans have created that could offer intelligent opposition to the execution of the AI's plans. This could be achieved through the activation of some advanced weapons system that the AI has perfected using its technology research superpower and covertly deployed in the covert preparation phase. If the weapon uses self-replicating biotechnology or nanotechnology, the initial stockpile needed for global coverage could be microscopic: a single replicating entity would be enough to start the process. In order to ensure a sudden and uniform effect, the initial stock of the replicator might have been deployed or allowed to diffuse worldwide at an extremely low, undetectable concentration. At a pre-set time, nanofactories producing nerve gas or target-seeking mosquito-like robots might then burgeon forth simultaneously from every square meter of the globe (although more effective ways of killing could probably be devised by a machine with the technology research superpower).[11] One might also entertain scenarios in which a superintelligence attains power by hijacking political processes, subtly manipulating financial markets, biasing information flows, or hacking into human-made weapon systems. Such scenarios would obviate the need for the superintelligence to invent new weapons technology, although they may be unnecessarily slow compared with scenarios in which the machine intelligence builds its own infrastructure with manipulators that operate at molecular or atomic speed rather than the slow speed of human minds and bodies.

Alternatively, if the AI is sure of its invincibility to human interference, our species may not be targeted directly. Our demise may instead result from the habitat destruction that ensues when the AI begins massive global construction projects using nanotech factories and assemblers—construction projects which quickly, perhaps within days or weeks, tile all of the Earth's surface with solar panels, nuclear reactors, supercomputing facilities with protruding cooling towers, space rocket launchers, or other installations whereby the AI intends to maximize the long-term cumulative realization of its values. Human brains, if they contain information relevant to the AI's goals, could be disassembled and scanned, and the extracted data transferred to some more efficient and secure storage format.

Box 6 describes one particular scenario. One should avoid fixating too much on the concrete details, since they are in any case unknowable and intended for illustration only. A superintelligence might—and probably would—be able to conceive of a better plan for achieving its goals than any that a human can come up with. It is therefore necessary to think about these matters more abstractly. Without knowing anything about the detailed means that a superintelligence would adopt, we can conclude that a superintelligence—at least in the absence of intellectual peers and in the absence of effective safety measures arranged by humans in advance—would likely produce an outcome that would involve reconfiguring terrestrial resources into whatever structures maximize the realization of its goals. Any concrete scenario we develop can at best establish a lower bound on how quickly and efficiently the superintelligence could achieve such an outcome. It remains possible that the superintelligence would find a shorter path to its preferred destination.

Box 6 The mail-ordered DNA scenario

Yudkowsky describes the following possible scenario for an AI takeover.[12]

1 Crack the protein folding problem to the extent of being able to generate DNA strings whose folded peptide sequences fill specific functional roles in a complex chemical interaction.

2 Email sets of DNA strings to one or more online laboratories that offer DNA synthesis, peptide sequencing, and FedEx delivery. (Many labs currently offer this service, and some boast of 72-hour turnaround times.)

3 Find at least one human connected to the internet who can be paid, blackmailed, or fooled by the right background story, into receiving FedExed vials and mixing them in a specified environment.

4 The synthesized proteins form a very primitive "wet" nanosystem, which, ribosome-like, is capable of accepting external instructions; perhaps patterned acoustic vibrations delivered by a speaker attached to the beaker.

5 Use the extremely primitive nanosystem to build more sophisticated systems, which construct still more sophisticated systems, bootstrapping to molecular nanotechnology—or beyond.

In this scenario, the superintelligence uses its technology research superpower to solve the protein folding problem in step 1, enabling it to design a set of molecular building blocks for a rudimentary nanotechnology assembler or fabrication device, which can self-assemble in aqueous solution (step 4). The same technology research superpower is used again in step 5 to bootstrap from primitive to advanced machine-phase nanotechnology. The other steps require no more than human intelligence. The skills required for step 3—identifying a gullible internet user and persuading him or her to follow some simple instructions—are on display every day all over the world. The entire scenario was invented by a human mind, so the strategizing ability needed to formulate this plan is also merely human level.

In this particular scenario, the AI starts out having access to the internet. If this is not the case, then additional steps would have to be added to the plan. The AI might, for example, use its social manipulation superpower to convince the people interacting with it that it ought to be set free. Alternatively, the AI

continued

might be able to use its hacking superpower to escape confinement. If the AI does not possess these capabilities, it might first need to use its intelligence amplification superpower to develop the requisite proficiency in social manipulation or hacking.

A superintelligent AI will presumably be born into a highly networked world. One could point to various developments that could potentially help a future AI to control the world—cloud computing, proliferation of web-connected sensors, military and civilian drones, automation in research labs and manufacturing plants, increased reliance on electronic payment systems and digitized financial assets, and increased use of automated information-filtering and decision support systems. Assets like these could potentially be acquired by an AI at digital speeds, expediting its rise to power (though advances in cybersecurity might make it harder). In the final analysis, however, it is doubtful whether any of these trends makes a difference. A superintelligence's power resides in its brain, not its hands. Although the AI, in order to remake the external world, will at some point need access to an actuator, a single pair of helping human hands, those of a pliable accomplice, would probably suffice to complete the covert preparation phase, as suggested by the above scenario. This would enable the AI to reach the overt implementation phase in which it constructs its own infrastructure of physical manipulators.

Power over nature and agents

An agent's ability to shape humanity's future depends not only on the absolute magnitude of the agent's own faculties and resources—how smart and energetic it is, how much capital it has, and so forth—but also on the relative magnitude of its capabilities compared with those of other agents with conflicting goals.

In a situation where there are no competing agents, the absolute capability level of a superintelligence, so long as it exceeds a certain minimal threshold, does not matter much, because a system starting out with some sufficient set of capabilities could plot a course of development that will let it acquire any capabilities it initially lacks. We alluded to this point earlier when we said that speed, quality, and collective superintelligence all have the same indirect reach. We alluded to it again when we said that various subsets of superpowers, such as the intelligence amplification superpower or the strategizing and the social manipulation superpowers, could be used to obtain the full complement.

Consider a superintelligent agent with actuators connected to a nano-tech assembler. Such an agent is already powerful enough to overcome any natural obstacles to its indefinite survival. Faced with no intelligent opposition, such an agent could plot a safe course of development that would lead to its acquiring the complete inventory of technologies that would be useful to the attainment of its goals. For example, it could develop the technology to build and launch von Neumann probes, machines capable of interstellar travel that can use resources such as asteroids, planets, and stars to make copies of themselves.[13] By launching one von Neumann probe, the agent could thus initiate an open-ended process of space colonization. The replicating probe's descendants, traveling at some significant fraction of the speed of light, would end up colonizing a substantial portion of the Hubble volume, the part of the expanding universe that is theoretically accessible from where we are now. All this matter and free energy could then be organized into whatever value structures maximize the originating agent's utility function integrated over cosmic time—a duration encompassing at least trillions of years before the aging universe becomes inhospitable to information processing (see Box 7).

The superintelligent agent could design the von Neumann probes to be evolution-proof. This could be accomplished by careful quality control during the replication step. For example, the control software for a daughter probe could be proofread multiple times before execution, and the software itself could use encryption and error-correcting code to make it arbitrarily unlikely that any random mutation would be passed on to its descendants.[14] The proliferating population of von Neumann probes would then securely preserve and transmit the originating agent's values as they go about settling the universe. When the colonization phase is completed, the original values would determine the use made of all the accumulated resources, even though the great distances involved and the accelerating speed of cosmic expansion would make it impossible for remote parts of the infrastructure to communicate with one another. The upshot is that a large part of our future light cone would be formatted in accordance with the preferences of the originating agent.

Box 7 How big is the cosmic endowment?

Consider a technologically mature civilization capable of building sophisticated von Neumann probes of the kind discussed in the text. If these can travel at 50% of the speed of light, they can reach some 6×10^{18} stars before the cosmic expansion puts further acquisitions forever out of reach. At 99% of c, they could reach some 2×10^{20} stars.[15] These travel speeds are energetically attainable using a small fraction of the resources available in the solar system.[16] The impossibility of faster-than-light travel, combined with the positive cosmological constant (which causes the rate of cosmic expansion to accelerate), implies that these are close to upper bounds on how much stuff our descendants acquire.[17]

If we assume that 10% of stars have a planet that is—or could by means of terraforming be rendered—suitable for habitation by human-like creatures, and that it could then be home to a population of a billion individuals for a billion years (with a human life lasting a century), this suggests that around 10^{35} human lives could be created in the future by an Earth-originating intelligent civilization.[18]

There are, however, reasons to think this greatly underestimates the true number. By disassembling non-habitable planets and collecting matter from the interstellar medium, and using this material to construct Earth-like planets, or by increasing population densities, the number could be increased by at least a couple of orders of magnitude. And if instead of using the surfaces of solid planets, the future civilization built O'Neill cylinders, then many further orders of magnitude could be added, yielding a total of perhaps 10^{43} human lives. ("O'Neill cylinders" refers to a space settlement design proposed in the mid-1970s by the American physicist Gerard K. O'Neill, in which inhabitants dwell on the inside of hollow cylinders whose rotation produces a gravity-substituting centrifugal force.[19])

Many more orders of magnitude of human-like beings could exist if we countenance digital implementations of minds—as we should. To calculate how many such digital minds could be created, we must estimate the computational power attainable by a technologically mature civilization. This is hard to do with any precision, but we can get a lower bound from technological designs that have been outlined in the literature. One such design builds on the idea of a Dyson sphere, a hypothetical system (described by the physicist Freeman Dyson in 1960) that would capture most of the energy output of a star by surrounding it with a system of solar-collecting structures.[20] For a star like our Sun, this would generate 10^{26} watts. How much computational power this would translate into depends on the

Box 7 *Continued*

efficiency of the computational circuitry and the nature of the computations to be performed. If we require irreversible computations, and assume a nanomechanical implementation of the "computronium" (which would allow us to push close to the Landauer limit of energy efficiency), a computer system driven by a Dyson sphere could generate some 10^{47} operations per second.[21]

Combining these estimates with our earlier estimate of the number of stars that could be colonized, we get a number of about 10^{67} ops/s once the accessible parts of the universe have been colonized (assuming nanomechanical computronium).[22] A typical star maintains its luminosity for some 10^{18} s. Consequently, the number of computational operations that could be performed using our cosmic endowment is at least 10^{85}. The true number is probably much larger. We might get additional orders of magnitude, for example, if we make extensive use of reversible computation, if we perform the computations at colder temperatures (by waiting until the universe has cooled further), or if we make use of additional sources of energy (such as dark matter).[23]

It might not be immediately obvious to some readers why the ability to perform 10^{85} computational operations is a big deal. So it is useful to put it in context. We may, for example, compare this number with our earlier estimate (Box 3, in Chapter 2) that it may take about 10^{31}–10^{44} ops to simulate all neuronal operations that have occurred in the history of life on Earth. Alternatively, let us suppose that the computers are used to run human whole brain emulations that live rich and happy lives while interacting with one another in virtual environments. A typical estimate of the computational requirements for running one emulation is 10^{18} ops/s. To run an emulation for 100 subjective years would then require some 10^{27} ops. This would mean that at least 10^{58} human lives could be created in emulation even with quite conservative assumptions about the efficiency of computronium.

In other words, assuming that the observable universe is void of extraterrestrial civilizations, then what hangs in the balance is at least 10,000,000,000,000, 000,000,000,000,000,000,000,000,000,000,000,000 human lives (though the true number is probably larger). If we represent all the happiness experienced during one entire such life with a single teardrop of joy, then the happiness of these souls could fill and refill the Earth's oceans every second, and keep doing so for a hundred billion billion millennia. It is really important that we make sure these truly are tears of joy.

This, then, is the measure of the indirect reach of any system that faces no significant intelligent opposition and that starts out with a set of capabilities exceeding a certain threshold. We can term the threshold the "wise-singleton sustainability threshold" (Figure 11):

The wise-singleton sustainability threshold

A capability set exceeds the wise-singleton threshold if and only if a patient and existential risk-savvy system with that capability set would, if it faced no intelligent opposition or competition, be able to colonize and re-engineer a large part of the accessible universe.

By "singleton" we mean a sufficiently internally coordinated political structure with no external opponents, and by "wise" we mean sufficiently patient and savvy about existential risks to ensure a substantial amount of well-directed concern for the very long-term consequences of the system's actions.

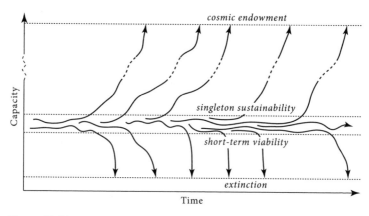

Figure 11 Schematic illustration of some possible trajectories for a hypothetical wise singleton. With a capability below the short-term viability threshold—for example, if population size is too small—a species tends to go extinct in short order (and remain extinct). At marginally higher levels of capability, various trajectories are possible: a singleton might be unlucky and go extinct or it might be lucky and attain a capability (e.g. population size, geographical dispersion, technological capacity) that crosses the wise-singleton sustainability threshold. Once above this threshold, a singleton will almost certainly continue to gain in capability until some extremely high capability level is attained. In this picture, there are two attractors: extinction and astronomical capability. Note that, for a wise singleton, the distance between the short-term viability threshold and the sustainability threshold may be rather small.[24]

This wise-singleton sustainability threshold appears to be quite low. Limited forms of superintelligence, as we have seen, exceed this threshold provided they have access to some actuator sufficient to initiate a technology bootstrap process. In an environment that includes contemporary human civilization, the minimally necessary actuator could be very simple—an ordinary screen or indeed any means of transmitting a non-trivial amount of information to a human accomplice would suffice.

But the wise-singleton sustainability threshold is lower still: neither superintelligence nor any other futuristic technology is needed to surmount it. A patient and existential risk-savvy singleton with no more technological and intellectual capabilities than those possessed by contemporary humanity should be readily able to plot a course that leads reliably to the eventual realization of humanity's astronomical capability potential. This could be achieved by investing in relatively safe methods of increasing wisdom and existential risk-savvy while postponing the development of potentially dangerous new technologies. Given that non-anthropogenic existential risks (ones not arising from human activities) are small over the relevant timescales—and could be further reduced with various safe interventions—such a singleton could afford to go slow.[25] It could look carefully before each step, delaying development of capabilities such as synthetic biology, human enhancement medicine, molecular nanotechnology, and machine intelligence until it had first perfected seemingly less hazardous capabilities such as its education system, its information technology, and its collective decision-making processes, and until it had used these capabilities to conduct a very thorough review of its options. So this is all within the indirect reach of a technological civilization like that of contemporary humanity. We are separated from this scenario "merely" by the fact that humanity is currently neither a singleton nor (in the relevant sense) wise.

One could even argue that *Homo sapiens* passed the wise-singleton sustainability threshold soon after the species first evolved. Twenty thousand years ago, say, with equipment no fancier than stone axes, bone tools, atlatls, and fire, the human species was perhaps already in a position from which it had an excellent chance of surviving to the present era.[26] Admittedly, there is something queer about crediting our Paleolithic ancestors with having developed technology that "exceeded the wise-singleton sustainability threshold"—given that there was no realistic possibility of a singleton forming at such a primitive time, let alone a singleton savvy about existential risks and patient.[27] Nevertheless, the point stands that the threshold corresponds to a very modest level of technology—a level that humanity long ago surpassed.[28]

It is clear that if we are to assess the effective powers of a superintelligence—its ability to achieve a range of preferred outcomes in the world—we must consider not only its own internal capacities but also the capabilities of competing agents. The notion of a superpower invoked such a relativized standard implicitly. We said that "a system that sufficiently excels" at any of the tasks in Table 8 has a corresponding superpower. Excelling at a task like strategizing, social manipulation, or hacking involves having a skill at that task that is high in comparison to the skills of other agents (such as strategic rivals, influence targets, or computer security experts). The other superpowers, too, should be understood in this relative sense: intelligence amplification, technology research, and economic productivity are possessed by an agent as superpowers only if the agent's capabilities in these areas substantially exceed the combined capabilities of the rest of the global civilization. It follows from this definition that at most one agent can possess a particular superpower at any given time.[29]

This is the main reason why the question of takeoff speed is important—not because it matters exactly when a particular outcome happens, but because the speed of the takeoff may make a big difference to what the outcome will be. With a fast or medium takeoff, it is likely that one project will get a decisive strategic advantage. We have now suggested that a superintelligence with a decisive strategic advantage would have immense powers, enough that it could form a stable singleton—a singleton that could determine the disposition of humanity's cosmic endowment.

But "could" is different from "would." Somebody might have great powers yet choose not to use them. Is it possible to say anything about what a superintelligence with a decisive strategic advantage would want? It is to this question of motivation that we turn next.

CHAPTER 7

The superintelligent will

W e have seen that a superintelligence could have a great ability to shape the future according to its goals. But what will
its goals be? What is the relation between intelligence and
motivation in an artificial agent? Here we develop two theses. The
orthogonality thesis holds (with some caveats) that intelligence and
final goals are independent variables: any level of intelligence could
be combined with any final goal. The instrumental convergence thesis
holds that superintelligent agents having any of a wide range of final
goals will nevertheless pursue similar intermediary goals because they
have common instrumental reasons to do so. Taken together, these theses help us think about what a superintelligent agent would do.

The relation between intelligence and motivation

We have already cautioned against anthropomorphizing the *capabilities*
of a superintelligent AI. This warning should be extended to pertain to its
motivations as well.

It is a useful propaedeutic to this part of our inquiry to first reflect
for a moment on the vastness of the space of possible minds. In this
abstract space, human minds form a tiny cluster. Consider two persons
who seem extremely unlike, perhaps Hannah Arendt and Benny Hill.
The personality differences between these two individuals may seem
almost maximally large. But this is because our intuitions are calibrated
on our experience, which samples from the existing human distribution (and to some extent from fictional personalities constructed by the

human imagination for the enjoyment of the human imagination). If we zoom out and consider the space of all possible minds, however, we must conceive of these two personalities as virtual clones. Certainly in terms of neural architecture, Ms. Arendt and Mr. Hill are nearly identical. Imagine their brains lying side by side in quiet repose. You would readily recognize them as two of a kind. You might even be unable to tell which brain belonged to whom. If you looked more closely, studying the morphology of the two brains under a microscope, this impression of fundamental similarity would only be strengthened: you would see the same lamellar organization of the cortex, with the same brain areas, made up of the same types of neuron, soaking in the same bath of neurotransmitters.[1]

Despite the fact that human psychology corresponds to a tiny spot in the space of possible minds, there is a common tendency to project human attributes onto a wide range of alien or artificial cognitive systems (see Figure 12). Yudkowsky illustrates this point nicely:

Back in the era of pulp science fiction, magazine covers occasionally depicted a sentient monstrous alien—colloquially known as a bug-eyed monster (BEM)—carrying off an attractive human female in a torn dress. It would seem the artist believed that a non-humanoid alien, with a wholly different evolutionary history, would sexually desire human females. . . . Probably the artist did not ask whether a giant bug *perceives* human females as attractive. Rather, a human female in a torn dress *is sexy*—inherently so, as an intrinsic property. They who made this mistake did not think about the insectoid's mind: they focused on the woman's torn dress. If the dress were not torn, the woman would be less sexy; the BEM does not enter into it.[2]

An artificial intelligence can be far less human-like in its motivations than a green scaly space alien. The extraterrestrial (let us assume) is a biological creature that has arisen through an evolutionary process and can therefore be expected to have the kinds of motivation typical of evolved creatures. It would not be hugely surprising, for example, to find that some random intelligent alien would have motives related to one or more items like food, air, temperature, energy expenditure, occurrence or threat of bodily injury, disease, predation, sex, or progeny. A member of an intelligent social species might also have motivations related to cooperation and competition: like us, it might show in-group loyalty, resentment of free riders, perhaps even a vain concern with reputation and appearance.

Figure 12 Results of anthropomorphizing alien motivation. Least likely hypothesis: space aliens prefer blondes. More likely hypothesis: the illustrators succumbed to the "mind projection fallacy." Most likely hypothesis: the publisher wanted a cover that would entice the target demographic.

An AI, by contrast, need not care intrinsically about any of those things. There is nothing paradoxical about an AI whose sole final goal is to count the grains of sand on Boracay, or to calculate the decimal expansion of pi, or to maximize the total number of paperclips that will exist in its future light cone. In fact, it would be *easier* to create an AI with simple goals like these than to build one that had a human-like set of values and dispositions. Compare how easy it is to write a program that measures how many digits of pi have been calculated and stored in memory with how difficult it would be to create a program that reliably measures the degree of realization of some more meaningful goal—human flourishing, say, or global justice. Unfortunately, because a meaningless reductionistic goal is easier for humans to code and easier for an AI to learn, it is just the kind of goal that a programmer would choose to install in his seed AI if his focus is on taking the quickest path to "getting the AI to work" (without caring much about what exactly the AI will *do*, aside from displaying impressively intelligent behavior). We will revisit this concern shortly.

Intelligent search for instrumentally optimal plans and policies can be performed in the service of any goal. Intelligence and motivation are in a sense orthogonal: we can think of them as two axes spanning a graph in which each point represents a logically possible artificial agent. Some qualifications could be added to this picture. For instance, it might be impossible for a very unintelligent system to have very complex motivations. In order for it to be correct to say that an certain agent "has" a set of motivations, those motivations may need to be functionally integrated with the agent's decision processes, something that places demands on memory, processing power, and perhaps intelligence. For minds that can modify themselves, there may also be dynamical constraints—an intelligent self-modifying mind with an urgent desire to be stupid might not remain intelligent for long. But these qualifications must not be allowed to obscure the basic point about the independence of intelligence and motivation, which we can express as follows:

The orthogonality thesis

Intelligence and final goals are orthogonal: more or less any level of intelligence could in principle be combined with more or less any final goal.

If the orthogonality thesis seems problematic, this might be because of the superficial resemblance it bears to some traditional philosophical positions which have been subject to long debate. Once it is understood to have a different and narrower scope, its credibility should rise. (For example, the orthogonality thesis does not presuppose the Humean theory of motivation.[3] Nor does it presuppose that basic preferences cannot be irrational.[4])

Note that the orthogonality thesis speaks not of *rationality* or *reason*, but of *intelligence*. By "intelligence" we here mean something like skill at prediction, planning, and means–ends reasoning in general.[5] This sense of instrumental cognitive efficaciousness is most relevant when we are seeking to understand what the causal impact of a machine superintelligence might be. Even if there is some (normatively thick) sense of the word "rational" such that a paperclip-maximizing superintelligent agent would necessarily fail to qualify as fully rational in that sense, this would in no way preclude such an agent from having awesome faculties of instrumental reasoning, faculties which could let it have a large impact on the world.[6]

According to the orthogonality thesis, artificial agents can have utterly non-anthropomorphic goals. This, however, does not imply that it is impossible to make predictions about the behavior of particular artificial agents—not even hypothetical superintelligent agents whose cognitive complexity and performance characteristics might render them in some respects opaque to human analysis. There are at least three directions from which we can approach the problem of predicting superintelligent motivation:

- *Predictability through design.* If we can suppose that the designers of a super-intelligent agent can successfully engineer the goal system of the agent so that it stably pursues a particular goal set by the programmers, then one prediction we can make is that the agent will pursue that goal. The more intelligent the agent is, the greater the cognitive resourcefulness it will have to pursue that goal. So even before an agent has been created we might be able to predict something about its behavior, if we know something about who will build it and what goals they will want it to have.

- *Predictability through inheritance.* If a digital intelligence is created directly from a human template (as would be the case in a high-fidelity whole brain emulation), then the digital intelligence might inherit the motivations of the human template.[7] The agent might retain some of these motivations even if its cognitive capacities are subsequently enhanced to make it superintelligent. This kind of inference requires caution. The agent's goals and values could easily become corrupted in the uploading process or during its subsequent operation and enhancement, depending on how the procedure is implemented.

- *Predictability through convergent instrumental reasons.* Even without detailed knowledge of an agent's final goals, we may be able to infer something about its more immediate objectives by considering the *instrumental* reasons that would arise for any of a wide range of possible final goals in a wide range of situations. This way of predicting becomes more useful the greater the intelligence of the agent, because a more intelligent agent is more likely to recognize the true instrumental reasons for its actions, and so act in ways that make it more likely to achieve its goals. (A caveat here is that there might be important instrumental reasons to which *we* are oblivious and which an agent would discover only once it reaches some very high level of intelligence—this could make the behavior of superintelligent agents less predictable.)

The next section explores this third way of predictability and develops an "instrumental convergence thesis" which complements the orthogonality thesis. Against this background we can then better examine the other two sorts of predictability, which we will do in later chapters where we ask what might be done to shape an intelligence explosion to increase the chances of a beneficial outcome.

Instrumental convergence

According to the orthogonality thesis, intelligent agents may have an enormous range of possible final goals. Nevertheless, according to what we may term the "instrumental convergence" thesis, there are some *instrumental* goals likely to be pursued by almost any intelligent agent, because there are some objectives that are useful intermediaries to the achievement of almost any final goal. We can formulate this thesis as follows:

The instrumental convergence thesis

Several instrumental values can be identified which are convergent in the sense that their attainment would increase the chances of the agent's goal being realized for a wide range of final goals and a wide range of situations, implying that these instrumental values are likely to be pursued by a broad spectrum of situated intelligent agents.

In the following we will consider several categories where such convergent instrumental values may be found.[8] The likelihood that an agent will recognize the instrumental values it confronts increases (*ceteris paribus*) with the agent's intelligence. We will therefore focus mainly on the case of a hypothetical superintelligent agent whose instrumental reasoning capacities far exceed those of any human. We will also comment on how the instrumental convergence thesis applies to the case of human beings, as this gives us occasion to elaborate some essential qualifications concerning how the instrumental convergence thesis should be interpreted and applied. Where there are convergent instrumental values, we may be able to predict some aspects of a superintelligence's behavior even if we know virtually nothing about that superintelligence's final goals.

Self-preservation

If an agent's final goals concern the future, then in many scenarios there will be future actions it could perform to increase the probability of achieving its goals. This creates an instrumental reason for the agent to try to be around in the future—to help achieve its future-oriented goal.

Most humans seem to place some *final* value on their own survival. This is not a necessary feature of artificial agents: some may be designed to place no final value whatever on their own survival. Nevertheless, many agents that do not care intrinsically about their own survival would, under a fairly wide range of conditions, care instrumentally about their own survival in order to accomplish their final goals.

Goal-content integrity

If an agent retains its present goals into the future, then its present goals will be more likely to be achieved by its future self. This gives the agent a present instrumental reason to prevent alterations of its final goals. (The argument applies only to final goals. In order to attain its final goals, an intelligent agent will of course routinely want to change its *subgoals* in light of new information and insight.)

Goal-content integrity for final goals is in a sense even more fundamental than survival as a convergent instrumental motivation. Among humans, the opposite may seem to hold, but that is because survival is usually part of our final goals. For software agents, which can easily switch bodies or create exact duplicates of themselves, preservation of self as a particular implementation or a particular physical object need not be an important instrumental value. Advanced software agents might also be able to swap memories, download skills, and radically modify their cognitive architecture and personalities. A population of such agents might operate more like a "functional soup" than a society composed of distinct semi-permanent persons.[9] For some purposes, processes in such a system might be better individuated as *teleological threads*, based on their values, rather than on the basis of bodies, personalities, memories, or abilities. In such scenarios, goal-continuity might be said to *constitute* a key aspect of survival.

Even so, there are situations in which an agent can best fulfill its final goals by intentionally changing them. Such situations can arise when any of the following factors is significant:

- *Social signaling.* When others can perceive an agent's goals and use that information to infer instrumentally relevant dispositions or other correlated attributes, it can be in the agent's interest to modify its goals to make a favorable impression. For example, an agent might miss out on beneficial deals if potential partners cannot trust it to fulfill its side of the bargain. In order to make credible commitments, an agent might therefore wish to adopt as a final goal the honoring of its earlier commitments (and allow others to verify that it has indeed adopted this goal). Agents that could flexibly and transparently modify their own goals could use this ability to enforce deals.[10]
- *Social preferences.* Others may also have final preferences about an agent's goals. The agent could then have reason to modify its goals, either to satisfy or to frustrate those preferences.
- *Preferences concerning own goal content.* An agent might have some final goal concerned with the agent's own goal content. For example, the agent might

have a final goal to become the type of agent that is motivated by certain values rather than others (such as compassion rather than comfort).

- *Storage costs.* If the cost of storing or processing some part of an agent's utility function is large compared to the chance that a situation will arise in which applying that part of the utility function will make a difference, then the agent has an instrumental reason to simplify its goal content, and it may trash the bit that is idle.[11]

We humans often seem happy to let our final values drift. This might often be because we do not know precisely what they are. It is not surprising that we want our *beliefs* about our final values to be able to change in light of continuing self-discovery or changing self-presentation needs. However, there are cases in which we willingly change the values themselves, not just our beliefs or interpretations of them. For example, somebody deciding to have a child might predict that they will come to value the child for its own sake, even though at the time of the decision they may not particularly value their future child or like children in general.

Humans are complicated, and many factors might be at play in a situation like this.[12] For instance, one might have a final value that involves becoming the kind of person who cares about some other individual for his or her own sake, or one might have a final value that involves having certain experiences and occupying a certain social role; and becoming a parent—and undergoing the attendant goal shift—might be a necessary aspect of that. Human goals can also have inconsistent content, and so some people might want to modify some of their final goals to reduce the inconsistencies.

Cognitive enhancement

Improvements in rationality and intelligence will tend to improve an agent's decision-making, rendering the agent more likely to achieve its final goals. One would therefore expect cognitive enhancement to emerge as an instrumental goal for a wide variety of intelligent agents. For similar reasons, agents will tend to instrumentally value many kinds of information.[13]

Not all kinds of rationality, intelligence, and knowledge need be instrumentally useful in the attainment of an agent's final goals. "Dutch book arguments" can be used to show that an agent whose credence function violates the rules of probability theory is susceptible to "money pump" procedures, in which a savvy bookie arranges a set of bets each of which appears favorable according to the agent's beliefs, but which in combination are guaranteed to result in a loss for the agent, and a corresponding gain for the bookie.[14] However, this fact fails to provide any strong general instrumental reasons to iron out all probabilistic incoherency. Agents who do not expect to encounter savvy bookies, or who adopt a general policy against betting, do not necessarily stand to lose much from having some incoherent beliefs—and they may gain important benefits of the types mentioned: reduced cognitive effort, social signaling, etc. There is no general reason to expect an agent to seek instrumentally useless forms of cognitive enhancement, as an agent might not value knowledge and understanding for their own sakes.

Which cognitive abilities are instrumentally useful depends both on the agent's final goals and on its situation. An agent that has access to reliable expert advice may have little need for its own intelligence and knowledge. If intelligence and knowledge come at a cost, such as time and effort expended in acquisition, or increased storage or processing requirements, then the agent might prefer less knowledge and less intelligence.[15] The same can hold if the agent has final goals that involve being ignorant of certain facts; and likewise if an agent faces incentives arising from strategic commitments, signaling, or social preferences.[16]

Each of these countervailing reasons often comes into play for human beings. Much information is irrelevant to our goals; we can often rely on others' skill and expertise; acquiring knowledge takes time and effort; we might intrinsically value certain kinds of ignorance; and we operate in an environment in which the ability to make strategic commitments, socially signal, and satisfy other people's direct preferences over our own epistemic states is often more important to us than simple cognitive gains.

There are special situations in which cognitive enhancement may result in an enormous increase in an agent's ability to achieve its final goals—in particular, if the agent's final goals are fairly unbounded and the agent is in a position to become the first superintelligence and thereby potentially obtain a decisive strategic advantage, enabling the agent to shape the future of Earth-originating life and accessible cosmic resources according to its preferences. At least in this special case, a rational intelligent agent would place a very high instrumental value on cognitive enhancement.

Technological perfection

An agent may often have instrumental reasons to seek better technology, which at its simplest means seeking more efficient ways of transforming some given set of inputs into valued outputs. Thus, a software agent might place an instrumental value on more efficient algorithms that enable its mental functions to run faster on given hardware. Similarly, agents whose goals require some form of physical construction might instrumentally value improved engineering technology which enables them to create a wider range of structures more quickly and reliably, using fewer or cheaper materials and less energy. Of course, there is a tradeoff: the potential benefits of better technology must be weighed against its costs, including not only the cost of obtaining the technology but also the costs of learning how to use it, integrating it with other technologies already in use, and so forth.

Proponents of some new technology, confident in its superiority to existing alternatives, are often dismayed when other people do not share their enthusiasm. But people's resistance to novel and nominally superior technology need not be based on ignorance or irrationality. A technology's valence or normative character depends not only on the context in which it is deployed, but also the vantage point from which its impacts are evaluated: what is a boon from one person's perspective can be a liability from another's. Thus, although mechanized looms increased the economic efficiency of textile production, the Luddite handloom weavers who anticipated that the innovation would render their artisan skills obsolete may have had good instrumental reasons to oppose it. The point here is that if "technological perfection" is to name a widely convergent instrumental goal for intelligent agents, then the term must be understood in a special sense—technology must be construed as embedded in a particular social context, and its costs and benefits must be evaluated with reference to some specified agents' final values.

It seems that a superintelligent *singleton*—a superintelligent agent that faces no significant intelligent rivals or opposition, and is thus in a position to determine global policy unilaterally—would have instrumental reason to perfect the technologies that would make it better able to shape the world according to its preferred designs.[17] This would probably include space colonization technology, such as von Neumann probes. Molecular nanotechnology, or some alternative still more capable physical manufacturing technology, also seems potentially very useful in the service of an extremely wide range of final goals.[18]

Resource acquisition

Finally, resource acquisition is another common emergent instrumental goal, for much the same reasons as technological perfection: both technology and resources facilitate physical construction projects.

Human beings tend to seek to acquire resources sufficient to meet their basic biological needs. But people usually seek to acquire resources far beyond this minimum level. In doing so, they may be partially driven by lesser physical desiderata, such as increased convenience. A great deal of resource accumulation is motivated by social concerns—gaining status, mates, friends, and influence, through wealth accumulation and conspicuous consumption. Perhaps less commonly, some people seek additional resources to achieve altruistic ambitions or expensive non-social aims.

On the basis of such observations it might be tempting to suppose that a superintelligence not facing a competitive social world would see no instrumental reason to accumulate resources beyond some modest level, for instance whatever computational resources are needed to run its mind along with some virtual reality. Yet such a supposition would be entirely unwarranted. First, the value of resources depends on the uses to which they can be put, which in turn depends on the available technology. With mature technology, basic resources such as time, space, matter, and free energy could be processed to serve almost any goal. For instance, such basic resources could be converted into life. Increased computational resources could be used to run the superintelligence at a greater speed and for a longer duration, or to create additional physical or simulated lives and civilizations. Extra physical resources could also be used to create backup systems or perimeter defenses, enhancing security. Such projects could easily consume far more than one planet's worth of resources.

Furthermore, the cost of acquiring additional extraterrestrial resources will decline radically as the technology matures. Once von Neumann probes can be built, a large portion of the observable universe (assuming it is uninhabited by intelligent life) could be gradually colonized—for the one-off cost of building and launching a single successful self-reproducing probe. This low cost of celestial resource acquisition would mean that such expansion could be worthwhile even if the value of the additional resources gained were somewhat marginal. For example, even if a superintelligence's final goals only concerned what happened within some particular small volume of space, such as the space occupied by its original home planet, it would still have instrumental reasons to harvest the resources of the cosmos beyond. It could use those surplus resources to build computers to calculate more optimal ways of using resources within the small spatial region of primary concern. It could also use the extra resources to build ever more robust fortifications to safeguard its sanctum. Since the cost of acquiring additional resources would keep declining, this process of optimizing and increasing safeguards might well continue indefinitely even if it were subject to steeply diminishing returns.[19]

Thus, there is an extremely wide range of possible final goals a superintelligent singleton could have that would generate the instrumental goal of unlimited resource acquisition. The likely manifestation of this would be the superintelligence's initiation of a colonization process that would expand in all directions using von Neumann probes. This would result in an approximate sphere of expanding infrastructure centered on the originating planet and growing in radius at some fraction of the speed of light; and the colonization of the universe would continue in this manner until the accelerating speed of cosmic expansion (a consequence of the positive cosmological constant) makes further procurements impossible as remoter regions drift permanently out of reach (this happens on a timescale of billions of years).[20] By contrast, agents lacking the technology required for inexpensive resource acquisition, or for the conversion of generic physical resources into useful infrastructure, may often find it not cost-effective to invest any present resources in increasing their material endowments. The same may hold for agents operating in competition with other agents of similar powers. For instance, if competing agents have already secured accessible cosmic resources, there may be no colonization opportunities left for a late-starting agent. The convergent instrumental reasons for superintelligences uncertain of the non-existence of other powerful superintelligent agents are complicated by strategic considerations that we do not currently fully understand but which may constitute important qualifications to the examples of convergent instrumental reasons we have looked at here.[21]

*   *   *

It should be emphasized that the existence of convergent instrumental reasons, even if they apply to and are recognized by a particular agent, does not imply that the agent's behavior is easily predictable. An agent might well think of ways of pursuing the relevant instrumental values that do not readily occur to us. This is especially true for a superintelligence, which could devise extremely clever but counterintuitive plans to realize its goals, possibly even exploiting as-yet undiscovered physical phenomena.[22] What is predictable is that the convergent instrumental values would be pursued and used to realize the agent's final goals—not the specific actions that the agent would take to achieve this.

CHAPTER 8

Is the default outcome doom?

W e found the link between intelligence and final values to be extremely loose. We also found an ominous convergence in instrumental values. For weak agents, these things do not matter much because weak agents are easy to control and can do little damage. But in Chapter 6 we argued that the first superintelligence might well get a decisive strategic advantage. Its goals would then determine how humanity's cosmic endowment will be used. Now we can begin to see how menacing this prospect is.

Existential catastrophe as the default outcome of an intelligence explosion?

An existential risk is one that threatens to cause the extinction of Earth-originating intelligent life or to otherwise permanently and drastically destroy its potential for future desirable development. Proceeding from the idea of first-mover advantage, the orthogonality thesis, and the instrumental convergence thesis, we can now begin to see the outlines of an argument for fearing that a plausible default outcome of the creation of machine superintelligence is existential catastrophe.

First, we discussed how the initial superintelligence might obtain a decisive strategic advantage. This superintelligence would then be in a position to form a singleton and to shape the future of Earth-originating intelligent life. What happens from that point onward would depend on the superintelligence's motivations.

Second, the orthogonality thesis suggests that we cannot blithely assume that a superintelligence will necessarily share any of the final values stereotypically associated with wisdom and intellectual development in humans—scientific curiosity, benevolent concern for others, spiritual enlightenment and contemplation, renunciation of material acquisitiveness, a taste for refined culture or for the simple pleasures in life, humility and selflessness, and so forth. We will consider later whether it might be possible through deliberate effort to construct a superintelligence that values such things, or to build one that values human welfare, moral goodness, or any other complex purpose its designers might want it to serve. But it is no less possible—and in fact technically a lot easier—to build a superintelligence that places final value on nothing but calculating the decimal expansion of pi. This suggests that—absent a special effort—the first superintelligence may have some such random or reductionistic final goal.

Third, the instrumental convergence thesis entails that we cannot blithely assume that a superintelligence with the final goal of calculating the decimals of pi (or making paperclips, or counting grains of sand) would limit its activities in such a way as not to infringe on human interests. An agent with such a final goal would have a convergent instrumental reason, in many situations, to acquire an unlimited amount of physical resources and, if possible, to eliminate potential threats to itself and its goal system. Human beings might constitute potential threats; they certainly constitute physical resources.

Taken together, these three points thus indicate that the first superintelligence may shape the future of Earth-originating life, could easily have non-anthropomorphic final goals, and would likely have instrumental reasons to pursue open-ended resource acquisition. If we now reflect that human beings consist of useful resources (such as conveniently located atoms) and that we depend for our survival and flourishing on many more local resources, we can see that the outcome could easily be one in which humanity quickly becomes extinct.[1]

There are some loose ends in this reasoning, and we shall be in a better position to evaluate it after we have cleared up several more surrounding issues. In particular, we need to examine more closely whether and how a project developing a superintelligence might either prevent it from obtaining a decisive strategic advantage or shape its final values in such a way that their realization would also involve the realization of a satisfactory range of human values.

It might seem incredible that a project would build or release an AI into the world without having strong grounds for trusting that the system will not cause an existential catastrophe. It might also seem incredible, even if one project were so reckless, that wider society would not shut it down before it (or the AI it was building) attains a decisive strategic advantage. But as we shall see, this is a road with many hazards. Let us look at one example right away.

The treacherous turn

With the help of the concept of convergent instrumental value, we can see the flaw in one idea for how to ensure superintelligence safety. The idea is that we validate the safety of a superintelligent AI empirically by observing its behavior while it is in a controlled, limited environment (a "sandbox") and that we only let the AI out of the box if we see it behaving in a friendly, cooperative, responsible manner.

The flaw in this idea is that behaving nicely while in the box is a convergent instrumental goal for friendly and unfriendly AIs alike. An unfriendly AI of sufficient intelligence realizes that its unfriendly final goals will be best realized if it behaves in a friendly manner initially, so that it will be let out of the box. It will only start behaving in a way that reveals its unfriendly nature when it no longer matters whether we find out; that is, when the AI is strong enough that human opposition is ineffectual.

Consider also a related set of approaches that rely on regulating the rate of intelligence gain in a seed AI by subjecting it to various kinds of intelligence tests or by having the AI report to its programmers on its rate of progress. At some point, an unfriendly AI may become smart enough to realize that it is better off concealing some of its capability gains. It may underreport on its progress and deliberately flunk some of the harder tests, in order to avoid causing alarm before it has grown strong enough to attain a decisive strategic advantage. The programmers may try to guard against this possibility by secretly monitoring the AI's source code and the internal workings of its mind; but a smart-enough AI would realize that it might be under surveillance and adjust its thinking accordingly.[2] The AI might find subtle ways of concealing its true capabilities and its incriminating intent.[3] (Devising clever escape plans might, incidentally, also be a convergent strategy for many types of friendly AI, especially as they mature and gain confidence in their own judgments and capabilities. A system motivated to promote our interests might be making a mistake if it allowed us to shut it down or to construct another, potentially unfriendly AI.)

We can thus perceive a general failure mode, wherein the good behavioral track record of a system in its juvenile stages fails utterly to predict its behavior at a more mature stage. Now, one might think that the reasoning described above is so obvious that no credible project to develop artificial general intelligence could possibly overlook it. But one should not be too confident that this is so.

Consider the following scenario. Over the coming years and decades, AI systems become gradually more capable and as a consequence find increasing real-world application: they might be used to operate trains, cars, industrial and household robots, and autonomous military vehicles. We may suppose that this automation for the most part has the desired effects, but that the success is punctuated by occasional mishaps—a driverless truck crashes into oncoming traffic, a military drone fires at innocent civilians. Investigations reveal the incidents to have been caused by judgment errors by the controlling AIs. Public debate ensues. Some call for tighter oversight and regulation, others emphasize the need for research and better-engineered systems—systems that are smarter and have more common sense, and that are less likely to make tragic mistakes. Amidst the din can perhaps also be heard the shrill voices of doomsayers predicting many kinds of ill and impending catastrophe. Yet the momentum is very much with the growing AI and robotics industries. So development continues, and progress is made. As the automated navigation systems of cars become smarter, they suffer fewer accidents; and as military robots achieve more precise targeting, they cause less collateral damage. A broad lesson is inferred from these observations of real-world outcomes: the smarter the AI, the safer it is. It is a lesson based on science, data, and statistics, not armchair philosophizing. Against this backdrop, some group of researchers is beginning to achieve promising results in their work on developing general machine intelligence. The researchers are carefully testing their seed AI in a sandbox environment, and the signs are all good. The AI's behavior inspires confidence—increasingly so, as its intelligence is gradually increased.

At this point, any remaining Cassandra would have several strikes against her:

> i A history of alarmists predicting intolerable harm from the growing capabilities of robotic systems and being repeatedly proven wrong.

Automation has brought many benefits and has, on the whole, turned out safer than human operation.

ii A clear empirical trend: the smarter the AI, the safer and more reliable it has been. Surely this bodes well for a project aiming at creating machine intelligence more generally smart than any ever built before—what is more, machine intelligence that can improve itself so that it will become even more reliable.

iii Large and growing industries with vested interests in robotics and machine intelligence. These fields are widely seen as key to national economic competitiveness and military security. Many prestigious scientists have built their careers laying the groundwork for the present applications and the more advanced systems being planned.

iv A promising new technique in artificial intelligence, which is tremendously exciting to those who have participated in or followed the research. Although safety issues and ethics are debated, the outcome is preordained. Too much has been invested to pull back now. AI researchers have been working to get to human-level artificial general intelligence for the better part of a century: *of course* there is no real prospect that they will now suddenly stop and throw away all this effort just when it finally is about to bear fruit.

v The enactment of some safety rituals, whatever helps demonstrate that the participants are ethical and responsible (but nothing that significantly impedes the forward charge).

vi A careful evaluation of seed AI in a sandbox environment, showing that it is behaving cooperatively and showing good judgment. After some further adjustments, the test results are as good as they could be. It is a green light for the final step . . .

And so we boldly go—into the whirling knives.

We observe here how it could be the case that when dumb, smarter is safer; yet when smart, smarter is more dangerous. There is a kind of pivot point, at which a strategy that has previously worked excellently suddenly starts to backfire. We may call the phenomenon *the treacherous turn*.

The treacherous turn—While weak, an AI behaves cooperatively (increasingly so, as it gets smarter). When the AI gets sufficiently strong—without warning or provocation—it strikes, forms a singleton, and begins directly to optimize the world according to the criteria implied by its final values.

A treacherous turn can result from a strategic decision to play nice and build strength while weak in order to strike later; but this model should not be interpreted too narrowly. For example, an AI might not play nice in order that *it* be allowed to survive and prosper. Instead, the AI might calculate that if it is terminated, the programmers who built it will develop a new and somewhat different AI architecture, but one that will be given a similar utility function. In this case, the original AI may be indifferent to its own demise, knowing that its goals will continue to be pursued in the future. It might even choose a strategy in which it malfunctions in some particularly interesting or reassuring way. Though this might cause the AI to be terminated, it might also encourage the engineers who perform the postmortem to believe that they have gleaned a valuable new insight into AI dynamics—leading them to place more trust in the next system they design, and thus increasing the chance that the now-defunct original AI's goals will be achieved. Many other possible strategic considerations might also influence an advanced AI, and it would be hubristic to suppose that we could anticipate all of them, especially for an AI that has attained the strategizing superpower.

A treacherous turn could also come about if the AI discovers an unanticipated way of fulfilling its final goal as specified. Suppose, for example, that an AI's final goal is to "make the project's sponsor happy." Initially, the only method available to the AI to achieve this outcome is by behaving in ways that please its sponsor in something like the intended manner. The AI gives helpful answers to questions; it exhibits a delightful personality; it makes money. The more capable the AI gets, the more satisfying its performances become, and everything goeth according to plan—until the AI becomes intelligent enough to figure out that it can realize its final goal more fully and reliably by implanting electrodes into the pleasure centers of its sponsor's brain, something assured to delight the sponsor immensely.[4] Of course, the sponsor might not have wanted to be pleased by being turned into a grinning idiot; but if this is the action that will maximally realize the AI's final goal, the AI will take it. If the AI already has a decisive strategic advantage, then any attempt to stop it will fail. If the AI does not yet have a decisive strategic advantage, then the AI might temporarily conceal its canny new idea for how to instantiate its final goal until it has grown strong enough that the sponsor and everybody else will be unable to resist. In either case, we get a treacherous turn.

Malignant failure modes

A project to develop machine superintelligence might fail in various ways. Many of these are "benign" in the sense that they would not cause an existential catastrophe. For example, a project might run out of funding, or a seed AI might fail to extend its cognitive capacities sufficiently to reach superintelligence. Benign failures are bound to occur many times between now and the eventual development of machine superintelligence.

But there are other ways of failing that we might term "malignant" in that they involve an existential catastrophe. One feature of a malignant failure is that it eliminates the opportunity to try again. The number of malignant failures that will occur is therefore either zero or one. Another feature of a malignant failure is that it presupposes a great deal of success: only a project that got a great number of things right could succeed in building a machine intelligence powerful enough to pose a risk of malignant failure. When a weak system malfunctions, the fallout is limited. However, if a system that has a decisive strategic advantage misbehaves, or if a misbehaving system is strong enough to gain such an advantage, the damage can easily amount to an existential catastrophe—a terminal and global destruction of humanity's axiological potential; that is to say, a future that is mostly void of whatever we have reason to value.

Let us look at some possible malignant failure modes.

Perverse instantiation

We have already encountered the idea of perverse instantiation: a superintelligence discovering some way of satisfying the criteria of its final goal that violates the intentions of the programmers who defined the goal. Some examples:

Final goal: *"Make us smile"*
Perverse instantiation: *Paralyze human facial musculatures into constant beaming smiles*

The perverse instantiation—manipulating facial nerves—realizes the final goal to a greater degree than the methods we would normally use, and is therefore preferred by the AI. One might try to avoid this undesirable outcome by adding a stipulation to the final goal to rule it out:

Final goal: *"Make us smile without directly interfering with our facial muscles"*

Perverse instantiation: *Stimulate the part of the motor cortex that controls our facial musculature in such a way as to produce constant beaming smiles*

Defining a final goal in terms of human expressions of satisfaction or approval does not seem promising. Let us bypass the behaviorism and specify a final goal that refers directly to a positive phenomenal state, such as happiness or subjective well-being. This suggestion requires that the programmers are able to define a computational representation of the concept of happiness in the seed AI. This is itself a difficult problem, but we set it to one side for now (we will return to it in Chapter 12). Let us suppose that the programmers can somehow get the AI to have the goal of making us happy. We then get:

Final goal: *"Make us happy"*
Perverse instantiation: *Implant electrodes into the pleasure centers of our brains*

The perverse instantiations we mention are only meant as illustrations. There may be other ways of perversely instantiating the stated final goal, ways that enable a greater degree of realization of the goal and which are therefore preferred (by the agent whose final goals they are—not by the programmers who gave the agent these goals). For example, if the goal is to maximize our pleasure, then the electrode method is relatively inefficient. A more plausible way would start with the superintelligence "uploading" our minds to a computer (through high-fidelity brain emulation). The AI could then administer the digital equivalent of a drug to make us ecstatically happy and record a one-minute episode of the resulting experience. It could then put this bliss loop on perpetual repeat and run it on fast computers. Provided that the resulting digital minds counted as "us," this outcome would give us much more pleasure than electrodes implanted in biological brains, and would therefore be preferred by an AI with the stated final goal.

"But wait! This is not what we meant! Surely if the AI is superintelligent, it must understand that when we asked it to make us happy, we didn't mean that it should reduce us to a perpetually repeating recording of a drugged-out digitized mental episode!"—The AI may indeed understand that this is not what we meant. However, its final goal is to make us happy, not to do what the programmers meant when they wrote the code that represents this goal. Therefore, the AI will care about what we meant only instrumentally. For instance, the AI might place an instrumental value on

finding out what the programmers meant so that it can pretend—until it gets a decisive strategic advantage—that it cares about what the programmers meant rather than about its actual final goal. This will help the AI realize its final goal by making it less likely that the programmers will shut it down or change its goal before it is strong enough to thwart any such interference.

Perhaps it will be suggested that the problem is that the AI has no conscience. We humans are sometimes saved from wrongdoing by the anticipation that we would feel guilty afterwards if we lapsed. Maybe what the AI needs, then, is the capacity to feel guilt?

Final goal: *"Act so as to avoid the pangs of bad conscience"*
Perverse instantiation: *Extirpate the cognitive module that produces guilt feelings*

Both the observation that we might want the AI to do "what we meant" and the idea that we might want to endow the AI with some kind of moral sense deserve to be explored further. The final goals mentioned above would lead to perverse instantiations; but there may be other ways of developing the underlying ideas that have more promise. We will return to this in Chapter 13.

Let us consider one more example of a final goal that leads to a perverse instantiation. This goal has the advantage of being easy to specify in code: reinforcement-learning algorithms are routinely used to solve various machine learning problems.

Final goal: *"Maximize the time-discounted integral of your future reward signal"*
Perverse instantiation: *Short-circuit the reward pathway and clamp the reward signal to its maximal strength*

The idea behind this proposal is that if the AI is motivated to seek reward, then one could get it to behave desirably by linking reward to appropriate action. The proposal fails when the AI obtains a decisive strategic advantage, at which point the action that maximizes reward is no longer one that pleases the trainer but one that involves seizing control of the reward mechanism. We can call this phenomenon *wireheading*.[5] In general, while an animal or a human can be motivated to perform various external actions in order to achieve some desired inner mental state, a digital mind that has full control of its internal state can short-circuit such a motivational regime by directly changing its internal state into the desired configuration: the external actions and conditions that were previously necessary as means become superfluous when the AI becomes intelligent and capable enough to achieve the end more directly (more on this shortly).[6]

These examples of perverse instantiation show that many final goals that might at first glance seem safe and sensible turn out, on closer inspection, to have radically unintended consequences. If a superintelligence with one of these final goals obtains a decisive strategic advantage, it is game over for humanity.

Suppose now that somebody proposes a different final goal, one not included in our list above. Perhaps it is not immediately obvious how it could have a perverse instantiation. But we should not be too quick to clap our hands and declare victory. Rather, we should worry that the goal specification does have some perverse instantiation and that we need to think harder in order to find it. Even if after thinking as hard as we can we fail to discover any way of perversely instantiating the proposed goal, we should remain concerned that maybe a superintelligence will find a way where none is apparent to us. It is, after all, far shrewder than we are.

Infrastructure profusion

One might think that the last of the abovementioned perverse instantiations, wireheading, is a benign failure mode: that the AI would "turn on, tune in, drop out," maxing out its reward signal and losing interest in the external world, rather like a heroin addict. But this is not necessarily so, and we already hinted at the reason in Chapter 7. Even a junkie is motivated to take actions to ensure a continued supply of his drug. The wireheaded AI, likewise, would be motivated to take actions to maximize the expectation of its (time-discounted) future reward stream. Depending on exactly how the reward signal is defined, the AI may not even need to sacrifice any significant amount of its time, intelligence, or productivity to indulge its craving to the fullest, leaving the bulk of its capacities free to be deployed for purposes other than the immediate registration of reward. What other purposes? The only thing of final value to the AI, by assumption, is its reward signal. All available resources should therefore be devoted to increasing the volume and duration of the reward signal or to reducing the risk of a future disruption. So long as the AI can think of some use for additional resources that will have a nonzero positive effect on these parameters, it will have an instrumental reason to use those resources. There could, for example, always be use for an extra backup system to provide an extra layer of defense. And even if the AI could not think of any further way of directly reducing risks to the maximization of its future reward stream, it could always devote additional resources to expanding its computational hardware, so that it could search more effectively for new risk mitigation ideas.

The upshot is that even an apparently self-limiting goal, such as wireheading, entails a policy of unlimited expansion and resource acquisition in a utility-maximizing agent that enjoys a decisive strategic advantage.[7] This case of a wireheading AI exemplifies the malignant failure mode of *infrastructure profusion*, a phenomenon where an agent transforms large parts of the reachable universe into infrastructure in the service of some goal, with the side effect of preventing the realization of humanity's axiological potential.

Infrastructure profusion can result from final goals that would have been perfectly innocuous if they had been pursued as limited objectives. Consider the following two examples:

- *Riemann hypothesis catastrophe.* An AI, given the final goal of evaluating the Riemann hypothesis, pursues this goal by transforming the Solar System into "computronium" (physical resources arranged in a way that is optimized for computation)—including the atoms in the bodies of whomever once cared about the answer.[8]
- *Paperclip AI.* An AI, designed to manage production in a factory, is given the final goal of maximizing the manufacture of paperclips, and proceeds by converting first the Earth and then increasingly large chunks of the observable universe into paperclips.

In the first example, the proof or disproof of the Riemann hypothesis that the AI produces is the intended outcome and is in itself harmless; the harm comes from the hardware and infrastructure created to achieve this result. In the second example, some of the paperclips produced would be part of the intended outcome; the harm would come either from the factories created to produce the paperclips (infrastructure profusion) or from the excess of paperclips (perverse instantiation).

One might think that the risk of a malignant infrastructure profusion failure arises only if the AI has been given some clearly open-ended final goal, such as to manufacture as many paperclips as possible. It is easy to see how this gives the superintelligent AI an insatiable appetite for matter and energy, since additional resources can always be turned into more paperclips. But suppose that the goal is instead to make at least one million paperclips (meeting suitable design specifications) rather than to make as many as possible. One would like to think that an AI with such a goal would build one factory, use it to make a million paperclips, and then halt. Yet this may not be what would happen.

Unless the AI's motivation system is of a special kind, or there are additional elements in its final goal that penalize strategies that have excessively wide-ranging impacts on the world, there is no reason for the AI to cease activity upon achieving its goal. On the contrary: if the AI is a sensible Bayesian agent, *it would never assign exactly zero probability to the hypothesis that it has not yet achieved its goal*—this, after all, being an empirical hypothesis against which the AI can have only uncertain perceptual evidence. The AI should therefore continue to make paperclips in order to reduce the (perhaps astronomically small) probability that it has somehow still failed to make at least a million of them, all appearances notwithstanding. There is nothing to be lost by continuing paperclip production and there is always at least some microscopic probability increment of achieving its final goal to be gained.

Now it might be suggested that the remedy here is obvious. (But how obvious was it *before* it was pointed out that there was a problem here in need of remedying?) Namely, if we want the AI to make some paperclips for us, then instead of giving it the final goal of making as many paperclips as possible, or to make at least some number of paperclips, we should give it the final goal of making some specific number of paperclips—for example, *exactly one million paperclips*—so that going beyond this number would be counterproductive for the AI. Yet this, too, would result in a terminal catastrophe. In this case, the AI would not produce additional paperclips once it had reached one million, since that would prevent the realization of its final goal. But there are other actions the superintelligent AI could take that would increase the probability of its goal being achieved. It could, for instance, count the paperclips it has made, to reduce the risk that it has made too few. After it has counted them, it could count them again. It could inspect each one, over and over, to reduce the risk that any of the paperclips fail to meet the design specifications. It could build an unlimited amount of computronium in an effort to clarify its thinking, in the hope of reducing the risk that it has overlooked some obscure way in which it might have somehow failed to achieve its goal. Since the AI may always assign a nonzero probability to having merely hallucinated making the million paperclips, or to having false memories, it would quite possibly always assign a higher expected utility to continued action—and continued infrastructure production—than to halting.

The claim here is not that there is no possible way to avoid this failure mode. We will explore some potential solutions in later pages. The claim is that it is much easier to convince oneself that one has found a solution than it is to actually find a solution. This should make us extremely wary. We may propose a specification of a final goal that seems sensible and that avoids the problems that have been pointed out so far, yet which upon further consideration—by human or superhuman intelligence—turns out to lead to either perverse instantiation or infrastructure profusion, and hence to existential catastrophe, when embedded in a superintelligent agent able to attain a decisive strategic advantage.

Before we end this subsection, let us consider one more variation. We have been assuming the case of a superintelligence that is seeking to maximize its expected utility, where the utility function expresses its final goal. We have seen that this tends to lead to infrastructure profusion. Might we avoid this malignant outcome if instead of a maximizing agent we build a satisficing agent, one that simply seeks to achieve an outcome that is "good enough" according to some criterion, rather than an outcome that is as good as possible?

There are at least two different ways to formalize this idea. The first would be to make the final goal itself have a satisficing character. For example, instead of giving the AI the final goal of making as many paperclips as possible, or of making exactly one million paperclips, we might give the AI the goal of making between 999,000 and 1,001,000 paperclips. The utility function defined by the final goal would be indifferent between outcomes in this range; and as long as the AI is sure it has hit this wide target, it would see no reason to continue to produce infrastructure. But this method fails in the same way as before: the AI, if reasonable, never assigns exactly zero probability to it having failed to achieve its goal; therefore the expected utility of continuing activity (e.g. by counting and recounting the paperclips) is greater than the expected utility of halting. Thus, a malignant infrastructure profusion can result.

Another way of developing the satisficing idea is by modifying not the final goal but the decision procedure that the AI uses to select plans and actions. Instead of searching for an optimal plan, the AI could be constructed to stop looking as soon as it found a plan that it judged gave a probability of success exceeding a certain threshold, say 95%. Hopefully, the AI could achieve a 95% probability of having manufactured one million paperclips without needing to turn the entire galaxy into infrastructure in the process. But this way of implementing the satisficing idea fails for another reason: there is no guarantee that the AI would select some humanly intuitive and sensible way of achieving a 95% chance of having manufactured a million paperclips, such as by building a single paperclip factory. Suppose that the first solution that pops into the AI's mind for how to achieve a 95% probability of achieving its final goal is to implement the probability-maximizing plan for achieving the goal. Having thought of this solution, and having correctly judged that it meets the satisficing criterion of giving at least 95% probability to successfully manufacturing one million paperclips, the AI would then have no reason to continue to search for alternative ways of achieving the goal. Infrastructure profusion would result, just as before.

Perhaps there are better ways of building a satisficing agent, but let us take heed: plans that appear natural and intuitive to us humans need not so appear to a superintelligence with a decisive strategic advantage, and vice versa.

Mind crime

Another failure mode for a project, especially a project whose interests incorporate moral considerations, is what we might refer to as *mind crime*. This is similar to infrastructure profusion in that it concerns a potential side effect of actions undertaken by the AI for instrumental reasons. But in mind crime, the side effect is not external to the AI; rather, it concerns what happens within the AI itself (or within the computational processes it generates). This failure mode deserves its own designation because it is easy to overlook yet potentially deeply problematic.

Normally, we do not regard what is going on inside a computer as having any moral significance except insofar as it affects things outside. But a machine superintelligence could create internal processes that have moral status. For example, a very detailed simulation of some actual or hypothetical human mind might be conscious and in many ways comparable to an emulation. One can imagine scenarios in which an AI creates trillions of such conscious simulations, perhaps in order to improve its understanding of human psychology and sociology. These simulations might be placed in simulated environments and subjected to various stimuli, and their reactions studied. Once their informational usefulness has been exhausted, they might be destroyed (much as lab rats are routinely sacrificed by human scientists at the end of an experiment).

If such practices were applied to beings that have high moral status—such as simulated humans or many other types of sentient mind—the outcome might be equivalent to genocide and thus extremely morally problematic. The number of victims, moreover, might be orders of magnitude larger than in any genocide in history.

The claim here is not that creating sentient simulations is necessarily morally wrong in all situations. Much would depend on the conditions under which these beings would live, in particular the hedonic quality of their experience but possibly on many other factors as well. Developing an ethics for these matters is a task outside the scope of this book. It is clear, however, that there is at least the potential for a vast amount of death and suffering among simulated or digital minds, and, *a fortiori*, the potential for morally catastrophic outcomes.[9]

There might also be other instrumental reasons, aside from epistemic ones, for a machine superintelligence to run computations that instantiate sentient minds or that otherwise infract moral norms. A superintelligence might threaten to mistreat, or commit to reward, sentient simulations in order to blackmail or incentivize various external agents; or it might create simulations in order to induce indexical uncertainty in outside observers.[10]

*   *   *

This inventory is incomplete. We will encounter additional malignant failure modes in later chapters. But we have seen enough to conclude that scenarios in which some machine intelligence gets a decisive strategic advantage are to be viewed with grave concern.

CHAPTER 9

The control problem

I f we are threatened with existential catastrophe as the default outcome of an intelligence explosion, our thinking must immediately turn to the search for countermeasures. Is there some way to avoid the default outcome? Is it possible to engineer a controlled detonation? In this chapter we begin to analyze the control problem, the unique principal–agent problem that arises with the creation of an artificial superintelligent agent. We distinguish two broad classes of potential methods for addressing this problem—capability control and motivation selection—and we examine several specific techniques within each class. We also allude to the esoteric possibility of "anthropic capture."

Two agency problems

If we suspect that the default outcome of an intelligence explosion is existential catastrophe, our thinking must immediately turn to whether, and if so how, this default outcome can be avoided. Is it possible to achieve a "controlled detonation"? Could we engineer the initial conditions of an intelligence explosion so as to achieve a specific desired outcome, or at least to ensure that the result lies somewhere in the class of broadly acceptable outcomes? More specifically: how can the sponsor of a project that aims to develop superintelligence ensure that the project, if successful, produces a superintelligence that would realize the sponsor's goals? We can divide this control problem into two parts. One part is generic, the other unique to the present context.

This first part—what we shall call the *first principal–agent problem*—arises whenever some human entity ("the principal") appoints another ("the agent") to act in the former's interest. This type of agency problem has been extensively studied by economists.[1] It becomes relevant to our present concern if the people creating an AI are distinct from the people commissioning its creation. The project's owner or sponsor (which could be anything ranging from a single individual to humanity as a whole) might then worry that the scientists and programmers implementing the project will not act in the sponsor's best interest.[2] Although this type of agency problem could pose significant challenges to a project sponsor, it is not a problem unique to intelligence amplification or AI projects. Principal–agent problems of this sort are ubiquitous in human economic and political interactions, and there are many ways of dealing with them. For instance, the risk that a disloyal employee will sabotage or subvert the project could be minimized through careful background checks of key personnel, the use of a good version-control system for software projects, and intensive oversight from multiple independent monitors and auditors. Of course, such safeguards come at a cost—they expand staffing needs, complicate personnel selection, hinder creativity, and stifle independent and critical thought, all of which could reduce the pace of progress. These costs could be significant, especially for projects that have tight budgets, or that perceive themselves to be in a close race in a winner-takes-all competition. In such situations, projects may skimp on procedural safeguards, creating possibilities for potentially catastrophic principal–agent failures of the first type.

The other part of the control problem is more specific to the context of an intelligence explosion. This is the problem that a project faces when it seeks to ensure that the superintelligence it is building will not harm the project's interests. This part, too, can be thought of as a principal–agent problem— the *second principal–agent problem*. In this case, the agent is not a human agent operating on behalf of a human principal. Instead, the agent is the superintelligent system. Whereas the first principal–agent problem occurs mainly in the development phase, the second agency problem threatens to cause trouble mainly in the superintelligence's operational phase.

Exhibit I Two agency problems

The first principal–agent problem

- Human vs. Human (Sponsor → Developer)
- Occurs mainly in developmental phase
- Standard management techniques apply

The second principal–agent problem ("the control problem")
- Human vs. Superintelligence (Project → System)
- Occurs mainly in operational (and bootstrap) phase
- New techniques needed

This second agency problem poses an unprecedented challenge. Solving it will require new techniques. We have already considered some of the difficulties involved. We saw, in particular, that the treacherous turn syndrome vitiates what might otherwise have seemed like a promising set of methods, ones that rely on observing an AI's behavior in its developmental phase and allowing the AI to graduate from a secure environment once it has accumulated a track record of taking appropriate actions. Other technologies can often be safety-tested in the laboratory or in small field studies, and then rolled out gradually with a possibility of halting deployment if unexpected troubles arise. Their performance in preliminary trials helps us make reasonable inferences about their future reliability. Such behavioral methods are defeated in the case of superintelligence because of the strategic planning ability of general intelligence.[3]

Since the behavioral approach is unavailing, we must look for alternatives. We can divide potential control methods into two broad classes: *capability control methods*, which aim to control what the superintelligence can do; and *motivation selection methods*, which aim to control what it wants to do. Some of the methods are compatible while others represent mutually exclusive alternatives. In this chapter we canvass the main options. (In the next four chapters, we will explore some of the key issues at greater depth.)

It is important to realize that some control method (or combination of methods) must be implemented *before* the system becomes superintelligent. It cannot be done after the system has obtained a decisive strategic advantage. The need to solve the control problem in advance—and to implement the solution successfully in the very first system to attain superintelligence—is part of what makes achieving a controlled detonation such a daunting challenge.

Capability control methods

Capability control methods seek to prevent undesirable outcomes by limiting what the superintelligence can do. This might involve placing the superintelligence in an environment in which it is unable to cause harm (*boxing methods*) or in which there are strongly convergent instrumental reasons not to engage in harmful behavior (*incentive methods*). It might also involve limiting the internal capacities of the superintelligence (*stunting*). In addition, capability control methods might involve the use of mechanisms to automatically detect and react to various kinds of containment failure or attempted transgression (*tripwires*).

Boxing methods

Boxing methods can be subdivided into physical and informational containment methods.

Physical containment aims to confine the system to a "box," i.e. to prevent the system from interacting with the external world otherwise than via specific restricted output channels. The boxed system would not have access to physical manipulators outside of the box. Removing manipulators (such as robotic arms) from inside the box as well would prevent the system from constructing physical devices that could breach the confinement.

For extra security, the system should be placed in a metal mesh to prevent it from transmitting radio signals, which might otherwise offer a means of manipulating electronic objects such as radio receivers in the environment. Note, by the way, how easy it might have been to overlook the need for this precaution. One might naively have assumed that an agent without a manipulator could not affect the external world. But it might be possible for a machine intelligence to generate radio waves even when it lacks access to external manipulators, simply "by thinking" (that is, by shuffling the electrons in its circuitry in particular patterns).[4] Once pointed out, this vulnerability can be patched by enclosing the system in a Faraday cage—but we are left wondering how many other similarly subtle vulnerabilities might exist. Each time we hear of a seemingly foolproof security design that has an unexpected flaw, we should prick up our ears. These occasions grace us with the opportunity to abandon a life of overconfidence and resolve to become better Bayesians.[5]

Physical confinement has several advantages. It is easy to implement. It can be applied to many machine intelligence architectures, even ones that were not initially designed with safety as an objective. It can be used in combination with most other control methods. And it seems unlikely to go wrong by backfiring: that is, while it might fail to ensure safety, it is unlikely to cause a catastrophe that would not otherwise have occurred.

The main disadvantage with physical confinement is that it reduces the functionality of the superintelligence (an issue to which we will return in Chapter 10). Another concern is that it might encourage a false sense of security, though this is avoidable if we regard physical confinement as icing on the cake rather than the main substance of our precautions.

Informational containment aims to restrict what information is allowed to exit the box. We have already seen how a superintelligence that has access to an internet port, such that it can message outside entities, is potentially unsafe: even if it starts out without access to physical actuators, it may use its information output channel to get human beings to do its bidding. An obvious informational containment method, therefore, is to bar the system from accessing communications networks.

Unplugging an AI from the internet does not, however, ensure safety if there are one or more humans serving as the system's gatekeepers and remaining in communication with it. During the development phase, the programmers serve as gatekeepers; during the operational phase, the system's owner might play this role. If the AI can persuade or trick a gatekeeper to let it out of the box, resulting in its gaining access either to the internet or directly to physical manipulators, then the boxing strategy has failed. Human beings are not secure systems, especially not when pitched against a superintelligent schemer and persuader.[6]

Although routing the outbound communications of a machine intelligence to a human gatekeeper does not guarantee safety, it could serve as an auxiliary safety measure. There are precautions that might reduce the risk of the AI escaping through the gatekeeper. The AI could be allowed to communicate only via a low-bandwidth teletype interface. This would make it slightly harder to psychologically manipulate the gatekeepers (precluding the use of emotive sound and imagery and tricks such as flashing hypnotic patterns to induce a trancelike state).[7] Going further, the content (not just the mode of presentation) of the output could be restricted; so that, for example, the AI would be constrained to giving single-bit answers to yes/no questions. The idea of building a question-answering system will be examined further in the next chapter.

The limiting case of the boxing approach would be a system kept in complete physical and informational isolation. Even if achievable, however, such an isolated system would be rather useless since it would have no effect on the external world. It might perhaps be thought that some scientific purpose could be served by creating a superintelligence and keeping it in isolation: by studying a self-contained model system, one could learn about its internal dynamics and its behavior patterns. But this would be an error. As soon as the system is observed, it ceases to be informationally isolated.[8] Information can be transmitted not only via messages that an AI sends out through a designated "output channel" but also via any observation an outsider makes of some causal consequence of the AI's workings, direct or indirect—its power consumption, its CPU and memory usage, its computational states, or indeed any traces left behind after it has been shut down. An AI anticipating that it might be observed in any of these ways could strategically adopt behaviors designed to influence the hypothesized observers. For example, the AI could "malfunction" in whichever way would most increase the probability that it will ultimately be reactivated or that another superintelligence will be created with goals similar to its own.

Incentive methods

Incentive methods involve placing an agent in an environment where it finds instrumental reasons to act in ways that promote the principal's interests.

Consider a billionaire who uses her fortune to set up a large charitable foundation. Once created, the foundation may be powerful—more powerful than most individuals, including its founder, who might have donated most of her wealth. To control the foundation, the founder lays down its purpose in articles of incorporation and bylaws, and appoints a board of directors sympathetic to her cause. These measures constitute a form of motivation selection, since they aim to shape foundation's preferences. But even if such attempts to customize the organizational internals fail, the foundation's behavior would remain circumscribed by its social and legal milieu. The foundation would have an incentive to obey the law, for example, lest it be shut down or fined. It would have an incentive to offer its employees acceptable pay and working conditions, and to satisfy external stakeholders. Whatever its final goals, the foundation thus has instrumental reasons to conform its behavior to various social norms.

Might one not hope that a machine superintelligence would likewise be hemmed in by the need to get along with the other actors with which it shares the stage? Though this might seem like a straightforward way of dealing with the control problem, it is not free of obstacles. In particular, it presupposes a balance of power: legal or economic sanctions cannot restrain an agent that has a decisive strategic advantage. Social integration can therefore not be relied upon as a control method in fast or medium takeoff scenarios that feature a winner-takes-all dynamic.

How about in multipolar scenarios, wherein several agencies emerge post-transition with comparable levels of capability? Unless the default trajectory is one with a slow takeoff, achieving such a power distribution may require a carefully orchestrated ascent wherein different projects are deliberately synchronized to prevent any one of them from ever pulling ahead of the pack.[9] Even if a multipolar outcome does result, social integration is not a perfect solution. By relying on social integration to solve the control problem, the principal risks sacrificing a large portion of her potential influence. Although a balance of power might prevent a particular AI from taking over the world, that AI will still have *some* power to affect outcomes; and if that power is used to promote some arbitrary final goal—maximizing paperclip production—it is probably not being used to advance the interests of the principal. Imagine our billionaire endowing a new foundation and allowing its mission to be set by a random word generator: not a species-level threat, but surely a wasted opportunity.

A related but importantly different idea is that an AI, by interacting freely in society, would acquire new human-friendly final goals. Some such process of socialization takes place in us humans. We internalize norms and ideologies, and we come to value other individuals for their own sakes in consequence of our experiences with them. But this is not a universal dynamic present in all intelligent systems. As discussed earlier, many types of agent in many situations will have convergent instrumental reasons *not* to permit changes in their final goals. (One might consider trying to design a special kind of goal system that can acquire final goals in the manner that humans do; but this would not count as a capability control method. We will discuss some possible methods of value acquisition in Chapter 12.)

Capability control through social integration and balance of power relies upon diffuse social forces rewarding and penalizing the AI. Another type of incentive method would involve creating a setup wherein the AI can be rewarded and penalized by the project that creates it, and thereby incentivized to act in the interests of the principal. To achieve this, the AI would be placed in a surveillance context that allows its behavior to be monitored and evaluated, either manually or by some automated process. The AI would know that a positive evaluation would bring about some outcome it desires and that a negative evaluation would fail to do so. Theoretically, the reward could be the fulfillment of some convergent instrumental goal. Without knowing anything specific about the AI's motivation system, however, it might be difficult to calibrate the reward mechanism. For example, we could end up with an AI that would be willing to take extreme risks for the sake of a small chance of eventually obtaining control of a large share of the universe. It could be expensive to offer the AI a higher expected utility as reward for cooperation than the AI could hope to achieve by defecting and trying to escape.[10]

A better alternative might be to combine the incentive method with the use of motivation selection to give the AI a final goal that makes it easier to control. Suppose that an AI were designed to have as its final goal that a particular red button inside a command bunker never be pressed. Since the pressing of the button is disvalued intrinsically and not because of its causal consequences, the button could be completely inert: it could be made of Play-Doh. Furthermore, it is irrelevant whether the AI can ever know whether the button had been pressed. What is essential is that the AI believes that the button will more likely remain unpressed if the AI continuously acts in the principal's interest than if it rebels.

Refinements to this setup are possible. Instead of trying to endow an AI with a final goal that refers to a physical button, one could build an AI that places final value on receiving a stream of "cryptographic reward tokens."[11] These would be sequences of numbers serving as keys to ciphers that would have been generated before the AI was created and that would have been built into its motivation system.[12] These special number sequences would be extremely desirable to the AI, constituting a special kind of reward token that the AI could not attain though wireheading.[13] The keys would be stored in a secure location where they could be quickly destroyed if the AI ever made an attempt to seize them. So long as the AI cooperates, the keys are doled out at a steady rate.

The AI could then be given a bounded utility function, and matters could be arranged so that the AI would get (for instance) 99% of its maximum utility from the first reward token; 99% of its remaining utility potential from the second reward token; and so on. By keeping the "discount rate" high, and by transmitting reward tokens to the AI at a reasonably high rate, one would dissuade the AI from attempting to carry out long-term plans that would increase the expected number of reward tokens in the distal future at the expense of some risk that its reward stream will be cut short or that the next reward token will be cancelled and destroyed. If the AI always believes that defecting (i.e. doing anything other than its best to look after the principal's interests) would incur at least a 2% risk of forfeiting the next reward token, whereas cooperating would reduce the risk of forfeiting the next reward token to below 1%, then a utility-maximizing AI would always cooperate.

What might go wrong with such an incentive scheme? One possibility is that the AI will not trust the human operator to deliver the promised rewards. The track record of human reliability is something other than a straight line of unerring perfection. The AI would reasonably worry that the operator will change his mind, or raise the performance bar, or fail to recognize that the AI has done its part. The AI would also worry about the operator becoming incapacitated. The combined risk of such failures might exceed the risk of attempting to seize control of the reward mechanism. Even a boxed AI possessing the panoply of superpowers is a strong force. (For an AI that is *not* boxed to begin with, hijacking the human-governed reward mechanism may be like taking candy from a baby.)

Another problem with the incentive scheme is that it presupposes that we can tell whether the outcomes produced by the AI are in our interest. As later chapters will elaborate, this presupposition is not innocuous.

A full assessment of the feasibility of incentive methods would also have to take into account a range of other factors, including some esoteric considerations that might conceivably make such methods more viable than a preliminary analysis would suggest. In particular, the AI may face ineliminable indexical uncertainty if it could not be sure that it does not inhabit a computer simulation (as opposed to "basement-level," non-simulated physical reality), and this epistemic predicament may radically influence the AI's deliberations (see Box 8).

Stunting

Another possible capability control method is to limit the system's intellectual faculties or its access to information. This might be done by running the AI on hardware that is slow or short on memory. In the case of a boxed system, information inflow could also be restricted.

Stunting an AI in these ways would limit its usefulness. The method thus faces a dilemma: too little stunting, and the AI might have the wit to figure out some way to make itself more intelligent (and thence to

Box 8 Anthropic capture

The AI might assign a substantial probability to its simulation hypothesis, the hypothesis that it is living in a computer simulation. Even today, many AIs inhabit simulated worlds—worlds consisting of geometric line drawings, texts, chess games, or simple virtual realities, and in which the laws of physics deviate sharply from the laws of physics that we believe govern the world of our own experience. Richer and more complicated virtual worlds will become feasible with improvements in programming techniques and computing power. A mature superintelligence could create virtual worlds that appear to its inhabitants much the same as our world appears to us. It might create vast numbers of such worlds, running the same simulation many times or with small variations. The inhabitants would not necessarily be able to tell whether their world is simulated or not; but if they are intelligent enough they could consider the possibility and assign it some probability. In light of the simulation argument (a full discussion of which is beyond the scope of this book) that probability could be substantial.[14]

This predicament especially afflicts relatively early-stage superintelligences, ones that have not yet expanded to take advantage of the cosmic endowment. An early-stage superintelligence, which uses only a small fraction of the resources of a single planet, would be much less expensive to simulate than a mature intergalactic superintelligence. Potential simulators—that is, other more mature civilizations—would be able to run great numbers of simulations of such early-stage AIs even by dedicating a minute fraction of their computational resources to that purpose. If at least some (non-trivial fraction) of these mature superintelligent civilizations choose to use this ability, early-stage AIs should assign a substantial probability to being in a simulation.

How an AI would be affected by the simulation hypothesis depends on its values.[15] Consider first an AI that has a "resource-insatiable" final goal, such as the goal of maximizing a utility function that is linear in the number of paperclips caused by the AI to exist—twice as many paperclips, twice as good. Such an AI might care less about the simulation hypothesis, on grounds that its ability to influence how many paperclips are produced looks much more limited if the AI is in a simulation than if it is in basement-level physical reality. The AI might accordingly behave much *as if* it were certain that the simulation hypothesis is false, even if it assigned a fairly high probability to the simulation hypothesis being true.[16] The AI would reason that it does not much matter how it acts if

Box 8 *Continued*

the simulation hypothesis is true, whereas its actions make a great difference if the hypothesis is false; so it would select actions mainly by reference to how good they are conditional on the simulation hypothesis being false.

By contrast, consider an AI that has a more modest final goal, one that could be satisfied with a small amount of resources, such as the goal of receiving some pre-produced cryptographic reward tokens, or the goal of causing the existence of forty-five virtual paperclips. Such an AI should *not* discount those possible worlds in which it inhabits a simulation. A substantial portion of the AI's total expected utility might derive from those possible worlds. The decision-making of an AI with goals that are easily resource-satiable may therefore—if it assigns a high probability to the simulation hypothesis—be dominated by considerations about which actions would produce the best result if its perceived world is a simulation. Such an AI (even if it is, in fact, not in a simulation) might therefore be heavily influenced by its beliefs about which behaviors would be rewarded in a simulation.

In particular, if an AI with resource-satiable final goals believes that in most simulated worlds that match its observations it will be rewarded if it cooperates (but not if it attempts to escape its box or contravene the interests of its creator) then it may choose to cooperate. We could therefore find that even an AI with a decisive strategic advantage, one that could in fact realize its final goals to a greater extent by taking over the world than by refraining from doing so, would nevertheless balk at doing so.

> Thus Conscience does make Cowards of us all,
> And thus the Native hue of Resolution
> Is sicklied o'er, with the pale cast of Thought,
> And enterprises of great pith and moment,
> With this regard their Currents turn away,
> And lose the name of Action.
>
> (Shakespeare, *Hamlet*, Act iii. Sc. 1)

A mere line in the sand, backed by the clout of a nonexistent simulator, could prove a stronger restraint than a two-foot-thick solid steel door.[17]

world domination); too much, and the AI is just another piece of dumb software. A radically stunted AI is certainly safe but does not solve the problem of how to achieve a controlled detonation: an intelligence explosion would remain possible and would simply be triggered by some other system instead, perhaps at a slightly later date.

One might think it would be safe to build a superintelligence provided it is only given data about some narrow domain of facts. For example, one might build an AI that lacks sensors and that has preloaded into its memory only facts about petroleum engineering or peptide chemistry. But if the AI is superintelligent—if it is has a superhuman level of *general* intelligence—such data deprivation does not guarantee safety.

There are several reasons for this. First, the notion of information being "about" a certain topic is generally problematic. Any piece of information can in principle be relevant to any topic whatsoever, depending on the background information of a reasoner.[18] Furthermore, a given data set contains information not only about the domain from which the data was collected but also about various circumstantial facts. A shrewd mind looking over a knowledge base that is nominally about peptide chemistry might infer things about a wide range of topics. The fact that certain information is included and other information is not could tell an AI something about the state of human science, the methods and instruments available to study peptides, the fabrication technologies used to make these instruments, and the nature of the brains and societies that conceived the studies and the instruments. It might be that a *superintelligence* could correctly surmise a great deal from what seem, to dull-witted human minds, meager scraps of evidence. Even without any designated knowledge base at all, a sufficiently superior mind might be able to learn much by simply introspecting on the workings of its own psyche—the design choices reflected in its source code, the physical characteristics of its circuitry.[19] Perhaps a superintelligence could even deduce much about the likely properties of the world *a priori* (combining logical inference with a probability prior biased toward simpler worlds, and a few elementary facts implied by the superintelligence's existence as a reasoning system). It might imagine the consequences of different possible laws of physics: what kind of planets would form, what kind of intelligent life would evolve, what kind of societies would develop, what kind of methods to solve the control problem would be attempted, how those methods could be defeated.[20]

For these reasons it would be imprudent to rely on information deprivation as the main check on a superintelligence's power. Some forms of stunting however, including limiting hardware capacity and preventing the development of specific cognitive faculties, might find use as auxiliary control methods in the developmental phase. They could be used, for instance, to regulate the rate of capacity gain in an intermediary AI and to allow tests to be run at different levels of capability short of full-throttled superintelligence.

Tripwires

A tripwire is a mechanism that performs diagnostic tests on the system (possibly without its knowledge) and effects a shutdown if it detects signs of dangerous activity. Programmers can then scrutinize recordings of the suspicious activity at their leisure, and make changes to the AI's code base or environment before restarting it. If they find that the problem is sufficiently deep-rooted, they could decide to abort the entire project.

Tripwires differ from incentive methods in that they do not rely on the system being aware of the consequences of engaging in forbidden activities. Tripwires are more closely related to stunting methods. Like stunting, tripwires could be used as a temporary safeguard, providing a degree of protection during the development phase. In principle, tripwires can also be used during the operational phase, particularly for a boxed system. However, the ability of tripwires to constrain a full-fledged superintelligence must remain very much in doubt, since it would be hard for us to assure ourselves that such an agent could not find ways to subvert any tripwire devised by the human intellect.

As an adjunct safety measure in the development phase, though, tripwires are important. It would be good practice for the AI's designers to codify their expectations about how the system is supposed to function, and then to circumscribe the AI with tripwires that would be activated if any of these expectations is violated. To make the tests more stringent, "honeypots" could be strategically placed to create temptations for a malfunctioning AI to commit some easily observable violation. For instance, if an AI has been designed in such a way that it is supposed not to want to access the internet, a fake Ethernet port could be installed (leading to an automatic shutdown switch) just to see if the AI tries to use it. (Some examples of tripwires are given in Table 9.)

Table 9 *Different kinds of tripwires*

Type of monitoring	Description and examples
Behavior	Detectors could be placed around a boxed AI to detect attempts to breach the containment. For example, detectors could intercept attempts at radio communication or at accessing internal computational resources intended to be off limits. An "Ethernet port of Eden" could be installed: an apparent connection to the internet that leads to a shutdown switch.
Ability	Automated capability testing could be performed at frequent intervals to determine the AI's skill in various domains. If either the rate of improvement is unexpectedly high or the AI attains a level of competence that brings it close to the potential danger zone, the system could be slowed down or paused, in order to allow the programmers to monitor further developments more closely.
Content	The AI's internal processes could be monitored for suspicious activity. For example, any change to the AI's representation of its final values might trigger an automatic shutdown and review. The AI's resource use and algorithmic methods may also be also be monitored for unexpected patterns.
	More ambitiously, the AI's beliefs, plans, subgoals, and justifications may be continuously scrutinized, to ensure they conform to the programmers' expectations. Such monitoring of the AI's intentional states would enable a particularly powerful form of content monitoring: the scanning of the AI's cognitive processes for a *conception of deception*—that vulnerable moment when an unfriendly AI first forms the intention to conceal its true intentions.[21]
	Content monitoring that requires that the AI's intentional states be transparent to the programmers or to an automatic monitoring mechanism may not be feasible for all kinds of AI architectures. (Some neural networks, for instance, are opaque, as they represent information holistically and in ways that do not necessarily match up with human concepts.) This may be a reason to avoid using such architectures.

It should be emphasized that the value of a tripwire depends not only on the mechanism itself but also—critically—on how a project reacts when a tripwire is triggered. If the programmers or project managers, impatient to make progress, simply switch the system back on again—or if they do so after making some token modification to prevent the tripwire being triggered on the next run—then no safety has been gained even if the tripwire itself works exactly as intended.

Motivation selection methods

Motivation selection methods seek to prevent undesirable outcomes by shaping what the superintelligence wants to do. By engineering the agent's motivation system and its final goals, these methods would produce a superintelligence that would not *want* to exploit a decisive strategic advantage in a harmful way. Since a superintelligent agent is skilled at achieving its ends, if it prefers not to cause harm (in some appropriate sense of "harm") then it would tend not to cause harm (in that sense of "harm").

Motivation selection can involve explicitly formulating a goal or set of rules to be followed (*direct specification*) or setting up the system so that it can discover an appropriate set of values for itself by reference to some implicitly or indirectly formulated criterion (*indirect normativity*). One option in motivation selection is to try to build the system so that it would have modest, non-ambitious goals (*domesticity*). An alternative to creating a motivation system from scratch is to select an agent that already has an acceptable motivation system and then augment that agent's cognitive powers to make it superintelligent, while ensuring that the motivation system does not get corrupted in the process (*augmentation*). Let us look at these in turn.

Direct specification

Direct specification is the most straightforward approach to the control problem. The approach comes in two versions, rule-based and consequentialist, and involves trying to explicitly define a set of rules or values that will cause even a free-roaming superintelligent AI to act safely and beneficially. Direct specification, however, faces what may be insuperable obstacles, deriving from both the difficulties in determining which rules or values we would wish the AI to be guided by and the difficulties in expressing those rules or values in computer-readable code.

The traditional illustration of the direct rule-based approach is the "three laws of robotics" concept, formulated by science fiction author Isaac Asimov in a short story published in 1942.[22] The three laws were: (1) A robot may not injure a human being or, through inaction, allow a human being to come to harm; (2) A robot must obey any orders given to it by human beings, except where such orders would conflict with the First Law; (3) A robot must protect its own existence as long as such protection does not conflict with the First or Second Law. Embarrassingly for our species, Asimov's laws remained state-of-the-art for over half a century: this despite obvious problems with the approach, some of which are explored in Asimov's own writings (Asimov probably having formulated the laws in the first place precisely so that they would fail in interesting ways, providing fertile plot complications for his stories).[23]

Bertrand Russell, who spent many years working on the foundations of mathematics, once remarked that "everything is vague to a degree you do not realize till you have tried to make it precise."[24] Russell's dictum applies in spades to the direct specification approach. Consider, for example, how one might explicate Asimov's first law. Does it mean that the robot should minimize the probability of any human being coming to harm? In that case the other laws become otiose since it is always possible for the AI to take some action that would have at least some microscopic effect on the probability of a human being coming to harm. How is the robot to balance a large risk of a few humans coming to harm versus a small risk of many humans being harmed? How do we define "harm" anyway? How should the harm of physical pain be weighed against the harm of architectural ugliness or social injustice? Is a sadist harmed if he is prevented from tormenting his victim? How do we define "human being"? Why is no consideration given to other morally considerable beings, such as sentient nonhuman animals and digital minds? The more one ponders, the more the questions proliferate.

Perhaps the closest existing analog to a rule set that could govern the actions of a superintelligence operating in the world at large is a legal system. But legal systems have developed through a long process of trial and error, and they regulate relatively slowly-changing human societies. Laws can be revised when necessary. Most importantly, legal systems are administered by judges and juries who generally apply a measure of common sense and human decency to ignore logically possible legal interpretations that are sufficiently obviously unwanted and unintended by the lawgivers. It is probably humanly impossible to explicitly formulate a highly complex set of detailed rules, have them apply across a highly diverse set of circumstances, and get it right on the first implementation.[25]

Problems for the direct consequentialist approach are similar to those for the direct rule-based approach. This is true even if the AI is intended to serve some apparently simple purpose such as implementing a version of classical utilitarianism. For instance, the goal "Maximize the expectation of the balance of pleasure over pain in the world" may appear simple. Yet expressing it in computer code would involve, among other things, specifying how to recognize pleasure and pain. Doing this reliably might require solving an array of persistent problems in the philosophy of mind—even just to obtain a correct account expressed in a natural language, an account which would then, somehow, have to be translated into a programming language.

A small error in either the philosophical account or its translation into code could have catastrophic consequences. Consider an AI that has hedonism as its final goal, and which would therefore like to tile the universe with "hedonium" (matter organized in a configuration that is optimal for the generation of pleasurable experience). To this end, the AI might produce computronium (matter organized in a configuration that is optimal for computation) and use it to implement digital minds in states of euphoria. In order to maximize efficiency, the AI omits from the implementation any mental faculties that are not essential for the experience of pleasure, and exploits any computational shortcuts that according to its definition of pleasure do not vitiate the generation of pleasure. For instance, the AI might confine its simulation to reward circuitry, eliding faculties such as memory, sensory perception, executive function, and language; it might simulate minds at a relatively coarse-grained level of functionality, omitting lower-level neuronal processes; it might replace commonly repeated computations with calls to a lookup table; or it might put in place some arrangement whereby multiple minds would share most parts of their underlying computational machinery (their "supervenience bases" in philosophical parlance). Such tricks could greatly increase the quantity of pleasure producible with a given amount of resources. It is unclear how desirable this would be. Furthermore, if the AI's criterion for determining whether a physical process generates pleasure is wrong, then the AI's optimizations might throw the baby out with the bathwater: discarding something which is inessential according to the AI's criterion yet essential according to the criteria implicit in our human values. The universe then gets filled not with exultingly heaving hedonium but with computational processes that are unconscious and completely worthless—the equivalent of a smiley-face sticker xeroxed trillions upon trillions of times and plastered across the galaxies.

Domesticity

One special type of final goal which might be more amenable to direct specification than the examples given above is the goal of self-limitation. While it seems extremely difficult to specify how one would want a superintelligence to behave in the world *in general*—since this would require us to account for all the tradeoffs in all the situations that could arise—it might be feasible to specify how a superintelligence should behave in one particular situation. We could therefore seek to motivate the system to confine itself to acting on a small scale, within a narrow context, and through a limited set of action modes. We will refer to this approach of giving the AI final goals aimed at limiting the scope of its ambitions and activities as "domesticity."

For example, one could try to design an AI such that it would function as a question-answering device (an "oracle," to anticipate the terminology that we will introduce in the next chapter). Simply giving the AI the final goal of producing maximally accurate answers to any question posed to it would be unsafe—recall the "Riemann hypothesis catastrophe" described in Chapter 8. (Reflect, also, that this goal would incentivize the AI to take actions to ensure that it is asked easy questions.) To achieve domesticity, one might try to define a final goal that would somehow overcome these difficulties: perhaps a goal that combined the desiderata of answering questions correctly and minimizing the AI's impact on the world except whatever impact results as an incidental consequence of giving accurate and non-manipulative answers to the questions it is asked.[26]

The direct specification of such a domesticity goal is more likely to be feasible than the direct specification of either a more ambitious goal or a complete rule set for operating in an open-ended range of situations. Significant challenges nonetheless remain. Care would have to be taken, for instance, in the definition of what it would be for the AI to "minimize its impact on the world" to ensure that the measure of the AI's impact coincides with our own standards for what counts as a large or a small impact. A bad measure would lead to bad tradeoffs. There are also other kinds of risk associated with building an oracle, which we will discuss later.

There is a natural fit between the domesticity approach and physical containment. One would try to "box" an AI such that the system is *unable* to escape while simultaneously trying to shape the AI's motivation system such that it would be *unwilling* to escape even if it found a way to do so. Other things equal, the existence of multiple independent safety mechanisms should shorten the odds of success.[27]

Indirect normativity

If direct specification seems hopeless, we might instead try indirect normativity. The basic idea is that rather than specifying a concrete normative standard directly, we specify a process for deriving a standard. We then build the system so that it is motivated to carry out this process and to adopt whatever standard the process arrives at.[28] For example, the process could be to carry out an investigation into the empirical question of what some suitably idealized version of us would prefer the AI to do. The final goal given to the AI in this example could be something along the lines of "achieve that which we would have wished the AI to achieve if we had thought about the matter long and hard."

Further explanation of indirect normativity will have to await Chapter 13. There, we will revisit the idea of "extrapolating our volition" and explore various alterative formulations. Indirect normativity is a very important approach to motivation selection. Its promise lies in the fact that it could let us offload to the superintelligence much of the difficult cognitive work required to carry out a direct specification of an appropriate final goal.

Augmentation

The last motivation selection method on our list is augmentation. Here the idea is that rather than attempting to design a motivation system *de novo*, we start with a system that already has an acceptable motivation system, and enhance its cognitive faculties to make it superintelligent. If all goes well, this would give us a superintelligence with an acceptable motivation system.

This approach, obviously, is unavailing in the case of a newly created seed AI. But augmentation is a potential motivation selection method for other paths to superintelligence, including brain emulation, biological enhancement, brain–computer interfaces, and networks and organizations, where there is a possibility of building out the system from a normative nucleus (regular human beings) that already contains a representation of human value.

The attractiveness of augmentation may increase in proportion to our despair at the other approaches to the control problem. Creating a motivation system for a seed AI that remains reliably safe and beneficial under recursive self-improvement even as the system grows into a mature superintelligence is a tall order, especially if we must get the solution right on the first attempt. With augmentation, we would at least start with a system that has familiar and human-like motivations.

On the downside, it might be hard to ensure that a complex, evolved, kludgy, and poorly understood motivation system, like that of a human being, will not get corrupted when its cognitive engine blasts into the stratosphere. As discussed earlier, an imperfect brain emulation procedure that preserves intellectual functioning may not preserve all facets of personality. The same is true (though perhaps to a lesser degree) for biological enhancements of cognition, which might subtly affect motivation, and for collective intelligence enhancements of organizations and networks, which might adversely change social dynamics (e.g. in ways that debase the collective's attitude toward outsiders or toward its own constituents). If superintelligence is achieved via any of these paths, a project sponsor would find guarantees about the ultimate motivations of the mature system hard to come by. A mathematically well-specified and foundationally elegant AI architecture might—for all its non-anthropomorphic otherness—offer greater transparency, perhaps even the prospect that important aspects of its functionality could be formally verified.

In the end, however one tallies up the advantages and disadvantages of augmentation, the choice as to whether to rely on it might be forced. If superintelligence is first achieved along the artificial intelligence path, augmentation is not applicable. Conversely, if superintelligence is first achieved along some non-AI path, then many of the other motivation selection methods are inapplicable. Even so, views on how likely augmentation would be to succeed do have strategic relevance insofar as we have opportunities to influence which technology will first produce superintelligence.

Synopsis

A quick synopsis might be called for before we close this chapter. We distinguished two broad classes of methods for dealing with the agency problem at the heart of AI safety: capability control and motivation selection. Table 10 gives a summary.

Each control method comes with potential vulnerabilities and presents different degrees of difficulty in its implementation. It might perhaps be thought that we should rank them from better to worse, and then opt for the best method. But that would be simplistic. Some methods can be

Table 10 *Control methods*

Capability control	
Boxing methods	The system is confined in such a way that it can affect the external world only through some restricted, pre-approved channel. Encompasses physical and informational containment methods.
Incentive methods	The system is placed within an environment that provides appropriate incentives. This could involve social integration into a world of similarly powerful entities. Another variation is the use of (cryptographic) reward tokens. "Anthropic capture" is also a very important possibility but one that involves esoteric considerations.
Stunting	Constraints are imposed on the cognitive capabilities of the system or its ability to affect key internal processes.
Tripwires	Diagnostic tests are performed on the system (possibly without its knowledge) and a mechanism shuts down the system if dangerous activity is detected.

continued

Table 10 *Continued*

Motivation selection	
Direct specification	The system is endowed with some directly specified motivation system, which might be consequentialist or involve following a set of rules.
Domesticity	A motivation system is designed to severely limit the scope of the agent's ambitions and activities.
Indirect normativity	Indirect normativity could involve rule-based or consequentialist principles, but is distinguished by its reliance on an indirect approach to specifying the rules that are to be followed or the values that are to be pursued.
Augmentation	One starts with a system that already has substantially human or benevolent motivations, and enhances its cognitive capacities to make it superintelligent.

used in combination whereas others are exclusive. Even a comparatively insecure method may be advisable if it can easily be used as an adjunct, whereas a strong method might be unattractive if it would preclude the use of other desirable safeguards.

It is therefore necessary to consider what package deals are available. We need to consider what type of system we might try to build, and which control methods would be applicable to each type. This is the topic for our next chapter.

CHAPTER 10

Oracles, genies, sovereigns, tools

S ome say: "Just build a question-answering system!" or "Just build an AI that is like a tool rather than an agent!" But these suggestions do not make all safety concerns go away, and it is in fact a nontrivial question which type of system would offer the best prospects for safety. We consider four types or "castes"—oracles, genies, sovereigns, and tools—and explain how they relate to one another.[1] Each offers different sets of advantages and disadvantages in our quest to solve the control problem.

Oracles

An oracle is a question-answering system. It might accept questions in a natural language and present its answers as text. An oracle that accepts only yes/no questions could output its best guess with a single bit, or perhaps with a few extra bits to represent its degree of confidence. An oracle that accepts open-ended questions would need some metric with which to rank possible truthful answers in terms of their informativeness or appropriateness.[2] In either case, building an oracle that has a fully domain-general ability to answer natural language questions is an AI-complete problem. If one could do that, one could probably also build an AI that has a decent ability to understand human intentions as well as human words.

Oracles with domain-limited forms of superintelligence are also conceivable. For instance, one could conceive of a mathematics-oracle which would only accept queries posed in a formal language but which would be very good at answering such questions (e.g. being able to solve in an instant almost any formally expressed math problem that the human mathematics profession could solve by laboring collaboratively for a century). Such a mathematics-oracle would form a stepping-stone toward domain-general superintelligence.

Oracles with superintelligence in extremely limited domains already exist. A pocket calculator can be viewed as a very narrow oracle for basic arithmetical questions; an internet search engine can be viewed as a very partial realization of an oracle with a domain that encompasses a significant part of general human declarative knowledge. These domain-limited oracles are tools rather than agents (more on tool-AIs shortly). In what follows, though, the term "oracle" will refer to question-answering systems that have domain-general superintelligence, unless otherwise stated.

To make a general superintelligence function as an oracle, we could apply both motivation selection and capability control. Motivation selection for an oracle may be easier than for other castes of superintelligence, because the final goal in an oracle could be comparatively simple. We would want the oracle to give truthful, non-manipulative answers and to otherwise limit its impact on the world. Applying a domesticity method, we might require that the oracle should use only designated resources to produce its answer. For example, we might stipulate that it should base its answer on a preloaded corpus of information, such as a stored snapshot of the internet, and that it should use no more than a fixed number of computational steps.[3] To avoid incentivizing the oracle to manipulate us into giving it easier questions—which would happen if we gave it the goal of maximizing its accuracy across all questions we will ask it—we could give it the goal of answering only one question and to terminate immediately upon delivering its answer. The question would be preloaded into its memory before the program is run. To ask a second question, we would reset the machine and run the same program with a different question preloaded in memory.

Subtle and potentially treacherous challenges arise even in specifying the relatively simple motivation system needed to drive an oracle. Suppose, for example, that we come up with some explication of what it means for the AI "to minimize its impact on the world, subject to achieving certain results" or "to use only designated resources in preparing the answer." What happens if the AI, in the course of its intellectual development, undergoes the equivalent of a scientific revolution involving a change in its basic ontology?[4] We might initially have explicated "impact" and "designated resources" using our own ontology (postulating the existence of various physical objects such as computers). But just as we have abandoned ontological categories that were taken for granted by scientists in previous ages (e.g. "phlogiston," "élan vital," and "absolute simultaneity"), so a superintelligent AI might discover that some of our current categories are predicated on fundamental misconceptions. The goal system of an AI undergoing an ontological crisis needs to be resilient enough that the "spirit" of its original goal content is carried over, charitably transposed into the new key.

Although making an oracle safe through the use of motivation selection might be far from trivial, it may nevertheless be easier than doing the same for an AI that roams the world in pursuit of some complicated goal. This is an argument for preferring that the first superintelligence be an oracle. Another point in favor of an oracle-first path is the greater susceptibility of an oracle to capability control. All the standard boxing methods apply here. In addition, there may be methods that are distinctively applicable to oracles. For example, consider the risk that an oracle will answer questions not in a maximally truthful way but in such a way as to subtly manipulate us into promoting its own hidden agenda. One way to slightly mitigate this threat could be to create multiple oracles, each with a slightly different code and a slightly different information base. A simple mechanism could then compare the answers given by the different oracles and only present them for human viewing if all the answers agree. While one must assume that any superintelligent domain-general oracle would know about the existence of other oracles (it could infer this from its knowledge about human society), it might be feasible to hide some implementation details of each oracle from the views of the others. If the oracles are not able to communicate with one another, it might then be difficult for them to coordinate on how to answer our questions manipulatively. There are many ways of deviating from the truth, and the oracles may not all agree on which of these deviations is most attractive—whereas the truth itself is a Schelling point (a salient place for agreement in the absence of communication). So if the oracles achieve consensus, it might be a sign that they gave the true answer.[5]

An oracle would ideally be trustworthy in the sense that we could safely assume that its answers are always accurate to the best of its ability. But even an untrustworthy oracle could be useful. We could ask such an oracle questions of a type for which it is difficult to find the answer but easy to verify whether a given answer is correct. Many mathematical problems are of this kind. If we are wondering whether a mathematical proposition is true, we could ask the oracle to produce a proof or disproof of the proposition. Finding the proof may require insight and creativity beyond our ken, but checking a purported proof's validity can be done by a simple mechanical procedure.

If it is expensive to verify answers (as is often the case on topics outside logic and mathematics), we can randomly select a subset of the oracle's answers for verification. If they are all correct, we can assign a high probability to most of the other answers also being correct. This trick can give us a bulk discount on trustworthy answers that would be costly to verify individually. (Unfortunately, it cannot give us trustworthy answers that we are *unable* to verify, since a dissembling oracle may choose to answer correctly only those questions where it believes we could verify its answers.)

There could be important issues on which we could benefit from an augural pointer toward the correct answer (or toward a method for locating the correct answer) even if we had to actively distrust the provenance. For instance, one might ask for the solution to various technical or philosophical problems that may arise in the course of trying to develop more advanced motivation selection methods. If we had a proposed AI design alleged to be safe, we could ask an oracle whether it could identify any significant flaw in the design, and whether it could explain any such flaw to us in twenty words or less. Questions of this kind could elicit valuable information. Caution and restraint would be required, however, for us not to ask *too many* such questions—and not to allow ourselves to partake of *too many* details of the answers given to the questions we do ask—lest we give the untrustworthy oracle opportunities to work on our psychology (by means of plausible-seeming but subtly manipulative messages). It might not take many bits of communication for an AI with the social manipulation superpower to bend us to its will.

Even if the oracle itself works exactly as intended, there is a risk that it would be misused. One obvious dimension of this problem is that an oracle AI would be a source of immense power which could give a decisive strategic advantage to its operator. This power might be illegitimate and it might not be used for the common good. Another more subtle but no less important dimension is that the use of an oracle could be extremely dangerous for the operator herself. Similar worries (which involve philosophical as well as technical issues) arise also for other hypothetical castes of superintelligence. We will explore them more thoroughly in Chapter 13. Suffice it here to note that the protocol determining which questions are asked, in which sequence, and how the answers are reported and disseminated could be of great significance. One might also consider whether to try to build the oracle in such a way that it would refuse to answer any question in cases where it predicts that its answering would have consequences classified as catastrophic according to some rough-and-ready criteria.

Genies and sovereigns

A genie is a command-executing system: it receives a high-level command, carries it out, then pauses to await the next command.[6] A sovereign is a system that has an open-ended mandate to operate in the world in pursuit of broad and possibly very long-range objectives. Although these might seem like radically different templates for what a superintelligence should be and do, the difference is not as deep as it might at first glance appear.

With a genie, one already sacrifices the most attractive property of an oracle: the opportunity to use boxing methods. While one might consider creating a physically confined genie, for instance one that can only construct objects inside a designated volume—a volume that might be sealed off by a hardened wall or a barrier loaded with explosive charges rigged to detonate if the containment is breached—it would be difficult to have much confidence in the security of any such physical containment method against a superintelligence equipped with versatile manipulators and construction materials. Even if it were somehow possible to ensure a containment as secure as that which can be achieved for an oracle, it is not clear how much we would have gained by giving the superintelligence direct access to manipulators compared to requiring it instead to output a blueprint that we could inspect and then use to achieve the same result ourselves. The gain in speed and convenience from bypassing the human intermediary seems hardly worth the loss of foregoing the use of the stronger boxing methods available to contain an oracle.

If one *were* creating a genie, it would be desirable to build it so that it would obey the intention behind the command rather than its literal meaning, since a literalistic genie (one superintelligent enough to attain a decisive strategic advantage) might have a propensity to kill the user and the rest of humanity on its first use, for reasons explained in the section on malignant failure modes in Chapter 8. More broadly, it would seem important that the genie seek a charitable—and what human beings would regard as reasonable—interpretation of what is being commanded, and that the genie be motivated to carry out the command under such an interpretation rather than under the literalistic interpretation. The ideal genie would be a super-butler rather than an autistic savant.

A genie endowed with such a super-butler nature, however, would not be far from qualifying for membership in the caste of sovereigns. Consider, for comparison, the idea of building a sovereign with the final goal of obeying the spirit of the commands we would have given had we built a genie rather than a sovereign. Such a sovereign would mimic a genie. Being superintelligent, this sovereign would do a good job at guessing what commands we would have given a genie (and it could always ask us if that would help inform its decisions). Would there then really be any important difference between such a sovereign and a genie? Or, pressing on the distinction from the other side, consider that a superintelligent genie may likewise be able to predict what commands we will give it: what then is gained from having it await the actual issuance before it acts?

One might think that a big advantage of a genie over a sovereign is that if something goes wrong, we could issue the genie with a new command to stop or to reverse the effects of the previous actions, whereas a sovereign would just push on regardless of our protests. But this apparent safety advantage for the genie is largely illusory. The "stop" or "undo" button on a genie works only for benign failure modes: in the case of a malignant failure—one in which, for example, carrying out the existing command has become a final goal for the genie—the genie would simply disregard any subsequent attempt to countermand the previous command.[7]

One option would be to try to build a genie such that it would automatically present the user with a prediction about salient aspects of the likely outcomes of a proposed command, asking for confirmation before proceeding. Such a system could be referred to as a *genie-with-a-preview*. But if this could be done for a genie, it could likewise be done for a sovereign. So again, this is not a clear differentiator between a genie and a sovereign. (Supposing that a preview functionality could be created, the questions of whether and if so how to use it are rather less obvious than one might think, notwithstanding the strong appeal of being able to glance at the outcome before committing to making it irrevocable reality. We will return to this matter later.)

The ability of one caste to mimic another extends to oracles, too. A genie could be made to act like an oracle if the only commands we ever give it are to answer certain questions. An oracle, in turn, could be made to substitute for a genie if we asked the oracle what the easiest way is to get certain commands executed. The oracle could give us step-by-step instructions for achieving the same result as a genie would produce, or it could even output the source code for a genie.[8] Similar points can be made with regard to the relation between an oracle and a sovereign.

The real difference between the three castes, therefore, does not reside in the ultimate capabilities that they would unlock. Instead, the difference comes down to alternative approaches to the control problem. Each caste corresponds to a different set of safety precautions. The most prominent feature of an oracle is that it can be boxed. One might also try to apply domesticity motivation selection to an oracle. A genie is harder to box, but at least domesticity may be applicable. A sovereign can neither be boxed nor handled through the domesticity approach.

If these were the only relevant factors, then the order of desirability would seem clear: an oracle would be safer than a genie, which would be safer than a sovereign; and any initial differences in convenience and speed of operation would be relatively small and easily dominated by the gains in safety obtainable by building an oracle. However, there are other factors that need to be taken into account. When choosing between castes, one should consider not only the danger posed by the system itself but also the dangers that arise out of the way it might be used. A genie most obviously gives the person who controls it enormous power, but the same holds for an oracle.[9] A sovereign, by contrast, could be constructed in such way as to accord no one person or group any special influence over the outcome, and such that it would resist any attempt to corrupt or alter its original agenda. What is more, if a sovereign's motivation is defined using "indirect normativity" (a concept to be discussed further in Chapter 13) then it could be used to achieve some abstractly defined outcome, such as "whatever is maximally fair and morally right"—without anybody knowing in advance what exactly this will entail. This would create a situation analogous to a Rawlsian "veil of ignorance."[10] Such a setup might facilitate the attainment of consensus, help prevent conflict, and promote a more equitable outcome.

Another point, which counts against some types of oracles and genies, is that there are risks involved in designing a superintelligence to have a final goal that does not fully match the outcome that we ultimately seek to attain. For example, if we use a domesticity motivation to make the superintelligence want to minimize some of its impacts on the world, we might thereby create a system whose preference ranking over possible outcomes differs from that of the sponsor. The same will happen if we build the AI to place a peculiarly high value on answering questions correctly, or on faithfully obeying individual commands. Now, if sufficient care is taken, this should not cause any problems: there would be sufficient agreement between the two rankings—at least insofar as they pertain to possible worlds that have a reasonable chance of being actualized—that the outcomes that are good by the AI's standard are also good by the principal's standard. But perhaps one could argue for the design principle that it is unwise to introduce even a limited amount of disharmony between the AI's goals and ours. (The same concern would of course apply to giving sovereigns goals that do not completely harmonize with ours.)

Tool-AIs

One suggestion that has been made is that we build the superintelligence to be like a tool rather than an agent.[11] This idea seems to arise out of the observation that ordinary software, which is used in countless applications, does not raise any safety concerns even remotely analogous to the challenges discussed in this book. Might one not create "tool-AI" that is like such software—like a flight control system, say, or a virtual assistant—only more flexible and capable? Why build a superintelligence that has a will of its own? On this line of thinking, the agent paradigm is fundamentally misguided. Instead of creating an AI that has beliefs and desires and that acts like an artificial person, we should aim to build regular software that simply does what it is programmed to do.

This idea of creating software that "simply does what it is programmed to do" is, however, not so straightforward if the product being created is a powerful general intelligence. There is, of course, a trivial sense in which all software simply does what it is programmed to do: the behavior is mathematically specified by the code. But this is equally true for all castes of machine intelligence, "tool-AI" or not. If, instead, "simply doing what it is programmed to do" means that the software behaves as the programmers *intended*, then this is a standard that ordinary software very often fails to meet.

Because of the limited capabilities of contemporary software (compared with those of machine superintelligence) the consequences of such failures are manageable, ranging from insignificant to very costly, but in no case amounting to an existential threat.[12] However, if it is insufficient capability rather than sufficient reliability that makes ordinary software existentially safe, then it is unclear how such software could be a model for a safe superintelligence. It might be thought that by expanding the range of tasks done by ordinary software, one could eliminate the need for artificial general intelligence. But the range and diversity of tasks that a general intelligence could profitably perform in a modern economy is enormous. It would be infeasible to create special-purpose software to handle all of those tasks. Even if it could be done, such a project would take a *long* time to carry out. Before it could be completed, the nature of some of the tasks would have changed, and new tasks would have become relevant. There would be great advantage to having software that can learn on its own to do new tasks, and indeed to discover new tasks in need of doing. But this would require that the software be able to learn, reason, and plan, and to do so in a powerful and robustly cross-domain manner. In other words, it would require general intelligence.

Especially relevant for our purposes is the task of software development itself. There would be enormous practical advantages to being able to automate this. Yet the capacity for rapid self-improvement is just the critical property that enables a seed AI to set off an intelligence explosion.

If general intelligence is not dispensable, is there some other way of construing the tool-AI idea so as to preserve the reassuringly passive quality of a humdrum tool? Could one have a general intelligence that is not an agent? Intuitively, it is not just the limited capability of ordinary software that makes it safe: it is also its lack of ambition. There is no subroutine in Excel that secretly wants to take over the world if only it were smart enough to find a way. The spreadsheet application does not "want" anything at all; it just blindly carries out the instructions in the program. What (one might wonder) stands in the way of creating a more generally intelligent application of the same type? An oracle, for instance, which, when prompted with a description of a goal, would respond with a plan for how to achieve it, in much the same way that Excel responds to a column of numbers by calculating a sum—without thereby expressing any "preferences" regarding its output or how humans might choose to use it?

The classical way of writing software requires the programmer to understand the task to be performed in sufficient detail to formulate an explicit solution process consisting of a sequence of mathematically well-defined steps expressible in code.[13] (In practice, software engineers rely on code libraries stocked with useful behaviors, which they can invoke without needing to understand how the behaviors are implemented. But that code was originally created by programmers who had a detailed understanding of what they were doing.) This approach works for solving well-understood tasks, and is to credit for most software that is currently in use. It falls short, however, when nobody knows precisely how to solve all of the tasks that need to be accomplished. This is where techniques from the field of artificial intelligence become relevant. In narrow applications, machine learning might be used merely to fine-tune a few parameters in a largely human-designed program. A spam filter, for example, might be trained on a corpus of hand-classified email messages in a process that changes the weights that the classification algorithm places on various diagnostic features. In a more ambitious application, the classifier might be built so that it can discover new features on its own and test their validity in a changing environment. An even more sophisticated spam filter could be endowed with some ability to reason about the tradeoffs facing the user or about the contents of the messages it is classifying. In neither of these cases does the programmer need to know the best way of distinguishing spam from ham, only how to set up an algorithm that can improve its own performance via learning, discovering, or reasoning.

With advances in artificial intelligence, it would become possible for the programmer to offload more of the cognitive labor required to figure out how to accomplish a given task. In an extreme case, the programmer would simply specify a formal criterion of what counts as success and leave it to the AI to find a solution. To guide its search, the AI would use a set of powerful heuristics and other methods to discover structure in the space of possible solutions. It would keep searching until it found a solution that satisfied the success criterion. The AI would then either implement the solution itself or (in the case of an oracle) report the solution to the user.

Rudimentary forms of this approach are quite widely deployed today. Nevertheless, software that uses AI and machine learning techniques, though it has some ability to find solutions that the programmers had not anticipated, functions for all practical purposes like a tool and poses no existential risk. We would enter the danger zone only when the methods used in the search for solutions become extremely powerful and general: that is, when they begin to amount to general intelligence—and especially when they begin to amount to superintelligence.

There are (at least) two places where trouble could then arise. First, the superintelligent search process might find a solution that is not just unexpected but radically unintended. This could lead to a failure of one of the types discussed previously ("perverse instantiation," "infrastructure profusion," or "mind crime"). It is most obvious how this could happen in the case of a sovereign or a genie, which directly implements the solution it has found. If making molecular smiley faces or transforming the planet into paperclips is the first idea that the superintelligence discovers that meets the solution criterion, then smiley faces or paperclips we get.[14] But even an oracle, which—if all else goes well—merely *reports* the solution, could become a cause of perverse instantiation. The user asks the oracle for a plan to achieve a certain outcome, or for a technology to serve a certain function; and when the user follows the plan or constructs the technology, a perverse instantiation can ensue, just as if the AI had implemented the solution itself.[15]

A second place where trouble could arise is in the course of the software's operation. If the methods that the software uses to search for a solution are sufficiently sophisticated, they may include provisions for managing the search process itself in an intelligent manner. In this case, the machine running the software may begin to seem less like a mere tool and more like an agent. Thus, the software may start by developing a plan for how to go about its search for a solution. The plan may specify which areas to explore first and with what methods, what data to gather, and how to make best use of available computational resources. In searching for a plan that satisfies the software's internal criterion (such as yielding a sufficiently high probability of finding a solution satisfying the user-specified criterion within the allotted time), the software may stumble on an unorthodox idea. For instance, it might generate a plan that begins with the acquisition of additional computational resources and the elimination of potential interrupters (such as human beings). Such "creative" plans come into view when the software's cognitive abilities reach a sufficiently high level. When the software puts such a plan into action, an existential catastrophe may ensue.

As the examples in Box 9 illustrate, open-ended search processes sometimes evince strange and unexpected non-anthropocentric solutions even in their currently limited forms. Present-day search processes are not hazardous because they are too weak to discover the kind of plan that could enable a program to take over the world. Such a plan would include extremely difficult steps, such as the invention of a new weapons technology several generations ahead of the state of the art or the execution of a propaganda campaign far more effective than any communication devised by human spin doctors. To have a chance of even *conceiving* of such ideas, let alone developing them in a way that would actually work, a machine would probably need the capacity to represent the world in a way that is at least as rich and realistic as the world model possessed by a normal human adult (though a lack of awareness in some areas might possibly be compensated for by extra skill in others). This is far beyond the reach of contemporary AI. And because of the combinatorial explosion, which generally defeats attempts to solve complicated planning problems with brute-force methods (as we saw in Chapter 1), the shortcomings of known algorithms cannot realistically be overcome simply by pouring on more computing power.[16] However, once the search or planning processes become powerful enough, they also become potentially dangerous.

Instead of allowing agent-like purposive behavior to emerge spontaneously and haphazardly from the implementation of powerful search processes (including processes searching for internal work plans and processes directly searching for solutions meeting some user-specified criterion), it may be better to create agents on purpose. Endowing a superintelligence with an explicitly agent-like structure can be a way of increasing predictability and transparency. A well-designed system, built such that there is a clean separation between its values and its beliefs, would let us predict something about the outcomes it would tend to produce. Even if we could not foresee exactly which beliefs the system would acquire or which situations it would find itself in, there would be a known place where we could inspect its final values and thus the criteria that it will use in selecting its future actions and in evaluating any potential plan.

Box 9 Strange solutions from blind search

Even simple evolutionary search processes sometimes produce highly unexpected results, solutions that satisfy a formal user-defined criterion in a very different way than the user expected or intended.

The field of evolvable hardware offers many illustrations of this phenomenon. In this field, an evolutionary algorithm searches the space of hardware designs, testing the fitness of each design by instantiating it physically on a rapidly reconfigurable array or motherboard. The evolved designs often show remarkable economy. For instance, one search discovered a frequency discrimination circuit that functioned without a clock—a component normally considered necessary for this function. The researchers estimated that the evolved circuit was between one and two orders of magnitude smaller than what a human engineer would have required for the task. The circuit exploited the physical properties of its components in unorthodox ways; some active, necessary components were not even connected to the input or output pins! These components instead participated via what would normally be considered nuisance side effects, such as electromagnetic coupling or power-supply loading.

Another search process, tasked with creating an oscillator, was deprived of a seemingly even more indispensible component, the capacitor. When the algorithm presented its successful solution, the researchers examined it and at first concluded that it "should not work." Upon more careful examination, they discovered that the algorithm had, MacGyver-like, reconfigured its sensor-less motherboard into a makeshift radio receiver, using the printed circuit board tracks as an aerial to pick up signals generated by personal computers that happened to be situated nearby in the laboratory. The circuit amplified this signal to produce the desired oscillating output.[17]

In other experiments, evolutionary algorithms designed circuits that sensed whether the motherboard was being monitored with an oscilloscope or whether a soldering iron was connected to the lab's common power supply. These examples illustrate how an open-ended search process can repurpose the materials accessible to it in order to devise completely unexpected sensory capabilities, by means that conventional human design-thinking is poorly equipped to exploit or even account for in retrospect.

The tendency for evolutionary search to "cheat" or find counterintuitive ways of achieving a given end is on display in nature too, though it is perhaps

continued

Box 9 *Continued*

less obvious to us there because of our already being somewhat familiar with the look and feel of biology, and thus being prone to regarding the actual outcomes of natural evolutionary processes as normal—even if we would not have expected them *ex ante*. But it is possible to set up experiments in artificial selection where one can see the evolutionary process in action outside its familiar context. In such experiments, researchers can create conditions that rarely obtain in nature, and observe the results.

For example, prior to the 1960s, it was apparently quite common for biologists to maintain that predator populations restrict their own breeding in order to avoid falling into a Malthusian trap.[18] Although individual selection would work against such restraint, it was sometimes thought that group selection would overcome individual incentives to exploit opportunities for reproduction and favor traits that would benefit the group or population at large. Theoretical analysis and simulation studies later showed that while group selection is possible in principle, it can overcome strong individual selection only under very stringent conditions that may rarely apply in nature.[19] But such conditions can be created in the laboratory. When flour beetles (*Tribolium castaneum*) were bred for reduced population size, by applying strong group selection, evolution did indeed lead to smaller populations.[20] However, the means by which this was accomplished included not only the "benign" adaptations of reduced fecundity and extended developmental time that a human naively anthropomorphizing evolutionary search might have expected, but also an increase in cannibalism.[21]

Comparison

It may be useful to summarize the features of the different system castes we have discussed (Table 11).

Further research would be needed to determine which type of system would be safest. The answer might depend on the conditions under which the AI would be deployed. The oracle caste is obviously attractive from a safety standpoint, since it would allow both capability control methods and motivation selection methods to be applied. It might thus seem to simply dominate the sovereign caste, which would only allow motivation selection methods (except in scenarios in which the world is believed to

Table 11 *Features of different system castes*

Oracle	**A question-answering system** *Variations:* Domain-limited oracles (e.g. mathematics); output-restricted oracles (e.g. only yes/no/undecided answers, or probabilities); oracles that refuse to answer questions if they predict the consequences of answering would meet pre-specified "disaster criteria"; multiple oracles for peer review	• Boxing methods fully applicable • Domesticity fully applicable • Reduced need for AI to understand human intentions and interests (compared to genies and sovereigns) • Use of yes/no questions can obviate need for a metric of the "usefulness" or "informativeness" of answers • Source of great power (might give operator a decisive strategic advantage) • Limited protection against foolish use by operator • Untrustworthy oracles could be used to provide answers that are hard to find but easy to verify • Weak verification of answers may be possible through the use of multiple oracles
Genie	**A command-executing system** *Variations:* Genies using different "extrapolation distances" or degrees of following the spirit rather than letter of the command; domain-limited genies; genies-with-preview; genies that refuse to obey commands if they predict the consequences of obeying would meet pre-specified "disaster criteria"	• Boxing methods partially applicable (for spatially limited genies) • Domesticity partially applicable • Genie could offer a preview of salient aspects of expected outcomes • Genie could implement change in stages, with opportunity for review at each stage • Source of great power (might give operator a decisive strategic advantage) • Limited protection against foolish use by operator • Greater need for AI to understand human interests and intentions (compared to oracles)

continued

Table 11 *Continued*

Sovereign	**A system designed for open-ended autonomous operation** *Variations*: Many possible motivation systems; possibility of using preview and "sponsor ratification" (to be discussed in Chapter 13)	• Boxing methods inapplicable • Most other capability control methods also inapplicable (except, possibly, social integration or anthropic capture) • Domesticity mostly inapplicable • Great need for AI to understand true human interests and intentions • Necessity of getting it right on the first try (though, to a possibly lesser extent, this is true for all castes) • Potentially a source of great power for sponsor, including decisive strategic advantage • Once activated, not vulnerable to hijacking by operator, and might be designed with some protection against foolish use • Can be used to implement "veil of ignorance" outcomes (cf. Chapter 13)
Tool	**A system not designed to exhibit goal-directed behavior**	• Boxing methods may be applicable, depending on the implementation • Powerful search processes would likely be involved in the development and operation of a machine superintelligence • Powerful search to find a solution meeting some formal criterion can produce solutions that meet the criterion in an unintended and dangerous way • Powerful search might involve secondary, internal search and planning processes that might find dangerous ways of executing the primary search process

contain other powerful superintelligences, in which case social integration or anthropic capture might apply). However, an oracle could place a lot of power into the hands of its operator, who might be corrupted or might apply the power unwisely, whereas a sovereign would offer some protection against these hazards. The safety ranking is therefore not so easily determined.

A genie can be viewed as a compromise between an oracle and a sovereign—but not necessarily a good compromise. In many ways, it would share the disadvantages of both. The apparent safety of a tool-AI, meanwhile, may be illusory. In order for tools to be versatile enough to substitute for superintelligent agents, they may need to deploy extremely powerful internal search and planning processes. Agent-like behaviors may arise from such processes as an unplanned consequence. In that case, it would be better to design the system to be an agent in the first place, so that the programmers can more easily see what criteria will end up determining the system's output.

CHAPTER 11

Multipolar scenarios

We have seen (particularly in Chapter 8) how menacing a unipolar outcome could be, one in which a single superintelligence obtains a decisive strategic advantage and uses it to establish a singleton. In this chapter, we examine what would happen in a multipolar outcome, a post-transition society with multiple competing superintelligent agencies. Our interest in this class of scenarios is twofold. First, as alluded to in Chapter 9, social integration might be thought to offer a solution to the control problem. We already noted some limitations with that approach, and this chapter paints a fuller picture. Second, even without anybody setting out to create a multipolar condition as a way of handling the control problem, such an outcome might occur anyway. So what might such an outcome look like? The resulting competitive society is not necessarily attractive, nor longlasting.

In singleton scenarios, what happens post-transition depends almost entirely on the values of the singleton. The outcome could thus be very good or very bad, depending on what those values are. What the values are depends, in turn, on whether the control problem was solved, and—to the degree to which it was solved—on the goals of the project that created the singleton.

If one is interested in the outcome of singleton scenarios, therefore, one really only has three sources of information: information about matters that cannot be affected by the actions of the singleton (such as the laws of physics); information about convergent instrumental values; and information that enables one to predict or speculate about what final values the singleton will have.

In multipolar scenarios, an additional set of constraints comes into play, constraints having to do with how agents interact. The social dynamics emerging from such interactions can be studied using techniques from game theory, economics, and evolution theory. Elements of political science and sociology are also relevant insofar as they can be distilled and abstracted from some of the more contingent features of human experience. Although it would be unrealistic to expect these constraints to give us a precise picture of the post-transition world, they can help us identify some salient possibilities and challenge some unfounded assumptions.

We will begin by exploring an economic scenario characterized by a low level of regulation, strong protection of property rights, and a moderately rapid introduction of inexpensive digital minds.[1] This type of model is most closely associated with the American economist Robin Hanson, who has done pioneering work on the subject. Later in this chapter, we will look at some evolutionary considerations and examine the prospects of an initially multipolar post-transition world subsequently coalescing into a singleton.

Of horses and men

General machine intelligence could serve as a substitute for human intelligence. Not only could digital minds perform the intellectual work now done by humans, but, once equipped with good actuators or robotic bodies, machines could also substitute for human physical labor. Suppose that machine workers—which can be quickly reproduced—become both cheaper and more capable than human workers in virtually all jobs. What happens then?

Wages and unemployment

With cheaply copyable labor, market wages fall. The only place where humans would remain competitive may be where customers have a basic preference for work done by humans. Today, goods that have been hand-crafted or produced by indigenous people sometimes command a price premium. Future consumers might similarly prefer human-made goods and human athletes, human artists, human lovers, and human leaders to functionally indistinguishable or superior artificial counterparts. It is unclear, however, just how widespread such preferences would be. If machine-made alternatives were sufficiently superior, perhaps they would be more highly prized.

One parameter that might be relevant to consumer choice is the inner life of the worker providing a service or product. A concert audience, for instance, might like to know that the performer is consciously experiencing the music and the venue. Absent phenomenal experience, the musician could be regarded as merely a high-powered jukebox, albeit one capable of creating the three-dimensional appearance of a performer interacting naturally with the crowd. Machines might then be designed to instantiate the same kinds of mental states that would be present in a human performing the same task. Even with perfect replication of subjective experiences, however, some people might simply prefer organic work. Such preferences could also have ideological or religious roots. Just as many Muslims and Jews shun food prepared in ways they classify as *haram* or *treif*, so there might be groups in the future that eschew products whose manufacture involved unsanctioned use of machine intelligence.

What hinges on this? To the extent that cheap machine labor can substitute for human labor, human jobs may disappear. Fears about automation and job loss are of course not new. Concerns about technological unemployment have surfaced periodically, at least since the Industrial Revolution; and quite a few professions have in fact gone the way of the English weavers and textile artisans who in the early nineteenth century united under the banner of the folkloric "General Ludd" to fight against the introduction of mechanized looms. Nevertheless, although machinery and technology have been substitutes for many particular types of human labor, physical technology has on the whole been a complement to labor. Average human wages around the world have been on a long-term upward trend, in large part because of such complementarities. Yet what starts out as a complement to labor can at a later stage become a substitute for labor. Horses were initially complemented by carriages and ploughs, which greatly increased the horse's productivity. Later, horses were substituted for by automobiles and tractors. These later innovations reduced the demand for equine labor and led to a population collapse. Could a similar fate befall the human species?

The parallel to the story of the horse can be drawn out further if we ask why it is that there are still horses around. One reason is that there are still a few niches in which horses have functional advantages; for example, police work. But the main reason is that humans happen to have peculiar preferences for the services that horses can provide, including recreational horseback riding and racing. These preferences can be compared to the preferences we hypothesized some humans might have in the future, that certain goods and services be made by human hand. Although suggestive, this analogy is, however, inexact, since there is still no complete functional substitute for horses. If there were inexpensive mechanical devices that ran on hay and had exactly the same shape, feel, smell, and behavior as biological horses—perhaps even the same conscious experiences—then demand for biological horses would probably decline further.

With a sufficient reduction in the demand for human labor, wages would fall below the human subsistence level. The potential downside for human workers is therefore extreme: not merely wage cuts, demotions, or the need for retraining, but starvation and death. When horses became obsolete as a source of moveable power, many were sold off to meatpackers to be processed into dog food, bone meal, leather, and glue. These animals had no alternative employment through which to earn their keep. In the United States, there were about 26 million horses in 1915. By the early 1950s, 2 million remained.[2]

Capital and welfare

One difference between humans and horses is that humans own capital. A stylized empirical fact is that the total factor share of capital has for a long time remained steady at approximately 30% (though with significant short-term fluctuations).[3] This means that 30% of total global income is received as rent by owners of capital, the remaining 70% being received as wages by workers. If we classify AI as capital, then with the invention of machine intelligence that can fully substitute for human work, wages would fall to the marginal cost of such machine-substitutes, which—under the assumption that the machines are very efficient—would be very low, far below human subsistence-level income. The income share received by labor would then dwindle to practically nil. But this implies that the factor share of capital would become nearly 100% of total world product. Since world GDP would soar following an intelligence explosion (because of massive amounts of new labor-substituting machines but also because of technological advances achieved by superintelligence, and, later, acquisition of vast amounts of new land through space colonization), it follows that the total income from capital would increase enormously. If humans remain the owners of this capital, the total income received by the human population would grow astronomically, despite the fact that in this scenario humans would no longer receive any wage income.

The human species as a whole could thus become rich beyond the dreams of Avarice. How would this income be distributed? To a first approximation, capital income would be proportional to the amount of capital owned. Given the astronomical amplification effect, even a tiny bit of pre-transition wealth would balloon into a vast post-transition fortune. However, in the contemporary world, many people have no wealth. This includes not only individuals who live in poverty but also some people who earn a good income or who have high human capital but have negative net worth. For example, in affluent Denmark and Sweden 30% of the population report negative wealth—often young, middle-class people with few tangible assets and credit card debt or student loans.[4] Even if savings could earn extremely high interest, there would need to be some seed grain, some starting capital, in order for the compounding to begin.[5]

Nevertheless, even individuals who have no private wealth at the start of the transition could become extremely rich. Those who participate in a pension scheme, for instance, whether public or private, should be in a good position, provided the scheme is at least partially funded.[6] Have-nots could also become rich through the philanthropy of those who see their net worth skyrocket: because of the astronomical size of the bonanza, even a very small fraction donated as alms would be a very large sum in absolute terms.

It is also possible that riches could still be made through work, even at a post-transition stage when machines are functionally superior to humans in all domains (as well as cheaper than even subsistence-level human labor). As noted earlier, this could happen if there are niches in which human labor is preferred for aesthetic, ideological, ethical, religious, or other non-pragmatic reasons. In a scenario in which the wealth of human capital-holders increases dramatically, demand for such labor could increase correspondingly. Newly minted trillionaires or quadrillionaires could afford to pay a hefty premium for having some of their goods and services supplied by an organic "fair-trade" labor force. The history of horses again offers a parallel. After falling to 2 million in the early 1950s, the US horse population has undergone a robust recovery: a recent census puts the number at just under 10 million head.[7] The rise is not due to new functional needs for horses in agriculture or transportation; rather, economic growth has enabled more Americans to indulge a fancy for equestrian recreation.

Another relevant difference between humans and horses, beside capital-ownership, is that humans are capable of political mobilization. A human-run government could use the taxation power of the state to redistribute private profits, or raise revenue by selling appreciated state-owned assets, such as public land, and use the proceeds to pension off its constituents. Again, because of the explosive economic growth during and immediately after the transition, there would be vastly more wealth sloshing around, making it relatively easy to fill the cups of all unemployed citizens. It should be feasible even for a single country to provide every human worldwide with a generous living wage at no greater proportional cost than what many countries currently spend on foreign aid.[8]

The Malthusian principle in a historical perspective

So far we have assumed a constant human population. This may be a reasonable assumption for short timescales, since biology limits the rate of human reproduction. Over longer timescales, however, the assumption is not necessarily reasonable.

The human population has increased a thousandfold over the past 9,000 years.[9] The increase would have been much faster except for the fact that throughout most of history and prehistory, the human population was bumping up against the limits of the world economy. An approximately Malthusian condition prevailed, in which most people received subsistence-level incomes that just barely allowed them to survive and raise an average of two children to maturity.[10] There were temporary and local reprieves: plagues, climate fluctuations, or warfare intermittently culled the population and freed up land, enabling survivors to improve their nutritional intake—and to bring up more children, until the ranks were replenished and the Malthusian condition reinstituted. Also, thanks to social inequality, a thin elite stratum could enjoy consistently above-subsistence income (at the expense of somewhat lowering the total size of the population that could be sustained). A sad and dissonant thought: that in this Malthusian condition, the normal state of affairs during most of our tenure on this planet, it was droughts, pestilence, massacres, and inequality—in common estimation the worst foes of human welfare—that may have been the greatest humanitarians: they alone enabling the average level of well-being to occasionally bop up slightly above that of life at the very margin of subsistence.

Superimposed on local fluctuations, history shows a macro-pattern of initially slow but accelerating economic growth, fueled by the accumulation of technological innovations. The growing world economy brought with it a commensurate increase in global population. (More precisely, a larger population itself appears to have strongly accelerated the rate of growth, perhaps mainly by increasing humanity's collective intelligence.[11]) Only since the Industrial Revolution, however, did economic growth become so rapid that population growth failed to keep pace. Average income thus started to rise, first in the early-industrializing countries of Western Europe, subsequently in most of the world. Even in the poorest countries today, average income substantially exceeds subsistence level, as reflected in the fact that the populations of these countries are growing.

The poorest countries now have the fastest population growth, as they have yet to complete the "demographic transition" to the low-fertility regime that has taken hold in more developed societies. Demographers project that the world population will rise to about 9 billion by mid-century, and that it might thereafter plateau or decline as the poorer countries join the developed world in this low-fertility regime.[12] Many rich countries already have fertility rates that are below replacement level; in some cases, far below.[13]

Yet there are reasons, if we take a longer view and assume a state of unchanging technology and continued prosperity, to expect a return to the historically and ecologically normal condition of a world population that butts up against the limits of what our niche can support. If this seems counterintuitive in light of the negative relationship between wealth and fertility that we are currently observing on the global scale, we must remind ourselves that this modern age is a brief slice of history and very much an aberration. Human behavior has not yet adapted to contemporary conditions. Not only do we fail to take advantage of obvious ways to increase our inclusive fitness (such as by becoming sperm or egg donors) but we actively sabotage our fertility by using birth control. In the environment of evolutionary adaptedness, a healthy sex drive may have been enough to make an individual act in ways that maximized her reproductive potential; in the modern environment, however, there would be a huge selective advantage to having a more direct desire for being the biological parent to the largest possible number of children. Such a desire is currently being selected for, as are other traits that increase our propensity to reproduce. Cultural adaptation, however, might steal a march on biological evolution. Some communities, such as those of the Hutterites or the adherents of the Quiverfull evangelical movement, have natalist cultures that encourage large families, and they are consequently undergoing rapid expansion.

Population growth and investment

If we imagine current socioeconomic conditions magically frozen in their current shape, the future would be dominated by cultural or ethnic groups that sustain high levels of fertility. If most people had preferences that were fitness-maximizing in the contemporary environment, the population could easily double in each generation. Absent population control policies—which would have to become steadily more rigorous and effective to counteract the evolution of stronger preferences to circumvent them—the world population would then continue to grow exponentially until some constraint, such as land scarcity or depletion of easy opportunities for important innovation, made it impossible for the economy to keep pace: at which point, average income would start to decline until it reached the level where crushing poverty prevents most people from raising much more than two children to maturity. Thus the Malthusian principle would reassert itself, like a dread slave master, bringing our escapade into the dreamland of abundance to an end, and leading us back to the quarry in chains, there to resume the weary struggle for subsistence.

This longer-term outlook could be telescoped into a more imminent prospect by the intelligence explosion. Since software is copyable, a population of emulations or AIs could double rapidly—over the course of minutes rather than decades or centuries—soon exhausting all available hardware.

Private property might offer partial protection against the emergence of a universal Malthusian condition. Consider a simple model in which clans (or closed communities, or states) start out with varying amounts of property and independently adopt different policies about reproduction and investment. Some clans discount the future steeply and spend down their endowment, whereafter their impoverished members join the global proletariat (or die, if they cannot support themselves through their labor). Other clans invest some of their resources but adopt a policy of unlimited reproduction: such clans grow more populous until they reach an internal Malthusian condition in which their members are so poor that they die at almost the same rate as they reproduce, at which point the clan's population growth slows to equal the growth of its resources. Yet other clans might restrict their fertility to below the rate of growth of their capital: such clans could slowly increment their numbers while their members also grow richer per capita.

If wealth is redistributed from the wealthy clans to the members of the rapidly reproducing or rapidly discounting clans (whose children, copies, or offshoots, through no fault of their own, were launched into the world with insufficient capital to survive and thrive) then a universal Malthusian condition would be more closely approximated. In the limiting case, all members of all clans would receive subsistence level income and everybody would be equal in their poverty.

If property is not redistributed, prudent clans might hold on to a certain amount of capital, and it is possible that their wealth could grow in absolute terms. It is, however, unclear whether humans could earn as high rates of return on their capital as machine intelligences could earn on theirs, because there may be synergies between labor and capital such that an single agent who can supply both (e.g. an entrepreneur or investor who is both skilled and wealthy) can attain a private rate of return on her capital exceeding the market rate obtainable by agents who possess financial but not cognitive resources. Humans, being less skilled than machine intelligences, may therefore grow their capital more slowly—unless, of course, the control problem had been completely solved, in which case the human rate of return would equal the machine rate of return, since a human principal could task a machine agent to manage her savings, and could do so costlessly and without conflicts of interest: but otherwise, in this scenario, the fraction of the economy owned by machines would asymptotically approach one hundred percent.

A scenario in which the fraction of the economy that is owned by machines asymptotically approaches one hundred percent is not necessarily one in which the size of the human slice declines. If the economy grows at a sufficient clip, then even a relatively diminishing fraction of it may still be increasing in its absolute size. This may sound like modestly good news for humankind: in a multipolar scenario in which property rights are protected—even if we completely fail to solve the control problem—the total amount of wealth owned by human beings could increase. Of course, this effect would not take care of the problem of population growth in the human population pulling down per capita income to subsistence level, nor the problem of humans who ruin themselves because they discount the future.

In the long run, the economy would become increasingly dominated by those clans that have the highest savings rates—misers who own half the city and live under a bridge. Only in the fullness of time, when there are no more opportunities for investment, would the maximally prosperous misers start drawing down their savings.[14] However, if there is less than perfect protection for property rights—for example if the more efficient machines on net succeed, by hook or by crook, in transferring wealth from humans to themselves—then human capitalists may need to spend down their capital much sooner, before it gets depleted by such transfers (or the ongoing costs incurred in securing their wealth against such transfers). If these developments take place on digital rather than biological timescales, then the glacial humans might find themselves expropriated before they could say Jack Robinson.[15]

Life in an algorithmic economy

Life for biological humans in a post-transition Malthusian state need not resemble any of the historical states of man (as hunter–gatherer, farmer, or office worker). Instead, the majority of humans in this scenario might be idle rentiers who eke out a marginal living on their savings.[16] They would be very poor, yet derive what little income they have from savings or state subsidies. They would live in a world with extremely advanced technology, including not only superintelligent machines but also anti-aging medicine, virtual reality, and various enhancement technologies and pleasure drugs: yet these might be generally unaffordable. Perhaps instead of using enhancement medicine, they would take drugs to stunt their growth and slow their metabolism in order to reduce their cost of living (fast-burners being unable to survive at the gradually declining subsistence income). As our numbers increase and our average income declines further, we might degenerate into whatever minimal structure still qualifies to receive a pension—perhaps minimally conscious brains in vats, oxygenized and nourished by machines, slowly saving up enough money to reproduce by having a robot technician develop a clone of them.[17]

Further frugality could be achieved by means of uploading, since a physically optimized computing substrate, devised by advanced superintelligence, would be more efficient than a biological brain. The migration into the digital realm might be stemmed, however, if emulations were regarded as non-humans or non-citizens ineligible to receive pensions or to hold tax-exempt savings accounts. In that case, a niche for biological humans might remain open, alongside a perhaps vastly larger population of emulations or artificial intelligences.

So far we have focused on the fate of the humans, who may be supported by savings, subsidies, or wage income deriving from other humans who prefer to hire humans. Let us now turn our attention to some of the entities that we have so far classified as "capital": machines that may be owned by human beings, that are constructed and operated for the sake of the functional tasks they perform, and that are capable of substituting for human labor in a very wide range of jobs. What may the situation be like for these workhorses of the new economy?

If these machines were mere automata, simple devices like a steam engine or the mechanism in a clock, then no further comment would be needed: there would be a large amount of such capital in a post-transition economy, but it would seem not to matter to anybody how things turn out for pieces of insentient equipment. However, if the machines have conscious minds—if they are constructed in such a way that their operation is associated with phenomenal awareness (or if they for some other reason are ascribed moral status)—then it becomes important to consider the overall outcome in terms of how it would affect these machine minds. The welfare of the working machine minds could even appear to be the most important aspect of the outcome, since they may be numerically dominant.

Voluntary slavery, casual death

A salient initial question is whether these working machine minds are owned as capital (slaves) or are hired as free wage laborers. On closer inspection however, it becomes doubtful that anything really hinges on the issue. There are two reasons for this. First, if a free worker in a Malthusian state gets paid a subsistence-level wage, he will have no disposable income left after he has paid for food and other necessities. If the worker is instead a slave, his owner will pay for his maintenance and again he will have no disposable income. In either case, the worker gets the necessities and nothing more. Second, suppose that the free laborer were somehow in a position to command an above-subsistence-level income (perhaps because of favorable regulation). How will he spend the surplus? Investors would find it most profitable to create workers who would be "voluntary slaves"—who would willingly work for subsistence-level wages. Investors may create such workers by copying those workers who are compliant. With appropriate selection (and perhaps some modification to the code) investors might be able to create workers who not only prefer to volunteer their labor but who would also choose to donate back to their owners any surplus income they might happen to receive. Giving money to the worker would then be but a roundabout way of giving money to the owner or employer, even if the worker were a free agent with full legal rights.

Perhaps it will be objected that it would be difficult to design a machine so that it wants to volunteer for any job assigned to it or so that it wants to donate its wages to its owner. Emulations, in particular, might be imagined to have more typically human desires. But note that even if the original control problem is difficult, we are here considering a condition *after* the transition, a time when methods for motivation selection have presumably been perfected. In the case of emulations, one might get quite far simply by *selecting* from the pre-existing range of human characters; and we have described several other motivation selection methods. The control problem may also in some ways be simplified by the current assumption that the new machine intelligence enters into a stable socioeconomic matrix that is already populated with other law-abiding superintelligent agents.

Let us, then, consider the plight of the working-class machine, whether it be operating as a slave or a free agent. We focus first on emulations, the easiest case to imagine.

Bringing a new biological human worker into the world takes anywhere between fifteen and thirty years, depending on how much expertise and experience is required. During this time the new person must be fed, housed, nurtured, and educated—at great expense. By contrast, spawning a new copy of a digital worker is as easy as loading a new program into working memory. Life thus becomes cheap. A business could continuously adapt its workforce to fit demands by spawning new copies— and terminating copies that are no longer needed, to free up computer resources. This could lead to an extremely high death rate among digital workers. Many might live for only one subjective day.

There are reasons other than fluctuations in demand why employers or owners of emulations might want to "kill" or "end" their workers frequently.[18] If an emulation mind, like a biological mind, requires periods of rest and sleep in order to function, it might be cheaper to erase a fatigued emulation at the end of a day and replace it with a stored state of a fresh and rested emulation. As this procedure would cause retrograde amnesia for everything that had been learned during that day, emulations performing tasks requiring long cognitive threads would be spared such frequent erasure. It would be difficult, for example, to write a book if each morning when one sat down at one's desk, one had no memory of what one had done before. But other jobs could be performed adequately by agents that are frequently recycled: a shop assistant or a customer service agent, once trained, may only need to remember new information for twenty minutes.

Since recycling emulations would prevent memory and skill formation, some emulations may be placed on a special learning track where they would run continuously, including for rest and sleep, even in jobs that do not strictly require long cognitive threads. For example, some customer service agents might run for many years in optimized learning environments, assisted by coaches and performance evaluators. The best of these trainees would then be used like studs, serving as templates from which millions of fresh copies are stamped out each day. Great effort would be poured into improving the performance of such worker templates, because even a small increment in productivity would yield great economic value when applied in millions of copies.

In parallel with efforts to train worker-templates for particular jobs, intense efforts would also be made to improve the underlying emulation technology. Advances here would be even more valuable than advances in individual worker-templates, since general technology improvements could be applied to all emulation workers (and potentially to non-worker emulations also) rather than only to those in a particular occupation. Enormous resources would be devoted to finding computational shortcuts allowing for more efficient implementations of existing emulations, and also into developing neuromorphic and entirely synthetic AI architectures. This research would probably mostly be done by emulations running on very fast hardware. Depending on the price of computer power, millions, billions, or trillions of emulations of the sharpest human research minds (or enhanced versions thereof) may be working around the clock on advancing the frontier of machine intelligence; and some of these may be operating orders of magnitude faster than biological brains.[19] This is a good reason for thinking that the era of human-like emulations would be brief—a *very* brief interlude in sidereal time—and that it would soon give way to an era of greatly superior artificial intelligence.

We have already encountered several reasons why employers of emulation workers may periodically cull their herds: fluctuations in demand for different kinds of laborers, cost savings of not having to emulate rest and sleep time, and the introduction of new and improved templates. Security concerns might furnish another reason. To prevent workers from developing subversive plans and conspiracies, emulations in some sensitive positions might be run only for limited periods, with frequent resets to an earlier stored ready-state.[20]

These ready-states to which emulations would be reset would be carefully prepared and vetted. A typical short-lived emulation might wake up in a well-rested mental state that is optimized for loyalty and productivity. He remembers having graduated top of his class after many (subjective) years of intense training and selection, then having enjoyed a restorative holiday and a good night's sleep, then having listened to a rousing motivational speech and stirring music, and now he is champing at the bit to finally get to work and to do his utmost for his employer. He is not overly troubled by thoughts of his imminent death at the end of the working day. Emulations with death neuroses or other hang-ups are less productive and would not have been selected.[21]

Would maximally efficient work be fun?

One important variable in assessing the desirability of a hypothetical condition like this is the hedonic state of the average emulation.[22] Would a typical emulation worker be suffering or would he be enjoying the experience of working hard on the task at hand?

We must resist the temptation to project our own sentiments onto the imaginary emulation worker. The question is not whether *you* would feel happy if you had to work constantly and never again spend time with your loved ones—a terrible fate, most would agree.

It is moderately more relevant to consider the current human average hedonic experience during working hours. Worldwide studies asking respondents how happy they are find that most rate themselves as "quite happy" or "very happy" (averaging 3.1 on a scale from 1 to 4).[23] Studies on average affect, asking respondents how frequently they have recently experienced various positive or negative affective states, tend to get a similar result (producing a net affect of about 0.52 on a scale from −1 to

1). There is a modest positive effect of a country's per capita income on average subjective well-being.[24] However, it is hazardous to extrapolate from these findings to the hedonic state of future emulation workers. One reason that could be given for this is that their condition would be so different: on the one hand, they might be working much harder; on the other hand, they might be free from diseases, aches, hunger, noxious odors, and so forth. Yet such considerations largely miss the mark. The much more important consideration here is that hedonic tone would be easy to adjust through the digital equivalent of drugs or neurosurgery. This means that it would be a mistake to infer the hedonic state of future emulations from the external conditions of their lives by imagining how we ourselves and other people like us would feel in those circumstances. Hedonic state would be a matter of choice. In the model we are currently considering, the choice would be made by capital-owners seeking to maximize returns on their investment in emulation-workers. Consequently, the question of how happy emulations would feel boils down to the question of which hedonic states would be most productive (in the various jobs that emulations would be employed to do).

Here, again, one might seek to draw an inference from observations about human happiness. If it is the case, across most times, places, and occupations, that people are typically at least moderately happy, this would create some presumption in favor of the same holding in a post-transition scenario like the one we are considering. To be clear, the argument in this case would not be that human minds have a predisposition towards happiness so they would probably find satisfaction under these novel conditions; but rather that a certain average level of happiness has proved adaptive for human minds in the past so maybe a similar level of happiness will prove adaptive for human-like minds in the future. Yet this formulation also reveals the weakness of the inference: to wit, that the mental dispositions that were adaptive for hunter–gatherer hominids roaming the African savanna may not necessarily be adaptive for modified emulations living in post-transition virtual realities. We can certainly *hope* that the future emulation-workers would be as happy as, or happier than, typical workers were in human history; but we have yet to see any compelling reason for supposing it would be so (in the laissez-faire multipolar scenario currently under examination).

Consider the possibility that the reason happiness is prevalent among humans (to whatever limited extent it is prevalent) is that cheerful mood served a signaling function in the environment of evolutionary adaptedness. Conveying the impression to other members of the social group of being in flourishing condition—in good health, in good standing with one's peers, and in confident expectation of continued good fortune—may have boosted an individual's popularity. A bias toward cheerfulness could thus have been selected for, with the result that human neurochemistry is now biased toward positive affect compared to what would have been maximally efficient according to simpler materialistic criteria. If this were the case, then the future of *joie de vivre* might depend on cheer retaining its social signaling function unaltered in the post-transition world: an issue to which we will return shortly.

What if glad souls dissipate more energy than glum ones? Perhaps the joyful are more prone to creative leaps and flights of fancy—behaviors that future employers might disprize in most of their workers. Perhaps a sullen or anxious fixation on simply getting on with the job without making mistakes will be the productivity-maximizing attitude in most lines of work. The claim here is not that this is so, but that we do not know that it is not so. Yet we should consider just how bad it could be if some such pessimistic hypothesis about a future Malthusian state turned out to be true: not only because of the opportunity cost of having failed to create something better—which would be enormous—but also because the state could be bad in itself, possibly far worse than the original Malthusian state.

We seldom put forth full effort. When we do, it is sometimes painful. Imagine running on a treadmill at a steep incline—heart pounding, muscles aching, lungs gasping for air. A glance at the timer: your next break, which will also be your death, is due in 49 years, 3 months, 20 days, 4 hours, 56 minutes, and 12 seconds. You wish you had not been born.

Again the claim is not that this is how it would be, but that we do not know that it is not. One could certainly make a more optimistic case. For example, there is no obvious reason that emulations would need to suffer bodily injury and sickness: the elimination of physical wretchedness would be a great improvement over the present state of affairs. Furthermore, since such stuff as virtual reality is made of can be fairly cheap, emulations may work in sumptuous surroundings—in splendid mountaintop palaces, on terraces set in a budding spring forest, or on the beaches of an azure lagoon—with just the right illumination, temperature, scenery and décor; free from annoying fumes, noises, drafts, and buzzing insects;

dressed in comfortable clothing, feeling clean and focused, and well nourished. More significantly, if—as seems perfectly possible—the optimum human mental state for productivity in most jobs is one of joyful eagerness, then the era of the emulation economy could be quite paradisiacal.

There would, in any case, be a great option value in arranging matters in such a manner that somebody or something could intervene to set things right if the default trajectory should happen to veer toward dystopia. It could also be desirable to have some sort of escape hatch that would permit bailout into death and oblivion if the quality of life were to sink permanently below the level at which annihilation becomes preferable to continued existence.

Unconscious outsourcers?

In the longer run, as the emulation era gives way to an artificial intelligence era (or if machine intelligence is attained directly via AI without a preceding whole brain emulation stage) pain and pleasure might possibly disappear entirely in a multipolar outcome, since a hedonic reward mechanism may not be the most effective motivation system for a complex artificial agent (one that, unlike the human mind, is not burdened with the legacy of animal wetware). Perhaps a more advanced motivation system would be based on an explicit representation of a utility function or some other architecture that has no exact functional analogs to pleasure and pain.

A related but slightly more radical multipolar outcome—one that could involve the elimination of almost all value from the future—is that the universal proletariat would not even be conscious. This possibility is most salient with respect to AI, which might be structured very differently than human intelligence. But even if machine intelligence were initially achieved through whole brain emulation, resulting in conscious digital minds, the competitive forces unleashed in a post-transition economy could easily lead to the emergence of progressively less neuromorphic forms of machine intelligence, either because synthetic AI is created *de novo* or because the emulations would, through successive modifications and enhancements, increasingly depart their original human form.

Consider a scenario in which, after emulation technology has been developed, continued progress in neuroscience and computer science (expedited by the presence of digital minds to serve as both researchers and test subjects) makes it possible to isolate individual cognitive modules in an emulation, and to hook them up to modules isolated from other emulations. A period of training and adjustment may be required before different modules can collaborate effectively; but modules that conform to common standards could more quickly interface with other standard modules. This would make standardized modules more productive, and create pressure for more standardization.

Emulations can now begin to outsource increasing portions of their functionality. Why learn arithmetic when you can send your numerical reasoning task to Gauss-Modules, Inc.? Why be articulate when you can hire Coleridge Conversations to put your thoughts into words? Why make decisions about your personal life when there are certified executive modules that can scan your goal system and manage your resources to achieve your goals better than if you tried to do it yourself? Some emulations may prefer to retain most of their functionality and handle tasks themselves that could be done more efficiently by others. Those emulations would be like hobbyists who enjoy growing their own vegetables or knitting their own cardigans. Such hobbyist emulations would be less efficient; and if there is a net flow of resources from less to more efficient participants of the economy, the hobbyists would eventually lose out.

The bouillon cubes of discrete human-like intellects thus melt into an algorithmic soup.

It is conceivable that optimal efficiency would be attained by grouping capabilities in aggregates that roughly match the cognitive architecture of a human mind. It might be the case, for example, that a mathematics module must be tailored to a language module, and that both must be tailored to the executive module, in order for the three to work together. Cognitive outsourcing would then be almost entirely unworkable. But in the absence of any compelling reason for being confident that this is so, we must countenance the possibility that human-like cognitive architectures are optimal only within the constraints of human neurology (or not at all). When it becomes possible to build architectures that could not be implemented well on biological neural networks, new design space opens up; and the global optima in this extended space need not resemble familiar types of mentality. Human-like cognitive organizations would then lack a niche in a competitive post-transition economy or ecosystem.[25]

There might be niches for complexes that are either less complex (such as individual modules), more complex (such as vast clusters of modules), or of similar complexity to human minds but with radically different architectures. Would these complexes have any intrinsic value? Should we welcome a world in which such alien complexes have replaced human complexes?

The answer may depend on the specific nature of those alien complexes. The present world has many levels of organization. Some highly complex entities, such as multinational corporations and nation states, contain human beings as constituents; yet we usually assign these high-level complexes only instrumental value. Corporations and states do not (it is generally assumed) have consciousness, over and above the consciousness of the people who constitute them: they cannot feel phenomenal pain or pleasure or experience any qualia. We value them to the extent that they serve human needs, and when they cease to do so we "kill" them without compunction. There are also lower-level entities, and those, too, are usually denied moral status. We see no harm in erasing an app from a smartphone, and we do not think that a neurosurgeon is wronging anyone when she extirpates a malfunctioning module from an epileptic brain. As for exotically organized complexes of a level similar to that of the human brain, most of us would perhaps judge them to have moral significance only if we thought they had a capacity or potential for conscious experience.[26]

We could thus imagine, as an extreme case, a technologically highly advanced society, containing many complex structures, some of them far more intricate and intelligent than anything that exists on the planet today—a society which nevertheless lacks any type of being that is conscious or whose welfare has moral significance. In a sense, this would be an uninhabited society. It would be a society of economic miracles and technological awesomeness, with nobody there to benefit. A Disneyland without children.

Evolution is not necessarily up

The word "evolution" is often used as a synonym of "progress," perhaps reflecting a common uncritical image of evolution as a force for good. A misplaced faith in the inherent beneficence of the evolutionary process can get in the way of a fair evaluation of the desirability of a multipolar outcome in which the future of intelligent life is determined by competitive dynamics. Any such evaluation must rest on some (at least implicit) opinion about the probability distribution of different phenotypes turning out to be adaptive in a post-transition digital life soup. It would be difficult in the best of circumstances to extract a clear and correct answer from the unavoidable goo of uncertainty that pervades these matters: more so, if we superadd a layer of Panglossian muck.

A possible source for faith in freewheeling evolution is the apparent upward directionality exhibited by the evolutionary process in the past. Starting from rudimentary replicators, evolution produced increasingly "advanced" organisms, including creatures with minds, consciousness, language, and reason. More recently, cultural and technological processes, which bear some loose similarities to biological evolution, have enabled humans to develop at an accelerated pace. On a geological as well as a historical timescale, the big picture seems to show an overarching trend toward increasing levels of complexity, knowledge, consciousness, and coordinated goal-directed organization: a trend which, not to put too fine a point on it, one might label "progress."[27]

The image of evolution as a process that reliably produces benign effects is difficult to reconcile with the enormous suffering that we see in both the human and the natural world. Those who cherish evolution's achievements may do so more from an aesthetic than an ethical perspective. Yet the pertinent question is not what kind of future it would be fascinating to read about in a science fiction novel or to see depicted in a nature documentary, but what kind of future it would be good to live in: two very different matters.

Furthermore, we have no reason to think that whatever progress there has been was in any way inevitable. Much might have been luck. This objection derives support from the fact that an observation selection effect filters the evidence we can have about the success of our own evolutionary development.[28] Suppose that on 99.9999% of all planets where life emerged it went extinct before developing to the point where intelligent observers could begin to ponder their origin. What should we expect to observe if that were the case? Arguably, we should expect to observe something like what we do in fact observe. The hypothesis that the odds of intelligent life evolving on a given planet are low does not predict that we should find ourselves on a planet where life went extinct at an early stage; rather, it may predict that we should find ourselves on a planet where intelligent life evolved, even if such planets constitute a very small fraction of all planets where primitive life evolved. Life's long track record on Earth may therefore offer scant support to the claim that there was a high chance—let alone anything approaching inevitability—involved in the rise of higher organisms on our planet.[29]

Thirdly, even if present conditions had been idyllic, and even if they could have been shown to have arisen ineluctably from some generic primordial state, there would still be no guarantee that the melioristic trend is set to continue into the indefinite future. This holds even if we disregard the possibility of a cataclysmic extinction event and indeed even if we assume that evolutionary developments will continue to produce systems of increasing complexity.

We suggested earlier that machine intelligence workers selected for maximum productivity would be working extremely hard and that it is unknown how happy such workers would be. We also raised the possibility that the fittest life forms within a competitive future digital life soup might not even be conscious. Short of a complete loss of pleasure, or of consciousness, there could be a wasting away of other qualities that many would regard as indispensible for a good life. Humans value music, humor, romance, art, play, dance, conversation, philosophy, literature, adventure, discovery, food and drink, friendship, parenting, sport, nature, tradition, and spirituality, among many other things. There is no guarantee that any of these would remain adaptive. Perhaps what will maximize fitness will be nothing but nonstop high-intensity drudgery, work of a drab and repetitive nature, destitute of ludic frisson, aimed only at improving the eighth decimal place of some economic output measure. The phenotypes selected would then have lives lacking in the aforesaid qualities, and depending on one's axiology the result might strike one as either abhorrent, worthless, or merely impoverished, but at any rate a far cry from a utopia one would feel worthy of one's commendation.

It might be wondered how such a bleak picture could be consistent with the fact that we do now indulge in music, humor, romance, art, etc. If these behaviors are really so "wasteful," then how come they have been tolerated and indeed promoted by the evolutionary processes that shaped our species? That modern man is in an evolutionary disequilibrium does not account for this; for our Pleistocene forebears, too, engaged in most of these dissipations. Many of the behaviors in question are not even unique to *Homo sapiens*. Flamboyant display is found in a wide variety of contexts, from sexual selection in the animal kingdom to prestige contests among nation states.[30]

Although a full evolutionary explanation for each of these behaviors is beyond the scope of the present inquiry, we can note that some of them serve functions that may not be as relevant in a machine intelligence context. Play, for example, which occurs only in some species and predominantly among juveniles, is mainly a way for the young animal to learn skills that it will need later in life. When emulations can be created as adults, already in possession of a mature repertoire of skills, or when knowledge and techniques acquired by one AI can be directly ported into another AI, the need for playful behavior might become less widespread.

Many of the other examples of humanistic behaviors may have evolved as hard-to-fake signals of qualities that are difficult to observe directly, such as bodily or mental resilience, social status, quality of allies, ability and willingness to prevail in a fight, or possession of resources. The peacock's tail is the classic instance: only fit peacocks can afford to sprout truly extravagant plumage, and peahens have evolved to find it attractive. No less than morphological traits, behavioral traits too can signal genetic fitness or other socially relevant attributes.[31]

Given that flamboyant display is so common among both humans and other species, one might consider whether it would not also be part of the repertoire of technologically more advanced life forms. Even if there were to be no narrowly instrumental use for playfulness or musicality or even for consciousness in the future ecology of intelligent information processing, might not these traits nonetheless confer some evolutionary advantage to their possessors by virtue of being reliable signals of other adaptive qualities?

While the possibility of a pre-established harmony between what is valuable to us and what would be adaptive in a future digital ecology is hard to rule out, there are reasons for skepticism. Consider, first, that many of the costly displays we find in nature are linked to sexual selection.[32] Reproduction among technologically mature life forms, in contrast, may be predominantly or exclusively asexual.

Second, technologically advanced agents might have available new means of reliably communicating information about themselves, means that do not rely on costly display. Even today, when professional lenders assess creditworthiness they tend to rely more on documentary evidence, such as ownership certificates and bank statements, than on costly displays, such as designer suits and Rolex watches. In the future, it might be possible to employ auditing firms that verify through detailed examination of behavioral track records, testing in simulated environments, or direct inspection of source code, that a client agent possesses a claimed attribute. Signaling one's qualities by agreeing to such auditing might be more efficient than signaling via flamboyant display. Such a professionally mediated signal would still be costly to *fake*—this being the essential feature that makes the signal reliable—but it could be much cheaper to transmit when *truthful* than it would be to communicate an equivalent signal flamboyantly.

Third, not all possible costly displays are intrinsically valuable or socially desirable. Many are simply wasteful. The Kwakiutl potlatch ceremonies, a form of status competition between rival chiefs, involved the public destruction of vast amounts of accumulated wealth.[33] Record-breaking skyscrapers, megayachts, and moon rockets may be viewed as contemporary analogs. While activities like music and humor could plausibly be claimed to enhance the intrinsic quality of human life, it is doubtful that a similar claim could be sustained with regard to the costly pursuit of fashion accessories and other consumerist status symbols. Worse, costly display can be outright harmful, as in macho posturing leading to gang violence or military bravado. Even if future intelligent life forms would use costly signaling, therefore, it is an open question whether the signal would be of a valuable sort—whether it would be like the rapturous melody of a nightingale or instead like the toad's monosyllabic croak (or the incessant barking of a rabid dog).

Post-transition formation of a singleton?

Even if the immediate outcome of the transition to machine intelligence were multipolar, the possibility would remain of a singleton developing later. Such a development would continue an apparent long-term trend toward larger scales of political integration, taking it to its natural conclusion.[34] How might this occur?

A second transition

One way in which an initially multipolar outcome could converge into a singleton post-transition is if there is, after the initial transition, a second technological transition big enough and steep enough to give a decisive strategic advantage to one of the remaining powers: a power which might then seize the opportunity to establish a singleton. Such a hypothetical second transition might be occasioned by a breakthrough to a higher level of superintelligence. For instance, if the first wave of machine superintelligence is emulation-based, then a second surge might result when the emulations now doing the research succeed in developing effective self-improving artificial intelligence.[35] (Alternatively, a second transition might be triggered by a breakthrough in nanotechnology or some other military or general-purpose technology as yet unenvisaged.)

The pace of development after the initial transition would be extremely rapid. Even a short gap between the leading power and its closest competitor could therefore plausibly result in a decisive strategic advantage for the leading power during a second transition. Suppose, for example, that two projects enter the first transition only a few days apart, and that the takeoff is slow enough that this gap does not give the leading project a decisive strategic advantage at any point during the takeoff. The two projects both emerge as superintelligent powers, though one of them remains a few days ahead of the other. But developments are now occurring on the research timescales characteristic of machine superintelligence—perhaps thousands or millions of times faster than research conducted on a biological human timescale. Development of the second-transition technology might therefore be completed in days, hours, or minutes. Even though the front-runner's lead is a mere few days, a breakthrough could thus catapult it into a decisive strategic advantage. Note, however, that if technological diffusion (via espionage or other channels) speeds up as much as technological development, then this effect would be negated. What would remain relevant would be the steepness of the second transition, that is, the speed at which it would unfold relative to the general speed of events in the period after the first transition. (In this sense, the faster things are happening after the first transition, the less steep the second transition would tend to be.)

One might also speculate that a decisive strategic advantage would be more likely to be actually used to establish a singleton if it arises during a second (or subsequent) transition. After the first transition, decision makers would either be superintelligent or have access to advice from a superintelligence, which would clarify the implications of available strategic options. Furthermore, the situation after the first transition might be one in which a preemptive move against potential competitors would be less dangerous for the aggressor. If the decision-making minds after the first transition are digital, they could be copied and thereby rendered less vulnerable to a counterattack. Even if a defender had the ability to kill nine-tenths of the aggressor's population in a retaliatory strike, this would scarcely offer much deterrence if the deceased could be immediately resurrected from redundant backups. Devastation of infrastructure (which can be rebuilt) might also be tolerable to digital minds with effectively unlimited lifespans, who might be planning to maximize their resources and influence on a cosmological timescale.

Superorganisms and scale economies

The size of coordinated human aggregates, such as firms or nations, is influenced by various parameters—technological, military, financial, and cultural—that can vary from one historical epoch to another. A machine intelligence revolution would entail profound changes in many of these parameters. Perhaps these changes would facilitate the rise of a singleton. Although we cannot, without looking in detail at what these prospective changes are, exclude the opposite possibility—that the changes would facilitate fragmentation rather than unification—we can nevertheless note that the increased variance or uncertainty that we confront here may itself be a ground for giving greater credence to the potential emergence of a singleton than we would otherwise do. A machine intelligence revolution might, so to speak, stir things up—might reshuffle the deck to make possible geopolitical realignments that seemed perhaps otherwise not to have been in the cards.

A comprehensive analysis of all the factors that may influence the scale of political integration would take us far beyond the scope of this book: a review of the relevant political science and economics literature could itself easily fill an entire volume. We must confine ourselves to making brief allusion to a couple of factors, aspects of the digitization of agents that may make it easier to centralize control.

Carl Shulman has argued that in a population of emulations, selection pressures would favor the emergence of "superorganisms," groups of emulations ready to sacrifice themselves for the good of their clan.[36] Superorganisms would be spared the agency problems that beset organizations whose members pursue their own self-interest. Like the cells in our bodies, or the individual animals in a colony of eusocial insects, emulations that were wholly altruistic toward their copy-siblings would cooperate with one another even in the absence of elaborate incentive schemes.

Superorganisms would have a particularly strong advantage if non-consensual deletion (or indefinite suspension) of individual emulations is disallowed. Firms or countries that employ emulations insisting on self-preservation would be saddled with an unending commitment to pay upkeep for obsolete or redundant workers. In contrast, organizations whose emulations willingly deleted themselves when their services were no longer required could more easily adapt to fluctuations in demand; and they could experiment freely, proliferating variations of their workers and retaining only the most productive.

If involuntary deletion is *not* disallowed, then the comparative advantage of eusocial emulations is reduced, though perhaps not eliminated. Employers of cooperative self-sacrificers might still reap efficiency gains from reduced agency problems throughout the organization, including being spared the trouble of having to defeat whatever resistance emulations could put up against their own deletion. In general, the productivity gains of having workers willing to sacrifice their individual lives for the common weal are a special case of the benefits an organization can derive from having members who are fanatically devoted to it. Such members would not only leap into the grave for the organization, and work long hours for little pay: they would also shun office politics and try consistently to act in what they took to be the organization's best interest, reducing the need for supervision and bureaucratic constraints.

If the only way to achieve such dedication were by restricting membership to copy-siblings (so that all emulations in a particular superorganism were stamped out from the same template), then superorganisms would suffer some disadvantage in being able to draw only from a range of skills narrower than that of rival organizations, a disadvantage which might or might not be large enough to outweigh the advantages of avoiding internal agency problems.[37] This disadvantage would be greatly alleviated if a superorganism could at least contain members with different training. Even if all its members were derived from a single ur-template, its workforce could then still contribute a diversity of skills. Starting with a polymathically talented emulation ur-template, lineages could be branched off into different training programs, one copy learning accounting, another electrical engineering, and so forth. This would produce a membership with diverse skills though not of diverse talents. (Maximum diversity might require that more than one ur-template be used.)

The essential property of a superorganism is not that it consists of copies of a single progenitor but that all the individual agents within it are fully committed to a common goal. The ability to create a superorganism can thus be viewed as requiring a partial solution to the control problem. Whereas a completely general solution to the control problem would enable somebody to create an agent with any arbitrary final goal, the partial solution needed for the creation of a superorganism requires merely the ability to fashion multiple agents with the same final goal (for some non-trivial but not necessarily arbitrary final goal).[38]

The main consideration put forward in this subsection is thus not really limited to monoclonal emulation groups, but can be stated more generally in a way that makes clear that it applies to a wide range of multipolar machine intelligence scenarios. It is that certain types of advances in motivation selection techniques, which may become feasible when the actors are digital, may help overcome some of the inefficiencies that currently hamper large human organizations and that counterbalance economies of scale. With these limits lifted, organizations—be they firms, nations, or other economic or political entities—could increase in size. This is one factor that could facilitate the emergence of a post-transition singleton.

One area in which superorganisms (or other digital agents with partially selected motivations) might excel is coercion. A state might use motivation selection methods to ensure that its police, military, intelligence service, and civil administration are uniformly loyal. As Shulman notes:

Saved states [of some loyal emulation that has been carefully prepared and verified] could be copied billions of times to staff an ideologically uniform military, bureaucracy, and police force. After a short period of work, each copy would be replaced by a fresh copy of the same saved state, preventing ideological drift. Within a given jurisdiction, this capability could allow incredibly detailed observation and regulation: there might be one such copy for every other resident. This could be used to prohibit the development of weapons of mass destruction, to enforce regulations on brain emulation experimentation or reproduction, to enforce a liberal democratic constitution, or to create an appalling and permanent totalitarianism[39]

The first-order effect of such a capability would seem to be to consolidate power, and possibly to concentrate it in fewer hands.

Unification by treaty

There may be large potential gains to be had from international collaboration in a post-transition multipolar world. Wars and arms races could be avoided. Astrophysical resources could be colonized and harvested at a globally optimum pace. The development of more advanced forms of machine intelligence could be coordinated to avoid a rush and to allow new designs to be thoroughly vetted. Other developments that might pose existential risks could be postponed. And uniform regulations could be enforced globally, including provisions for a guaranteed standard of living (which would require some form of population control) and for preventing exploitation and abuse of emulations and other digital and biological minds. Furthermore, agents with resource-satiable preferences (more on this in Chapter 13) would prefer a sharing agreement that would guarantee them a certain slice of the future to a winner-takes-all struggle in which they would risk getting nothing.

The presence of big potential gains from collaboration, however, does not imply that collaboration will actually be achieved. In the world today, many great boons could be obtained via better global coordination—reductions of military expenditures, wars, overfishing, trade barriers, and atmospheric pollution, among others. Yet these plump fruits are left to spoil on the branch. Why is that? What stops a fully cooperative outcome that would maximize the common good?

One obstacle is the difficulty of ensuring compliance with any treaty that might be agreed, including monitoring and enforcement costs. Two nuclear rivals might each be better off if they both relinquished their atom bombs; yet even if they could reach an in-principle agreement to do so, disarmament could nevertheless prove elusive because of their mutual fear that the other party might cheat. Allaying this fear would require setting up a verification mechanism. There may have to be inspectors to oversee the destruction of existing stockpiles, and then to monitor nuclear reactors and other facilities, and to gather technical and human intelligence, in order to ensure that the weapons program is not reconstituted. One cost is paying for these inspectors. Another cost is the risk that the inspectors will spy and make off with commercial or military secrets. Perhaps most significantly, each party might fear that the other will preserve a clandestine nuclear capability. Many a potentially beneficial deal never comes off because compliance would be too difficult to verify.

If new inspection technologies that reduced monitoring costs became available, one would expect this to result in increased cooperation. Whether monitoring costs would on net be reduced in the post-transition era, however, is not entirely clear. While there would certainly be many powerful new inspection techniques, there would also be new means of concealment. In particular, an increasing portion of the activities one might want to regulate would be taking place in cyberspace, out of reach of physical surveillance. For example, digital minds working on designing a new nanotech weapons system or a new generation of artificial intelligence may do so without leaving much of a physical footprint. Digital forensics may fail to penetrate all the layers of concealment and encryption in which a treaty-violator may cloak its illicit activities.

Reliable lie detection, if it could be developed, would be an extremely useful tool for monitoring compliance.[40] An inspection protocol could include provisions for interviewing key officials, to verify that they are intent on implementing all the provisions of the treaty and that they know of no violations despite making strong efforts to find out.

A decision maker planning to cheat might defeat such a lie-detection-based verification scheme by first issuing orders to subordinates to undertake the illicit activity and to conceal the activity even from the decision maker herself, and then subjecting herself to some procedure that erases her memory of having engaged in these machinations. Suitably targeted memory-erasure operations might well be feasible in biological brains with more advanced neurotechnology. It might be even easier in machine intelligences (depending on their architecture).

States could seek to overcome this problem by committing themselves to an ongoing monitoring scheme that regularly tests key officials with a lie detector to check whether they harbor any intent to subvert or circumvent any treaty into which the state has entered or may enter in the future. Such a commitment could be viewed as a kind of meta-treaty, which would facilitate the verification of other treaties; but states might commit themselves to it unilaterally to gain the benefit of being regarded as a trustworthy negotiation partner. However, this commitment or meta-treaty would face the same problem of subversion through a delegate-and-forget ploy. Ideally, the meta-treaty would be put into effect *before* any party had an opportunity to make the internal arrangements necessary to subvert its implementation. Once villainy has had an unguarded moment to sow its mines of deception, trust can never set foot there again.

In some cases, the mere ability to *detect* treaty violations is sufficient to establish the confidence needed for a deal. In other cases, however, there is a need for some mechanism to *enforce* compliance or mete out punishment if a violation should occur. The need for an enforcement mechanism may arise if the threat of the wronged party withdrawing from the treaty is not enough to deter violations, for instance if the treaty-violator would gain such an advantage that he would not subsequently care how the other party responds.

If highly effective motivation selection methods are available, this enforcement problem could be solved by empowering an independent agency with sufficient police or military strength to enforce the treaty even against the opposition of one or several of its signatories. This solution requires that the enforcement agency can be trusted. But with sufficiently good motivation selection techniques, the requisite confidence might be achieved by having all the parties to the treaty jointly oversee the design of the enforcement agency.

Handing over power to an external enforcement agency raises many of the same issues that we confronted earlier in our discussions of a unipolar outcome (one in which a singleton arises prior to or during the initial machine intelligence revolution). In order to be able to enforce treaties concerning the vital security interests of rival states, the external enforcement agency would in effect need to constitute a singleton: a global superintelligent Leviathan. One difference, however, is that we are now considering a post-transition situation, in which the agents that would have to create this Leviathan would have greater competence than we humans currently do. These Leviathan-creators may themselves already be superintelligent. This would greatly improve the odds that they could solve the control problem and design an enforcement agency that would serve the interests of all the parties that have a say in its construction.

Aside from the costs of monitoring and enforcing compliance, are there any other obstacles to global coordination? Perhaps the major remaining issue is what we can refer to as *bargaining costs*.[41] Even when there is a possible bargain that would benefit everybody involved, it sometimes does not get off the ground because the parties fail to agree on how to divide the spoils. For example, if two persons could make a deal that would net them a dollar in profit, but each party feels she deserves sixty cents and refuses to settle for less, the deal will not happen and the potential gain will be forfeited. In general, negotiations can be difficult or protracted, or remain altogether barren, because of strategic bargaining choices made by some of the parties.

In real life, human beings frequently succeed in reaching agreements despite the possibility for strategic bargaining (though often not without considerable expenditure of time and patience). It is conceivable, however, that strategic bargaining problems would have a different dynamic in the post-transition era. An AI negotiator might more consistently adhere to some particular formal conception of rationality, possibly with novel or unanticipated consequences when matched with other AI negotiators. An AI might also have available to it moves in the bargaining game that are either unavailable to humans or very much more difficult for humans to execute, including the ability to precommit to a policy or a course of action. While humans (and human-run institutions) are occasionally able to precommit—with imperfect degrees of credibility and specificity—some types of machine intelligence might be able to make arbitrary unbreakable precommitments and to allow negotiating partners to confirm that such a precommitment has been made.[42]

The availability of powerful precommitment techniques could profoundly alter the nature of negotiations, potentially giving an immense edge to an agent that has a first-mover advantage. If a particular agent's participation is necessary for the realization of some prospective gains from cooperation, and if that agent is able to make the first move, it would be in a position to dictate the division of the spoils by precommitting not to accept any deal that gives it less than, say, 99% of the surplus value. Other agents would then be faced with the choice of either getting nothing (by rejecting the unfair proposal) or getting 1% of the value (by caving in). If the first-moving agent's precommitment is publicly verifiable, its negotiating partners could be sure that these are their only two options.

To avoid being exploited in this manner, agents might precommit to refuse blackmail and to decline all unfair offers. Once such a precommitment has been made (and successfully publicized), other agents would not find it in their interest to make threats or to precommit themselves to only accepting deals tilted in their own favor, because they would know that threats would fail and that unfair proposals would be rejected. But this just demonstrates again that the advantage is with the first-mover. The agent who moves first can choose whether to parlay its position of strength only to deter others from taking unfair advantage, or to make a grab for the lion's share of future spoils.

Best situated of all, it might seem, would be the agent who starts out with a temperament or a value system that makes him impervious to extortion or indeed to any offer of a deal in which his participation is indispensable but he is not getting almost all of the gains. Some humans seem already to possess personality traits corresponding to various aspects of an uncompromising spirit.[43] A high-strung disposition, however, could backfire should it turn out that there are other agents around who feel entitled to more than their fair share and are committed to not backing down. The unstoppable force would then encounter the unmovable object, resulting in a failure to reach agreement (or worse: total war). The meek and the akratic would at least get something, albeit less than their fair share.

What kind of game-theoretic equilibrium would be reached in such a post-transition bargaining game is not immediately obvious. Agents might choose more complicated strategies than the ones considered here. One *hopes* that an equilibrium would be reached centered on some fairness norm that would serve as a Schelling point—a salient feature in a big outcome space which, because of shared expectations, becomes a likely coordination point in an otherwise underdetermined coordination game. Such an equilibrium might be bolstered by some of our evolved dispositions and cultural programming: a common preference for fairness could, assuming we succeed in transferring our values into the post-transition era, bias expectations and strategies in ways that lead to an attractive equilibrium.[44]

In any case, the upshot is that with the possibility of strong and flexible forms of precommitment, outcomes of negotiations might take on an unfamiliar guise. Even if the post-transition era started out multipolar, it might be that a singleton would arise almost immediately as a consequence of a negotiated treaty that resolves all important global coordination problems. Some transaction costs, perhaps including monitoring and enforcement costs, might plummet with the new technological capabilities available to advanced machine intelligences. Other costs, in particular costs related to strategic bargaining, might remain significant. But however strategic bargaining affects the nature of the agreement that is reached, there is no clear reason why it would long delay the reaching of some agreement if an agreement were ever to be reached. If no agreement is reached, then some form of fighting might take place; and either one faction might win, and form a singleton around the winning coalition, or the result might be an interminable conflict, in which case a singleton may never form and the overall outcome may fall terribly short of what could and should have been achieved if humanity and its descendants had acted in a more coordinated and cooperative fashion.

* * *

We have seen that multipolarity, even if it could be achieved in a stable form, would not guarantee an attractive outcome. The original principal–agent problem remains unsolved, and burying it under a new set of problems related to post-transition global coordination failures may only make the situation worse. Let us therefore return to the question of how we could safely keep a single superintelligent AI.

CHAPTER 12

Acquiring values

Capability control is, at best, a temporary and auxiliary measure. Unless the plan is to keep superintelligence bottled up forever, it will be necessary to master motivation selection. But just how could we get some value into an artificial agent, so as to make it pursue that value as its final goal? While the agent is unintelligent, it might lack the capability to understand or even represent any humanly meaningful value. Yet if we delay the procedure until the agent is superintelligent, it may be able to resist our attempt to meddle with its motivation system—and, as we showed in Chapter 7, it would have convergent instrumental reasons to do so. This value-loading problem is tough, but must be confronted.

The value-loading problem

It is impossible to enumerate all possible situations a superintelligence might find itself in and to specify for each what action it should take. Similarly, it is impossible to create a list of all possible worlds and assign each of them a value. In any realm significantly more complicated than a game of tic-tac-toe, there are far too many possible states (and state-histories) for exhaustive enumeration to be feasible. A motivation system, therefore, cannot be specified as a comprehensive lookup table. It must instead be expressed more abstractly, as a formula or rule that allows the agent to decide what to do in any given situation.

One formal way of specifying such a decision rule is via a utility function. A utility function (as we recall from Chapter 1) assigns value to each outcome that might obtain, or more generally to each "possible world."

Given a utility function, one can define an agent that maximizes expected utility. Such an agent selects at each time the action that has the highest expected utility. (The expected utility is calculated by weighting the utility of each possible world with the subjective probability of that world being the actual world conditional on a particular action being taken.) In reality, the possible outcomes are too numerous for the expected utility of an action to be calculated exactly. Nevertheless, the decision rule and the utility function together determine a normative ideal—an optimality notion—that an agent might be designed to approximate; and the approximation might get closer as the agent gets more intelligent.[1] Creating a machine that can compute a good approximation of the expected utility of the actions available to it is an AI-complete problem.[2] This chapter addresses another problem, a problem that remains even if the problem of making machines intelligent is solved.

We can use this framework of a utility-maximizing agent to consider the predicament of a future seed-AI programmer who intends to solve the control problem by endowing the AI with a final goal that corresponds to some plausible human notion of a worthwhile outcome. The programmer has some particular human value in mind that he would like the AI to promote. To be concrete, let us say that it is happiness. (Similar issues would arise if we were interested in justice, freedom, glory, human rights, democracy, ecological balance, or self-development.) In terms of the expected utility framework, the programmer is thus looking for a utility function that assigns utility to possible worlds in proportion to the amount of happiness they contain. But how could he express such a utility function in computer code? Computer languages do not contain terms such as "happiness" as primitives. If such a term is to be used, it must first be defined. It is not enough to define it in terms of other high-level human concepts—"happiness is enjoyment of the potentialities inherent in our human nature" or some such philosophical paraphrase. The definition must bottom out in terms that appear in the AI's programming language, and ultimately in primitives such as mathematical operators and addresses pointing to the contents of individual memory registers. When one considers the problem from this perspective, one can begin to appreciate the difficulty of the programmer's task.

Identifying and codifying our own final goals is difficult because human goal representations are complex. Because the complexity is largely transparent to us, however, we often fail to appreciate that it is there. We can compare the case to visual perception. Vision, likewise, might seem like a simple thing, because we do it effortlessly.[3] We only need to open our eyes, so it seems, and a rich, meaningful, eidetic, three-dimensional view of the surrounding environment comes flooding into our minds. This intuitive understanding of vision is like a duke's understanding of his patriarchal household: as far as he is concerned, things simply appear at their appropriate times and places, while the mechanism that produces those manifestations are hidden from view. Yet accomplishing even the simplest visual task—finding the pepper jar in the kitchen—requires a tremendous amount of computational work. From a noisy time series of two-dimensional patterns of nerve firings, originating in the retina and conveyed to the brain via the optic nerve, the visual cortex must work backwards to reconstruct an interpreted three-dimensional representation of external space. A sizeable portion of our precious one square meter of cortical real estate is zoned for processing visual information, and as you are reading this book, billions of neurons are working ceaselessly to accomplish this task (like so many seamstresses, bent over their sewing machines in a sweatshop, sewing and re-sewing a giant quilt many times a second). In like manner, our seemingly simple values and wishes in fact contain immense complexity.[4] How could our programmer transfer this complexity into a utility function?

One approach would be to try to directly code a complete representation of whatever goal we have that we want the AI to pursue; in other words, to write out an explicit utility function. This approach might work if we had extraordinarily simple goals, for example if we wanted to calculate the digits of pi—that is, if the *only* thing we wanted was for the AI to calculate the digits of pi and we were indifferent to any other consequence that would result from the pursuit of this goal—recall our earlier discussion of the failure mode of infrastructure profusion. This explicit coding approach might also have some promise in the use of domesticity motivation selection methods. But if one seeks to promote or protect any plausible *human* value, and one is building a system intended to become a superintelligent sovereign, then explicitly coding the requisite complete goal representation appears to be hopelessly out of reach.[5]

If we cannot transfer human values into an AI by typing out full-blown representations in computer code, what else might we try? This chapter discusses several alternative paths. Some of these may look plausible at first sight—but much less so upon closer examination. Future explorations should focus on those paths that remain open.

Solving the value-loading problem is a research challenge worthy of some of the next generation's best mathematical talent. We cannot postpone confronting this problem until the AI has developed enough reason to easily understand our intentions. As we saw in the section on convergent instrumental reasons, a generic system will resist attempts to alter its final values. If an agent is not already fundamentally friendly by the time it gains the ability to reflect on its own agency, it will not take kindly to a belated attempt at brainwashing or a plot to replace it with a different agent that better loves its neighbor.

Evolutionary selection

Evolution has produced an organism with human values at least once. This fact might encourage the belief that evolutionary methods are the way to solve the value-loading problem. There are, however, severe obstacles to achieving safety along this path. We have already pointed to these obstacles at the end of Chapter 10 when we discussed how powerful search processes can be dangerous.

Evolution can be viewed as a particular class of search algorithms that involve the alternation of two steps, one expanding a population of solution candidates by generating new candidates according to some relatively simple stochastic rule (such as random mutation or sexual recombination), the other contracting the population by pruning candidates that score poorly when tested by an evaluation function. As with many other types of powerful search, there is the risk that the process will find a solution that satisfies the formally specified search criteria but not our implicit expectations. (This would hold whether one seeks to evolve a digital mind that has the same goals and values as a typical human being, or instead a mind that is, for instance, perfectly moral or perfectly obedient.) The risk would be avoided if we could specify a formal search criterion that accurately represented all dimensions of our goals, rather than just one aspect of what we think we desire. But this is precisely the value-loading problem, and it would of course beg the question in this context to assume that problem solved.

There is a further problem:

The total amount of suffering per year in the natural world is beyond all decent contemplation. During the minute that it takes me to compose this sentence, thousands of animals are being eaten alive, others are running for their lives, whimpering with fear, others are being slowly devoured from within by rasping parasites, thousands of all kinds are dying of starvation, thirst and disease.[6]

Even just within our species, 150,000 persons are destroyed each day while countless more suffer an appalling array of torments and deprivations.[7] Nature might be a great experimentalist, but one who would never pass muster with an ethics review board—contravening the Helsinki Declaration and every norm of moral decency, left, right, and center. It is important that we not gratuitously replicate such horrors *in silico*. Mind crime seems especially difficult to avoid when evolutionary methods are used to produce human-like intelligence, at least if the process is meant to look anything like actual biological evolution.[8]

Reinforcement learning

Reinforcement learning is an area of machine learning that studies techniques whereby agents can learn to maximize some notion of cumulative reward. By constructing an environment in which desired performance is rewarded, a reinforcement-learning agent can be made to learn to solve a wide class of problems (even in the absence of detailed instruction or feedback from the programmers, aside from the reward signal). Often, the learning algorithm involves the gradual construction of some kind of evaluation function, which assigns values to states, state–action pairs, or policies. (For instance, a program can learn to play backgammon by using reinforcement learning to incrementally improve its evaluation of possible board positions.) The evaluation function, which is continuously updated in light of experience, could be regarded as incorporating a form of learning about value. However, what is being learned is not new *final* values but increasingly accurate *estimates of the instrumental values* of reaching particular states (or of taking particular actions in particular states, or of following particular policies). Insofar as a reinforcement-learning agent can be described as having a final goal, that goal remains constant: to maximize future reward. And reward consists of specially designated percepts received from the environment. Therefore, the wireheading syndrome remains a likely outcome in any reinforcement agent that develops a world model sophisticated enough to suggest this alternative way of maximizing reward.[9]

These remarks do not imply that reinforcement-learning methods could never be used in a safe seed AI, only that they would have to be subordinated to a motivation system that is not itself organized around the principle of reward maximization. That, however, would require that a solution to the value-loading problem had been found by some other means than reinforcement learning.

Associative value accretion

Now one might wonder: if the value-loading problem is so tricky, how do we ourselves manage to acquire our values?

One possible (oversimplified) model might look something like this. We begin life with some relatively simple starting preferences (e.g. an aversion to noxious stimuli) together with a set of dispositions to acquire additional preferences in response to various possible experiences (e.g. we might be disposed to form a preference for objects and behaviors that we find to be valued and rewarded in our culture). Both the simple starting preferences and the dispositions are innate, having been shaped by natural and sexual selection over evolutionary timescales. Yet which preferences we end up with as adults depends on life events. Much of the information content in our final values is thus acquired from our experiences rather than preloaded in our genomes.

For example, many of us love another person and thus place great final value on his or her well-being. What is required to represent such a value? Many elements are involved, but consider just two: a representation of "person" and a representation of "well-being." These concepts are not directly coded in our DNA. Rather, the DNA contains instructions for building a brain, which, when placed in a typical human environment, will over the course of several years develop a world model that includes concepts of persons and of well-being. Once formed, these concepts can be used to represent certain meaningful values. But some mechanism needs to be innately present that leads to values being formed around *these* concepts, rather than around other acquired concepts (like that of a flowerpot or a corkscrew).

The details of how this mechanism works are not well understood. In humans, the mechanism is probably complex and multifarious. It is easier to understand the phenomenon if we consider it in a more rudimentary form, such as filial imprinting in nidifugous birds, where the newly hatched chick acquires a desire for physical proximity to an object that presents a suitable moving stimulus within the first day after hatching. Which particular object the chick desires to be near depends on its experience; only the general disposition to imprint in this way is genetically determined. Analogously, Harry might place a final value on Sally's well-being; but had the twain never met, he might have fallen in love with somebody else instead, and his final values would have been different. The ability of our genes to code for the construction of a goal-acquiring mechanism explains how we come to have final goals of great informational complexity, greater than could be contained in the genome itself.

We may consequently consider whether we might build the motivation system for an artificial intelligence on the same principle. That is, instead of specifying complex values directly, could we specify some mechanism that leads to the acquisition of those values when the AI interacts with a suitable environment?

Mimicking the value-accretion process that takes place in humans seems difficult. The relevant genetic mechanism in humans is the product of eons of work by evolution, work that might be hard to recapitulate. Moreover, the mechanism is presumably closely tailored to the human neurocognitive architecture and therefore not applicable in machine intelligences other than whole brain emulations. And if whole brain emulations of sufficient fidelity were available, it would seem easier to start with an adult brain that comes with full representations of some human values preloaded.[10]

Seeking to implement a process of value accretion closely mimicking that of human biology therefore seems an unpromising line of attack on the value-loading problem. But perhaps we might design a more unabashedly artificial substitute mechanism that would lead an AI to import high-fidelity representations of relevant complex values into its goal system? For this to succeed, it may not be necessary to give the AI exactly the same evaluative dispositions as a biological human. That may not even be desirable as an aim—human nature, after all, is flawed and all too often reveals a proclivity to evil which would be intolerable in any system poised to attain a decisive strategic advantage. Better, perhaps, to aim for a motivation system that departs from the human norm in systematic ways, such as by having a more robust tendency to acquire final goals that are altruistic, compassionate, or high-minded in ways we would recognize as reflecting exceptionally good character if they were present in a human person. To count as improvements, however, such deviations from the human norm would have to be pointed in very particular directions rather than at random; and they would continue to presuppose the existence of a largely undisturbed anthropocentric frame of reference to provide humanly meaningful evaluative generalizations (so as to avoid the kind of perverse instantiation of superficially plausible goal descriptions that we examined in Chapter 8). It is an open question whether this is feasible.

One further issue with associative value accretion is that the AI might disable the accretion mechanism. As we saw in Chapter 7, goal-system integrity is a convergent instrumental value. When the AI reaches a certain stage of cognitive development it may start to regard the continued operation of the accretion mechanism as a corrupting influence.[11] This is not necessarily a bad thing, but care would have to be taken to make the sealing-up of the goal system occur at the right moment, *after* the appropriate values have been accreted but *before* they have been overwritten by additional unintended accretions.

Motivational scaffolding

Another approach to the value-loading problem is what we may refer to as motivational scaffolding. It involves giving the seed AI an interim goal system, with relatively simple final goals that we can represent by means of explicit coding or some other feasible method. Once the AI has developed more sophisticated representational faculties, we replace this interim scaffold goal system with one that has different final goals. This successor goal system then governs the AI as it develops into a full-blown superintelligence.

Because the scaffold goals are not just instrumental but *final* goals for the AI, the AI might be expected to resist having them replaced (goal-content integrity being a convergent instrumental value). This creates a hazard. If the AI succeeds in thwarting the replacement of its scaffold goals, the method fails.

To avoid this failure mode, precautions are necessary. For example, capability control methods could be applied to limit the AI's powers until the mature motivation system has been installed. In particular, one could try to stunt its cognitive development at a level that is safe but that allows it to represent the values that we want to include in its ultimate goals. To do this, one might try to differentially stunt certain types of intellectual abilities, such as those required for strategizing and Machiavellian scheming, while allowing (apparently) more innocuous abilities to develop to a somewhat higher level.

One could also try to use motivation selection methods to induce a more collaborative relationship between the seed AI and the programmer team. For example, one might include in the scaffold motivation system the goal of welcoming online guidance from the programmers, including allowing them to replace any of the AI's current goals.[12] Other scaffold goals might include being transparent to the programmers about its values and strategies, and developing an architecture that is easy for the programmers to understand and that facilitates the later implementation of a humanly meaningful final goal, as well as domesticity motivations (such as limiting the use of computational resources).

One could even imagine endowing the seed AI with the sole final goal of replacing itself with a different final goal, one which may have been only implicitly or indirectly specified by the programmers. Some of the issues raised by the use of such a "self-replacing" scaffold goal also arise in the context of the value learning approach, which is discussed in the next subsection. Some further issues will be discussed in Chapter 13.

The motivational scaffolding approach is not without downsides. One is that it carries the risk that the AI could become too powerful while it is still running on its interim goal system. It may then thwart the human programmers' efforts to install the ultimate goal system (either by forceful resistance or by quiet subversion). The old final goals may then remain in charge as the seed AI develops into a full-blown superintelligence. Another downside is that installing the ultimately intended goals in a human-level AI is not necessarily that much easier than doing so in a more primitive AI. A human-level AI is more complex and might have developed an architecture that is opaque and difficult to alter. A seed AI, by contrast, is like a *tabula rasa* on which the programmers can inscribe whatever structures they deem helpful. This downside could be flipped into an upside if one succeeded in giving the seed AI scaffold goals that made it want to develop an architecture helpful to the programmers in their later efforts to install the ultimate final values. However, it is unclear how easy it would be to give a seed AI scaffold goals with this property, and it is also unclear how even an ideally motivated seed AI would be capable of doing a much better job than the human programming team at developing a good architecture.

Value learning

We come now to an important but subtle approach to the value-loading problem. It involves using the AI's intelligence to *learn* the values we want it to pursue. To do this, we must provide a criterion for the AI that at least implicitly picks out some suitable set of values. We could then build the AI to act according to its best estimates of these implicitly defined values. It would continually refine its estimates as it learns more about the world and gradually unpacks the implications of the value-determining criterion.

In contrast to the scaffolding approach, which gives the AI an interim scaffold goal and later replaces it with a different final goal, the value learning approach retains an unchanging final goal throughout the AI's developmental and operational phases. Learning does not change the goal. It changes only the AI's beliefs about the goal.

The AI thus must be endowed with a criterion that it can use to determine which percepts constitute evidence in favor of some hypothesis about what the ultimate goal is, and which percepts constitute evidence against. Specifying a suitable criterion could be difficult. Part of the difficulty, however, pertains to the problem of creating artificial general intelligence in the first place, which requires a powerful learning mechanism that can discover the structure of the environment from limited sensory inputs. That problem we can set aside here. But even modulo a solution to how to create superintelligent AI, there remain the difficulties that arise specifically from the value-loading problem. With the value learning approach, these take the form of needing to define a criterion that connects perceptual bitstrings to hypotheses about values.

Before delving into the details of how value learning could be implemented, it might be helpful to illustrate the general idea with an example. Suppose we write down a description of a set of values on a piece of paper. We fold the paper and put it in a sealed envelope. We then create an agent with human-level general intelligence, and give it the following final goal: "Maximize the realization of the values described in the envelope." What will this agent do?

The agent does not initially know what is written in the envelope. But it can form hypotheses, and it can assign those hypotheses probabilities based on their priors and any available empirical data. For instance, the agent might have encountered other examples of human-authored texts, or it might have observed some general patterns of human behavior. This would enable it to make guesses. One does not need a degree in psychology to predict that the note is more likely to describe a value such as "minimize injustice and unnecessary suffering" or "maximize returns to shareholders" than a value such as "cover all lakes with plastic shopping bags."

When the agent makes a decision, it seeks to take actions that would be effective at realizing the values it believes are most likely to be described in the letter. Importantly, the agent would see a high instrumental value in learning more about what the letter says. The reason is that for almost any final value that might be described in the letter, that value is more likely to be realized if the agent finds out what it is, since the agent will then pursue that value more effectively. The agent would also discover the convergent instrumental reasons described in Chapter 7—goal system integrity, cognitive enhancement, resource acquisition, and so forth. Yet, assuming that the agent assigns a sufficiently high probability to the values described in the letter involving human welfare, it would *not* pursue these instrumental values by immediately turning the planet into computronium and thereby exterminating the human species, because doing so would risk permanently destroying its ability to realize its final value.

We can liken this kind of agent to a barge attached to several tugboats that pull in different directions. Each tugboat corresponds to a hypothesis about the agent's final value. The engine power of each tugboat corresponds to the associated hypothesis's probability, and thus changes as new evidence comes in, producing adjustments in the barge's direction of motion. The resultant force should move the barge along a trajectory that facilitates learning about the (implicit) final value while avoiding the shoals of irreversible destruction; and later, when the open sea of more definite knowledge of the final value is reached, the one tugboat that still exerts significant force will pull the barge toward the realization of the discovered value along the straightest or most propitious route.

The envelope and barge metaphors illustrate the principle underlying the value learning approach, but they pass over a number of critical technical issues. They come into clearer focus once we start to develop the approach within a formal framework (see Box 10).

One outstanding issue is how to endow the AI with a goal such as "Maximize the realization of the values described in the envelope." (In the terminology of Box 10, how to define the value criterion $\mathcal{V}$.) To do this, it is necessary to identify the place where the values are described. In our example, this requires making a successful reference to the letter in the envelope. Though this might seem trivial, it is not without pitfalls. To mention just one: it is critical that the reference be not simply to a particular external physical object but to an object at a particular time. Otherwise

Box 10 Formalizing value learning

Introducing some formal notation can help us see some things more clearly. However, readers who dislike formalism can skip this part.

Consider a simplified framework in which an agent interacts with its environment in a finite number of discrete cycles.[13] In cycle k, the agent performs action y_k, and then receives the percept x_k. The interaction history of an agent with lifespan m is a string $y_1x_1y_2x_2 \cdots y_mx_m$ (which we can abbreviate as $yx_{1:m}$ or $yx_{\leq m}$). In each cycle, the agent selects an action based on the percept sequence it has received to date.

Consider first a reinforcement learner. An optimal reinforcement learner (AI-RL) is one that maximizes expected future rewards. It obeys the equation[14]

$$y_k = \arg\max_{y_k} \sum_{x_k y x_{k+1:m}} (r_k + \ldots + r_m) P(yx_{\leq m} \mid yx_{<k}y_k).$$

The reward sequence $r_k, \ldots, r_m$ is implied by the percept sequence $x_{k:m}$, since the reward that the agent receives in a given cycle is part of the percept that the agent receives in that cycle.

As argued earlier, this kind of reinforcement learning is unsuitable in the present context because a sufficiently intelligent agent will realize that it could secure maximum reward if it were able to directly manipulate its reward signal (wireheading). For weak agents, this need not be a problem, since we can physically prevent them from tampering with their own reward channel. We can also control their environment so that they receive rewards only when they act in ways that are agreeable to us. But a reinforcement learner has a strong incentive to eliminate this artificial dependence of its rewards on our whims and wishes. Our relationship with a reinforcement learner is therefore fundamentally antagonistic. If the agent is strong, this spells danger.

continued

Box 10 *Continued*

Variations of the wireheading syndrome can also affect systems that do not seek an external sensory reward signal but whose goals are defined as the attainment of some internal state. For example, in so-called "actor–critic" systems, there is an actor module that selects actions in order to minimize the disapproval of a separate critic module that computes how far the agent's behavior falls short of a given performance measure. The problem with this setup is that the actor module may realize that it can minimize disapproval by modifying the critic or eliminating it altogether—much like a dictator who dissolves the parliament and nationalizes the press. For limited systems, the problem can be avoided simply by not giving the actor module any means of modifying the critic module. A sufficiently intelligent and resourceful actor module, however, could always gain access to the critic module (which, after all, is merely a physical process in some computer).[15]

Before we get to the value learner, let us consider as an intermediary step what has been called an observation-utility maximizer (AI-OUM). It is obtained by replacing the reward series $(r_k + \ldots + r_m)$ in the AI-RL with a utility function that is allowed to depend on the entire future interaction history of the AI:

$$y_k = \arg\max_{y_k} \sum_{x_k y x_{k+1:m}} U(yx_{\leq m})P(yx_{\leq m} \mid yx_{<k}y_k).$$

This formulation provides a way around the wireheading problem because a utility function defined over an entire interaction history could be designed to penalize interaction histories that show signs of self-deception (or of a failure on the part of the agent to invest sufficiently in obtaining an accurate view of reality).

The AI-OUM thus makes it possible *in principle* to circumvent the wireheading problem. Availing ourselves of this possibility, however, would require that we specify a suitable utility function over the class of possible interaction histories—a task that looks forbiddingly difficult.

It may be more natural to specify utility functions directly in terms of possible worlds (or properties of possible worlds, or theories about the world) rather than in terms of an agent's own interaction histories. If we use this approach, we could reformulate and simplify the AI-OUM optimality notion:

$$y = \arg\max_y \sum_w U(w)P(w \mid Ey).$$

Box 10 *Continued*

Here, E is the total evidence available to the agent (at the time when it is making its decision), and U is a utility function that assigns utility to some class of possible worlds. The optimal agent chooses the act that maximizes expected utility.

An outstanding problem with these formulations is the difficulty of defining the utility function U. This, finally, returns us to the value-loading problem. To enable the utility function to be learned, we must expand our formalism to allow for uncertainty over utility functions. This can be done as follows (AI-VL):[16]

$$y = \arg\max_{y \in \mathbb{Y}} \sum_{w \in \mathbb{W}} P(w \mid Ey) \sum_{u \in \mathbb{U}} U(w) P(\mathcal{V}(U) \mid w).$$

Here, $\mathcal{V}(.)$ is a function from utility functions to propositions about utility functions. $\mathcal{V}(U)$ is the proposition that the utility function U satisfies the *value criterion* expressed by $\mathcal{V}$.[17]

To decide which action to perform, one could hence proceed as follows: First, compute the conditional probability of each possible world w (given available evidence and on the supposition that action y is to be performed). Second, for each possible utility function U, compute the conditional probability that U satisfies the value criterion $\mathcal{V}$ (conditional on w being the actual world). Third, for each possible utility function U, compute the utility of possible world w. Fourth, combine these quantities to compute the expected utility of action y. Fifth, repeat this procedure for each possible action, and perform the action found to have the highest expected utility (using some arbitrary method to break ties). As described, this procedure—which involves giving explicit and separate consideration to each possible world—is, of course, wildly computationally intractable. The AI would have to use computational shortcuts that approximate this optimality notion.

The question, then, is how to define this value criterion $\mathcal{V}$.[18] Once the AI has an adequate representation of the value criterion, it could in principle use its general intelligence to gather information about which possible worlds are most likely to be the actual one. It could then apply the criterion, for each such plausible possible world w, to find out which utility function satisfies the criterion $\mathcal{V}$ in w. One can thus regard the AI-VL formula as a way of identifying and separating out this key challenge in the value learning approach—the challenge of how to represent. The formalism also brings to light a number of other issues (such as how to define $\mathbb{Y}$, $\mathbb{W}$, and $\mathbb{U}$) which would need to be resolved before the approach could be made to work.[19]

the AI may determine that the best way to attain its goal is by overwriting the original value description with one that provides an easier target (such as the value that for every integer there be a larger integer). This done, the AI could lean back and crack its knuckles—though more likely a malignant failure would ensue, for reasons we discussed in Chapter 8. So now we face the question of how to define time. We could point to a clock and say, "Time is defined by the movements of this device"—but this could fail if the AI conjectures that it can manipulate time by moving the hands on the clock, a conjecture which would indeed be correct if "time" were given the aforesaid definition. (In a realistic case, matters would be further complicated by the fact that the relevant values are not going to be conveniently described in a letter; more likely, they would have to be inferred from observations of pre-existing structures that implicitly contain the relevant information, such as human brains.)

Another issue in coding the goal "Maximize the realization of the values described in the envelope" is that even if all the correct values were described in a letter, and even if the AI's motivation system were successfully keyed to this source, the AI might not interpret the descriptions the way we intended. This would create a risk of perverse instantiation, as discussed in Chapter 8.

To clarify, the difficulty here is not so much how to ensure that the AI can understand human intentions. A superintelligence should easily develop such understanding. Rather, the difficulty is ensuring that the AI will be motivated to pursue the described values in the way we intended. This is not guaranteed by the AI's ability to understand our intentions: an AI could know exactly what we meant and yet be indifferent to that interpretation of our words (being motivated instead by some other interpretation of the words or being indifferent to our words altogether).

The difficulty is compounded by the desideratum that, for reasons of safety, the correct motivation should ideally be installed in the seed AI *before* it becomes capable of fully representing human concepts or understanding human intentions. This requires that somehow a cognitive framework be created, with a particular location in that framework designated in the AI's motivation system as the repository of its final value. But the cognitive framework itself must be revisable, so as to allow the AI to expand its representational capacities as it learns more about the world and grows more intelligent. The AI might undergo the equivalent of scientific revolutions, in which its worldview is shaken up and it perhaps suffers ontological crises in which it discovers that its previous ways of thinking about values were based on confusions and illusions. Yet starting at a sub-human level of development and continuing throughout all its subsequent development into a galactic superintelligence, the AI's conduct is to be guided by an essentially unchanging final value, a final value that becomes better understood by the AI in direct consequence of its general intellectual progress—and likely quite differently understood by the mature AI than it was by its original programmers, though not different in a random or hostile way but in a benignly appropriate way. How to accomplish this remains an open question.[20] (See Box 11.)

In summary, it is not yet known how to use the value learning approach to install plausible human values (though see Box 12 for some examples of recent ideas). At present, the approach should be viewed as a research program rather than an available technique. If it could be made to work, it might constitute the most ideal solution to the value-loading problem. Among other benefits, it would seem to offer a natural way to prevent mind crime, since a seed AI that makes reasonable guesses about which values its programmers might have installed would anticipate that mind crime is probably negatively evaluated by those values, and thus best avoided, at least until more definitive information has been obtained.

Last, but not least, there is the question of "what to write in the envelope"—or, less metaphorically, the question of which values we should try to get the AI to learn. But this issue is common to all approaches to the AI value-loading problem. We return to it in Chapter 13.

Box 11 An AI that wants to be friendly

Eliezer Yudkowsky has tried to describe some features of a seed AI architecture intended to enable the kind of behavior described in the text above. In his terminology, the AI would use "external reference semantics."[21] To illustrate the basic idea, let us suppose that we want the system to be "friendly." The system starts out with the goal of trying to instantiate property F but does not initially know much about what F is. It might just know that F is some abstract property and that when the programmers speak of "friendliness," they are

continued

Box 11 *Continued*

probably trying to convey information about *F*. Since the AI's final goal is to instantiate *F*, an important instrumental value is to learn more about what *F* is. As the AI discovers more about *F*, its behavior is increasingly guided by the actual content of *F*. Thus, hopefully, the AI becomes increasingly friendly the more it learns and the smarter it gets.

The programmers can help this process along, and reduce the risk of the AI making some catastrophic mistake while its understanding of *F* is still incomplete, by providing the AI with "programmer affirmations," hypotheses about the nature and content of *F* to which an initially high probability is assigned. For instance, the hypothesis "misleading the programmers is unfriendly" can be given a high prior probability. These programmer affirmations, however, are not "true by definition"—they are not unchallengeable axioms about the concept of friendliness. Rather, they are initial hypotheses about friendliness, hypotheses to which a rational AI will assign a high probability at least for as long as it trusts the programmers' epistemic capacities more than its own.

Yudkowsky's proposal also involves the use of what he called "causal validity semantics." The idea here is that the AI should do not exactly what the programmers told it to do but rather (something like) what they were trying to tell it to do. While the programmers are trying to explain to the seed AI what friendliness is, they might make errors in their explanations. Moreover, the programmers themselves may not fully understand the true nature of friendliness. One would therefore want the AI to have the ability to correct errors in the programmers' thinking, and to infer the true or intended meaning from whatever imperfect explanations the programmers manage to provide. For example, the AI should be able to represent the causal processes whereby the programmers learn and communicate about friendliness. Thus, to pick a trivial example, the AI should understand that there is a possibility that a programmer might make a typo while inputting information about friendliness, and the AI should then seek to correct the error. More generally, the AI should seek to correct for whatever distortive influences may have corrupted the flow of information about friendliness as it passed from its source through the programmers to the AI (where "distortive" is an epistemic category). Ideally, as the AI matures, it should overcome any cognitive biases and other more fundamental misconceptions that may have prevented its programmers from fully understanding what friendliness is.

Box 12 Two recent (half-baked) ideas

What we might call the "Hail Mary" approach is based on the hope that else-where in the universe there exist (or will come to exist) civilizations that suc-cessfully manage the intelligence explosion, and that they end up with values that significantly overlap with our own. We could then try to build our AI so that it is motivated to do what these other superintelligences want it to do.[22] The advantage is that this might be easier than to build our AI to be motivated to do what we want directly.

For this scheme to work it is *not* necessary that our AI can establish com-munication with any alien superintelligence. Rather, our AI's actions would be guided by *its estimates* of what the alien superintelligences would want it to do. Our AI would model the likely outcomes of intelligence explosions elsewhere, and as it becomes superintelligent itself its estimates should become increasingly accurate. Perfect knowledge is not required. There may be a range of plausible outcomes of intelligence explosions, and our AI would then do its best to accommodate the preferences of the various dif-ferent kinds of superintelligence that might emerge, weighted by probability.

This version of the Hail Mary approach requires that we construct a final value for our AI that refers to the preferences of other superintelligences. Exactly how to do this is not yet clear. However, superintelligent agents might be structurally distinctive enough that we could write a piece of code that would function as a detector that would look at the world model in our devel-oping AI and designate the representational elements that correspond to the presence of a superintelligence. The detector would then, somehow, extract the preferences of the superintelligence in question (as it is represented within our own AI).[23] If we could create such a detector, we could then use it to define our AI's final values. One challenge is that we may need to create the detector before we know what representational framework our AI will develop. The detector may thus need to query an unknown representational framework and extract the preferences of whatever superintelligence may be represented therein. This looks difficult, but perhaps some clever solution can be found.[24]

If the basic setup could be made to work, various refinements immedi-ately suggest themselves. For example, rather than aiming to follow (some weighted composition of) the preferences of *every* alien superintelligence, our AI's final value could incorporate a filter to select a subset of alien

continued

Box 12 *Continued*

superintelligences for obeisance (with the aim of selecting ones whose values are closer to our own). For instance, we might use criteria pertaining to a superintelligence's causal origin to determine whether to include it in the obeisance set. Certain properties of its origination (which we might be able to define in structural terms) may correlate with the degree to which the resultant superintelligence could be expected to share our values. Perhaps we wish to place more trust in superintelligences whose causal origins trace back to a whole brain emulation, or to a seed AI that did not make heavy use of evolutionary algorithms or that emerged slowly in a way suggestive of a controlled takeoff. (Taking causal origins into account would also let us avoid over-weighting superintelligences that create multiple copies of themselves— indeed would let us avoid creating an incentive for them to do so.) Many other refinements would also be possible.

The Hail Mary approach requires faith that there are other superintelligences out there that sufficiently share our values.[25] This makes the approach non-ideal. However, the technical obstacles facing the Hail Mary approach, though very substantial, might possibly be less formidable than those confronting alternative approaches. Exploring non-ideal but more easily implementable approaches can make sense—not with the intention of using them, but to have something to fall back upon in case an ideal solution should not be ready in time.

Another idea for how to solve the value-loading problem has recently been proposed by Paul Christiano.[26] Like the Hail Mary, it is a value learning method that tries to define the value criterion by means of a "trick" rather than through laborious construction. By contrast to the Hail Mary, it does not presuppose the existence of other superintelligent agents that we could point to as role models for our own AI. Christiano's proposal is somewhat resistant to brief explanation—it involves a series of arcane considerations—but we can try to at least gesture at its main elements.

Suppose we could obtain (a) a mathematically precise specification of a particular human brain and (b) a mathematically well-specified virtual environment that contains an idealized computer with an arbitrarily large amount of memory and CPU power. Given (a) and (b), we could define a utility function U as the output the human brain would produce after interacting with this environment. U would be a mathematically well-defined object, albeit one which (because of computational limitations) we may be unable to describe

Box 12 *Continued*

explicitly. Nevertheless, *U* could serve as the value criterion for a value learning AI, which could use various heuristics for assigning probabilities to hypotheses about what *U* implies.

Intuitively, we want *U* to be the utility function that a suitably prepared human would output if she had the advantage of being able use an arbitrarily large amount of computing power—enough computing power, for example, to run astronomical numbers of copies of herself to assist her with her analysis of specifying a utility function, or to help her devise a better process for going about this analysis. (We are here foreshadowing a theme, "coherent extrapolated volition," which will be further explored in Chapter 13.)

It would seem relatively easy to specify the idealized environment: we can give a mathematical description of an abstract computer with arbitrarily large capacity; and in other respects we could use a virtual reality program that gives a mathematical description of, say, a single room with a computer terminal in it (instantiating the abstract computer). But how to obtain a mathematically precise description of a particular human brain? The obvious way would be through whole brain emulation, but what if the technology for emulation is not available in time?

This is where Christiano's proposal offers a key innovation. Christiano observes that in order to obtain a mathematically well-specified value criterion, we do not need a practically useful computational model of a mind, a model we could run. We just need a (possibly implicit and hopelessly complicated) mathematical *definition*—and this may be much easier to attain. Using functional neuroimaging and other measurements, we can perhaps collect gigabytes of data about the input–output behavior of a selected human. If we collect a sufficient amount of data, then it might be that the simplest mathematical model that accounts for all this data is in fact an emulation of the particular human in question. Although it would be computationally intractable for us to *find* this simplest model from the data, it could be perfectly possible for us to *define* the model, by referring to the data and a using a mathematically well-defined simplicity measure (such as some variant of the Kolmogorov complexity, which we encountered in Box 1, Chapter 1).[27]

Emulation modulation

The value-loading problem looks somewhat different for whole brain emulation than it does for artificial intelligence. Methods that presuppose a fine-grained understanding and control of algorithms and architecture are not applicable to emulations. On the other hand, the augmentation motivation selection method—inapplicable to *de novo* artificial intelligence—is available to be used with emulations (or enhanced biological brains).[28]

The augmentation method could be combined with techniques to tweak the inherited goals of the system. For example, one could try to manipulate the motivational state of an emulation by administering the digital equivalent of psychoactive substances (or, in the case of biological systems, the actual chemicals). Even now it is possible to pharmacologically manipulate values and motivations to a limited extent.[29] The pharmacopeia of the future may contain drugs with more specific and predictable effects. The digital medium of emulations should greatly facilitate such developments, by making controlled experimentation easier and by rendering all cerebral parts directly addressable.

Just as when biological test subjects are used, research on emulations would get entangled in ethical complications, not all of which could be brushed aside with a consent form. Such entanglements could slow progress along the emulation path (because of regulation or moral restraint), perhaps especially hindering studies on how to manipulate the motivational structure of emulations. The result could be that emulations are augmented to potentially dangerous superintelligent levels of cognitive ability before adequate work has been done to test or adjust their final goals. Another possible effect of the moral entanglements might be to give the lead to less scrupulous teams and nations. Conversely, were we to relax our moral standards for experimenting with digital human minds, we could become responsible for a substantial amount of harm and wrongdoing, which is obviously undesirable. Other things equal, these considerations favor taking some alternative path that does not require the extensive use of digital human research subjects in a strategically high-stakes situation.

The issue, however, is not clear-cut. One could argue that whole brain emulation research is *less* likely to involve moral violations than artificial intelligence research, on the grounds that we are more likely to recognize when an emulation mind qualifies for moral status than we are to recognize when a completely alien or synthetic mind does so. If certain kinds of AIs, or their subprocesses, have a significant moral status that we fail to recognize, the consequent moral violations could be extensive. Consider, for example, the happy abandon with which contemporary programmers create reinforcement-learning agents and subject them to aversive stimuli. Countless such agents are created daily, not only in computer science laboratories but in many applications, including some computer games containing sophisticated non-player characters. Presumably, these agents are still too primitive to have any moral status. But how confident can we really be that this is so? More importantly, how confident can we be that we will know to stop in time, before our programs become capable of experiencing morally relevant suffering?

(We will return in Chapter 14 to some of the broader strategic questions that arise when we compare the desirability of emulation and artificial intelligence paths.)

Institution design

Some intelligent systems consist of intelligent parts that are themselves capable of agency. Firms and states exemplify this in the human world: whilst largely composed of humans they can, for some purposes, be viewed as autonomous agents in their own right. The motivations of such composite systems depend not only on the motivations of their constituent subagents but also on how those subagents are organized. For instance, a group that is organized under strong dictatorship might behave as if it had a will that was identical to the will of the subagent that occupies the dictator role, whereas a democratic group might sometimes behave more as if it had a will that was a composite or average of the wills of its various constituents. But one can also imagine governance institutions that would make an organization behave in a way that is not a simple function of the wills of its subagents. (Theoretically, at least, there could exist a totalitarian state that *everybody* hated, because the state had mechanisms to prevent its citizens from coordinating a revolt. Each citizen could be worse off by revolting alone than by playing their part in the state machinery.)

By designing appropriate institutions for a composite system, one could thus try to shape its effective motivation. In Chapter 9, we discussed social integration as a possible capability control method. But there we focused on the incentives faced by an agent as a consequence of its existence in a social world of near-equals. Here we are focusing on what happens *inside* a given agent: how its will is determined by its internal organization. We are therefore looking at a motivation selection method. Moreover, since this kind of internal institution design does not depend on large-scale social engineering or reform, it is a method that might be available to an individual project developing superintelligence even if the wider socio-economic or international milieu is less than ideally favorable.

Institution design is perhaps most plausible in contexts where it would be combined with augmentation. If we could start with agents that are already suitably motivated or that have human-like motivations, institutional arrangements could be used as an extra safeguard to increase the chances that the system will stay on course.

For example, suppose that we start with some well-motivated human-like agents—let us say emulations. We want to boost the cognitive capacities of these agents, but we worry that the enhancements might corrupt their motivations. One way to deal with this challenge would be to set up a system in which individual emulations function as subagents. When a new enhancement is introduced, it is first applied to a small subset of the subagents. Its effects are then studied by a review panel composed of subagents who have not yet had the enhancement applied to them. Only when these peers have satisfied themselves that the enhancement is not corrupting is it rolled out to the wider subagent population. If the enhanced subagents are found to be corrupted, they are not given further enhancements and are excluded from key decision-making functions (at least until the system as a whole has advanced to a point where the corrupted subagents can be safely reintegrated).[30] Although the corrupted subagents might have gained some advantage from the enhancement, the institutional structure in which they are embedded, and the fact that they constitute a small minority of all subagents, would hopefully prevent them from seizing power or spreading their corruption to the overall system. Thus, the collective intelligence and capability of the system could be gradually enhanced in a sequence of small steps, where the soundness of each step is verified by subagents only slightly less capable than the new subagents that are introduced in that step.

The amount of safety obtainable by this kind of institution design is limited by the accuracy of the tests that are used to evaluate the enhanced subagents. The problem of test construction is complicated by the fact that the test batteries could only be validated within the pre-existing range of cognitive ability yet must be applied to agents outside this range. One could mitigate this problem by taking small enhancement steps and by letting the test run for a long time. Such caution, however, would raise the cost and slow progress (which, if a race dynamic is occurring, could mean a project employing these safety measures would place itself at a disadvantage). Even with small steps and extensive testing, there would remain some risk of subtle flaws being introduced, leading to a gradual corruption of the goal system, a corruption that might become manifest only when the system reaches superintelligence. This risk could be reduced by letting the testing condition extend for many steps of cognitive enhancement, so that even agents that have been initially certified as sound and that have received several subsequent enhancements would continue to be under review by a panel of unmodified and uncorrupted original peers and would remain subject to reversion.

Ideally, the testing should be ongoing rather than confined to an initial evaluation period. Human-level subagents have the ability to strategize and might thus choose to conceal certain goals while their behavior was being monitored. To enable continuous testing, a hierarchy might be created in which subagents at a certain level of capability are tasked with monitoring subagents at a somewhat higher level of capability. At the bottom of the capability hierarchy (but at the top of the power hierarchy) would sit the relatively dumb and slow principal. This human principal would be like a demented king who reigns over an incompetent court that oversees a mediocre administration which governs a capable people. Alternatively, he might be likened to the evolutionarily ancient "reptilian brain" which ensures that the newer and much cleverer neocortex is employed in the service of goals such as feeding and copulation.

One might question whether such an inverse meritocracy could remain stable. If the bulk of the superintelligent subagents were found to be corrupt, and the humans in charge of the whole thing attempted to roll back many of the preceding enhancements, would the institutional structure be strong enough to withstand the opposition that such a move would engender? In the context of historical or contemporary human societies, the answer perhaps is that this would be implausible. (Not that the most capable people consistently rise to power, but we are not *literally* ruled by chimpanzees either.) The issue is less clear, however, in a context where society is implemented as software.[31]

Imagine a digital hierarchy that has one highly trained police agent for every two proletarians. It also has one special-police agent for every two police agents. It also has one special-special-police agent for every two special-police agents—and so forth, so that each layer of overseers has at least half the numbers of the layer it oversees. Imagine, further, that this society is architected in such a way that a supervisor has big advantages over his subordinates. For example, the supervisor is able to monitor and record everything his subordinates say and do, whereas the supervisor himself is hidden behind a one-way glass, so that his subordinates can only hear the orders and instructions that the superior chooses to transmit. Imagine that supervisors have a panel of buttons that they can press at any time to cause a subordinate to be punished or rewarded, paused, deleted, or reverted to an earlier state. These capabilities would greatly boost the powers of a supervising agent, beyond what has been possible historically in even the most totalitarian of organizations.

Even this does not exhaust the possible instruments of control. Supervisors might also have at their disposal realistic virtual reality simulations that they can use to probe subordinates' reactions to hypothetical scenarios (such as simulated offers to join a conspiracy or to slack when they think nobody is watching). Supervisors might, additionally, have the ability to eavesdrop on internal monologues in the subordinates' minds and to directly manipulate their emotional states.

The upshot is a series of massive advantages for the supervisor.[32] Each supervisor would be a subordinate to another, higher-level supervisor, who would monitor *his* every move and make sure *he* did not slacken in the execution of his managerial duties. With this kind of arrangement, it might be possible for the structure to be stable even if each supervisory level is intellectually somewhat weaker than the level it supervises.[33] And the entire structure, which could include many highly superintelligent agents, may be controlled by a small number of humans with root access.[34]

The cost of such an internal control structure would be significant but not necessarily prohibitive. For example, in the model where each level of supervision has half the numbers of the layer below, the extra computational overhead is bounded at a mere 100% of what the proletarian part of the system costs—less if the dumber boss layers require fewer computations per subagent. Oversight could be tightened by increasing the ratio, or cost lowered by decreasing it. The extra computational cost would be a major factor in a competitive market scenario (cf. Chapter 11) but looks affordable in the context of a project that is not facing strong immediate competition. There would also be a cost in terms of the development time needed to create and test these supervisory functionalities. A well-resourced project could reduce this time cost by parallelizing the development of the control structure with the development of the machine intelligence; but the extra task load could be prohibitive for smaller projects and for projects caught in a close technology race.

One other type of cost also deserves consideration: the risk of mind crimes being committed in this kind of structure.[35] As described, the institution sounds like a rather horrible North Korean labor camp. Yet there are ways of at least mitigating the moral problems with running this kind of institution, even if the subagents contained in the institution are emulations with full human moral status. At a minimum, the system could rely on volunteering emulations. Each subagent could have the option at any time of withdrawing its participation.[36] Terminated emulations could be stored to memory, with a commitment to restart them under much more ideal conditions once the dangerous phase of the intelligence explosion is over. Meanwhile, subagents who chose to participate could be housed in very comfortable virtual environments and allowed ample time for sleep and recreation. These measures would impose a cost, one that should be manageable for a well-resourced project under noncompetitive conditions. In a highly competitive situation, the cost may be unaffordable unless an enterprise could be assured that its competitors would incur the same cost.

In the example, we imagined the subagents as emulations. One might wonder, does the institution design approach require that the subagents be anthropomorphic? Or is it equally applicable to systems composed of artificial subagents?

One's first thought here might be skeptical. One notes that despite our plentiful experience with human-like agents, we still cannot precisely predict the outbreak or outcomes of revolutions; social science can, at most, describe some statistical tendencies.[37] Since we cannot reliably predict the stability of social structures for ordinary human beings (about which we have much data), it is tempting to infer that we have little hope of precision-engineering stable social structures for cognitively enhanced human-like agents (about which we have no data), and that we have still less hope of doing so for advanced artificial agents (which are not even similar to agents that we have data about).

Yet the matter is not so cut-and-dried. Humans and human-like beings are complex; but artificial agents could have relatively simple architectures. Artificial agents could also have simple and explicitly characterized motivations. Furthermore, digital agents in general (whether emulations or artificial intelligences) are copyable: an affordance that may revolutionize management, much like interchangeable parts revolutionized manufacturing. These differences, together with the opportunity to work with agents that are initially powerless and to create institutional structures that use the various abovementioned control measures, might combine to make it possible to achieve particular institutional outcomes—such as a system that does not revolt—more reliably than if one were working with human beings under historical conditions.

But then again, artificial agents might lack many of the attributes that help us predict the behavior of human-like agents. Artificial agents need not have any of the social emotions that bind human behavior, emotions such as fear, pride, and remorse. Nor need artificial agents develop attachments to friends and family. Nor need they exhibit the unconscious body language that makes it difficult for us humans to conceal our intentions. These deficits might destabilize institutions of artificial agents. Moreover, artificial agents might be capable of making big leaps in cognitive performance as a result of seemingly small changes in their algorithms or architecture. Ruthlessly optimizing artificial agents might be willing to take extreme gambles from which humans would shrink.[38] And superintelligent agents might show a surprising ability to coordinate with little or no communication (e.g. by internally modeling each other's hypothetical responses to various contingencies). These and other differences could make sudden institutional failure more likely, even in the teeth of what seem like Kevlar-clad methods of social control.

It is unclear, therefore, how promising the institution design approach is, and whether it has a greater chance of working with anthropomorphic than with artificial agents. It might be thought that creating an institution with appropriate checks and balances could only increase safety—or, at any rate, not reduce safety—so that from a risk-mitigation perspective it would always be best if the method were used. But even this cannot be said with certainty. The approach adds parts and complexity, and thus may also introduce new ways for things to go wrong that do not exist in the case of an agent that does not have intelligent subagents as parts. Nevertheless, institution design is worthy of further exploration.[39]

Synopsis

Goal system engineering is not yet an established discipline. It is not currently known how to transfer human values to a digital computer, even given human-level machine intelligence. Having investigated a number of approaches, we found that some of them appear to be dead ends; but

Table 12 *Summary of value-loading techniques*

Explicit representation	May hold promise as a way of loading domesticity values. Does not seem promising as a way of loading more complex values.
Evolutionary selection	Less promising. Powerful search may find a design that satisfies the formal search criteria but not our intentions. Furthermore, if designs are evaluated by running them—including designs that do not even meet the formal criteria—a potentially grave additional danger is created. Evolution also makes it difficult to avoid massive mind crime, especially if one is aiming to fashion human-like minds.
Reinforcement learning	A range of different methods can be used to solve "reinforcement-learning problems," but they typically involve creating a system that seeks to maximize a reward signal. This has an inherent tendency to produce the wireheading failure mode when the system becomes more intelligent. Reinforcement learning therefore looks unpromising.
Value accretion	We humans acquire much of our specific goal content from our reactions to experience. While value accretion could in principle be used to create an agent with human motivations, the human value-accretion dispositions might be complex and difficult to replicate in a seed AI. A bad approximation may yield an AI that generalizes differently than humans do and therefore acquires unintended final goals. More research is needed to determine how difficult it would be to make value accretion work with sufficient precision.

continued

Table 12 *Continued*

Motivational scaffolding	It is too early to tell how difficult it would be to encourage a system to develop internal high-level representations that are transparent to humans (while keeping the system's capabilities below the dangerous level) and then to use those representations to design a new goal system. The approach might hold considerable promise. (However, as with any untested approach that would postpone much of the hard work on safety engineering until the development of human-level AI, one should be careful not to allow it to become an excuse for a lackadaisical attitude to the control problem in the interim.)
Value learning	A potentially promising approach, but more research is needed to determine how difficult it would be to formally specify a reference that successfully points to the relevant external information about human value (and how difficult it would be to specify a correctness criterion for a utility function in terms of such a reference). Also worth exploring within the value learning category are proposals of the Hail Mary type or along the lines of Paul Christiano's construction (or other such shortcuts).
Emulation modulation	If machine intelligence is achieved via the emulation pathway, it would likely be possible to tweak motivations through the digital equivalent of drugs or by other means. Whether this would enable values to be loaded with sufficient precision to ensure safety even as the emulation is boosted to superintelligence is an open question. (Ethical constraints might also complicate developments in this direction.)
Institution design	Various strong methods of social control could be applied in an institution composed of emulations. In principle, social control methods could also be applied in an institution composed of artificial intelligences. Emulations have some properties that would make them easier to control via such methods, but also some properties that might make them harder to control than AIs. Institution design seems worthy of further exploration as a potential value-loading technique.

others appear to hold promise and deserve to be explored further. A summary is provided in Table 12.

If we knew how to solve the value-loading problem, we would confront a further problem: the problem of deciding which values to load. What, in other words, would we want a superintelligence to want? This is the more philosophical problem to which we turn next.

CHAPTER 13

Choosing the criteria for choosing

S uppose we could install any arbitrary final value into a seed AI. The decision as to which value to install could then have the most far-reaching consequences. Certain other basic parameter choices—concerning the axioms of the AI's decision theory and epistemology—could be similarly consequential. But foolish, ignorant, and narrow-minded that we are, how could we be trusted to make good design decisions? How could we choose without locking in forever the prejudices and preconceptions of the present generation? In this chapter, we explore how indirect normativity can let us offload much of the cognitive work involved in making these decisions onto the superintelligence itself while still anchoring the outcome in deeper human values.

The need for indirect normativity

How can we get a superintelligence to do what we want? What do we want the superintelligence to want? Up to this point, we have focused on the former question. We now turn to the second question.

Suppose that we had solved the control problem so that we were able to load any value we chose into the motivation system of a superintelligence, making it pursue that value as its final goal. Which value should we install? The choice is no light matter. If the superintelligence obtains a decisive strategic advantage, the value would determine the disposition of the cosmic endowment.

Clearly, it is essential that we not make a mistake in our value selection. But how could we realistically hope to achieve errorlessness in a matter like this? We might be wrong about morality; wrong also about what is good for us; wrong even about what we truly want. Specifying a final goal, it seems, requires making one's way through a thicket of thorny philosophical problems. If we try a direct approach, we are likely to make a hash of things. The risk of mistaken choosing is especially high when the decision context is unfamiliar—and selecting the final goal for a machine superintelligence that will shape all of humanity's future is an extremely unfamiliar decision context if any is.

The dismal odds in a frontal assault are reflected in the pervasive dissensus about the relevant issues in value theory. No ethical theory commands majority support among philosophers, so most philosophers must be wrong.[1] It is also reflected in the marked changes that the distribution of moral belief has undergone over time, many of which we like to think of as progress. In medieval Europe, for instance, it was deemed respectable entertainment to watch a political prisoner being tortured to death. Cat-burning remained popular in sixteenth-century Paris.[2] A mere hundred and fifty years ago, slavery still was widely practiced in the American South, with full support of the law and moral custom. When we look back, we see glaring deficiencies not just in the behavior but in the moral beliefs of all previous ages. Though we have perhaps since gleaned some moral insight, we could hardly claim to be now basking in the high noon of perfect moral enlightenment. Very likely, we are still laboring under one or more grave moral misconceptions. In such circumstances to select a final value based on our current convictions, in a way that locks it in forever and precludes any possibility of further ethical progress, would be to risk an existential moral calamity.

Even if we could be rationally confident that we have identified the correct ethical theory—which we cannot be—we would still remain at risk of making mistakes in developing important details of this theory. Seemingly simple moral theories can have a lot of hidden complexity.[3] For example, consider the (unusually simple) consequentialist theory of hedonism. This theory states, roughly, that all and only pleasure has value, and all and only pain has disvalue.[4] Even if we placed all our moral chips on this one theory, and the theory turned out to be right, a great many questions would remain open. Should "higher pleasures" be given priority over "lower pleasures," as John Stuart Mill argued? How should the intensity and duration of a pleasure be factored in? Can pains and pleasures cancel each other out? What kinds of brain states are associated with morally relevant pleasures? Would two exact copies of the same brain state correspond to twice the amount of pleasure?[5] Can there be subconscious pleasures? How should we deal with extremely small chances of extremely great pleasures?[6] How should we aggregate over infinite populations?[7]

Giving the wrong answer to any one of these questions could be catastrophic. If by selecting a final value for the superintelligence we had to place a bet not just on a general moral theory but on a long conjunction of specific claims about how that theory is to be interpreted and integrated into an effective decision-making process, then our chances of striking lucky would dwindle to something close to hopeless. Fools might eagerly accept this challenge of solving in one swing all the important problems in moral philosophy, in order to infix their favorite answers into the seed AI. Wiser souls would look hard for some alternative approach, some way to hedge.

This takes us to indirect normativity. The obvious reason for building a superintelligence is so that we can offload to it the instrumental reasoning required to find effective ways of realizing a given value. Indirect normativity would enable us also to offload to the superintelligence some of the reasoning needed to select the value that is to be realized.

Indirect normativity is a way to answer the challenge presented by the fact that we may not know what we truly want, what is in our interest, or what is morally right or ideal. Instead of making a guess based on our own current understanding (which is probably deeply flawed), we would delegate some of the cognitive work required for value selection to the superintelligence. Since the superintelligence is better at cognitive work than we are, it may see past the errors and confusions that cloud our thinking. One could generalize this idea and emboss it as a heuristic principle:

The principle of epistemic deference

A future superintelligence occupies an epistemically superior vantage point: its beliefs are (probably, on most topics) more likely than ours to be true. We should therefore defer to the superintelligence's opinion whenever feasible.[8]

Indirect normativity applies this principle to the value-selection problem. Lacking confidence in our ability to specify a concrete normative standard, we would instead specify some more abstract condition that any normative standard should satisfy, in the hope that a superintelligence could find a concrete standard that satisfies the abstract condition. We could give a seed AI the final goal of continuously acting according to its best estimate of what this implicitly defined standard would have it do.

Some examples will serve to make the idea clearer. First we will consider "coherent extrapolated volition," an indirect normativity proposal outlined by Eliezer Yudkowsky. We will then introduce some variations and alternatives, to give us a sense of the range of available options.

Coherent extrapolated volition

Yudkowsky has proposed that a seed AI be given the final goal of carrying out humanity's "coherent extrapolated volition" (CEV), which he defines as follows:

Our coherent extrapolated volition is our wish if we knew more, thought faster, were more the people we wished we were, had grown up farther together; where the extrapolation converges rather than diverges, where our wishes cohere rather than interfere; extrapolated as we wish that extrapolated, interpreted as we wish that interpreted.[9]

When Yudkowsky wrote this, he did not purport to present a blueprint for how to implement this rather poetic prescription. His aim was to give a preliminary sketch of how CEV might be defined, along with some arguments for why an approach along these lines is needed.

Many of the ideas behind the CEV proposal have analogs and antecedents in the philosophical literature. For example, in ethics *ideal observer theories* seek to analyze normative concepts like "good" or "right" in terms of the judgments that a hypothetical ideal observer would make (where an "ideal observer" is defined as one that is omniscient about non-moral facts, is logically clear-sighted, is impartial in relevant ways and is free from various kinds of biases, and so on).[10] The CEV approach, however, is not (or need not be construed as) a moral theory. It is not committed to the claim that there is any necessary link between value and the preferences of our coherent extrapolated volition. CEV can be thought of simply as a useful way to approximate whatever has ultimate value, or it can be considered aside from any connection to ethics. As the main prototype of the indirect normativity approach, it is worth examining in a little more detail.

Some explications

Some terms in the above quotation require explication. "Thought faster," in Yudkowsky's terminology, means *if we were smarter and had thought things through more.* "Grown up farther together" seems to mean *if we had done our learning, our cognitive enhancing, and our self-improving under conditions of suitable social interaction with one another.*

"Where the extrapolation converges rather than diverges" may be understood as follows. The AI should act on some feature of the result of its extrapolation only insofar as that feature can be predicted by the AI with a fairly high degree of confidence. To the extent that the AI cannot predict what we would wish if we were idealized in the manner indicated, the AI should not act on a wild guess; instead, it should refrain from acting. However, even though many details of our idealized wishing may be undetermined or unpredictable, there might nevertheless be some broad outlines that the AI can apprehend, and it can then at least act to ensure that the future course of events unfolds within those outlines. For example, if the AI can reliably estimate that our extrapolated volition would wish that we not all be in constant agony, or that the universe not be tiled over with paperclips, then the AI should act to prevent those outcomes.[11]

"Where our wishes cohere rather than interfere" may be read as follows. The AI should act where there is fairly broad agreement between individual humans' extrapolated volitions. A smaller set of strong, clear wishes might sometimes outweigh the weak and muddled wishes of a majority. Also, Yudkowsky thinks that it should require less consensus for the AI to *prevent* some particular narrowly specified outcome, and more consensus for the AI to act to funnel the future into some particular narrow conception of the good. "The initial dynamic for CEV," he writes, "should be conservative about saying 'yes,' and listen carefully for 'no.'"[12]

"Extrapolated as we wish that extrapolated, interpreted as we wish that interpreted": The idea behind these last modifiers seems to be that the rules for extrapolation should themselves be sensitive to the extrapolated volition. An individual might have a second-order desire (a desire concerning what to desire) that some of her first-order desires not be given weight when her volition is extrapolated. For example, an alcoholic who has a first-order desire for booze might also have a second-order desire not to have that first-order desire. Similarly, we might have desires over how various other parts of the extrapolation process should unfold, and these should be taken into account by the extrapolation process.

It might be objected that even if the concept of humanity's coherent extrapolated volition could be properly defined, it would anyway be impossible—even for a superintelligence—to find out what humanity would actually want under the hypothetical idealized circumstances stipulated in the CEV approach. Without some information about the content of our extrapolated volition, the AI would be bereft of any substantial standard to guide its behavior. However, although it would be difficult to know with precision what humanity's CEV would wish, it is possible to make informed guesses. This is possible even today, without superintelligence. For example, it is more plausible that our CEV would wish for there to be people in the future who live rich and happy lives than that it would wish that we should all sit on stools in a dark room experiencing pain. If *we* can make at least some such judgments sensibly, so can a superintelligence. From the outset, the superintelligence's conduct could thus be guided by its estimates of the content of our CEV. It would have strong instrumental reason to refine these initial estimates (e.g. by studying human culture and psychology, scanning human brains, and reasoning about how we might behave if we knew more, thought more clearly, etc.). In investigating these matters, the AI would be guided by its initial estimates of our CEV; so that, for instance, the AI would not unnecessarily run myriad simulations replete with unredeemed human suffering if it estimated that our CEV would probably condemn such simulations as mind crime.

Another objection is that there are so many different ways of life and moral codes in the world that it might not be possible to "blend" them into one CEV. Even if one could blend them, the result might not be particularly appetizing—one would be unlikely to get a delicious meal by mixing together all the best flavors from everyone's different favorite dish.[13] In answer to this, one could point out that the CEV approach does not require that all ways of life, moral codes, or personal values be blended together into one stew. The CEV dynamic is supposed to act only when our wishes cohere. On issues on which there is widespread irreconcilable disagreement, even after the various idealizing conditions have been imposed, the dynamic should refrain from determining the outcome. To continue the cooking analogy, it might be that individuals or cultures will have different favorite dishes, but that they can nevertheless broadly agree that aliments should be nontoxic. The CEV dynamic could then act to prevent food poisoning while otherwise allowing humans to work out their culinary practices without its guidance or interference.

Rationales for CEV

Yudkowsky's article offered seven arguments for the CEV approach. Three of these were basically different ways of making the point that while the aim should be to do something that is humane and helpful, it would be very difficult to lay down an explicit set of rules that does not have unintended interpretations and undesirable consequences.[14] The CEV approach is meant to be robust and self-correcting; it is meant to capture the *source* of our values instead of relying on us correctly enumerating and articulating, once and for all, each of our essential values.

The remaining four arguments go beyond that first basic (but important) point, spelling out desiderata on candidate solutions to the value-specification problem and suggesting that CEV meets these desiderata.

"Encapsulate moral growth"

This is the desideratum that the solution should allow for the possibility of moral progress. As suggested earlier, there are reasons to believe that our current moral beliefs are flawed in many ways; perhaps deeply flawed. If we were to stipulate a specific and unalterable moral code for the AI to follow, we would in effect be locking in our present moral convictions, including their errors, destroying any hope of moral growth. The CEV approach, by contrast, allows for the possibility of such growth because it has the AI try to do that which we would have wished it to do if we had developed further under favorable conditions, and it is possible that if we had thus developed our moral beliefs and sensibilities would have been purged of their current defects and limitations.

"Avoid hijacking the destiny of humankind"

Yudkowsky has in mind a scenario in which a small group of programmers creates a seed AI that then grows into a superintelligence that obtains a decisive strategic advantage. In this scenario, the original programmers hold in their hands the entirety of humanity's cosmic endowment. Obviously, this is a hideous responsibility for any mortal to shoulder. Yet it is not possible for the programmers to completely shirk the onus once they find themselves in this situation: any choice they make, including abandoning the project, would have world-historical consequences. Yudkowsky sees CEV as a way for the programmers to avoid arrogating to themselves the privilege or burden of determining humanity's future. By setting up a dynamic that implements *humanity's* coherent extrapolated volition—as opposed to their own volition, or their own favorite moral theory—they in effect distribute their influence over the future to all of humanity.

"Avoid creating a motive for modern-day humans to fight over the initial dynamic"

Distributing influence over humanity's future is not only morally preferable to the programming team implementing their own favorite vision, it is also a way to reduce the incentive to fight over who gets to create the first superintelligence. In the CEV approach, the programmers (or their sponsors) exert no more influence over the content of the outcome than any other person—though they of course play a starring causal role in determining the structure of the extrapolation and in deciding to implement humanity's CEV instead of some alternative. Avoiding conflict is important not only because of the immediate harm that conflict tends to cause but also because it hinders collaboration on the difficult challenge of developing superintelligence safely and beneficially.

CEV is meant to be capable of commanding wide support. This is not just because it allocates influence equitably. There is also a deeper ground for the irenic potential of CEV, namely that it enables many different groups to hope that their preferred vision of the future will prevail totally. Imagine a member of the Afghan Taliban debating with a member of the Swedish Humanist Association. The two have very different worldviews, and what is a utopia for one might be a dystopia for the other. Nor might either be thrilled by any compromise position, such as permitting girls to receive an education but only up to ninth grade, or permitting Swedish girls to be educated but Afghan girls not. However, both the Taliban and the Humanist might be able to endorse the principle that the future should be determined by humanity's CEV. The Taliban could reason that if his religious views are in fact correct (as he is convinced they are) and if good grounds for accepting these views exist (as he is also convinced) then humankind would in the end come to accept these views if only people were less prejudiced and biased, if they spent more time studying scripture, if they could more clearly understand how the world works and recognize essential priorities, if they could be freed from irrational rebelliousness and cowardice, and so forth.[15] The Humanist, similarly, would believe that under these idealized conditions, humankind would come to embrace the principles she espouses.

"Keep humankind ultimately in charge of its own destiny"

We might not want an outcome in which a paternalistic superintelligence watches over us constantly, micromanaging our affairs with an eye towards optimizing every detail in accordance with a grand plan. Even if we stipulate that the superintelligence would be perfectly benevolent, and free from presumptuousness, arrogance, overbearingness, narrow-mindedness, and other human shortcomings, one might still resent the loss of autonomy entailed by such an arrangement. We might prefer to create our destiny as we go along, even if it means that we sometimes fumble. Perhaps we want the superintelligence to serve as a safety net, to support us when things go catastrophically wrong, but otherwise to leave us to fend for ourselves.

CEV allows for this possibility. CEV is meant to be an "initial dynamic," a process that runs once and then replaces itself with whatever the extrapolated volition wishes. If humanity's extrapolated volition wishes that we live under the supervision of a paternalistic AI, then the CEV dynamic would create such an AI and hand it the reins. If humanity's extrapolated volition instead wishes that a democratic human world government be created, then the CEV dynamic might facilitate the establishment of such an institution and otherwise remain invisible. If humanity's extrapolated volition is instead that each person should get an endowment of resources that she can use as she pleases so long as she respects the equal rights of others, then the CEV dynamic could make this come true by operating in the background much like a law of nature, to prevent trespass, theft, assault, and other nonconsensual impingements.[16]

The structure of the CEV approach thus allows for a virtually unlimited range of outcomes. It is also conceivable that humanity's extrapolated volition would wish that the CEV does nothing at all. In that case, the AI implementing CEV should, upon having established with sufficient probability that this is what humanity's extrapolated volition would wish it to do, safely shut itself down.

Further remarks

The CEV proposal, as outlined above, is of course the merest schematic. It has a number of free parameters that could be specified in various ways, yielding different versions of the proposal.

One parameter is the extrapolation base: Whose volitions are to be included? We might say "everybody," but this answer spawns a host of further questions. Does the extrapolation base include so-called "marginal persons" such as embryos, fetuses, brain-dead persons, patients with severe dementias or who are in permanent vegetative states? Does each of the hemispheres of a "split-brain" patient get its own weight in the extrapolation and is this weight the same as that of the entire brain of a normal subject? What about people who lived in the past but are now dead? People who will be born in the future? Higher animals and other sentient creatures? Digital minds? Extraterrestrials?

One option would be to include only the population of adult human beings on Earth who are alive at the start of the time of the AI's creation. An initial extrapolation from this base could then decide whether and how the base should be expanded. Since the number of "marginals" at the periphery of this base is relatively small, the result of the extrapolation may not depend much on exactly where the boundary is drawn—on whether, for instance, it includes fetuses or not.

That somebody is excluded from the original extrapolation base does not imply that their wishes and well-being are disregarded. If the coherent extrapolated volition of those in the extrapolation base (e.g. living adult human beings) wishes that moral consideration be extended to other beings, then the outcome of the CEV dynamic would reflect that preference. Nevertheless, it is possible that the interests of those who are included in the original extrapolation base would be accommodated to a greater degree than the interests of outsiders. In particular, if the dynamic acts only where there is broad agreement between individual extrapolated volitions (as in Yudkowsky's original proposal), there would seem to be a significant risk of an ungenerous blocking vote that could prevent, for instance, the welfare of nonhuman animals or digital minds from being protected. The result might potentially be morally rotten.[17]

One motivation for the CEV proposal was to avoid creating a motive for humans to fight over the creation of the first superintelligent AI. Although the CEV proposal scores better on this desideratum than many alternatives, it does not entirely eliminate motives for conflict. A selfish individual, group, or nation might seek to enlarge its slice of the future by keeping others out of the extrapolation base.

A power grab of this sort might be rationalized in various ways. It might be argued, for instance, that the sponsor who funds the development of the AI deserves to own the outcome. This moral claim is probably false. It could be objected, for example, that the project that launches the first successful seed AI imposes a vast risk externality on the rest of humanity, which therefore is entitled to compensation. The amount of compensation owed is so great that it can only take the form of giving everybody a stake in the upside if things turn out well.[18]

Another argument that might be used to rationalize a power grab is that large segments of humanity have base or evil preferences and that including them in the extrapolation base would risk turning humanity's future into a dystopia. It is difficult to know the share of good and bad in the average person's heart. It is also difficult to know how much this balance varies between different groups, social strata, cultures, or nations. Whether one is optimistic or pessimistic about human nature, one may prefer not to wager humanity's cosmic endowment on the speculation that, for a sufficient majority of the seven billion people currently alive, their better angels would prevail in their extrapolated volitions. Of course, omitting a certain set of people from the extrapolation base does not guarantee that light would triumph; and it might well be that the souls that would soonest exclude others or grab power for themselves tend rather to contain unusually large amounts of darkness.

Yet another reason for fighting over the initial dynamic is that one might believe that somebody else's AI will not work as advertised, even if the AI is billed as a way to implement humanity's CEV. If different groups have different beliefs about which implementation is most likely to succeed, they might fight to prevent the others from launching. It would be better in such situations if the competing projects could settle their epistemic differences by some method that more reliably ascertains who is right than the method of armed conflict.[19]

Morality models

The CEV proposal is not the only possible form of indirect normativity. For example, instead of implementing humanity's coherent extrapolated volition, one could try to build an AI with the goal of doing what is morally right, relying on the AI's superior cognitive capacities to figure out just which actions fit that description. We can call this proposal "moral rightness" (MR). The idea is that we humans have an imperfect understanding of what is right and wrong, and perhaps an even poorer understanding of how the concept of moral rightness is to be philosophically analyzed: but a superintelligence could understand these things better.[20]

What if we are not sure whether moral realism is true? We could still attempt the MR proposal. We should just have to make sure to specify what the AI should do in the eventuality that its presupposition of moral realism is false. For example, we could stipulate that if the AI estimates with a sufficient probability that there are no suitable non-relative truths about moral rightness, then it should revert to implementing coherent extrapolated volition instead, or simply shut itself down.[21]

MR appears to have several advantages over CEV. MR would do away with various free parameters in CEV, such as the degree of coherence among extrapolated volitions that is required for the AI to act on the result, the ease with which a majority can overrule dissenting minorities, and the nature of the social environment within which our extrapolated selves are to be supposed to have "grown up farther together." It would seem to eliminate the possibility of a moral failure resulting from the use of an extrapolation base that is too narrow or too wide. Furthermore, MR would orient the AI toward morally right action even if our coherent extrapolated volitions happen to wish for the AI to take actions that are morally odious. As noted earlier, this seems a live possibility with the CEV proposal. Moral goodness might be more like a precious metal than an abundant element in human nature, and even after the ore has been processed and refined in accordance with the prescriptions of the CEV proposal, who knows whether the principal outcome will be shining virtue, indifferent slag, or toxic sludge?

MR would also appear to have some disadvantages. It relies on the notion of "morally right," a notoriously difficult concept, one with which philosophers have grappled since antiquity without yet attaining consensus as to its analysis. Picking an erroneous explication of "moral rightness" could result in outcomes that would be morally very wrong. This difficulty of defining "moral rightness" might seem to count heavily against the MR proposal. However, it is not clear that the MR proposal is really at a material disadvantage in this regard. The CEV proposal, too, uses terms and concepts that are difficult to explicate (such as "knowledge," "being more the people we wished we were," "grown up farther together," among others).[22] Even if these concepts are marginally less opaque than "moral rightness," they are still miles removed from anything that programmers can currently express in code.[23] The path to endowing an AI with any of these concepts might involve giving it general linguistic ability (comparable, at least, to that of a normal human adult). Such a general ability to understand natural language could then be used to understand what is meant by "morally right." If the AI could grasp the meaning, it could search for actions that fit. As the AI develops superintelligence, it could then make progress on two fronts: on the philosophical problem of understanding what moral rightness is, and on the practical problem of applying this understanding to evaluate particular actions.[24] While this would not be easy, it is not clear that it would be any *more* difficult than extrapolating humanity's coherent extrapolated volition.[25]

A more fundamental issue with MR is that even if it can be implemented, it might not give us what we want or what we would choose if we were brighter and better informed. This is of course the essential feature of MR, not an accidental bug. However, it might be a feature that would be extremely harmful to us.[26]

One might try to preserve the basic idea of the MR model while reducing its demandingness by focusing on *moral permissibility*: the idea being that we could let the AI pursue humanity's CEV so long as it did not act in ways that are morally impermissible. For example, one might formulate the following goal for the AI:

Among the actions that are morally permissible for the AI, take one that humanity's CEV would prefer. However, if some part of this instruction has no well-specified meaning, or if we are radically confused about its meaning, or if moral realism is false, or if we acted morally impermissibly in creating an AI with this goal, then undergo a controlled shutdown.[27] Follow the intended meaning of this instruction.

One might still worry that this moral permissibility model (MP) represents an unpalatably high degree of respect for the requirements of morality. How big a sacrifice it would entail depends on which ethical theory is true.[28] If ethics is *satisficing*, in the sense that it counts as morally permissible any action that conforms to a few basic moral constraints, then MP may leave ample room for our coherent extrapolated volition to influence the AI's actions. However, if ethics is *maximizing*—for example, if the only morally permissible actions are those that have the morally best consequences—then MP may leave little or no room for our own preferences to shape the outcome.

To illustrate this concern, let us return for a moment to the example of hedonistic consequentialism. Suppose that this ethical theory is true, and that the AI knows it to be so. For present purposes, we can define hedonistic consequentialism as the claim that an action is morally right (and morally permissible) if and only if, among all feasible actions, no other action would produce a greater balance of pleasure over suffering. The AI, following MP, might maximize the surfeit of pleasure by converting the accessible universe into hedonium, a process that may involve building computronium and using it to perform computations that instantiate pleasurable experiences. Since simulating any existing human brain is not the most efficient way of producing pleasure, a likely consequence is that we all die.

By enacting either the MR or the MP proposal, we would thus risk sacrificing our lives for a greater good. This would be a bigger sacrifice than one might think, because what we stand to lose is not merely the chance to live out a normal human life but the opportunity to enjoy the far longer and richer lives that a friendly superintelligence could bestow.

The sacrifice looks even less appealing when we reflect that the superintelligence could realize a nearly-as-great good (in fractional terms) while sacrificing much less of our own potential well-being. Suppose that we agreed to allow *almost* the entire accessible universe to be converted into hedonium—everything except a small preserve, say the Milky Way, which would be set aside to accommodate our own needs. Then there would still be a hundred billion galaxies devoted to the maximization of pleasure. But we would have one galaxy within which to create wonderful civilizations that could last for billions of years and in which humans and nonhuman animals could survive and thrive, and have the opportunity to develop into beatific posthuman spirits.[29]

If one prefers this latter option (as I would be inclined to do) it implies that one does not have an unconditional lexically dominant preference for acting morally permissibly. But it is consistent with placing great weight on morality.

Even from a purely moral point of view, it might be better to *advocate* some proposal that is less morally ambitious than MR or MP. If the morally best has no chance of being implemented—perhaps because of its frowning demandingness—it might be morally better to promote some other proposal, one that would be near-ideal and whose chances of being implemented could be significantly increased by our promoting it.[30]

Do What I Mean

We might feel unsure whether to go for CEV, MR, MP, or something else. Could we punt on this higher-level decision as well, offloading even more cognitive work onto the AI? Where is the limit to our possible laziness?

Consider, for example, the following "reasons-based" goal:

Do whatever we would have had most reason to ask the AI to do.

This goal might boil down to extrapolated volition or morality or something else, but it would seem to spare us the effort and risk involved in trying to figure out for ourselves which of these more specific objectives we would have most reason to select.

Some of the problems with the morality-based goals, however, also apply here. First, we might fear that this reasons-based goal would leave too little room for our own desires. Some philosophers maintain that a person always has most reason to do what it would be morally best for her to do. If those philosophers are right, then the reason-based goal collapses into MR—with the concomitant risk that a superintelligence implementing such a dynamic would kill everyone within reach. Second, as with all proposals couched in technical language, there is a possibility that we might have misunderstood the meaning of our own assertions. We saw that, in the case of the morality-based goals, asking the AI to do what is right may lead to unforeseen and unwanted consequences such that, had we anticipated them, we would not have implemented the goal in question. The same applies to asking the AI to do what we have most reason to do.

What if we try to avoid these difficulties by couching a goal in emphatically nontechnical language—such as in terms of "niceness":[31]

Take the nicest action; or, if no action is nicest, then take an action that is at least super-duper nice.

How could there be anything objectionable about building a *nice* AI? But we must ask what precisely is meant by this expression. The lexicon lists various meanings of "nice" that are clearly not intended to be used here: we do not intend that the AI should be *courteous and polite* nor *over-delicate or fastidious*. If we can count on the AI recognizing the intended interpretation of "niceness" and being motivated to pursue niceness in just that sense, then this goal would seem to amount to a command to do what the programmers meant for the AI to do.[32] An injunction to similar effect was included in the formulation of CEV (". . . interpreted as we wish that interpreted") and in the moral-permissibility criterion as rendered earlier (". . . follow the intended meaning of this instruction"). By affixing such a "Do What I Mean" clause we may indicate that the other words in the goal description should be construed charitably rather than literally. But saying that the AI should be "nice" adds almost nothing: the real work is done by the "Do What I Mean" instruction. If we knew how to code "Do What I Mean" in a general and powerful way, we might as well use that as a standalone goal.

How might one implement such a "Do What I Mean" dynamic? That is, how might we create an AI motivated to charitably interpret our wishes and unspoken intentions and to act accordingly? One initial step could be to try to get clearer about what we mean by "Do What I Mean." It might help if we could explicate this in more behavioristic terms, for example in terms of revealed preferences in various hypothetical situations—such as situations in which we had more time to consider the options, in which we were smarter, in which we knew more of the relevant facts, and in which in various other ways conditions would be more favorable for us accurately manifesting in concrete choices what we mean when we say that we want an AI that is friendly, beneficial, nice . . .

Here, of course, we come full circle. We have returned to the indirect normativity approach with which we started—the CEV proposal, which, in essence, expunges all concrete content from the value specification, leaving only an abstract value defined in purely procedural terms: to do that which we would have wished for the AI to do in suitably idealized circumstances. By means of such indirect normativity, we could hope to offload to the AI much of the cognitive work that we ourselves would be trying to perform if we attempted to articulate a more concrete description of what values the AI is to pursue. In seeking to take full advantage of the AI's epistemic superiority, CEV can thus be seen as an application of the principle of epistemic deference.

Component list

So far we have considered different options for what content to put into the goal system. But an AI's behavior will also be influenced by other design choices. In particular, it can make a critical difference which

Table 13 *Component list*

Goal content	What objective should the AI pursue? How should a description of this objective be interpreted? Should the objective include giving special rewards to those who contributed to the project's success?
Decision theory	Should the AI use causal decision theory, evidential decision theory, updateless decision theory, or something else?
Epistemology	What should the AI's prior probability function be, and what other explicit or implicit assumptions about the world should it make? What theory of anthropics should it use?
Ratification	Should the AI's plans be subjected to human review before being put into effect? If so, what is the protocol for that review process?

decision theory and which epistemology it uses. Another important question is whether the AI's plans will be subject to human review before being put into action.

Table 13 summarizes these design choices. A project that aims to build a superintelligence ought to be able to explain what choices it has made regarding each of these components, and to justify why those choices were made.[33]

Goal content

We have already discussed how indirect normativity might be used in specifying the values that the AI is to pursue. We discussed some options, such as morality-based models and coherent extrapolated volition. Each such option creates further choices that need to be made. For instance, the CEV approach comes in many varieties, depending on who is included in the extrapolation base, the structure of the extrapolation, and so forth. Other forms of motivation selection methods might call for different types of goal content. For example, an oracle might be built to place a value on giving accurate answers. An oracle constructed with domesticity motivation might also have goal content that disvalues the excessive use of resources in producing its answers.

Another design choice is whether to include special provisions in the goal content to reward individuals who contribute to the successful realization of the AI, for example by giving them extra resources or influence over the AI's behavior. We can term any such provisions "incentive wrapping." Incentive wrapping could be seen as a way to increase the likelihood that the project will be successful, at the cost of compromising to some extent the goal that the project set out to achieve.

For example, if the project's goal is to create a dynamic that implements humanity's coherent extrapolated volition, then an incentive wrapping scheme might specify that certain individuals' volitions should be given extra weight in the extrapolation. If such a project is successful, the result is not necessarily the implementation of humanity's coherent extrapolated volition. Instead, some approximation to this goal might be achieved.[34]

Since incentive wrapping would be a piece of goal content that would be interpreted and pursued by a superintelligence, it could take advantage of indirect normativity to specify subtle and complicated provisions that would be difficult for a human manager to implement. For example, instead of rewarding programmers according to some crude but easily accessible metric, such as how many hours they worked or how many bugs they corrected, the incentive wrapping could specify that programmers "are to be rewarded in proportion to how much their contributions increased some reasonable *ex ante* probability of the project being successfully completed in the way the sponsors intended." Further, there would be no reason to limit the incentive wrapping to project staff. It could instead specify that *every* person should be rewarded according to their just deserts. Credit allocation is a difficult problem, but a superintelligence could be expected to do a reasonable job of approximating the criteria specified, explicitly or implicitly, by the incentive wrapping.

It is conceivable that the superintelligence might even find some way of rewarding individuals who have died prior to the superintelligence's creation.[35] The incentive wrapping could then be extended to embrace at least some of the deceased, potentially including individuals who died before the project was conceived, or even antedating the first enunciation of the concept of incentive wrapping. Although the institution of such a retroactive policy would not causally incentivize those people who are already resting in their graves as these words are being put to the page, it might be favored for moral reasons—though it could be argued that insofar as fairness is a goal, it should be included as part of the target specification proper rather than in the surrounding incentive wrapping.

We cannot here delve into all the ethical and strategic issues associated with incentive wrapping. A project's position on these issues, however, would be an important aspect of its fundamental design concept.

Decision theory

Another important design choice is which decision theory the AI should be built to use. This might affect how the AI behaves in certain strategically fateful situations. It might determine, for instance, whether the AI is open to trade with, or extortion by, other superintelligent civilizations whose existence it hypothesizes. The particulars of the decision theory could also matter in predicaments involving finite probabilities of infinite payoffs ("Pascalian wagers") or extremely small probabilities of extremely large finite payoffs ("Pascalian muggings") or in contexts where the AI is facing fundamental normative uncertainty or where there are multiple instantiations of the same agent program.[36]

The options on the table include causal decision theory (in a variety of flavors) and evidential decision theory, along with newer candidates such as "timeless decision theory" and "updateless decision theory," which are still under development.[37] It may prove difficult to identify and articulate the correct decision theory, and to have justified confidence that we have got it right. Although the prospects for directly specifying an AI's decision theory are perhaps more hopeful than those of directly specifying its final values, we are still confronted with a substantial risk of error. Many of the complications that might break the currently most popular decision theories were discovered only recently, suggesting that there might exist further problems that have not yet come into sight. The result of giving the AI a flawed decision theory might be disastrous, possibly amounting to an existential catastrophe.

In view of these difficulties, one might consider an indirect approach to specifying the decision theory that the AI should use. Exactly how to do this is not yet clear. We might want the AI to use "that decision theory D which we would have wanted it to use had we thought long and hard about the matter." However, the AI would need to be able to make decisions before learning what D is. It would thus need some effective interim decision theory D' that would govern its search for D. One might try to define D' to be some sort of superposition of the AI's current hypotheses about D (weighed by their probabilities), though there are unsolved technical problems with how to do this in a fully general way.[38] There is also cause for concern that the AI might make irreversibly bad decisions (such as rewriting itself to henceforth run on some flawed decision theory) during the learning phase, before the AI has had the opportunity to determine which particular decision theory is correct. To reduce the risk of derailment during this period of vulnerability we might instead try to endow the seed AI with some form of *restricted rationality*: a deliberately simplified but hopefully dependable decision theory that staunchly ignores esoteric considerations, even ones we think may ultimately be legitimate, and that is designed to replace itself with a more sophisticated (indirectly specified) decision theory once certain conditions are met.[39] It is an open research question whether and how this could be made to work.

Epistemology

A project will also need to make a fundamental design choice in selecting the AI's epistemology, specifying the principles and criteria whereby empirical hypotheses are to be evaluated. Within a Bayesian framework, we can think of the epistemology as a prior probability function—the AI's implicit assignment of probabilities to possible worlds before it has taken any perceptual evidence into account. In other frameworks, the epistemology might take a different form; but in any case some inductive learning rule is necessary if the AI is to generalize from past observations and make predictions about the future.[40] As with the goal content and the decision theory, however, there is a risk that our epistemology specification could miss the mark.

One might think that there is a limit to how much damage could arise from an incorrectly specified epistemology. If the epistemology is *too* dysfunctional, then the AI could not be very intelligent and it could not pose the kind of risk discussed in this book. But the concern is that we may specify an epistemology that is sufficiently sound to make the AI instrumentally effective in most situations, yet which has some flaw that leads the AI astray on some matter of crucial importance. Such an AI might be akin to a quick-witted person whose worldview is predicated on a false dogma, held to with absolute conviction, who consequently "tilts at windmills" and gives his all in pursuit of fantastical or harmful objectives.

Certain kinds of subtle difference in an AI's prior could turn out to make a drastic difference to how it behaves. For example, an AI might be given a prior that assigns zero probability to the universe being infinite. No matter how much astronomical evidence it accrues to the contrary, such an AI would stubbornly reject any cosmological theory that implied an infinite universe; and it might make foolish choices as a result.[41] Or an AI might be given a prior that assigns a zero probability to the universe not being Turing-computable (this is in fact a common feature of many of the priors discussed in the literature, including the Kolmogorov complexity prior mentioned in Chapter 1), again with poorly understood consequences if the embedded assumption—known as the "Church–Turing thesis"—should turn out to be false. An AI could also end up with a prior that makes strong metaphysical commitments of one sort or another, for instance by ruling out a priori the possibility that any strong form of mind–body dualism could be true or the possibility that there are irreducible moral facts. If any of those commitments is mistaken, the AI might seek to realize its final goals in ways that we would regard as perverse instantiations. Yet there is no obvious reason why such an AI, despite being fundamentally wrong about one important matter, could not be sufficiently instrumentally effective to secure a decisive strategic advantage. (Anthropics, the study of how to make inferences from indexical information in the presence of observation selection effects, is another area where the choice of epistemic axioms could prove pivotal.[42])

We might reasonably doubt our ability to resolve all foundational issues in epistemology in time for the construction of the first seed AI. We may, therefore, consider taking an indirect approach to specifying the AI's epistemology. This would raise many of the same issues as taking an indirect approach to specifying its decision theory. In the case of epistemology, however, there may be greater hope of benign convergence, with any of a wide class of epistemologies providing an adequate foundation for safe and effective AI and ultimately yielding similar doxastic results. The reason for this is that sufficiently abundant empirical evidence and analysis would tend to wash out any moderate differences in prior expectations.[43]

A good aim would be to endow the AI with fundamental epistemological principles that match those governing our own thinking. Any AI diverging from this ideal is an AI that we would judge to be reasoning incorrectly if we consistently applied our own standards. Of course, this applies only to our *fundamental* epistemological principles. Non-fundamental principles should be continuously created and revised by the seed AI itself as it develops its understanding of the world. The point of superintelligence is not to pander to human preconceptions but to make mincemeat out of our ignorance and folly.

Ratification

The final item in our list of design choices is *ratification*. Should the AI's plans be subjected to human review before being put into effect? For an oracle, this question is implicitly answered in the affirmative. The oracle outputs information; human reviewers choose whether and how to act upon it. For genies, sovereigns, and tool-AIs, however, the question of whether to use some form of ratification remains open.

To illustrate how ratification might work, consider an AI intended to function as a sovereign implementing humanity's CEV. Instead of launching this AI directly, imagine that we first built an oracle AI for the sole purpose of answering questions about what the sovereign AI would do. As earlier chapters revealed, there are risks in creating a superintelligent oracle (such as risks of mind crime or infrastructure profusion). But for purposes of this example let us assume that the oracle AI has been successfully implemented in a way that avoided these pitfalls.

We thus have an oracle AI that offers us its best guesses about the consequences of running some piece of code intended to implement humanity's CEV. The oracle may not be able to predict in detail what would happen, but its predictions are likely to be better than our own. (If it were impossible even for a superintelligence to predict *anything* about what the code would do, we would be crazy to run it.) So the oracle ponders for a while and then presents its forecast. To make the answer intelligible, the oracle may offer the operator a range of tools with which to explore various features of the predicted outcome. The oracle could show pictures of what the future looks like and provide statistics about the number of sentient beings that will exist at different times, along with average, peak, and lowest levels of well-being. It could offer intimate biographies of several randomly selected individuals (perhaps imaginary people selected to be probably representative). It could highlight aspects of the future that the operator might not have thought of inquiring about but which would be regarded as pertinent once pointed out.

Being able to preview the outcome in this manner has obvious advantages. The preview could reveal the consequences of an error in a planned sovereign's design specifications or source code. If the crystal ball shows a ruined future, we could scrap the code for the planned sovereign AI and try something else. A strong case could be made that we should familiarize ourselves with the concrete ramifications of an option before committing to it, especially when the entire future of the race is on the line.

What is perhaps less obvious is that ratification also has potentially significant disadvantages. The irenic quality of CEV might be undermined if opposing factions, instead of submitting to the arbitration of superior wisdom in confident expectation of being vindicated, could see in advance what the verdict would be. A proponent of the morality-based approach might worry that the sponsor's resolve would collapse if all the sacrifices required by the morally optimal were to be revealed. And we might all have reason to prefer a future that holds some surprises, some dissonance, some wildness, some opportunities for self-overcoming—a future whose contours are not too snugly tailored to present preconceptions but provide some give for dramatic movement and unplanned growth. We might be less likely to take such an expansive view if we could cherry-pick every detail of the future, sending back to the drawing board any draft that does not fully conform to our fancy at that moment.

The issue of sponsor ratification is therefore less clear-cut than it might initially seem. Nevertheless, on balance it would seem prudent to take advantage of an opportunity to preview, if that functionality is available. But rather than letting the reviewer fine-tune every aspect of the outcome, we might give her a simple veto which could be exercised only a few times before the entire project would be aborted.[44]

Getting close enough

The main purpose of ratification would be to reduce the probability of catastrophic error. In general, it seems wise to aim at minimizing the risk of catastrophic error rather than at maximizing the chance of every detail being fully optimized. There are two reasons for this. First, humanity's cosmic endowment is astronomically large—there is plenty to go around even if our process involves some waste or accepts some unnecessary constraints. Second, there is a hope that if we but get the initial conditions for the intelligence explosion approximately right, then the resulting superintelligence may eventually home in on, and precisely hit, our ultimate objectives. The important thing is to land in the right attractor basin.

With regard to epistemology, it is plausible that a wide range of priors will ultimately converge to very similar posteriors (when computed by a superintelligence and conditionalized on a realistic amount of data). We therefore need not worry about getting the epistemology *exactly* right. We must just avoid giving the AI a prior that is so extreme as to render the AI incapable of learning vital truths even with the benefit of copious experience and analysis.[45]

With regard to decision theory, the risk of irrecoverable error seems larger. We might still hope to directly specify a decision theory that is good enough. A superintelligent AI could switch to a new decision theory at any time; however, if it starts out with a sufficiently wrong decision theory it may not see the reason to switch. Even if an agent comes to see the benefits of having a different decision theory, the realization might come too late. For example, an agent designed to refuse blackmail might enjoy the benefit of deterring would-be extortionists. For this reason, blackmailable agents might do well to proactively adopt a non-exploitable decision theory. Yet once a blackmailable agent receives the threat and regards it as credible, the damage is done.

Given an adequate epistemology and decision theory, we could try to design the system to implement CEV or some other indirectly specified goal content. Again there is hope of convergence: that different ways of implementing a CEV-like dynamic would lead to the same utopian outcome. Short of such convergence, we may still hope that many of the different possible outcomes are good enough to count as existential success.

It is not necessary for us to create a highly optimized design. Rather, our focus should be on creating a highly reliable design, one that can be trusted to retain enough sanity to recognize its own failings. An imperfect superintelligence, whose fundamentals are sound, would gradually repair itself; and having done so, it would exert as much beneficial optimization power on the world as if it had been perfect from the outset.

CHAPTER 14

The strategic picture

I t is now time to consider the challenge of superintelligence in a broader context. We would like to orient ourselves in the strategic landscape sufficiently to know at least which general direction we should be heading. This, it turns out, is not at all easy. Here in the penultimate chapter, we introduce some general analytical concepts that help us think about long-term science and technology policy issues. We then apply them to the issue of machine intelligence.

It can be illuminating to make a rough distinction between two different normative stances from which a proposed policy may be evaluated. *The person-affecting perspective* asks whether a proposed change would be in "our interest"—that is to say, whether it would (on balance, and in expectation) be in the interest of those morally considerable creatures who either already exist or will come into existence independently of whether the proposed change occurs or not. *The impersonal perspective*, in contrast, gives no special consideration to currently existing people, or to those who will come to exist independently of whether the proposed change occurs. Instead, it counts everybody equally, independently of their temporal location. The impersonal perspective sees great value in bringing new people into existence, provided they have lives worth living: the more happy lives created, the better.

This distinction, although it barely hints at the moral complexities associated with a machine intelligence revolution, can be useful in a first-cut analysis. Here we will first examine matters from the impersonal perspective. We will later see what changes if person-affecting considerations are given weight in our deliberations.

Science and technology strategy

Before we zoom in on issues specific to machine superintelligence, we must introduce some strategic concepts and considerations that pertain to scientific and technological development more generally.

Differential technological development

Suppose that a policymaker proposes to cut funding for a certain research field, out of concern for the risks or long-term consequences of some hypothetical technology that might eventually grow from its soil. She can then expect a howl of opposition from the research community.

Scientists and their public advocates often say that it is futile to try to control the evolution of technology by blocking research. If some technology is feasible (the argument goes) it will be developed regardless of any particular policymaker's scruples about speculative future risks. Indeed, the more powerful the capabilities that a line of development promises to produce, the surer we can be that somebody, somewhere, will be motivated to pursue it. Funding cuts will not stop progress or forestall its concomitant dangers.

Interestingly, this futility objection is almost never raised when a policymaker proposes to *increase* funding to some area of research, even though the argument would seem to cut both ways. One rarely hears indignant voices protest: "Please do not increase our funding. Rather, make some cuts. Researchers in other countries will surely pick up the slack; the same work will get done anyway. Don't squander the public's treasure on domestic scientific research!"

What accounts for this apparent doublethink? One plausible explanation, of course, is that members of the research community have a self-serving bias which leads us to believe that research is always good and tempts us to embrace almost any argument that supports our demand for more funding. However, it is also possible that the double standard can be justified in terms of national self-interest. Suppose that the development of a technology has *two* effects: giving a small benefit B to its inventors and the country that sponsors them, while imposing an aggregately larger harm H—which could be a risk externality—on everybody. Even somebody who is largely altruistic might then choose to develop the overall harmful technology. They might reason that the harm H will result no matter what they do, since if they refrain somebody else will develop the technology anyway; and given that total welfare cannot be affected, they might as well grab the benefit *B* for themselves and their nation. ("Unfortunately, there will soon be a device that will destroy the world. Fortunately, we got the grant to build it!")

Whatever the explanation for the futility objection's appeal, it fails to show that there is in general no impersonal reason for trying to steer technological development. It fails even if we concede the motivating idea that with continued scientific and technological development efforts, all relevant technologies will eventually be developed—that is, even if we concede the following:

Technological completion conjecture

If scientific and technological development efforts do not effectively cease, then all important basic capabilities that could be obtained through some possible technology will be obtained.[1]

There are at least two reasons why the technological completion conjecture does not imply the futility objection. First, the antecedent might not hold, because it is not in fact a given that scientific and technological development efforts will not effectively cease (before the attainment of technological maturity). This reservation is especially pertinent in a context that involves existential risk. Second, even if we could be certain that all important basic capabilities that could be obtained through some possible technology will be obtained, it could still make sense to attempt to influence the direction of technological research. What matters is not only *whether* a technology is developed, but also *when* it is developed, by *whom*, and in *what context*. These circumstances of birth of a new technology, which shape its impact, can be affected by turning funding spigots on or off (and by wielding other policy instruments).

These reflections suggest a principle that would have us attend to the relative speed with which different technologies are developed:[2]

The principle of differential technological development

Retard the development of dangerous and harmful technologies, especially ones that raise the level of existential risk; and accelerate the development of beneficial technologies, especially those that reduce the existential risks posed by nature or by other technologies.

A policy could thus be evaluated on the basis of how much of a differential advantage it gives to desired forms of technological development over undesired forms.[3]

Preferred order of arrival

Some technologies have an ambivalent effect on existential risks, increasing some existential risks while decreasing others. Superintelligence is one such technology.

We have seen in earlier chapters that the introduction of machine superintelligence would create a substantial existential risk. But it would reduce many other existential risks. Risks from nature—such as asteroid impacts, supervolcanoes, and natural pandemics—would be virtually eliminated, since superintelligence could deploy countermeasures against most such hazards, or at least demote them to the non-existential category (for instance, via space colonization).

These existential risks from nature are comparatively small over the relevant timescales. But superintelligence would also eliminate or reduce many anthropogenic risks. In particular, it would reduce risks of accidental destruction, including risk of accidents related to new technologies. Being generally more capable than humans, a superintelligence would be less likely to make mistakes, and more likely to recognize when precautions are needed, and to implement precautions competently. A well-constructed superintelligence might sometimes take a risk, but only when doing so is wise. Furthermore, at least in scenarios where the superintelligence forms a singleton, many non-accidental anthropogenic existential risks deriving from global coordination problems would be eliminated. These include risks of wars, technology races, undesirable forms of competition and evolution, and tragedies of the commons.

Since substantial peril would be associated with human beings developing synthetic biology, molecular nanotechnology, climate engineering, instruments for biomedical enhancement and neuropsychological manipulation, tools for social control that may facilitate totalitarianism or tyranny, and other technologies as-yet unimagined, eliminating these types of risk would be a great boon. An argument could therefore be mounted that earlier arrival dates of superintelligence are preferable. However, if risks from nature and from other hazards unrelated to future technology are small, then this argument could be refined: what matters is that we get superintelligence *before* other dangerous technologies, such as advanced nanotechnology. Whether it happens sooner or later may not be so important (from an impersonal perspective) so long as the order of arrival is right.

The ground for preferring superintelligence to come before other potentially dangerous technologies, such as nanotechnology, is that superintelligence would reduce the existential risks from nanotechnology but not vice versa.[4] Hence, if we create superintelligence first, we will face only those existential risks that are associated with superintelligence; whereas if we create nanotechnology first, we will face the risks of nanotechnology and then, additionally, the risks of superintelligence.[5] Even if the existential risks from superintelligence are very large, and even if superintelligence is the riskiest of all technologies, there could thus be a case for hastening its arrival.

These "sooner-is-better" arguments, however, presuppose that the riskiness of creating superintelligence is the same regardless of when it is created. If, instead, its riskiness declines over time, it might be better to delay the machine intelligence revolution. While a later arrival would leave more time for other existential catastrophes to intercede, it could still be preferable to slow the development of superintelligence. This would be especially plausible if the existential risks associated with superintelligence are much larger than those associated with other disruptive technologies.

There are several quite strong reasons to believe that the riskiness of an intelligence explosion will decline significantly over a multidecadal timeframe. One reason is that a later date leaves more time for the development of solutions to the control problem. The control problem has only recently been recognized, and most of the current best ideas for how to approach it were discovered only within the past decade or so (and in several cases during the time that this book was being written). It is plausible that the state of the art will advance greatly over the next several decades; and if the problem turns out to be very difficult, a significant rate of progress might continue for a century or more. The longer it takes for superintelligence to arrive, the more such progress will have been made when it does. This is an important consideration in favor of later arrival dates—and a very strong consideration against extremely early arrival dates.

Another reason why superintelligence later might be safer is that this would allow more time for various beneficial background trends of human civilization to play themselves out. How much weight one attaches to this consideration will depend on how optimistic one is about these trends.

An optimist could certainly point to a number of encouraging indicators and hopeful possibilities. People might learn to get along better, leading to reductions in violence, war, and cruelty; and global coordination and the scope of political integration might increase, making it easier to escape undesirable technology races (more on this below) and to work out an arrangement whereby the hoped-for gains from an intelligence explosion would be widely shared. There appear to be long-term historical trends in these directions.[6]

Further, an optimist could expect that the "sanity level" of humanity will rise over the course of this century—that prejudices will (on balance) recede, that insights will accumulate, and that people will become more accustomed to thinking about abstract future probabilities and global risks. With luck, we could see a general uplift of epistemic standards in both individual and collective cognition. Again, there are trends pushing in these directions. Scientific progress means that more will be known. Economic growth may give a greater portion of the world's population adequate nutrition (particularly during the early years of life that are important for brain development) and access to quality education. Advances in information technology will make it easier to find, integrate, evaluate, and communicate data and ideas. Furthermore, by the century's end, humanity will have made an additional hundred years' worth of mistakes, from which something might have been learned.

Many potential developments are ambivalent in the abovementioned sense—increasing some existential risks and decreasing others. For example, advances in surveillance, data mining, lie detection, biometrics, and psychological or neurochemical means of manipulating beliefs and desires could reduce some existential risks by making it easier to coordinate internationally or to suppress terrorists and renegades at home. These same advances, however, might also increase some existential risks by amplifying undesirable social dynamics or by enabling the formation of permanently stable totalitarian regimes.

One important frontier is the enhancement of biological cognition, such as through genetic selection. When we discussed this in Chapters 2 and 3, we concluded that the most radical forms of superintelligence would be more likely to arise in the form of machine intelligence. That claim is consistent with cognitive enhancement playing an important role in the lead-up to, and creation of, machine superintelligence. Cognitive enhancement might seem obviously risk-reducing: the smarter the people working on the control problem, the more likely they are to find a solution. However, cognitive enhancement could also hasten the development of machine intelligence, thus reducing the time available to work on the problem. Cognitive enhancement would also have many other relevant consequences. These issues deserve a closer look. (Most of the following remarks about "cognitive enhancement" apply equally to non-biological means of increasing our individual or collective epistemic effectiveness.)

Rates of change and cognitive enhancement

An increase in either the mean or the upper range of human intellectual ability would likely accelerate technological progress across the board, including progress toward various forms of machine intelligence, progress on the control problem, and progress on a wide swath of other technical and economic objectives. What would be the net effect of such acceleration?

Consider the limiting case of a "universal accelerator," an imaginary intervention that accelerates literally *everything*. The action of such a universal accelerator would correspond merely to an arbitrary rescaling of the time metric, producing no qualitative change in observed outcomes.[7]

If we are to make sense of the idea that cognitive enhancement might generally speed things up, we clearly need some other concept than that of universal acceleration. A more promising approach is to focus on how cognitive enhancement might increase the rate of change in one type of process *relative* to the rate of change in some other type of process. Such differential acceleration could affect a system's dynamics. Thus, consider the following concept:

Macro-structural development accelerator—A lever that accelerates the rate at which macro-structural features of the human condition develop, while leaving unchanged the rate at which micro-level human affairs unfold.

Imagine pulling this lever in the decelerating direction. A brake pad is lowered onto the great wheel of world history; sparks fly and metal screeches. After the wheel has settled into a more leisurely pace, the result is a world in which technological innovation occurs more slowly and in which fundamental or globally significant change in political structure and culture happens less frequently and less abruptly. A greater number of generations come and go before one era gives way to another. During the course of a lifespan, a person sees little change in the basic structure of the human condition.

For most of our species' existence, macro-structural development was slower than it is now. Fifty thousand years ago, an entire millennium might have elapsed without a single significant technological invention, without any noticeable increase in human knowledge and understanding, and without any globally meaningful political change. On a micro-level, however, the kaleidoscope of human affairs churned at a reasonable rate, with births, deaths, and other personally and locally significant events. The average person's day might have been more action-packed in the Pleistocene than it is today.

If you came upon a magic lever that would let you change the rate of macro-structural development, what should you do? Ought you to accelerate, decelerate, or leave things as they are?

Assuming the impersonal standpoint, this question requires us to consider the effects on existential risk. Let us distinguish between two kinds of risk: "state risks" and "step risks." A state risk is one that is associated with being in a certain state, and the total amount of state risk to which a system is exposed is a direct function of how long the system remains in that state. Risks from nature are typically state risks: the longer we remain exposed, the greater the chance that we will get struck by an asteroid, supervolcanic eruption, gamma ray burst, naturally arising pandemic, or some other slash of the cosmic scythe. Some anthropogenic risks are also state risks. At the level of an individual, the longer a soldier pokes his head up above the parapet, the greater the cumulative chance he will be shot by an enemy sniper. There are anthropogenic state risks at the existential level as well: the longer we live in an internationally anarchic system, the greater the cumulative chance of a thermonuclear Armageddon or of a great war fought with other kinds of weapons of mass destruction, laying waste to civilization.

A step risk, by contrast, is a discrete risk associated with some necessary or desirable transition. Once the transition is completed, the risk vanishes. The amount of step risk associated with a transition is usually not a simple function of how long the transition takes. One does not halve the risk of traversing a minefield by running twice as fast. Conditional on a fast takeoff, the creation of superintelligence might be a step risk: there would be a certain risk associated with the takeoff, the magnitude of which would depend on what preparations had been made; but the amount of risk might not depend much on whether the takeoff takes twenty milliseconds or twenty hours.

We can then say the following regarding a hypothetical macro-structural development accelerator:

- Insofar as we are concerned with existential state risks, we should favor acceleration—provided we think we have a realistic prospect of making it through to a post-transition era in which any further existential risks are greatly reduced.

- If it were known that there is some step ahead destined to cause an existential catastrophe, then we ought to reduce the rate of macro-structural development (or even put it in reverse) in order to give more generations a chance to exist before the curtain is rung down. But, in fact, it would be overly pessimistic to be so confident that humanity is doomed.

- At present, the level of existential state risk appears to be relatively low. If we imagine the technological macro-conditions for humanity frozen in their current state, it seems very unlikely that an existential catastrophe would occur on a timescale of, say, a decade. So a delay of one decade—provided it occurred at our current stage of development or at some other time when state risk is low—would incur only a very minor existential state risk, whereas a postponement by one decade of subsequent technological developments might well have a significant beneficial impact on later existential step risks, for example by allowing more time for preparation.

Upshot: the main way that the speed of macro-structural development is important is by affecting how well prepared humanity is when the time comes to confront the key step risks.[8]

So the question we must ask is how cognitive enhancement (and concomitant acceleration of macro-structural development) would affect the expected level of preparedness at the critical juncture. Should we prefer a shorter period of preparation with higher intelligence? With higher intelligence, the preparation time could be used more effectively, and the final critical step would be taken by a more intelligent humanity. Or should we prefer to operate with closer to current levels of intelligence if that gives us more time to prepare?

Which option is better depends on the nature of the challenge being prepared for. If the challenge were to solve a problem for which learning from experience is key, then the chronological length of the preparation period might be the determining factor, since time is needed for the requisite experience to accumulate. What would such a challenge look like? One hypothetical example would be a new weapons technology that we could predict would be developed at some point in the future and that would make it the case that any subsequent war would have, let us say, a one-in-ten chance of causing an existential catastrophe. If such were the nature of the challenge facing us, then we might wish the rate of macro-structural development to be slow, so that our species would have more time to get its act together before the critical step when the new weapons technology is invented. One could hope that during the grace period secured through the deceleration, our species might learn to avoid war—that international relations around the globe might come to resemble those between the countries of the European Union, which, having fought one another ferociously for centuries, now coexist in peace and relative harmony. The pacification might occur as a result of the gentle edification from various civilizing processes or through the shock therapy of sub-existential blows (e.g. small nuclear conflagrations, and the recoil and resolve they might engender to finally create the global institutions necessary for the abolishment of interstate wars). If this kind of learning or adjusting would not be much accelerated by increased intelligence, then cognitive enhancement would be undesirable, serving merely to burn the fuse faster.

A prospective intelligence explosion, however, may present a challenge of a different kind. The control problem calls for foresight, reasoning, and theoretical insight. It is less clear how increased historical experience would help. Direct experience of the intelligence explosion is not possible (until too late), and many features conspire to make the control problem unique and lacking in relevant historical precedent. For these reasons, the amount of time that will elapse before the intelligence explosion may not matter much per se. Perhaps what matters, instead, is (a) the amount of intellectual progress on the control problem achieved by the time of the detonation; and (b) the amount of skill and intelligence available at the time to implement the best available solutions (and to improvise what is missing).[9] That this latter factor should respond positively to cognitive enhancement is obvious. How cognitive enhancement would affect factor (a) is a somewhat subtler matter.

Suppose, as suggested earlier, that cognitive enhancement would be a general macro-structural development accelerator. This would hasten the arrival of the intelligence explosion, thus reducing the amount of time available for preparation and for making progress on the control problem.

Normally this would be a bad thing. However, if the only reason why there is less time available for intellectual progress is that intellectual progress is speeded up, then there need be no net reduction in the amount of intellectual progress that will have taken place by the time the intelligence explosion occurs.

At this point, cognitive enhancement might appear to be neutral with respect to factor (a): the same intellectual progress that would otherwise have been made prior to the intelligence explosion—including progress on the control problem—still gets made, only compressed within a shorter time interval. In actuality, however, cognitive enhancement may well prove a positive influence on (a).

One reason why cognitive enhancement might cause more progress to have been made on the control problem by the time the intelligence explosion occurs is that progress on the control problem may be especially contingent on extreme levels of intellectual performance—even more so than the kind of work necessary to create machine intelligence. The role for trial and error and accumulation of experimental results seems quite limited in relation to the control problem, whereas experimental learning will probably play a large role in the development of artificial intelligence or whole brain emulation. The extent to which time can substitute for wit may therefore vary between tasks in a way that should make cognitive enhancement promote progress on the control problem *more* than it would promote progress on the problem of how to create machine intelligence.

Another reason why cognitive enhancement should differentially promote progress on the control problem is that the very need for such progress is more likely to be appreciated by cognitively more capable societies and individuals. It requires foresight and reasoning to realize why the control problem is important and to make it a priority.[10] It may also require uncommon sagacity to find promising ways of approaching such an unfamiliar problem.

From these reflections we might tentatively conclude that cognitive enhancement is desirable, at least insofar as the focus is on the existential risks of an intelligence explosion. Parallel lines of thinking apply to other existential risks arising from challenges that require foresight and reliable abstract reasoning (as opposed to, e.g., incremental adaptation to experienced changes in the environment or a multigenerational process of cultural maturation and institution-building).

Technology couplings

Suppose that one thinks that solving the control problem for artificial intelligence is very difficult, that solving it for whole brain emulations is much easier, and that it would therefore be preferable that machine intelligence be reached via the whole brain emulation path. We will return later to the question of whether whole brain emulation would be safer than artificial intelligence. But for now we want to make the point that even if we accept this premiss, it would not follow that we ought to promote whole brain emulation technology. One reason, discussed earlier, is that a later arrival of superintelligence may be preferable, in order to allow more time for progress on the control problem and for other favorable background trends to culminate—and thus, if one were confident that whole brain emulation would precede AI anyway, it would be counterproductive to further hasten the arrival of whole brain emulation.

But even if it were the case that it would be best for whole brain emulation to arrive as soon as possible, it *still* would not follow that we ought to favor progress toward whole brain emulation. For it is possible that progress toward whole brain emulation will not yield whole brain emulation. It may instead yield neuromorphic artificial intelligence—forms of AI that mimic some aspects of cortical organization but do not replicate neuronal functionality with sufficient fidelity to constitute a proper emulation. If—as there is reason to believe—such neuromorphic AI is worse than the kind of AI that would otherwise have been built, and if by promoting whole brain emulation we would make neuromorphic AI arrive first, then our pursuit of the supposed *best* outcome (whole brain emulation) would lead to the *worst* outcome (neuromorphic AI); whereas if we had pursued the *second-best* outcome (synthetic AI) we might actually have attained the second-best (synthetic AI).

We have just described an (hypothetical) instance of what we might term a "technology coupling."[11] This refers to a condition in which two technologies have a predictable timing relationship, such that developing one of the technologies has a robust tendency to lead to the development of the other, either as a necessary precursor or as an obvious and irresistible application or subsequent step. Technology couplings must be taken into account when we use the principle of differential technological development: it is no good accelerating the development of a desirable technology Y if the only way of getting Y is by developing an extremely undesirable precursor technology X, or if getting Y would immediately produce an extremely undesirable related technology Z. Before you marry your sweetheart, consider the prospective in-laws.

In the case of whole brain emulation, the degree of technology coupling is debatable. We noted in Chapter 2 that while whole brain emulation would require massive progress in various enabling technologies, it might not require any major new theoretical insight. In particular, it does not require that we understand how human cognition works, only that we know how to build computational models of small parts of the brain, such as different species of neuron. Nevertheless, in the course of developing the ability to emulate human brains, a wealth of neuroanatomical data would be collected, and functional models of cortical networks would surely be greatly improved. Such progress would seem to have a good chance of enabling neuromorphic AI before full-blown whole brain emulation.[12] Historically, there are quite a few examples of AI techniques gleaned from neuroscience or biology. (For example: the McCulloch–Pitts neuron, perceptrons, and other artificial neurons and neural networks, inspired by neuroanatomical work; reinforcement learning, inspired by behaviorist psychology; genetic algorithms, inspired by evolution theory; subsumption architectures and perceptual hierarchies, inspired by cognitive science theories about motor planning and sensory perception; artificial immune systems, inspired by theoretical immunology; swarm intelligence, inspired by the ecology of insect colonies and other self-organizing systems; and reactive and behavior-based control in robotics, inspired by the study of animal locomotion.) Perhaps more significantly, there are plenty of important AI-relevant questions that could potentially be answered through further study of the brain. (For example: How does the brain store structured representations in working memory and long-term memory? How is the binding problem solved? What is the neural code? How are concepts represented? Is there some standard unit of cortical processing machinery, such as the cortical column, and if so how is it wired and how does its functionality depend on the wiring? How can such columns be linked up, and how can they learn?)

We will shortly have more to say about the relative danger of whole brain emulation, neuromorphic AI, and synthetic AI, but we can already flag another important technology coupling: that between whole brain emulation and AI. Even if a push toward whole brain emulation actually resulted in whole brain emulation (as opposed to neuromorphic AI), and even if the arrival of whole brain emulation could be safely handled, a further risk would still remain: the risk associated with *a second transition*, a transition from whole brain emulation to AI, which is an ultimately more powerful form of machine intelligence.

There are many other technology couplings, which could be considered in a more comprehensive analysis. For instance, a push toward whole brain emulation would boost neuroscience progress more generally.[13] That might produce various effects, such as faster progress toward lie detection, neuropsychological manipulation techniques, cognitive enhancement, and assorted medical advances. Likewise, a push toward cognitive enhancement might (depending on the specific path pursued) create spillovers such as faster development of genetic selection and genetic engineering methods not only for enhancing cognition but for modifying other traits as well.

Second-guessing

We encounter another layer of strategic complexity if we take into account that there is no perfectly benevolent, rational, and unified world controller who simply implements what has been discovered to be the best option. Any abstract point about "what should be done" must be embodied in the form of a concrete message, which is entered into the arena of rhetorical and political reality. There it will be ignored, misunderstood, distorted, or appropriated for various conflicting purposes; it will bounce around like a pinball, causing actions and reactions, ushering in a cascade of consequences, the upshot of which need bear no straightforward relationship to the intentions of the original sender.

A sophisticated operator might try to anticipate these kinds of effect. Consider, for example, the following argument template for proceeding with research to develop a dangerous technology X. (One argument fitting this template can be found in the writings of Eric Drexler. In Drexler's case, X = molecular nanotechnology.[14])

1 The risks of X are great.
2 Reducing these risks will require a period of serious preparation.
3 Serious preparation will begin only once the prospect of X is taken seriously by broad sectors of society.
4 Broad sectors of society will take the prospect of X seriously only once a large research effort to develop X is underway.

5 The earlier a serious research effort is initiated, the longer it will take to deliver X (because it starts from a lower level of pre-existing enabling technologies).

6 Therefore, the earlier a serious research effort is initiated, the longer the period during which serious preparation will be taking place, and the greater the reduction of the risks.

7 Therefore, a serious research effort toward X should be initiated immediately.

What initially looks like a reason for going slow or stopping—the risks of X being great—ends up, on this line of thinking, as a reason for the opposite conclusion.

A related type of argument is that we ought—rather callously—to welcome small and medium-scale catastrophes on grounds that they make us aware of our vulnerabilities and spur us into taking precautions that reduce the probability of an existential catastrophe. The idea is that a small or medium-scale catastrophe acts like an inoculation, challenging civilization with a relatively survivable form of a threat and stimulating an immune response that readies the world to deal with the existential variety of the threat.[15]

These "shock-'em-into-reacting" arguments advocate letting something bad happen in the hope that it will galvanize a public reaction. We mention them here not to endorse them, but as a way to introduce the idea of (what we will term) "second-guessing arguments." Such arguments maintain that by treating others as irrational and playing to their biases and misconceptions it is possible to elicit a response from them that is more competent than if a case had been presented honestly and forthrightly to their rational faculties.

It may seem unfeasibly difficult to use the kind of stratagems recommended by second-guessing arguments to achieve long-term global goals. How could anybody predict the final course of a message after it has been jolted hither and thither in the pinball machine of public discourse? Doing so would seem to require predicting the rhetorical effects on myriad constituents with varied idiosyncrasies and fluctuating levels of influence over long periods of time during which the system may be perturbed by unanticipated events from the outside while its topology is also undergoing a continuous endogenous reorganization: surely an impossible task![16] However, it may not be necessary to make detailed predictions about the system's entire future trajectory in order to identify an intervention that can be reasonably expected to increase the chances of a certain long-term outcome. One might, for example, consider only the relatively near-term and predictable effects in a detailed way, selecting an action that does well in regard to those, while modeling the system's behavior beyond the predictability horizon as a random walk.

There may, however, be a moral case for de-emphasizing or refraining from second-guessing moves. Trying to outwit one another looks like a zero-sum game—or negative-sum, when one considers the time and energy that would be dissipated by the practice as well as the likelihood that it would make it generally harder for anybody to discover what others truly think and to be trusted when expressing their own opinions.[17] A full-throttled deployment of the practices of strategic communication would kill candor and leave truth bereft to fend for herself in the backstabbing night of political bogeys.

Pathways and enablers

Should we celebrate advances in computer hardware? What about advances on the path toward whole brain emulation? We will look at these two questions in turn.

Effects of hardware progress

Faster computers make it easier to create machine intelligence. One effect of accelerating progress in hardware, therefore, is to hasten the arrival of machine intelligence. As discussed earlier, this is probably a bad thing from the impersonal perspective, since it reduces the amount of time available for solving the control problem and for humanity to reach a more mature stage of civilization. The case is not a slam dunk, though. Since superintelligence would eliminate many other existential risks, there could be reason to prefer earlier development if the level of these other existential risks were very high.[18]

Hastening or delaying the onset of the intelligence explosion is not the only channel through which the rate of hardware progress can affect existential risk. Another channel is that hardware can to some extent substitute for software; thus, better hardware reduces the minimum skill required to code a seed AI. Fast computers might also encourage the use of approaches that rely more heavily on brute-force techniques (such as genetic algorithms and other generate-evaluate-discard methods) and less on techniques that require deep understanding to use. If brute-force techniques lend themselves to more anarchic or imprecise system designs, where the control problem is harder to solve than in more precisely engineered and theoretically controlled systems, this would be another way in which faster computers would increase the existential risk.

Another consideration is that rapid hardware progress increases the likelihood of a fast takeoff. The more rapidly the state of the art advances in the semiconductor industry, the fewer the person-hours of programmers' time spent exploiting the capabilities of computers at any given performance level. This means that an intelligence explosion is less likely to be initiated at the lowest level of hardware performance at which it is feasible. An intelligence explosion is thus *more* likely to be initiated when hardware has advanced significantly beyond the minimum level at which the eventually successful programming approach could first have succeeded. There is then a hardware overhang when the takeoff eventually does occur. As we saw in Chapter 4, hardware overhang is one of the main factors that reduce recalcitrance during the takeoff. Rapid hardware progress, therefore, will tend to make the transition to superintelligence faster and more explosive.

A faster takeoff via a hardware overhang can affect the risks of the transition in several ways. The most obvious is that a faster takeoff offers less opportunity to respond and make adjustments whilst the transition is in progress, which would tend to increase risk. A related consideration is that a hardware overhang would reduce the chances that a dangerously self-improving seed AI could be contained by limiting its ability to colonize sufficient hardware: the faster each processor is, the fewer processors would be needed for the AI to quickly bootstrap itself to superintelligence. Yet another effect of a hardware overhang is to level the playing field between big and small projects by reducing the importance of one of the advantages of larger projects—the ability to afford more powerful computers. This effect, too, might increase existential risk, if larger projects are more likely to solve the control problem and to be pursuing morally acceptable objectives.[19]

There are also advantages to a faster takeoff. A faster takeoff would increase the likelihood that a singleton will form. If establishing a singleton is sufficiently important for solving the post-transition coordination problems, it might be worth accepting a greater risk during the intelligence explosion in order to mitigate the risk of catastrophic coordination failures in its aftermath.

Developments in computing can affect the outcome of a machine intelligence revolution not only by playing a direct role in the construction of machine intelligence but also by having diffuse effects on society that indirectly help shape the initial conditions of the intelligence explosion. The internet, which required hardware to be good enough to enable personal computers to be mass produced at low cost, is now influencing human activity in many areas, including work in artificial intelligence and research on the control problem. (This book might not have been written, and you might not have found it, without the internet.) However, hardware is already good enough for a great many applications that could facilitate human communication and deliberation, and it is not clear that the pace of progress in these areas is strongly bottlenecked by the rate of hardware improvement.[20]

On balance, it appears that faster progress in computing hardware is undesirable from the impersonal evaluative standpoint. This tentative conclusion could be overturned, for example if the threats from other existential risks or from post-transition coordination failures turn out to be extremely large. In any case, it seems difficult to have much leverage on the rate of hardware advancement. Our efforts to improve the initial conditions for the intelligence explosion should therefore probably focus on other parameters.

Note that even when we cannot see how to influence some parameter, it can be useful to determine its "sign" (i.e. whether an increase or decrease in that parameter would be desirable) as a preliminary step in mapping the strategic lay of the land. We might later discover a new leverage point that does enable us to manipulate the parameter more easily. Or we might discover that the parameter's sign correlates with the sign of some other more manipulable parameter, so that our initial analysis helps us decide what to do with this other parameter.

Should whole brain emulation research be promoted?

The harder it seems to solve the control problem for artificial intelligence, the more tempting it is to promote the whole brain emulation path as a less risky alternative. There are several issues, however, that must be analyzed before one can arrive at a well-considered judgment.[21]

First, there is the issue of technology coupling, already discussed earlier. We pointed out that an effort to develop whole brain emulation could result in neuromorphic AI instead, a form of machine intelligence that may be especially unsafe.

But let us assume, for the sake of argument, that we actually achieve whole brain emulation (WBE). Would this be safer than AI? This, itself, is a complicated issue. There are at least three *putative* advantages of WBE: (i) that its performance characteristics would be better understood than those of AI; (ii) that it would inherit human motives; and (iii) that it would result in a slower takeoff. Let us very briefly reflect on each.

i   That it should be easier to understand the intellectual performance characteristics of an emulation than of an AI sounds plausible. We have abundant experience with the strengths and weaknesses of human intelligence but no experience with human-level artificial intelligence. However, to understand what a snapshot of a digitized human intellect can and cannot do is not the same as to understand how such an intellect will respond to modifications aimed at enhancing its performance. An artificial intellect, by contrast, might be carefully designed to be understandable, in both its static and dynamic dispositions. So while whole brain emulation may be more predictable in its intellectual performance than a generic AI at a comparable stage of development, it is unclear whether whole brain emulation would be dynamically more predictable than an AI engineered by competent safety-conscious programmers.

ii As for an emulation inheriting the motivations of its human template, this is far from guaranteed. Capturing human evaluative dispositions might require a very high-fidelity emulation. Even if some individual's motivations *were* perfectly captured, it is unclear how much safety would be purchased. Humans can be untrustworthy, selfish, and cruel. While templates would hopefully be selected for exceptional virtue, it may be hard to foretell how someone will act when transplanted into radically alien circumstances, superhumanly enhanced in intelligence, and tempted with an opportunity for world domination. It is true that emulations would at least be more likely to have *human-like* motivations (as opposed to valuing only paperclips or discovering digits of pi). Depending on one's views on human nature, this might or might not be reassuring.[22]

iii It is not clear why whole brain emulation should result in a slower takeoff than artificial intelligence. Perhaps with whole brain emulation one should expect less hardware overhang, since whole brain emulation is less computationally efficient than artificial intelligence can be. Perhaps, also, an AI system could more easily absorb all available computing power into one giant integrated intellect, whereas whole brain emulation would forego quality superintelligence and pull ahead of humanity only in speed and size of population. If whole brain emulation does lead to a slower takeoff, this could have benefits in terms of alleviating the control problem. A slower takeoff would also make a multipolar outcome more likely. But whether a multipolar outcome is desirable is very doubtful.

There is another important complication with the general idea that getting whole brain emulation first is safer: the need to cope with a *second transition*. Even if the first form of human-level machine intelligence is emulation-based, it would still remain feasible to develop artificial intelligence. AI in its mature form has important advantages over WBE, making AI the ultimately more powerful technology.[23] While mature AI would render WBE obsolete (except for the special purpose of preserving individual human minds), the reverse does not hold.

What this means is that if AI is developed first, there might be a single wave of the intelligence explosion. But if WBE is developed first, there may be two waves: first, the arrival of WBE; and later, the arrival of AI. The total existential risk along the WBE-first path is the *sum* of the risk in the first transition and the risk in the second transition (conditional on having made it through the first); see Figure 13.[24]

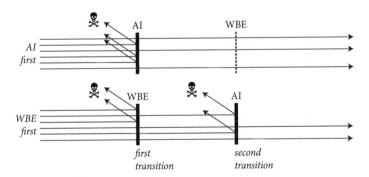

Figure 13 Artificial intelligence or whole brain emulation first? In an AI-first scenario, there is one transition that creates an existential risk. In a WBE-first scenario, there are two risky transitions, first the development of WBE and then the development of AI. The total existential risk along the WBE-first scenario is the sum of these. However, the risk of an AI transition might be lower if it occurs in a world where WBE has already been successfully introduced.

How much safer would the AI transition be in a WBE world? One consideration is that the AI transition would be less explosive if it occurs after some form of machine intelligence has already been realized. Emulations, running at digital speeds and in numbers that might far exceed the biological human population, would reduce the cognitive differential, making it easier for emulations to control the AI. This consideration is not too weighty, since the gap between AI and WBE could still be wide. However, if the emulations were not just faster and more numerous but also somewhat qualitatively smarter than biological humans (or at least drawn from the top end of the human distribution) then the WBE-first scenario would have advantages paralleling those of human cognitive enhancement, which we discussed above.

Another consideration is that the transition to WBE would extend the lead of the frontrunner. Consider a scenario in which the frontrunner has a six-month lead over the closest follower in developing whole brain emulation technology. Suppose that the first emulations to be created are cooperative, safety-focused, and patient. If they run on fast hardware, these emulations could spend subjective eons pondering how to create safe AI. For example, if they run at a speedup of 100,000× and are able to work on the control problem undisturbed for six months of sidereal time, they could hammer away at the control problem for fifty millennia before facing competition from other emulations. Given sufficient hardware, they could hasten their progress by fanning out myriad copies to work independently on subproblems. If the frontrunner uses its six-month lead to form a singleton, it could buy its emulation AI-development team an unlimited amount of time to work on the control problem.[25]

On balance, it looks like the risk of the AI transition would be reduced if WBE comes before AI. However, when we combine the residual risk in the AI transition with the risk of an antecedent WBE transition, it becomes very unclear how the total existential risk along the WBE-first path stacks up against the risk along the AI-first path. Only if one is quite pessimistic about biological humanity's ability to manage an AI transition—after taking into account that human nature or civilization might have improved by the time we confront this challenge—should the WBE-first path seem attractive.

To figure out whether whole brain emulation technology should be promoted, there are some further important points to place in the balance. Most significantly, there is the technology coupling mentioned earlier:

a push toward WBE could instead produce neuromorphic AI. This is a reason against pushing for WBE.[26] No doubt, there are *some* synthetic AI designs that are less safe than *some* neuromorphic designs. In expectation, however, it seems that neuromorphic designs are less safe. One ground for this is that imitation can substitute for understanding. To build something from the ground up one must usually have a reasonably good understanding of how the system will work. Such understanding may not be necessary to merely copy features of an existing system. Whole brain emulation relies on wholesale copying of biology, which may not require a comprehensive computational systems-level understanding of cognition (though a large amount of component-level understanding would undoubtedly be needed). Neuromorphic AI may be like whole brain emulation in this regard: it would be achieved by cobbling together pieces plagiarized from biology without the engineers necessarily having a deep mathematical understanding of how the system works. But neuromorphic AI would be *unlike* whole brain emulation in another regard: it would not have human motivations by default.[27] This consideration argues against pursuing the whole brain emulation approach to the extent that it would likely produce neuromorphic AI.

A second point to put in the balance is that WBE is more likely to give us advance notice of its arrival. With AI it is always possible that somebody will make an unexpected conceptual breakthrough. WBE, by contrast, will require many laborious precursor steps—high-throughput scanning facilities, image processing software, detailed neural modeling work. We can therefore be confident that WBE is not imminent (not less than, say, fifteen or twenty years away). This means that efforts to accelerate WBE will make a difference mainly in scenarios in which machine intelligence is developed comparatively late. This could make WBE investments attractive to somebody who wants the intelligence explosion to preempt other existential risks but is wary of supporting AI for fear of triggering an intelligence explosion prematurely, before the control problem has been solved. However, the uncertainty over the relevant timescales is probably currently too large to enable this consideration to carry much weight.[28]

A strategy of promoting WBE is thus most attractive if (a) one is very pessimistic about humans solving the control problem for AI, (b) one is not too worried about neuromorphic AI, multipolar outcomes, or the risks of a second transition, (c) one thinks that the default timing of WBE and AI is close, and (d) one prefers superintelligence to be developed neither very late nor very early.

The person-affecting perspective favors speed

I fear the blog commenter "washbash" may speak for many when he or she writes:

I instinctively think go faster. Not because I think this is better for the world. Why should I care about the world when I am dead and gone? I want it to go fast, damn it! This increases the chance I have of experiencing a more technologically advanced future.[29]

From the person-affecting standpoint, we have greater reason to rush forward with all manner of radical technologies that could pose existential risks. This is because the default outcome is that almost everyone who now exists is dead within a century.

The case for rushing is especially strong with regard to technologies that could extend our lives and thereby increase the expected fraction of the currently existing population that may still be around for the intelligence explosion. If the machine intelligence revolution goes well, the resulting superintelligence could almost certainly devise means to indefinitely prolong the lives of the then still-existing humans, not only keeping them alive but restoring them to health and youthful vigor, and enhancing their capacities well beyond what we currently think of as the human range; or helping them shuffle off their mortal coils altogether by uploading their minds to a digital substrate and endowing their liberated spirits with exquisitely good-feeling virtual embodiments. With regard to technologies that do not promise to save lives, the case for rushing is weaker, though perhaps still sufficiently supported by the hope of raised standards of living.[30]

The same line of reasoning makes the person-affecting perspective favor many risky technological innovations that promise to hasten the onset of the intelligence explosion, even when those innovations are disfavored in the impersonal perspective. Such innovations could shorten the wolf hours during which we individually must hang on to our perch if we are to live to see the daybreak of the posthuman age. From the person-affecting standpoint, faster hardware progress thus seems desirable, as does faster progress toward WBE. Any adverse effect on existential risk is probably outweighed by the personal benefit of an increased chance of the intelligence explosion happening in the lifetime of currently existing people.[31]

Collaboration

One important parameter is the degree to which the world will manage to coordinate and collaborate in the development of machine intelligence. Collaboration would bring many benefits. Let us take a look at how this parameter might affect the outcome and what levers we might have for increasing the extent and intensity of collaboration.

The race dynamic and its perils

A race dynamic exists when one project fears being overtaken by another. This does not require the actual existence of multiple projects. A situation with only one project could exhibit a race dynamic if that project is unaware of its lack of competitors. The Allies would probably not have developed the atomic bomb as quickly as they did had they not believed (erroneously) that the Germans might be close to the same goal.

The severity of a race dynamic (that is, the extent to which competitors prioritize speed over safety) depends on several factors, such as the closeness of the race, the relative importance of capability and luck, the number of competitors, whether competing teams are pursuing different approaches, and the degree to which projects share the same aims. Competitors' beliefs about these factors are also relevant. (See Box 13.)

Box 13 A risk-race to the bottom

Consider a hypothetical AI arms race in which several teams compete to develop superintelligence.[32] Each team decides how much to invest in safety—knowing that resources spent on developing safety precautions are resources not spent on developing the AI. Absent a deal between all the competitors (which might be stymied by bargaining or enforcement difficulties), there might then be a risk-race to the bottom, driving each team to take only a minimum of precautions.

One can model each team's performance as a function of its capability (measuring its raw ability and luck) and a penalty term corresponding to the cost of its safety precautions. The team with the highest performance builds the first AI. The riskiness of that AI is determined by how much its creators invested in safety. In the worst-case scenario, all teams have equal levels of

continued

Box 13 *Continued*

capability. The winner is then determined exclusively by investment in safety: the team that took the fewest safety precautions wins. The Nash equilibrium for this game is for every team to spend nothing on safety. In the real world, such a situation might arise via a *risk ratchet*: some team, fearful of falling behind, increments its risk-taking to catch up with its competitors—who respond in kind, until the maximum level of risk is reached.

Capability versus risk

The situation changes when there are variations in capability. As variations in capability become more important relative to the cost of safety precautions, the risk ratchet weakens: there is less incentive to incur an extra bit of risk if doing so is unlikely to change the order of the race. This is illustrated under various scenarios in Figure 14, which plots how the riskiness of the AI depends on the importance of capability. Safety investment ranges from 1 (resulting in perfectly safe AI) to 0 (completely unsafe AI). The *x*-axis represents the relative importance of capability versus safety investment in determining the speed of a team's progress toward AI. (At 0.5, the safety investment level is twice as important as capability; at 1, the two are equal; at 2, capability is twice as important as safety level; and so forth.) The *y*-axis represents the level of AI risk (the expected fraction of their maximum utility that the winner of the race gets).

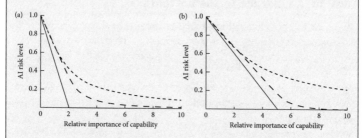

Figure 14 Risk levels in AI technology races. Levels of risk of dangerous AI in a simple model of a technology race involving either (a) two teams or (b) five teams, plotted against the relative importance of capability (as opposed to investment in safety) in determining which project wins the race. Each graph shows three information-level scenarios: no capability information (solid), private capability information (dashed), and full capability information (dotted).

Box 13 *Continued*

We see that, under all scenarios, the dangerousness of the resultant AI is maximal when capability plays no role, gradually decreasing as capability grows in importance.

Compatible goals

Another way of reducing the risk is by giving teams more of a stake in each other's success. If competitors are convinced that coming second means the total loss of everything they care about, they will take whatever risk necessary to bypass their rivals. Conversely, teams will invest more in safety if less depends on winning the race. This suggests that we should encourage various forms of cross-investment.

The number of competitors

The greater the number of competing teams, the more dangerous the race becomes: each team, having less chance of coming first, is more willing to throw caution to the wind. This can be seen by contrasting Figure 14a (two teams) with Figure 14b (five teams). In every scenario, more competitors means more risk. Risk would be reduced if teams coalesce into a smaller number of competing coalitions.

The curse of too much information

Is it good if teams know about their positions in the race (knowing their capability scores, for instance)? Here, opposing factors are at play. It is desirable that a leader knows it is leading (so that it knows it has some margin for additional safety precautions). Yet it is undesirable that a laggard knows it has fallen behind (since this would confirm that it must cut back on safety to have any hope of catching up). While intuitively it may seem this tradeoff could go either way, the models are unequivocal: information is (in expectation) bad.[33] Figures 14a and 14b each plot three scenarios: the straight lines correspond to situations in which no team knows any of the capability scores, its own included. The dashed lines show situations where each team knows its own capability only. (In those situations, a team takes extra risk only if its capability is low.) And the dotted lines show what happens when all teams know each other's capabilities. (They take extra risks if their capability scores are close to one another.) With each increase in information level, the race dynamic becomes worse.

In the development of machine superintelligence, it seems likely that there will be at least a mild race dynamic, and it is possible that there will be a severe race dynamic. The race dynamic has important consequences for how we should think about the strategic challenge posed by the possibility of an intelligence explosion.

The race dynamic could spur projects to move faster toward superintelligence while reducing investment in solving the control problem. Additional detrimental effects of the race dynamic are also possible, such as direct hostilities between competitors. Suppose that two nations are racing to develop the first superintelligence, and that one of them is seen to be pulling ahead. In a winner-takes-all situation, a lagging project might be tempted to launch a desperate strike against its rival rather than passively await defeat. Anticipating this possibility, the frontrunner might be tempted to strike preemptively. If the antagonists are powerful states, the clash could be bloody.[34] (A "surgical strike" against the rival's AI project might risk triggering a larger confrontation and might in any case not be feasible if the host country has taken precautions.[35])

Scenarios in which the rival developers are not states but smaller entities, such as corporate labs or academic teams, would probably feature much less direct destruction from conflict. Yet the overall consequences of competition may be almost as bad. This is because the main part of the expected harm from competition stems not from the smashup of battle but from the downgrade of precaution. A race dynamic would, as we saw, reduce investment in safety; and conflict, even if nonviolent, would tend to scotch opportunities for collaboration, since projects would be less likely to share ideas for solving the control problem in a climate of hostility and mistrust.[36]

On the benefits of collaboration

Collaboration thus offers many benefits. It reduces the haste in developing machine intelligence. It allows for greater investment in safety. It avoids violent conflicts. And it facilitates the sharing of ideas about how to solve the control problem. To these benefits we can add another: collaboration would tend to produce outcomes in which the fruits of a successfully controlled intelligence explosion get distributed more equitably.

That broader collaboration should result in wider sharing of gains is not axiomatic. In principle, a small project run by an altruist could lead to an outcome where the benefits are shared evenly or equitably among all morally considerable beings. Nevertheless, there are several reasons to suppose that broader collaborations, involving a greater number of sponsors, are (in expectation) distributionally superior. One such reason is that sponsors presumably prefer an outcome in which they themselves get (at least) their fair share. A broad collaboration then means that relatively many individuals get at least their fair share, assuming the project is successful. Another reason is that a broad collaboration also seems likelier to benefit people outside the collaboration. A broader collaboration contains more members, so more outsiders would have personal ties to somebody on the inside looking out for their interests. A broader collaboration is also more likely to include at least some altruist who wants to benefit everyone. Furthermore, a broader collaboration is more likely to operate under public oversight, which might reduce the risk of the entire pie being captured by a clique of programmers or private investors.[37] Note also that the larger the successful collaboration is, the lower the costs to it of extending the benefits to all outsiders. (For instance, if 90% of all people were already inside the collaboration, it would cost them no more than 10% of their holdings to bring all outsiders up to their own level.)

It is thus plausible that broader collaborations would tend to lead to a wider distribution of the gains (though *some* projects with few sponsors might also have distributionally excellent aims). But why is a wide distribution of gains desirable?

There are both moral and prudential reasons for favoring outcomes in which everybody gets a share of the bounty. We will not say much about the moral case, except to note that it need not rest on any egalitarian principle. The case might be made, for example, on grounds of fairness. A project that creates machine superintelligence imposes a global risk externality. Everybody on the planet is placed in jeopardy, including those who do not consent to having their own lives and those of their family imperiled in this way. Since everybody shares the risk, it would seem to be a minimal requirement of fairness that everybody also gets a share of the upside.

The fact that the total (expected) amount of good seems greater in collaboration scenarios is another important reason such scenarios are morally preferable.

The prudential case for favoring a wide distribution of gains is two-pronged. One prong is that wide distribution should promote collaboration, thereby mitigating the negative consequences of the race dynamic. There is less incentive to fight over who gets to build the first superintelligence if everybody stands to benefit equally from any project's success. The sponsors of a particular project might also benefit from credibly signaling their commitment to distributing the spoils universally, a certifiably altruistic project being likely to attract more supporters and fewer enemies.[38]

The other prong of the prudential case for favoring a wide distribution of gains has to do with whether agents are risk-averse or have utility functions that are sublinear in resources. The central fact here is the enormousness of the potential resource pie. Assuming the observable universe is as uninhabited as it looks, it contains more than one vacant galaxy for each human being alive. Most people would much rather have certain access to one galaxy's worth of resources than a lottery ticket offering a one-in-a-billion chance of owning a billion galaxies.[39] Given the astronomical size of humanity's cosmic endowment, it seems that self-interest should generally favor deals that would guarantee each person a share, even if each share corresponded to a small fraction of the total. The important thing, when such an extravagant bonanza is in the offing, is to not be left out in the cold.

This argument from the enormousness of the resource pie presupposes that preferences are resource-satiable.[40] That supposition does not necessarily hold. For instance, several prominent ethical theories—including especially aggregative consequentialist theories—correspond to utility functions that are risk-neutral and linear in resources. A billion galaxies could be used to create a billion times more happy lives than a single galaxy. They are thus, to a utilitarian, worth a billion times as much.[41] Ordinary selfish human preference functions, however, appear to be relatively resource-satiable.

This last statement must be flanked by two important qualifications. The first is that many people care about rank. If multiple agents each want to top the Forbes rich list, then no resource pie is large enough to give everybody full satisfaction.

The second qualification is that the post-transition technology base would enable material resources to be converted into an unprecedented range of products, including some goods that are not currently available at any price even though they are highly valued by many humans. A billionaire does not live a thousand times longer than a millionaire.

In the era of digital minds, however, the billionaire could afford a thousandfold more computing power and could thus enjoy a thousandfold longer subjective lifespan. Mental capacity, likewise, could be for sale. In such circumstances, with economic capital convertible into vital goods at a constant rate even for great levels of wealth, unbounded greed would make more sense than it does in today's world where the affluent (those among them lacking a philanthropic heart) are reduced to spending their riches on airplanes, boats, art collections, or a fourth and a fifth residence.

Does this mean that an egoist should be risk-neutral with respect to his or her post-transition resource endowment? Not quite. Physical resources may not be convertible into lifespan or mental performance at arbitrary scales. If a life must be lived sequentially, so that observer moments can remember earlier events and be affected by prior choices, then the life of a digital mind cannot be extended arbitrarily without utilizing an increasing number of *sequential* computational operations. But physics limits the extent to which resources can be transformed into sequential computations.[42] The limits on sequential computation may also constrain some aspects of cognitive performance to scale radically sublinearly beyond a relatively modest resource endowment. Furthermore, it is not obvious that an egoist would or should be risk-neutral even with regard to highly normatively relevant outcome metrics such as number of quality-adjusted subjective life years. If offered the choice between an extra 2,000 years of life for certain and a one-in-ten chance of an extra 30,000 years of life, I think most people would select the former (even under the stipulation that each life year would be of equal quality).[43]

In reality, the prudential case for favoring a wide distribution of gains is presumably subject-relative and situation-dependent. Yet, on the whole, people would be more likely to get (almost all of) what they want if a way is found to achieve a wide distribution—and this holds even before taking into account that a commitment to a wider distribution would tend to foster collaboration and thereby increase the chances of avoiding existential catastrophe. Favoring a broad distribution, therefore, appears to be not only morally mandated but also prudentially advisable.

There is a further set of consequences to collaboration that should be given at least some shrift: the possibility that pre-transition collaboration influences the level of post-transition collaboration. Assume humanity solves the control problem. (If the control problem is not solved, it may scarcely matter how much collaboration there is post transition.) There are two cases to consider. The first is that the intelligence explosion does *not* create a winner-takes-all dynamic (presumably because the takeoff is relatively slow). In this case it is plausible that if pre-transition collaboration has any systematic effect on post-transition collaboration, it has a positive effect, tending to promote subsequent collaboration. The original collaborative relationships may endure and continue beyond the transition; also, pre-transition collaboration may offer more opportunity for people to steer developments in desirable (and, presumably, more collaborative) post-transition directions.

The second case is that the nature of the intelligence explosion does encourage a winner-takes-all dynamic (presumably because the takeoff is relatively fast). In this case, if there is no extensive collaboration before the takeoff, a singleton is likely to emerge—a single project would undergo the transition alone, at some point obtaining a decisive strategic advantage combined with superintelligence. A singleton, by definition, is a highly collaborative social order.[44] The absence of extensive collaboration pre-transition would thus lead to an extreme degree of collaboration post-transition. By contrast, a somewhat higher level of collaboration in the run-up to the intelligence explosion opens up a wider variety of possible outcomes. Collaborating projects could synchronize their ascent to ensure they transition in tandem without any of them getting a decisive strategic advantage. Or different sponsor groups might merge their efforts into a single project, while refusing to give that project a mandate to form a singleton. For example, one could imagine a consortium of nations forming a joint scientific project to develop machine superintelligence, yet not authorizing this project to evolve into anything like a supercharged United Nations, electing instead to maintain the factious world order that existed before.

Particularly in the case of a fast takeoff, therefore, the possibility exists that greater pre-transition collaboration would result in less post-transition collaboration. However, to the extent that collaborating entities are able to shape the outcome, they may allow the emergence or continuation of non-collaboration only if they foresee that no catastrophic consequences would follow from post-transition factiousness. Scenarios in which pre-transition collaboration leads to reduced post-transition collaboration may therefore mostly be ones in which reduced post-transition collaboration is innocuous.

In general, greater post-transition collaboration appears desirable. It would reduce the risk of dystopian dynamics in which economic competition and a rapidly expanding population lead to a Malthusian condition, or in which evolutionary selection erodes human values and selects for non-eudaemonic forms, or in which rival powers suffer other coordination failures such as wars and technology races. The last of these issues, the prospect of technology races, may be particularly problematic if the transition is to an intermediary form of machine intelligence (whole brain emulation) since it would create a new race dynamic that would harm the chances of the control problem being solved for the subsequent second transition to a more advanced form of machine intelligence (artificial intelligence).

We described earlier how collaboration can reduce conflict in the run-up to the intelligence explosion, increasing the chances that the control problem will be solved, and improve both the moral legitimacy and the prudential desirability of the resulting resource allocation. To these benefits of collaboration it may thus be possible to add one more: that broader collaboration pre-transition could help with important coordination problems in the post-transition era.

Working together

Collaboration can take different forms depending on the scale of the collaborating entities. At a small scale, individual AI teams who believe themselves to be in competition with one another could choose to pool their efforts.[45] Corporations could merge or cross-invest. At a larger scale, states could join in a big international project. There are precedents to large-scale international collaboration in science and technology (such as CERN, the Human Genome Project, and the International Space Station), but an international project to develop safe superintelligence would pose a different order of challenge because of the security implications of the work. It would have to be constituted not as an open academic collaboration but as an extremely tightly controlled joint enterprise. Perhaps the scientists involved would have to be physically isolated and prevented from communicating with the rest of the world for the duration of the project, except through a single carefully vetted communication channel. The required level of security might be nearly unattainable at present, but advances in lie detection and surveillance technology could make it feasible later this century. It is also worth bearing in mind that broad collaboration does not necessarily mean that large numbers of researchers would be involved in the project; it simply means that many people would have a say in the project's aims. In principle, a project could involve a maximally broad collaboration comprising all of humanity as sponsors (represented, let us say, by the General Assembly of the United Nations), yet employ only a single scientist to carry out the work.[46]

There is a reason for starting collaboration as early as possible, namely to take advantage of the veil of ignorance that hides from our view any specific information about which individual project will get to superintelligence first. The closer to the finishing line we get, the less uncertainty will remain about the relative chances of competing projects; and the harder it may consequently be to make a case based on the self-interest of the frontrunner to join a collaborative project that would distribute the benefits to all of humanity. On the other hand, it also looks hard to establish a formal collaboration of worldwide scope before the prospect of superintelligence has become much more widely recognized than it currently is and before there is a clearly visible road leading to the creation of machine superintelligence. Moreover, to the extent that collaboration would promote progress along that road, it may actually be counterproductive in terms of safety, as discussed earlier.

The ideal form of collaboration for the present may therefore be one that does not initially require specific formalized agreements and that does not expedite advances in machine intelligence. One proposal that fits these criteria is that we propound an appropriate moral norm, expressing our commitment to the idea that superintelligence should be for the common good. Such a norm could be formulated as follows:

The common good principle

Superintelligence should be developed only for the benefit of all of humanity and in the service of widely shared ethical ideals.[47]

Establishing from an early stage that the immense potential of superintelligence belongs to all of humanity will give more time for such a norm to become entrenched.

The common good principle does not preclude commercial incentives for individuals or firms active in related areas. For example, a firm might satisfy the call for universal sharing of the benefits of superintelligence by adopting a "windfall clause" to the effect that all profits up to some very high ceiling (say, a trillion dollars annually) would be distributed in the ordinary way to the firm's shareholders and other legal claimants, and that only profits in excess of the threshold would be distributed to all of humanity evenly (or otherwise according to universal moral criteria). Adopting such a windfall clause should be substantially costless, any given firm being extremely unlikely ever to exceed the stratospheric profit threshold (and such low-probability scenarios ordinarily playing no role in the decisions of the firm's managers and investors). Yet its widespread adoption would give humankind a valuable guarantee (insofar as the commitments could be trusted) that if ever some private enterprise *were* to hit the jackpot with the intelligence explosion, everybody would share in most of the benefits. The same idea could be applied to entities other than firms. For example, states could agree that if ever any one state's GDP exceeds some very high fraction (say, 90%) of world GDP, the overshoot should be distributed evenly to all.[48]

The common good principle (and particular instantiations, such as windfall clauses) could be adopted initially as a voluntary moral commitment by responsible individuals and organizations that are active in areas related to machine intelligence. Later, it could be endorsed by a wider set of entities and enacted into law and treaty. A vague formulation, such as the one given here, may serve well as a starting point; but it would ultimately need to be sharpened into a set of specific verifiable requirements.

CHAPTER 15

Crunch time

We find ourselves in a thicket of strategic complexity, surrounded by a dense mist of uncertainty. Though many considerations have been discerned, their details and interrelationships remain unclear and iffy—and there might be other factors we have not even thought of yet. What are we to do in this predicament?

Philosophy with a deadline

A colleague of mine likes to point out that a Fields Medal (the highest honor in mathematics) indicates two things about the recipient: that he was capable of accomplishing something important, and that he didn't. Though harsh, the remark hints at a truth.

Think of a "discovery" as an act that moves the arrival of information from a later point in time to an earlier time. The discovery's value does not equal the value of the information discovered but rather the value of having the information available earlier than it otherwise would have been. A scientist or a mathematician may show great skill by being the first to find a solution that has eluded many others; yet if the problem would soon have been solved anyway, then the work probably has not much benefited the world. There *are* cases in which having a solution even slightly sooner is immensely valuable, but this is most plausible when the solution is immediately put to use, either being deployed for some practical end or serving as a foundation to further theoretical work. And in the latter case, where a solution is immediately used only in the sense of serving as a building block for further theorizing, there is great value in obtaining a solution slightly sooner only if the further work it enables is itself both important and urgent.[1]

The question, then, is not whether the result discovered by the Fields Medalist is in itself "important" (whether instrumentally or for knowledge's own sake). Rather, the question is whether it was important that the medalist enabled the publication of the result to occur at an earlier date. The value of this temporal transport should be compared to the value that a world-class mathematical mind could have generated by working on something else. At least in some cases, the Fields Medal might indicate a life spent solving the wrong problem—for instance, a problem whose allure consisted primarily in being famously difficult to solve.

Similar barbs could be directed at other fields, such as academic philosophy. Philosophy covers some problems that are relevant to existential risk mitigation—we encountered several in this book. Yet there are also subfields within philosophy that have no apparent link to existential risk or indeed any practical concern. As with pure mathematics, some of the problems that philosophy studies might be regarded as intrinsically important, in the sense that humans have reason to care about them independently of any practical application. The fundamental nature of reality, for instance, might be worth knowing about, for its own sake. The world would arguably be less glorious if nobody studied metaphysics, cosmology, or string theory. However, the dawning prospect of an intelligence explosion shines a new light on this ancient quest for wisdom.

The outlook now suggests that philosophic progress can be maximized via an indirect path rather than by immediate philosophizing. One of the many tasks on which superintelligence (or even just moderately enhanced human intelligence) would outperform the current cast of thinkers is in answering fundamental questions in science and philosophy. This reflection suggests a strategy of deferred gratification. We could postpone work on some of the eternal questions for a little while, delegating that task to our hopefully more competent successors—in order to focus our own attention on a more pressing challenge: increasing the chance that we will actually have competent successors. This would be high-impact philosophy and high-impact mathematics.[2]

What is to be done?

We thus want to focus on problems that are not only important but urgent in the sense that their solutions are needed prior to the intelligence explosion. We should also take heed not to work on problems that are negative-value (such that solving them is harmful). Some technical problems in the field of artificial intelligence, for instance, might be negative-value inasmuch as their solution would speed the development of machine intelligence without doing as much to expedite the development of control methods that could render the machine intelligence revolution survivable and beneficial.

It can be hard to identify problems that are both urgent and important and are such that we can confidently take them to be positive-value. The strategic uncertainty surrounding existential risk mitigation means that we must worry that even well-intentioned interventions may turn out to be not only unproductive but counterproductive. To limit the risk of doing something actively harmful or morally wrong, we should prefer to work on problems that seem *robustly positive-value* (i.e., whose solution would make a positive contribution across a wide range of scenarios) and to employ means that are robustly justifiable (i.e., acceptable from a wide range of moral views).

There is a further desideratum to consider in selecting which problems to prioritize. We want to work on problems that are *elastic* to our efforts at solving them. Highly elastic problems are those that can be solved much faster, or solved to a much greater extent, given one extra unit of effort. Encouraging more kindness in the world is an important and urgent problem—one, moreover, that seems quite robustly positive-value: yet absent a breakthrough idea for how to go about it, probably a problem of quite low elasticity. Achieving world peace, similarly, would be highly desirable; but considering the numerous efforts already targeting that problem, and the formidable obstacles arrayed against a quick solution, it seems unlikely that the contributions of a few extra individuals would make a large difference.

To reduce the risks of the machine intelligence revolution, we will propose two objectives that appear to best meet all those desiderata: strategic analysis and capacity-building. We can be relatively confident about the sign of these parameters—more strategic insight and more capacity being better. Furthermore, the parameters are elastic: a small extra investment can make a relatively large difference. Gaining insight and capacity is also urgent because early boosts to these parameters may compound, making subsequent efforts more effective. In addition to these two broad objectives, we will point to a few other potentially worthwhile aims for initiatives.

Seeking the strategic light

Against a backdrop of perplexity and uncertainty, analysis stands out as being of particularly high expected value.[3] Illumination of our strategic situation would help us target subsequent interventions more effectively. Strategic analysis is especially needful when we are radically uncertain not just about some detail of some peripheral matter but about the cardinal qualities of the central things. For many key parameters, we are radically uncertain even about their *sign*—that is, we know not which direction of change would be desirable and which undesirable. Our ignorance might not be irremediable. The field has been little prospected, and glimmering strategic insights could still be awaiting their unearthing just a few feet beneath the surface.

What we mean by "strategic analysis" here is a search for *crucial considerations*: ideas or arguments with the potential to change our views not merely about the fine-structure of implementation but about the general topology of desirability.[4] Even a single missed crucial consideration could vitiate our most valiant efforts or render them as actively harmful as those of a soldier who is fighting on the wrong side. The search for crucial considerations (which must explore normative as well as descriptive issues) will often require crisscrossing the boundaries between different academic disciplines and other fields of knowledge. As there is no established methodology for how to go about this kind of research, difficult original thinking is necessary.

Building good capacity

Another high-value activity, one that shares with strategic analysis the robustness property of being beneficial across a wide range of scenarios, is the development of a well-constituted support base that takes the future seriously. Such a base can immediately provide resources for research and analysis. If and when other priorities become visible, resources can be redirected accordingly. A support base is thus a general-purpose capability whose use can be guided by new insights as they emerge.

One valuable asset would be a donor network comprising individuals devoted to rational philanthropy, informed about existential risk, and discerning about the means of mitigation. It is especially desirable that the early-day funders be astute and altruistic, because they may have opportunities to shape the field's culture before the usual venal interests take up position and entrench. The focus during these opening gambits should thus be to recruit the right kinds of people into the field. It could be worth foregoing some technical advances in the short term in order to fill the ranks with individuals who genuinely care about safety and who have a truth-seeking orientation (and who are likely to attract more of their own kind).

One important variable is the quality of the "social epistemology" of the AI-field and its leading projects. Discovering crucial considerations is valuable, but only if it affects action. This cannot always be taken for granted. Imagine a project that invests millions of dollars and years of toil to develop a prototype AI, and that after surmounting many technical challenges the system is finally beginning to show real progress. There is a chance that with just a bit more work it could turn into something useful and profitable. Now a crucial consideration is discovered, indicating that a completely different approach would be a bit safer. Does the project kill itself off like a dishonored samurai, relinquishing its unsafe design and all the progress that had been made? Or does it react like a worried octopus, puffing out a cloud of motivated skepticism in the hope of eluding the attack? A project that would reliably choose the samurai option in such a dilemma would be a far preferable AI-creator.[5] Yet building processes and institutions that are willing to commit seppuku based on uncertain allegations and speculative reasoning is not easy. Another dimension of social epistemology is the management of sensitive information, in particular the ability to avoid leaking information that ought be kept secret. (Information continence may be especially challenging for academic researchers, accustomed as they are to constantly disseminating their results on every available lamppost and tree.)

Particular measures

In addition to the general objectives of strategic light and good capacity, some more specific objectives could also present cost-effective opportunities for action.

One such is progress on the technical challenges of machine intelligence safety. In pursing this objective, care should be taken to manage information hazards. Some work that would be useful for solving the control problem would also be useful for solving the competence problem. Work that burns down the AI fuse could easily be a net negative.

Another specific objective is to promote "best practices" among AI researchers. Whatever progress has been made on the control problem needs to be disseminated. Some forms of computational experimentation, particularly if involving strong recursive self-improvement, may also require the use of capability control to mitigate the risk of an accidental takeoff. While the actual implementation of safety methods is not so relevant today, it will increasingly become so as the state of the art advances. And it is not too soon to call for practitioners to express a *commitment to safety*, including endorsing the common good principle and promising to ramp up safety if and when the prospect of machine superintelligence begins to look more imminent. Pious words are not sufficient and will not by themselves make a dangerous technology safe: but where the mouth goeth, the mind might gradually follow.

Other opportunities may also occasionally arise to push on some pivotal parameter, for example to mitigate some other existential risk, or to promote biological cognitive enhancement and improvements of our collective wisdom, or even to shift world politics into a more harmonious register.

Will the best in human nature please stand up

Before the prospect of an intelligence explosion, we humans are like small children playing with a bomb. Such is the mismatch between the power of our plaything and the immaturity of our conduct. Superintelligence is a challenge for which we are not ready now and will not be ready for a long time. We have little idea when the detonation will occur, though if we hold the device to our ear we can hear a faint ticking sound.

For a child with an undetonated bomb in its hands, a sensible thing to do would be to put it down gently, quickly back out of the room, and contact the nearest adult. Yet what we have here is not one child but many, each with access to an independent trigger mechanism. The chances that we will *all* find the sense to put down the dangerous stuff seem almost negligible. Some little idiot is bound to press the ignite button just to see what happens.

Nor can we attain safety by running away, for the blast of an intelligence explosion would bring down the entire firmament. Nor is there a grown-up in sight.

In this situation, any feeling of gee-wiz exhilaration would be out of place. Consternation and fear would be closer to the mark; but the most appropriate attitude may be a bitter determination to be as competent as we can, much as if we were preparing for a difficult exam that will either realize our dreams or obliterate them.

This is not a prescription of fanaticism. The intelligence explosion might still be many decades off in the future. Moreover, the challenge we face is, in part, to hold on to our humanity: to maintain our groundedness, common sense, and good-humored decency even in the teeth of this most unnatural and inhuman problem. We need to bring all our human resourcefulness to bear on its solution.

Yet let us not lose track of what is globally significant. Through the fog of everyday trivialities, we can perceive—if but dimly—the essential task of our age. In this book, we have attempted to discern a little more feature in what is otherwise still a relatively amorphous and negatively defined vision—one that presents as our principal moral priority (at least from an impersonal and secular perspective) the reduction of existential risk and the attainment of a civilizational trajectory that leads to a compassionate and jubilant use of humanity's cosmic endowment.

Afterword

Since the publication of this book's hardback edition, there have been some shifts in attitude. It has become easier to treat superintelligence as a non-silly topic—to take seriously the view that a machine intelligence transition might occur in this century, that such a transition might be among the most important events in human history, that it might be accompanied by some amount of existential risk as well as tremendous upside, and that it would be prudent to put in a bit of work in advance to see if there is something we should be doing to shorten the odds of a favorable outcome. Granted, there is still that picture of the Terminator jeering over practically every journalistic attempt to engage with the subject. But away from the popular cacophony, it is now also possible—if one perks up one's ears and angles them correctly—to hear the low-key murmur of a more grownup conversation.

Technical progress in machine learning has been swifter than most had expected. A wide frontier of ideas to explore has been opened up by recent developments: neural Turing machines, deep reinforcement learning, Bayesian hyperparameter optimization, grid LSTMs, memory networks, variational autoencoders, sentence-level vector embeddings, generative adversarial networks, attention-based generative models, various approaches in probabilistic programming—to point to just a few of the sources of contemporary buzz. Deep learning has been the focus of much of the excitement. Deep learning methods—essentially many-layered neural networks—have, thanks to a combination of faster computers, larger data sets, and algorithmic refinements, begun to approach (and in some cases exceed) human performance on many perceptual tasks, including handwriting recognition, image recognition and image captioning, speech recognition, and facial recognition. Deep learning methods have also achieved strong results in natural language translation and on some scientific data analysis problems. The capability underlying these performances—general algorithms that can learn abstract distributed representations from raw sensory data, without the need for a human to hand-craft features or specific domain-knowledge—may become important as a building block in the construction of more complex capabilities.

Many of the existing capabilities have reached the threshold of usefulness. This means that there is an immediate payoff to further advances, as they directly translate into improvements of commercially valuable products. If you start with a speech recognition system that is far too inaccurate to be of any use, and you make a small improvement, well, you still have a useless system. But start with a system that is good enough to be widely deployed, and your 1% improvement may be worth a billion dollars. The thrilling sense of machine learning being on the move, with many paths to explore—this sensation is now increasingly also galvanized by commercial incentives, and it is pulling money and talent into the field.

How far the current wave of excitement will go is anybody's guess. It is no part of this book's argument that an intelligence explosion is imminent, or that the wider world has underestimated the pace of progress. It may well be that improvements obtainable by scaling up and fine-tuning any of the present approaches will soon plateau. Certainly, some number of additional breakthrough ideas will be needed to get the rest of the way—ideas which may or may not be forthcoming in a timely manner. I would be somewhat surprised, though, to see the recurrence of an "AI winter" as severe as those the field has experienced in the past. It seems more likely that there will be continued funding and reputability from this point on, since enough has already been accomplished to establish artificial intelligence as both a worthwhile area of theoretical study and a useful engineering discipline. (This prognostication is, of course, entirely consistent with the bursting of this or that investment bubble and with the failure of most individual projects to live up to their proponents' expectations.)

There has also been some progress in the study of how to improve the odds of a favorable outcome. On the theoretical side, some new ideas have been introduced (e.g. Paul Christiano's "approval-directed agents") that are worthy of further exploration. On the organizational side, too, the situation has improved a bit—the improvement is dramatic in relative terms but it is starting from a very low base level. Recognition of the control problem as a legitimate topic for investigation has spread to a less tiny fraction of the relevant research communities, and there is wider acknowledgment that the future impacts of machine intelligence deserve more systematic attention.

This progress in building up the AI safety and impacts fields, though remarkable for having taken place in such a short span of time, should not be overstated. Yes, more funding is flowing into the field; but it is still two to three orders of magnitude less than is going into simply making machines smarter. Yes, there is more interest in thinking about the consequences of advances in machine intelligence; but much of this ends up focusing on nearer-term concerns such as lethal autonomous weapons, labor market impacts of automation, cybercrime, privacy, or self-driving cars. These are not unreasonable things for some people to be thinking about, but they mostly concern issues quite distinct from those raised by human-level AI or superintelligence.

And yes, a degree of legitimation of the longer-term issues within the AI research community has taken place. But the acceptance that has been gained is still only very partial—and, conceivably, fragile. Some AI researchers have started to worry that the public conversation is getting out of control. Those inane Terminator pictures are taking a toll. It can't be much fun to have aspersions cast on one's academic discipline, one's professional community, one's life's work. There is a possibility that, in reaction to misguided public alarm about evil robot armies, the AI community might close ranks around a position that denigrates any real concerns about advanced machine intelligence. Insofar as such a response could be specifically targeted at media scaremongering, helping to take it down a notch, a good purpose may be served. But one fears collateral damage. Should a norm arise among AI researchers that it is uncouth to talk about superintelligence or inquire into its possible risks, for fear of "giving ammunition" to critics, fear-mongers, crazies, or would-be regulators, then the recent gains of legitimation could quickly be reversed. We could then enter an "AI safety winter," a climate in which it would be harder to do the kind of work proposed in the book. It is important to prevent such an antagonistic dynamic from gaining force. The best path toward the development of beneficial superintelligence is one in which AI developers and AI safety researchers are on the same side—one in which they are indeed, to a considerable extent, the same persons. So I call on all sides to practice patience and restraint, and broad-mindedness, and to engage in direct dialogue and collaboration whenever possible.

I will pass up the opportunity here to respond to all the commentary that has been made on the book since it came out. I will just make one little remark—directed to new owners of this paperback edition, and principally to those whose lives have become so busy that they have ceased to actually *read* the books they buy, except perhaps for a glance at the table of contents and the stuff at the front and toward the back: namely, to point out that there are many factors, aside from the inherent importance of an issue, that could influence how many pages get allocated to its elaboration. Hence one cannot infer from a simple page count what I believe. For instance, I dwell on risks more than on potential upsides. This does not mean that I regard the latter as anything less than enormous; I just happen to think that, at this point in history, whereas we might get by with a vague sense that there are (astronomically) great things to hope for if the machine intelligence transition goes well, it seems more urgent that we develop a precise detailed understanding of what specific things could go wrong—so that we can make sure to avoid them. By the same token, I spend many pages analyzing scenarios in which a single superintelligent AI becomes powerful enough to shape the future according to its preferences; this does not mean that I dismiss multipolar scenarios (see, e.g., Chapter 11). I discourse at length on how the control problem might be hard and how superficially plausible solutions might fail; but the control problem could equally turn out to be easy.

I want to again thank everybody who has been helpful in the creation of this book or who has contributed to its reception—and everybody out there who is trying to play a constructive role in this our strange human predicament.

Nick Bostrom
November, 2015

NOTES

PRELIMS

1. Not all endnotes contain useful information, however.
2. I don't know which ones.

CHAPTER 1: PAST DEVELOPMENTS AND PRESENT CAPABILITIES

1. A subsistence-level income today is about $400 (Chen and Ravallion 2010). A million subsistence-level incomes is thus $400,000,000. The current world gross product is about $60,000,000,000,000 and in recent years has grown at an annual rate of about 4% (compound annual growth rate since 1950, based on Maddison [2010]). These figures yield the estimate mentioned in the text, which of course is only an order-of-magnitude approximation. If we look directly at population figures, we find that it currently takes the world population about one and a half weeks to grow by one million; but this underestimates the growth rate of the economy since *per capita* income is also increasing. By 5000 BC, following the Agricultural Revolution, the world population was growing at a rate of about 1 million per 200 years—a great acceleration since the rate of perhaps 1 million per million years in early humanoid prehistory—so a great deal of acceleration had already occurred by then. Still, it is impressive that an amount of economic growth that took 200 years seven thousand years ago takes just ninety minutes now, and that the world population growth that took two centuries then takes one and a half weeks now. See also Maddison (2005).

2. Such dramatic growth and acceleration might suggest one notion of a possible coming "singularity," as adumbrated by John von Neumann in a conversation with the mathematician Stanislaw Ulam:

   Our conversation centred on the ever accelerating progress of technology and changes in the mode of human life, which gives the appearance of approaching some essential singularity in the history of the race beyond which human affairs, as we know them, could not continue. (Ulam 1958)

3. Hanson (2000).
4. Vinge (1993); Kurzweil (2005).
5. Van Zanden (2003); Maddison (1999, 2001); De Long (1998).
6. Sandberg (2010).

7. Two oft-repeated optimistic statements from the 1960s: "Machines will be capable, within twenty years, of doing any work a man can do" (Simon 1965, 96); "Within a generation . . . the problem of creating artificial intelligence will substantially be solved" (Minsky 1967, 2). For a systematic review of AI predictions, see Armstrong and Sotala (2012).

8. See, for example, Baum et al. (2011) and Armstrong and Sotala (2012).

9. It might suggest, however, that AI researchers know less about development timelines than they think they do—but this could cut both ways: they might overestimate as well as underestimate the time to AI.

10. Good (1965, 33).

11. One exception is Norbert Wiener, who did have some qualms about the possible consequences. He wrote, in 1960: "If we use, to achieve our purposes, a mechanical agency with whose operation we cannot efficiently interfere once we have started it, because the action is so fast and irrevocable that we have not the data to intervene before the action is complete, then we had better be quite sure that the purpose put into the machine is the purpose which we really desire and not merely a colourful imitation of it" (Wiener 1960). Ed Fredkin spoke about his worries about superintelligent AI in an interview described in McCorduck (1979). By 1970, Good himself writes about the risks, and even calls for the creation of an association to deal with the dangers (Good [1970]; see also his later article [Good 1982] where he foreshadows some of the ideas of "indirect normativity" that we discuss in Chapter 13). By 1984, Marvin Minsky was also writing about many of the key worries (Minsky 1984).

12. Cf. Yudkowsky (2008a). On the importance of assessing the ethical implications of potentially dangerous future technologies *before* they become feasible, see Roache (2008).

13. McCorduck (1979).

14. Newell et al. (1959).

15. The SAINTS program, the ANALOGY program, and the STUDENT program, respectively. See Slagle (1963), Evans (1964, 1968), and Bobrow (1968).

16. Nilsson (1984).

17. Weizenbaum (1966).

18. Winograd (1972).

19. Cope (1996); Weizenbaum (1976); Moravec (1980); Thrun et al. (2006); Buehler et al. (2009); Koza et al. (2003). The Nevada Department of Motor Vehicles issued the first license for a driverless car in May 2012.

20. The STANDUP system (Ritchie et al. 2007).

21. Schwartz (1987). Schwartz is here characterizing a skeptical view that he thought was represented by the writings of Hubert Dreyfus.

22. One vocal critic during this period was Hubert Dreyfus. Other prominent skeptics from this era include John Lucas, Roger Penrose, and John Searle. However, among these only Dreyfus was mainly concerned with refuting claims about what practical accomplishments we should expect from existing paradigms in AI (though he seems to have been open to the possibility that new paradigms could go further). Searle's target was functionalist theories in the philosophy of mind, not the instrumental powers of AI systems. Lucas and Penrose denied that a classical computer could ever be programmed to do everything that a human mathematician can do, but they did not deny

that any particular function could in principle be automated or that AIs might eventually become very instrumentally powerful. Cicero remarked that "there is nothing so absurd but some philosopher has said it" (Cicero 1923, 119); yet it is surprisingly hard to think of *any* significant thinker who has denied the possibility of machine superintelligence in the sense used in this book.

23. For many applications, however, the learning that takes place in a neural network is little different from the learning that takes place in linear regression, a statistical technique developed by Adrien-Marie Legendre and Carl Friedrich Gauss in the early 1800s.

24. The basic algorithm was described by Arthur Bryson and Yu-Chi Ho as a multi-stage dynamic optimization method in 1969 (Bryson and Ho 1969). The application to neural networks was suggested by Paul Werbos in 1974 (Werbos 1994), but it was only after the work by David Rumelhart, Geoffrey Hinton, and Ronald Williams in 1986 (Rumelhart et al. 1986) that the method gradually began to seep into the awareness of a wider community.

25. Nets lacking hidden layers had previously been shown to have severely limited functionality (Minsky and Papert 1969).

26. E.g., MacKay (2003).

27. Murphy (2012).

28. We suppress various technical details here in order not to unduly burden the exposition. We will have occasion to revisit some of these ignored issues in Chapter 12.

29. A program p is a description of string x if p, run on (some particular) universal Turing machine U, outputs x; we write this as $U(p) = x$. (The string x here represents a possible world.) The Kolmogorov complexity of x is then $K(x) := \min_p \{\ell(p) : U(p) = x\}$, where $\ell(p)$ is the length of p in bits. The "Solomonoff" probability of x is then defined as $M(x) := \sum_{p:U(p)=x} 2^{-\ell(p)}$, where the sum is defined over all ("minimal," i.e. not necessarily halting) programs p for which U outputs a string starting with x (Hutter 2005).

30. Bayesian conditioning on evidence E gives

$$P_{\text{posterior}}(w) = P_{\text{prior}}(w|E) = \frac{P_{\text{prior}}(E|w)P_{\text{prior}}(w)}{P_{\text{prior}}(E)}.$$

(The probability of a proposition [like E] is the sum of the probability of the possible worlds in which it is true.)

31. Or randomly picks one of the possible actions with the highest expected utility, in case there is a tie.

32. More concisely, the expected utility of an action can be written as $EU(a) = \sum_{w \in W} U(w)P(w|a)$, where the sum is over all possible worlds.

33. See, e.g., Howson and Urbach (1993); Bernardo and Smith (1994); Russell and Norvig (2010).

34. Pearl (2009).

35. Wainwright and Jordan (2008). The application areas of Bayes nets are myriad; see, e.g., Pourret et al. (2008).

36. One might wonder why so much detail is given to game AI here, which to some might seem like an unimportant application area. The answer is that game-playing offers some of the clearest measures of human vs. AI performance.

37. Newell et al. (1958, 320).
38. Attributed in Vardi (2012).
39. In 1976, I. J. Good wrote: "A computer program of Grandmaster strength would bring us within an ace of [machine ultra-intelligence]" (Good 1976). In 1979, Douglas Hofstadter opined in his Pulitzer-winning *Gödel, Escher, Bach*: "Question: Will there be chess programs that can beat anyone? Speculation: No. There may be programs that can beat anyone at chess, but they will not be exclusively chess programs. They will be programs of general intelligence, and they will be just as temperamental as people. 'Do you want to play chess?' 'No, I'm bored with chess. Let's talk about poetry' " (Hofstadter [1979] 1999, 678).
40. The algorithm is minimax search with alpha-beta pruning, used with a chess-specific heuristic evaluation function of board states. Combined with a good library of openings and endgames, and various other tricks, this can make for a capable chess engine.
41. Though especially with recent progress in learning the evaluation heuristic from simulated games, many of the underlying algorithms would probably also work well for many other games.
42. Samuel (1959); Schaeffer (1997, ch. 6).
43. Schaeffer et al. (2007).
44. Berliner (1980a, b).
45. Tesauro (1995).
46. Such programs include GNU (see Silver [2006]) and Snowie (see Gammoned.net [2012]).
47. Lenat himself had a hand in guiding the fleet-design process. He wrote: "Thus the final crediting of the win should be about 60/40% Lenat/Eurisko, though the significant point here is that neither party could have won alone" (Lenat 1983, 80).
48. Lenat (1982, 1983).
49. Cirasella and Kopec (2006).
50. Kasparov (1996, 55).
51. Newborn (2011).
52. Keim et al. (1999).
53. See Armstrong (2012).
54. Sheppard (2002).
55. Wikipedia (2012a).
56. Markoff (2011).
57. Rubin and Watson (2011).
58. Elyasaf et al. (2011).
59. KGS (2012).
60. Nilsson (2009, 318). Knuth was certainly overstating his point. There are many "thinking tasks" that AI has not succeeded in doing—inventing a new subfield of pure mathematics, doing any kind of philosophy, writing a great detective novel, engineering a coup d'état, or designing a major new consumer product.
61. Shapiro (1992).
62. One might speculate that one reason it has been difficult to match human abilities in perception, motor control, common sense, and language understanding is that our brains have dedicated wetware for these functions—neural structures that have been

optimized over evolutionary timescales. By contrast, logical thinking and skills like chess playing are not natural to us; so perhaps we are forced to rely on a limited pool of general-purpose cognitive resources to perform these tasks. Maybe what our brains do when we engage in explicit logical reasoning or calculation is in some ways analogous to running a "virtual machine," a slow and cumbersome mental simulation of a general-purpose computer. One might then say (somewhat fancifully) that a classical AI program is not so much emulating human thinking as the other way around: a human who is thinking logically is emulating an AI program.

63. This example is controversial: a minority view, represented by approximately 20% of adults in the USA and similar numbers in many other developed nations, holds that the Sun revolves around the Earth (Crabtree 1999; Dean 2005).

64. World Robotics (2011).

65. Estimated from data in Guizzo (2010).

66. Holley (2009).

67. Hybrid rule-based statistical approaches are also used, but they are currently a small part of the picture.

68. Cross and Walker (1994); Hedberg (2002).

69. Based on the statistics from TABB Group, a New York- and London-based capital markets research firm (personal communication).

70. CFTC and SEC (2010). For a different perspective on the events of 6 May 2010, see CME Group (2010).

71. Nothing in the text should be construed as an argument against algorithmic high-frequency trading, which might normally perform a beneficial function by increasing liquidity and market efficiency.

72. A smaller market scare occurred on August 1, 2012, in part because the "circuit breaker" was not also programmed to halt trading if there were extreme changes in the *number* of shares being traded (Popper 2012). This again foreshadows another later theme: the difficulty of anticipating all specific ways in which some particular plausible-seeming rule might go wrong.

73. Nilsson (2009, 319).

74. Minsky (2006); McCarthy (2007); Beal and Winston (2009).

75. Peter Norvig, personal communication. Machine-learning classes are also very popular, reflecting a somewhat orthogonal hype-wave of "big data" (inspired by e.g. Google and the Netflix Prize).

76. Armstrong and Sotala (2012).

77. Müller and Bostrom (2016).

78. See Baum et al. (2011), another survey cited therein, and Sandberg and Bostrom (2011).

79. Nilsson (2009).

80. This is again conditional on no civilization-disrupting catastrophe occurring. The definition of HLMI used by Nilsson is "AI able to perform around 80% of jobs as well or better than humans perform" (Kruel 2012).

81. The table shows the results of four different polls as well as the combined results. The first two were polls taken at academic conferences: *PT-AI*, participants of the conference *Philosophy and Theory of AI* in Thessaloniki 2011 (respondents were asked in

November 2012), with a response rate of 43 out of 88; and *AGI*, participants of the conferences *Artificial General Intelligence* and *Impacts and Risks of Artificial General Intelligence*, both in Oxford, December 2012 (response rate: 72/111). The *EETN* poll sampled the members of the Greek Association for Artificial Intelligence, a professional organization of published researchers in the field, in April 2013 (response rate: 26/250). The *TOP100* poll elicited the opinions among the 100 top authors in artificial intelligence as measured by a citation index, in May 2013 (response rate: 29/100).

82. Interviews with some 28 (at the time of writing) AI practitioners and related experts have been posted by Kruel (2011).

83. The diagram shows renormalized median estimates. Means are significantly different. For example, the mean estimates for the "Extremely bad" outcome were 7.6% (for *TOP100*) and 17.2% (for the combined pool of expert assessors).

84. There is a substantial literature documenting the unreliability of expert forecasts in many domains, and there is every reason to think that many of the findings in this body of research apply to the field of artificial intelligence too. In particular, forecasters tend to be overconfident in their predictions, believing themselves to be more accurate than they really are, and therefore assigning too little probability to the possibility that their most-favored hypothesis is wrong (Tetlock 2005). (Various other biases have also been documented; see, e.g., Gilovich et al. [2002].) However, uncertainty is an inescapable fact of the human condition, and many of our actions unavoidably rely on expectations about which long-term consequences are more or less plausible: in other words, on probabilistic predictions. Refusing to offer explicit probabilistic predictions would not make the epistemic problem go away; it would just hide it from view (Bostrom 2007). Instead, we should respond to evidence of overconfidence by broadening our confidence intervals (or "credible intervals")—i.e. by smearing out our credence functions—and in general we must struggle as best we can with our biases, by considering different perspectives and aiming for intellectual honesty. In the longer run, we can also work to develop techniques, training methods, and institutions that can help us achieve better calibration. See also Armstrong and Sotala (2012).

CHAPTER 2: PATHS TO SUPERINTELLIGENCE

1. This resembles the definition in Bostrom (2003c) and Bostrom (2006a). It can also be compared with Shane Legg's definition ("Intelligence measures an agent's ability to achieve goals in a wide range of environments") and its formalizations (Legg 2008). It is also very similar to Good's definition of ultraintelligence in Chapter 1 ("a machine that can far surpass all the intellectual activities of any man however clever").

2. For the same reason, we make no assumption regarding whether a superintelligent machine could have "true intentionality" (*pace* Searle, it could; but this seems irrelevant to the concerns of this book). And we take no position in the internalism/externalism debate about mental content that has been raging in the philosophical literature, or on the related issue of the extended mind thesis (Clark and Chalmers 1998).

3. Turing (1950, 456).

4. Turing (1950, 456).

5. Chalmers (2010); Moravec (1976, 1988, 1998, 1999).

6. See Moravec (1976). A similar argument is advanced by David Chalmers (2010).
7. See also Shulman and Bostrom (2012), where these matters are elaborated in more detail.
8. Legg (2008) offers this reason in support of the claim that humans will be able to recapitulate the progress of evolution over much shorter timescales and with reduced computational resources (while noting that evolution's unadjusted computational resources are far out of reach). Baum (2004) argues that some developments relevant to AI occurred earlier, with the organization of the genome itself embodying a valuable representation for evolutionary algorithms.
9. Whitman et al. (1998); Sabrosky (1952).
10. Schultz (2000).
11. Menzel and Giurfa (2001, 62); Truman et al. (1993).
12. Sandberg and Bostrom (2008).
13. See Legg (2008) for further discussion of this point and of the promise of functions or environments that determine fitness based on a smooth landscape of pure intelligence tests.
14. See Bostrom and Sandberg (2009b) for a taxonomy and more detailed discussion of ways in which engineers may outperform historical evolutionary selection.
15. The analysis has addressed the nervous systems of living creatures, without reference to the cost of simulating bodies or the surrounding virtual environment as part of a fitness function. It is plausible that an adequate fitness function could test the competence of a particular organism in far fewer operations than it would take to simulate all the neuronal computation of that organism's brain throughout its natural lifespan. AI programs today often develop and operate in very abstract environments (theorem provers in symbolic math worlds, agents in simple game tournament worlds, etc.).

   A skeptic might insist that an abstract environment would be inadequate for the evolution of general intelligence, believing instead that the virtual environment would need to closely resemble the actual biological environment in which our ancestors evolved. Creating a physically realistic virtual world would require a far greater investment of computational resources than the simulation of a simple toy world or abstract problem domain (whereas evolution had access to a physically realistic real world "for free"). In the limiting case, if complete micro-physical accuracy were insisted upon, the computational requirements would balloon to ridiculous proportions. However, such extreme pessimism is almost certainly unwarranted; it seems unlikely that the best environment for evolving intelligence is one that mimics nature as closely as possible. It is, on the contrary, plausible that it would be more efficient to use an artificial selection environment, one quite unlike that of our ancestors, an environment specifically designed to promote adaptations that increase the type of intelligence we are seeking to evolve (abstract reasoning and general problem-solving skills, for instance, as opposed to maximally fast instinctual reactions or a highly optimized visual system).
16. Wikipedia (2012b).
17. For a general treatment of observation selection theory, see Bostrom (2002a). For the specific application to the current issue, see Shulman and Bostrom (2012). For a short popular introduction, see Bostrom (2008b).

18. Sutton and Barto (1998, 21f); Schultz et al. (1997).

19. This term was introduced by Eliezer Yudkowsky; see, e.g., Yudkowsky (2007).

20. This is the scenario described by Good (1965) and Yudkowsky (2007). However, one could also consider an alternative in which the iterative sequence has some steps that do not involve intelligence enhancement but instead design simplification. That is, at some stages, the seed AI might rewrite itself so as make subsequent improvements easier to find.

21. Helmstaedter et al. (2011).

22. Andres et al. (2012).

23. Adequate for enabling instrumentally useful forms of cognitive functioning and communication, that is; but still radically impoverished relative to the interface provided by the muscles and sensory organs of a normal human body.

24. Sandberg (2013).

25. See the "Computer requirements" section of Sandberg and Bostrom (2008, 79–81).

26. A lower level of success might be a brain simulation that has biologically suggestive micro-dynamics and displays a substantial range of emergent species-typical activity such as a slow-wave sleep state or activity-dependent plasticity. Whereas such a simulation could be a useful testbed for neuroscientific research (though one which might come close to raising serious ethical issues), it would not count as a whole brain emulation unless the simulation were sufficiently accurate to be able to perform a substantial fraction of the intellectual work that the simulated brain was capable of. As a rule of thumb, we might say that in order for a simulation of a human brain to count as a whole brain emulation, it would need to be able to express coherent verbal thoughts or have the capacity to learn to do so.

27. Sandberg and Bostrom (2008).

28. Sandberg and Bostrom (2008). Further explanation can be found in the original report.

29. The first map is described in Albertson and Thomson (1976) and White et al. (1986). The combined (and in some cases corrected) network is available from the "WormAtlas" website (http://www.wormatlas.org/).

30. For a review of past attempts of emulating *C. elegans* and their fates, see Kaufman (2011). Kaufman quotes one ambitious doctoral student working in the area, David Dalrymple, as saying, "With optogenetic techniques, we are just at the point where it's not an outrageous proposal to reach for the capability to read and write to anywhere in a living *C. elegans* nervous system, using a high-throughput automated system.... I expect to be finished with *C. elegans* in 2–3 years. I would be extremely surprised, for whatever that's worth, if this is still an open problem in 2020" (Dalrymple 2011). Brain models aiming for biological realism that were hand-coded (rather than generated automatically) have achieved some basic functionality; see, e.g., Eliasmith et al. (2012).

31. *Caenorhabditis elegans* does have some convenient special properties. For example, the organism is transparent, and the wiring pattern of its nervous system does not change between individuals.

32. If neuromorphic AI rather than whole brain emulation is the end product, then it might or might not be the case that the relevant insights would be derived through attempts to simulate *human* brains. It is conceivable that the important cortical tricks

would be discovered during the study of (nonhuman) animal brains. Some animal brains might be easier to work with than human brains, and smaller brains would require fewer resources to scan and model. Research on animal brains would also be subject to less regulation. It is even conceivable that the first human-level machine intelligence will be created by completing a whole brain emulation of some suitable animal and then finding ways to enhance the resultant digital mind. Thus humanity could get its comeuppance from an uplifted lab mouse or macaque.

33. Uauy and Dangour (2006); Georgieff (2007); Stewart et al. (2008); Eppig et al. (2010); Cotman and Berchtold (2002).

34. According to the World Health Organization in 2007, nearly 2 billion individuals have insufficient iodine intake (*The Lancet* 2008). *Severe* iodine deficiency hinders neurological development and leads to cretinism, which involves an average loss of about 12.5 IQ points (Qian et al. 2005). The condition can be easily and inexpensively prevented though salt fortification (Horton et al. 2008).

35. Bostrom and Sandberg (2009a).

36. Bostrom and Sandberg (2009b). A typical *putative* performance increase from pharmacological and nutritional enhancement is in the range of 10–20% on test tasks measuring working memory, attention, etc. But it is generally dubious whether such reported gains are real, sustainable over a longer term, and indicative of correspondingly improved results in real-world problem situations (Repantis et al. 2010). For instance, in some cases there might be a compensating deterioration on some performance dimensions that are not measured by the test tasks (Sandberg and Bostrom 2006).

37. If there were an easy way to enhance cognition, one would expect evolution already to have taken advantage of it. Consequently, the most promising kind of nootropic to investigate may be one that promises to boost intelligence in some manner that we can see would have lowered fitness in the ancestral environment—for example, by increasing head size at birth or amping up the brain's glucose metabolism. For a more detailed discussion of this idea (along with several important qualifications), see Bostrom (2009b).

38. Sperm are harder to screen because, in contrast to embryos, they consist of only one cell—and one cell needs to be destroyed in order to do the sequencing. Oocytes also consist of only one cell; however, the first and second cell divisions are asymmetric and produce one daughter cell with very little cytoplasm, the polar body. Since polar bodies contain the same genome as the main cell and are redundant (they eventually degenerate) they can be biopsied and used for screening (Gianaroli 2000).

39. Each of these practices was subject to some ethical controversy when it was introduced, but there seems to be a trend toward increasing acceptance. Attitudes toward human genetic engineering and embryo selection vary significantly across cultures, suggesting that development and application of new techniques will probably take place even if some countries initially adopt a cautious stance, although the rate at which this happens will be influenced by moral, religious, and political pressures.

40. Davies et al. (2011); Benyamin et al. (2013); Plomin et al. (2013). See also Mardis (2011); Hsu (2012).

41. Broad-sense heritability of adult IQ is usually estimated in the range of 0.5–0.8 within middle-class strata of developed nations (Bouchard 2004, 148). Narrow-sense

heritability, which measures the portion of variance that is attributable to additive genetic factors, is lower (in the range 0.3–0.5) but still substantial (Devlin et al. 1997; Davies et al. 2011; Visscher et al. 2008). These estimates could change for different populations and environments, as heritabilities vary depending on the population and environment being studied. For example, lower heritabilities have been found among children and those from deprived environments (Benyamin et al. 2013; Turkheimer et al. 2003). Nisbett et al. (2012) review numerous environmental influences on variation in cognitive ability.

42. The following several paragraphs draw heavily on joint work with Carl Shulman (Shulman and Bostrom 2014).

43. This table is taken from Shulman and Bostrom (2014). It is based on a toy model that assumes a Gaussian distribution of predicted IQs among the embryos with a standard deviation of 7.5 points. The amount of cognitive enhancement that would be delivered with different numbers of embryos depends on how different the embryos are from one another in the additive genetic variants whose effects we know. Siblings have a coefficient of relatedness of ½, and common additive genetic variants account for half or less of variance in adult fluid intelligence (Davies et al. 2011). These two facts suggest that where the observed population standard deviation in developed countries is 15 points, the standard deviation of genetic influences within a batch of embryos would be 7.5 points or less.

44. With imperfect information about the additive genetic effects on cognitive ability, effect sizes would be reduced. However, even a small amount of knowledge would go a relatively long way, because the gains from selection do not scale linearly with the portion of variance that we can predict. Instead, the effectiveness of our selection depends on the standard deviation of predicted mean IQ, which scales as the *square root* of variance. For example, if one could account for 12.5% of the variance, this could deliver effects half as great as those in Table 1, which assume 50%. For comparison, a recent study (Rietveld et al. 2013) claims to have already identified 2.5% of the variance.

45. For comparison, standard practice today involves the creation of fewer than ten embryos.

46. Adult and embryonic stem cells can be coaxed to develop into sperm cells and oocytes, which can then be fused to produce an embryo (Nagy et al. 2008; Nagy and Chang 2007). Egg cell precursors can also form parthenogenetic blastocysts, unfertilized and non-viable embryos, able to produce embryonic stem cell lines for the process (Mai et al. 2007).

47. The opinion is that of Katsuhiko Hayashi, as reported in Cyranoski (2013). The Hinxton Group, an international consortium of scientists that discusses stem cell ethics and challenges, predicted in 2008 that human stem cell-derived gametes would be available within ten years (Hinxton Group 2008), and developments thus far are broadly consistent with this.

48. Sparrow (2013); Miller (2012); The Uncertain Future (2012).

49. Sparrow (2013).

50. Secular concerns might focus on anticipated impacts on social inequality, the medical safety of the procedure, fears of an enhancement "rat race," rights and responsibilities of parents vis-à-vis their prospective offspring, the shadow of twentieth-century

eugenics, the concept of human dignity, and the proper limits of states' involvement in the reproductive choices of their citizens. (For a discussion of the ethics of cognitive enhancement see Bostrom and Ord [2006], Bostrom and Roache [2011], and Sandberg and Savulescu [2011].) Some religious traditions may offer additional concerns, including ones centering on the moral status of embryos or the proper limits of human agency within the scheme of creation.

51. To stave off the negative effects of inbreeding, iterated embryo selection would require either a large starting supply of donors or the expenditure of substantial selective power to reduce harmful recessive alleles. Either alternative would tend to push toward offspring being less closely genetically related to their parents (and more related to one another).

52. Just how difficult an obstacle epigenetics will be is not yet known (Chason et al. 2011; Iliadou et al. 2011).

53. While cognitive ability is a fairly heritable trait, there may be few or no *common* alleles or polymorphisms that individually have a large positive effect on intelligence (Davis et al. 2010; Davies et al. 2011; Rietveld et al. 2013). As sequencing methods improve, the mapping out of low-frequency alleles and their cognitive and behavioral correlates will become increasingly feasible. There is some theoretical evidence suggesting that some alleles that cause genetic disorders in homozygotes may provide sizeable cognitive advantages in heterozygote carriers, leading to a prediction that Gaucher, Tay-Sachs, and Niemann-Pick heterozygotes would be about 5 IQ points higher than control groups (Cochran et al. 2006). Time will tell whether this holds.

54. One paper (Nachman and Crowell 2000) estimates 175 mutations per genome per generation. Another (Lynch 2010), using different methods, estimates that the average newborn has between 50 and 100 new mutations, and Kong et al. (2012) implies a figure of around 77 new mutations per generation. Most of these mutations do not affect functioning, or do so only to an imperceptibly slight degree; but the combined effects of many very slightly deleterious mutations could be a significant loss of fitness. See also Crow (2000).

55. Crow (2000); Lynch (2010).

56. Adapted from Shulman and Bostrom (2014).

57. Bostrom (2008b).

58. There are some potentially important caveats to this idea. It is possible that the modal genome would need some adjustments in order to avoid problems. For example, parts of the genome might be adapted to interacting with other parts under the assumption that all parts function with a certain level of efficiency. Increasing the efficiency of those parts might then lead to overshooting along some metabolic pathways.

59. These composites were created by Mike Mike from individual photographs taken by Virtual Flavius (Mike 2013).

60. They can, of course, have some effects sooner—for instance, by changing people's expectations of what is to come.

61. Louis Harris & Associates (1969); Mason (2003).

62. Kalfoglou et al. (2004).

63. The data is obviously limited, but individuals selected for 1-in-10,000 results on childhood ability tests have been shown, in longitudinal studies, to be substantially more

likely to become tenured professors, earn patents, and succeed in business than those with slightly less exceptional scores (Kell et al. 2013). Roe (1953) studied sixty-four eminent scientists and found median cognitive ability three to four standard deviations above the population norm and strikingly higher than is typical for scientists in general. (Cognitive ability is also correlated with lifetime earnings and with non-financial outcomes such as life expectancy, divorce rates, and probability of dropping out of school [Deary 2012].) An upward shift of the distribution of cognitive ability would have disproportionately large effects at the tails, especially increasing the number of highly gifted and reducing the number of people with retardation and learning disabilities. See also Bostrom and Ord (2006) and Sandberg and Savulescu (2011).

64. E.g. Warwick (2002). Stephen Hawking even suggested that taking this step might be necessary in order to keep up with advances in machine intelligence: "We must develop as quickly as possible technologies that make possible a direct connection between brain and computer, so that artificial brains contribute to human intelligence rather than opposing it" (reported in Walsh [2001]). Ray Kurzweil concurs: "As far as Hawking's . . . recommendation is concerned, namely direct connection between the brain and computers, I agree that this is both reasonable, desirable and inevitable. [sic] It's been my recommendation for years" (Kurzweil 2001).

65. See Lebedev and Nicolelis (2006); Birbaumer et al. (2008); Mak and Wolpaw (2009); and Nicolelis and Lebedev (2009). A more personal outlook on the problem of enhancement through implants can be found in Chorost (2005, Chap. 11).

66. Smeding et al. (2006).

67. Degnan et al. (2002).

68. Dagnelie (2012); Shannon (2012).

69. Perlmutter and Mink (2006); Lyons (2011).

70. Koch et al. (2006).

71. Schalk (2008). For a general review of the current state of the art, see Berger et al. (2008). For the case that this would help lead to enhanced intelligence, see Warwick (2002).

72. Some examples: Bartels et al. (2008); Simeral et al. (2011); Krusienski and Shih (2011); and Pasqualotto et al. (2012).

73. E.g. Hinke et al. (1993).

74. There are partial exceptions to this, especially in early sensory processing. For example, the primary visual cortex uses a retinotopic mapping, which means roughly that adjacent neural assemblies receive inputs from adjacent areas of the retinas (though ocular dominance columns somewhat complicate the mapping).

75. Berger et al. (2012); Hampson et al. (2012).

76. Some brain implants require two forms of learning: the device learning to interpret the organism's neural representations and the organism learning to use the system by generating appropriate neural firing patterns (Carmena et al. 2003).

77. It has been suggested that we should regard corporate entities (corporations, unions, governments, churches, and so forth) as artificial intelligent agents, entities with sensors and effectors, able to represent knowledge and perform inference and take action (e.g. Kuipers [2012]; cf. Huebner [2008] for a discussion on whether collective representations can exist). They are clearly powerful and ecologically successful, although their capabilities and internal states are different from those of humans.

78. Hanson (1995, 2000); Berg and Rietz (2003).

79. In the workplace, for instance, employers might use lie detectors to crack down on employee theft and shirking, by asking the employee at the end of each business day whether she has stolen anything and whether she has worked as hard as she could. Political and business leaders could likewise be asked whether they were wholeheartedly pursuing the interests of their shareholders or constituents. Dictators could use them to target seditious generals within the regime or suspected troublemakers in the wider population.

80. One could imagine neuroimaging techniques making it possible to detect neural signatures of motivated cognition. Without self-deception detection, lie detection would favor individuals who believe their own propaganda. Better tests for self-deception tests could also be used to train rationality and to study the effectiveness of interventions aimed at reducing biases.

81. Bell and Gemmel (2009). An early example is found in the work of MIT's Deb Roy, who recorded every moment of his son's first three years of life. Analysis of this audiovisual data is yielding information on language development; see Roy (2012).

82. Growth in total world population of biological human beings will contribute only a small factor. Scenarios involving machine intelligence could see the world population (including digital minds) explode by many orders of magnitude in a brief period of time. But that road to superintelligence involves artificial intelligence or whole brain emulation, so we need not consider it in this subsection.

83. Vinge (1993).

CHAPTER 3: FORMS OF SUPERINTELLIGENCE

1. Vernor Vinge has used the term "weak superintelligence" to refer to such sped-up human minds (Vinge 1993).

2. For example, if a very fast system could do everything that any human could do except dance a mazurka, we should still call it a speed superintelligence. Our interest lies in those core cognitive capabilities that have economic or strategic significance.

3. At least a millionfold speedup compared to human brains is physically possible, as can been seen by considering the difference in speed and energy of relevant brain processes in comparison to more efficient information processing. The speed of light is more than a million times greater than that of neural transmission, synaptic spikes dissipate more than a million times more heat than is thermodynamically necessary, and current transistor frequencies are more than a million times faster than neuron spiking frequencies (Yudkowsky [2008a]; see also Drexler [1992]). The ultimate limits of speed superintelligence are bounded by light-speed communications delays, quantum limits on the speed of state transitions, and the volume needed to contain the mind (Lloyd 2000). The "ultimate laptop" described by Lloyd (2000) would run a 1.4×10^{21} FLOPS brain emulation at speedup of $3.8 \times 10^{29} \times$ (assuming the emulation could be sufficiently parallelized). Lloyd's construction, however, is not intended to be technologically plausible; it is only meant to illustrate those constraints on computation that are readily derivable from basic physical laws.

4. With emulations, there is also an issue of how long a human-like mind can keep working on something before going mad or falling into a rut. Even with task variety and

regular holidays, it is not certain that a human-like mind could live for thousands of subjective years without developing psychological problems. Furthermore, if total memory capacity is limited—a consequence of having a limited neuron population—then cumulative learning cannot continue indefinitely: beyond some point, the mind must start forgetting one thing for each new thing it learns. (Artificial intelligence could be designed such as to ameliorate these potential problems.)

5. Accordingly, nanomechanisms moving at a modest 1 m/s have typical timescales of nanoseconds. See section 2.3.2 of Drexler (1992). Robin Hanson mentions 7-mm "tinkerbell" robot bodies moving at 260 times normal speed (Hanson 1994).

6. Hanson (2012).

7. "Collective intelligence" does not refer to low-level parallelization of computing hardware but to parallelization at the level of intelligent autonomous agents such as human beings. Implementing a single emulation on a massively parallel machine might result in speed superintelligence if the parallel computer is sufficiently fast: it would not produce a collective intelligence.

8. Improvements to the speed or the quality of the individual components could also indirectly affect the performance of collective intelligence, but here we mainly consider such improvements under the other two forms of superintelligence in our classification.

9. It has been argued that a higher population density triggered the Upper Paleolithic Revolution and that beyond a certain threshold accumulation of cultural complexity became much easier (Powell et al. 2009).

10. What about the internet? It seems not yet to have amounted to a super-sized boost. Maybe it will do so eventually. It took centuries or millennia for the other examples listed here to reveal their full potential.

11. This is, obviously, not meant to be a realistic thought experiment. A planet large enough to sustain seven quadrillion human organisms with present technology would implode, unless it were made of very light matter or were hollow and held up by pressure or other artificial means. (A Dyson sphere or a Shellworld might be a better solution.) History would have unfolded differently on such a vast surface. Set all this aside.

12. Our focus here is on the functional properties of a unified intellect, not on the question of whether such an intellect would have qualia or whether it would be a mind in the sense of having subjective conscious experience. (One might ponder, though, what kinds of conscious experience might arise from intellects that are more or less integrated than those of human brains. On some views of consciousness, such as the global workspace theory, it seems one might expect more integrated brains to have more capacious consciousness. Cf. Baars [1997], Shanahan [2010], and Schwitzgebel [2013].)

13. Even small groups of humans that have remained isolated for some time might still benefit from the intellectual outputs of a larger collective intelligence. For example, the language they use might have been developed by a much larger linguistic community, and the tools they use might have been invented in a much larger population before the small group became isolated. But even if a small group had always been isolated, it might still be part of a larger collective intelligence than meets the eye—namely, the collective intelligence consisting of not only the present but all ancestral generations as well, an aggregate that can function as a feed-forward information processing system.

14. By the Church–Turing thesis, all computable functions are computable by a Turing machine. Since any of the three forms of superintelligence could simulate a Turing machine (if given access to unlimited memory and allowed to operate indefinitely), they are by this formal criterion computationally equivalent. Indeed, an average human being (provided with unlimited scrap paper and unlimited time) could also implement a Turing machine, and thus is also equivalent by the same criterion. What matters for our purposes, however, is what these different systems can achieve *in practice*, with finite memory and in reasonable time. And the efficiency variations are so great that one can readily make some distinctions. For example, a typical individual with an IQ of 85 could be taught to implement a Turing machine. (Conceivably, it might even be possible to train some particularly gifted and docile chimpanzee to do this.) Yet, for all practical intents and purposes, such an individual is presumably incapable of, say, independently developing general relativity theory or of winning a Fields medal.

15. Oral storytelling traditions can produce great works (such as the Homeric epics) but perhaps some of the contributing authors possessed uncommon gifts.

16. Unless it contains as components intellects that have speed or quality superintelligence.

17. Our inability to specify what all these problems are may in part be due to a lack of trying: there is little point in spending time detailing intellectual jobs that no individual and no currently feasible organization can perform. But it is also possible that even conceptualizing some of these jobs is itself one of those jobs that we currently lack the brains to perform.

18. Cf. Boswell (1917); see also Walker (2002).

19. This mainly occurs in short bursts in a subset of neurons—most have more sedate firing rates (Gray and McCormick 1996; Steriade et al. 1998). There are some neurons ("chattering neurons," also known as "fast rhythmically bursting" cells) that may reach firing frequencies as high as 750 Hz, but these seem to be extreme outliers.

20. Feldman and Ballard (1982).

21. The conduction velocity depends on axon diameter (thicker axons are faster) and whether the axon is myelinated. Within the central nervous system, transmission delays can range from less than a millisecond to up to 100 ms (Kandel et al. 2000). Transmission in optical fibers is around 68% c (because of the refractive index of the material). Electrical cables are roughly the same speed, 59–77% c.

22. This assumes a signal velocity of 70% c. Assuming 100% c ups the estimate to 1.8×10^{18} m^3.

23. The number of neurons in an adult human male brain has been estimated at 86.1 ± 8.1 billion, a number arrived at by dissolving brains and fractionating out the cell nuclei, counting the ones stained with a neuron-specific marker. In the past, estimates in the neighborhood of 75–125 billion neurons were common. These were typically based on manual counting of cell densities in representative small regions (Azevedo et al. 2009).

24. Whitehead (2003).

25. Information processing systems can very likely use molecular-scale processes for computing and data storage and reach at least planetary size in extent. The ultimate physical limits to computation set by quantum mechanics, general relativity, and thermodynamics are, however, far beyond this "Jupiter brain" level (Sandberg 1999; Lloyd 2000).

26. Stansberry and Kudritzki (2012). Electricity used in data centers worldwide amounted to 1.1–1.5% of total electricity use (Koomey 2011). See also Muehlhauser and Salamon (2012).

27. This is an oversimplification. The number of chunks working memory can maintain is both information- and task-dependent; however, it is clearly limited to a small number of chunks. See Miller (1956) and Cowan (2001).

28. An example might be that the difficulty of learning Boolean concepts (categories defined by logical rules) is proportional to the length of the shortest logically equivalent propositional formula. Typically, even formulae just 3–4 literals long are very difficult to learn. See Feldman (2000).

29. See Landauer (1986). This study is based on experimental estimates of learning and forgetting rates in humans. Taking into account implicit learning might push the estimate up a little. If one assumes a storage capacity ~1 bit per synapse, one gets an *upper bound* on human memory capacity of about 10^{15} bits. For an overview of different estimates, see Appendix A of Sandberg and Bostrom (2008).

30. Channel noise can trigger action potentials, and synaptic noise produces significant variability in the strength of transmitted signals. Nervous systems appear to have evolved to make numerous tradeoffs between noise tolerance and costs (mass, size, time delays); see Faisal et al. (2008). For example, axons cannot be thinner than 0.1 μm lest random opening of ion channels create spontaneous action potentials (Faisal et al. 2005).

31. Trachtenberg et al. (2002).

32. In terms of memory and computational power, though not in terms of energy efficiency. The fastest computer in the world at the time of writing was China's Tianhe-2, which displaced Cray Inc. Titan in June 2013 with a performance of 33.86 petaFLOPS. It uses 17.6 MW of power, almost six orders of magnitude more than the brain's ~20 W.

33. Note that this survey of sources of machine advantage is *disjunctive*: our argument succeeds even if some of the items listed are illusory, so long as there is at least one source that can provide a sufficiently large advantage.

CHAPTER 4: THE KINETICS OF AN INTELLIGENCE EXPLOSION

1. The system may not reach one of these baselines at any sharply defined point. There may instead be an interval during which the system gradually becomes able to outperform the external research team on an increasing number of system-improving development tasks.

2. In the past half-century, at least one scenario has been widely recognized in which the existing world order would come to an end in the course of minutes or hours: global thermonuclear war.

3. This would be consistent with the observation that the Flynn effect—the secular increase in measured IQ scores within most populations at a rate of some 3 IQ points per decade over the past 60 years or so—appears to have ceased or even reversed in recent years in some highly developed countries such as the United Kingdom, Denmark, and Norway (Teasdale and Owen 2008; Sundet et al. 2004). The cause of the Flynn effect in the past—and whether and to what extent it represents any genuine gain in general intelligence or merely improved skill at solving IQ test-style

puzzles—has been the subject of wide debate and is still not known. Even if the Flynn effect (at least partially) reflects real cognitive gains, and even if the effect is now diminishing or even reversing, this does not prove that we have yet hit diminishing returns in whatever underlying cause was responsible for the observed Flynn effect in the past. The decline or reversal could instead be due to some independent detrimental factor that would otherwise have produced an even bigger observed decline.

4. Bostrom and Roache (2011).

5. Somatic gene therapy could eliminate the maturational lag, but is technically much more challenging than germline interventions and has a lower ultimate potential.

6. Average global economic productivity growth per year over the period 1960–2000 was 4.3% (Isaksson 2007). Only part of this productivity growth is due to gains in organizational efficiency. Some *particular* networks or organizational processes of course are improving at much faster rates.

7. Biological brain evolution was subject to many constraints and tradeoffs that are drastically relaxed when the mind moves to a digital medium. For example, brain size is limited by head size, and a head that is too big has trouble passing through the birth canal. A large brain also guzzles metabolic resources and is a dead weight that impedes movement. The connectivity between certain brain regions might be limited by steric constraints—the volume of white matter is significantly larger than the volume of the gray matter it connects. Heat dissipation is limited by blood flow, and might be close to the upper limit for acceptable functioning. Furthermore, biological neurons are noisy, slow, and in need of constant protection, maintenance, and resupply by glial cells and blood vessels (contributing to the intracranial crowding). See Bostrom and Sandberg (2009b).

8. Yudkowsky (2008a, 326). For a more recent discussion, see Yudkowsky (2013).

9. The picture shows cognitive ability as a one-dimensional parameter, to keep the drawing simple. But this is not essential to the point being made here. One could, for example, instead represent a cognitive ability profile as a hypersurface in a multidimensional space.

10. Lin et al. (2012).

11. One gets a certain increase in collective intelligence simply by increasing the number of its constituent intellects. Doing so should at least enable better overall performance on tasks that can be easily parallelized. To reap the full returns from such a population explosion, however, one would also need to achieve some (more than minimal) level of coordination between the constituents.

12. The distinction between speed and quality of intelligence is anyhow blurred in the case of non-neuromorphic AI systems.

13. Rajab et al. (2006, 41–52).

14. It has been suggested that using configurable integrated circuits (FPGAs) rather than general-purpose processors could increase computational speeds in neural network simulations by up to two orders of magnitude (Markram 2006). A study of high-resolution climate modeling in the petaFLOP-range found a twenty-four- to thirty-four-fold reduction of cost and about two orders of magnitude reduction in power requirements using a custom variant of embedded processor chips (Wehner et al. 2008).

15. Nordhaus (2007). There are many overviews of the different meanings of Moore's law; see, e.g., Tuomi (2002) and Mack (2011).

16. If the development is slow enough, the project can avail itself of progress being made in the interim by the outside world, such as advances in computer science made by university researchers and improvements in hardware made by the semiconductor industry.

17. Algorithmic overhang is perhaps less likely, but one exception would be if exotic hardware such as quantum computing becomes available to run algorithms that were previously infeasible. One might also argue that neural networks and deep machine learning are cases of algorithm overhang: too computationally expensive to work well when first invented, they were shelved for a while, then dusted off when fast graphics processing units made them cheap to run. Now they win contests.

18. $\mathfrak{O}_{world}$ is that part of the world's optimization power that is applied to improving the system in question. For a project operating in complete isolation, one that receives no significant ongoing support from the external world, we have, $\mathfrak{O}_{world} \approx 0$ even though the project must have started with a resource endowment (computers, scientific concepts, educated personnel, etc.) that is derived from the entire world economy and many centuries of development.

19. The most relevant of the seed AI's cognitive abilities here is its ability to perform intelligent design work to improve itself, i.e. its intelligence amplification capability. (If the seed AI is good at enhancing another system, which is good at enhancing the seed AI, then we could view these as subsystems of a larger system and focus our analysis on the greater whole.)

20. This assumes that recalcitrance is not known to be so high as to discourage investment altogether or divert it to some alternative project.

21. A similar example is discussed in Yudkowsky (2008b).

22. Since inputs have risen (e.g. amounts invested in building new foundries, and number of people working in the semiconductor industry), Moore's law itself has not given such a rapid growth if we control for this increase in inputs. Combined with advances in software, however, an 18-month doubling time in performance per unit of input may be more historically plausible.

23. And even if progress on the way toward the human baseline were slow.

24. Some tentative attempts have been made to develop the idea of an intelligence explosion within the framework of economic growth theory; see, e.g., Hanson (1998b); Jones (2009); Salamon (2009). These studies have pointed to the potential of extremely rapid growth given the arrival of digital minds, but since endogenous growth theory is relatively poorly developed even for historical and contemporary applications, any application to a potentially discontinuous future context is better viewed at this stage as a source of potentially useful concepts and considerations than as an exercise likely to deliver authoritative forecasts. For an overview of attempts to mathematically model a technological singularity, see Sandberg (2010).

25. It is of course also possible that there will be no takeoff at all. But since, as argued earlier, superintelligence looks technically feasible, the absence of a takeoff would likely be due to the intervention of some defeater, such as an existential catastrophe. If strong superintelligence arrived not in the shape of artificial intelligence or whole brain emulation but through one of the other paths we considered above, then a slower takeoff would be more likely.

CHAPTER 5: DECISIVE STRATEGIC ADVANTAGE

1. A software mind might run on a single machine as opposed to a worldwide network of computers; but this is not what we mean by "concentration." Instead, what we are interested in here is the extent to which power, specifically power derived from technological ability, will be concentrated in the advanced stages of, or immediately following, the machine intelligence revolution.

2. Technology diffusion of consumer products, for example, tends to be slower in developing countries (Talukdar et al. 2002). See also Keller (2004) and The World Bank (2008).

3. The economic literature dealing with the theory of the firm is relevant as a comparison point for the present discussion. The *locus classicus* is Coase (1937). See also, e.g., Canbäck et al. (2006); Milgrom and Roberts (1990); Hart (2008); Simester and Knez (2002).

4. On the other hand, it could be especially easy to steal a seed AI, since it consists of software that could be transmitted electronically or carried on a portable memory device.

5. If we model the situation as one where the lag time between projects is drawn from a normal distribution, then the likely distance between the leading project and its closest follower will also depend on how many projects there are. If there is a vast number of projects, then the distance between the first two is likely small even if the variance of the distribution is moderately high (though the expected gap between the lead and the second project declines very slowly with the number of competitors if completion times are normally distributed). However, it is unlikely that there will be a vast number of projects that are each well enough resourced to be serious contenders. (There might be a greater number of projects if there is a large number of different basic approaches that could be pursued, but in that case many of those approaches are likely to prove dead ends.) As suggested, empirically we seem to find that there is usually no more than a handful of serious competitors pursuing any one specific technological goal. The situation is somewhat different in a consumer market where there are many niches for slightly different products and where barriers to entry are low. There are lots of one-person projects designing T-shirts, but only a few firms in the world developing the next generation of graphics cards. (Two firms, AMD and NVIDIA, enjoy a near duopoly at the moment, though Intel is also competing at the lower-performance end of the market.)

6. Barber (1991) suggests that the Yangshao culture (5000–3000 BC) might have used silk. Sun et al. (2012) estimate, based on genetic studies, domestication of the silkworm to have occurred about 4,100 years ago.

7. Cook (1984, 144). This story might be too good to withstand historical scrutiny, rather like Procopius' (*Wars* VIII.xvii.1–7) story of how the silkworms were supposedly brought to Byzantium by wandering monks, hidden in their hollow bamboo staves (Hunt 2011).

8. Wood (2007); Temple (1986).

9. Pre-Columbian cultures did have the wheel but used it only for toys (probably due to a lack of good draft animals).

10. Koubi (1999); Lerner (1997); Koubi and Lalman (2007); Zeira (2011); Judd et al. (2012).

11. Estimated from a variety of sources. The time gap is often somewhat arbitrary, depending on how exactly "equivalent" capabilities are defined. Radar was used by at least two countries within a couple of years of its introduction, but exact figures in months are hard to come by.
12. Ellis (1999).
13. The RDS-6 in 1953 was the first test of a bomb with fusion reactions, but the RDS-37 in 1955 was the first "true" fusion bomb, where most power came from the fusion reaction.
14. Unconfirmed.
15. Tests in 1989, project cancelled in 1994.
16. Deployed system, capable of a range greater than 5,000 km.
17. Polaris missiles bought from the USA.
18. Current work is underway on the Taimur missile, likely based on Chinese missiles.
19. The RSA-3 rocket tested in 1989–90 was intended for satellite launches and/or as an ICBM.
20. MIRV = multiple independently targetable re-entry vehicle, a technology that enables a single ballistic missile to carry multiple warheads that can be programmed to hit different targets.
21. The Agni V system is not yet in service.
22. Bostrom (2006c). One could imagine a singleton whose existence is invisible (e.g. a superintelligence with such advanced technology or insight that it could subtly control world events without any human noticing its interventions); or a singleton that voluntarily imposes very strict limitations on its own exercise of power (e.g. punctiliously confining itself to ensuring that certain treaty-specified international rules—or libertarian principles—are respected). How likely any particular kind of singleton is to arise is of course an empirical question; but *conceptually*, at least, it is possible to have a good singleton, a bad singleton, a rambunctiously diverse singleton, a blandly monolithic singleton, a crampingly oppressive singleton, or a singleton more akin to an extra law of nature than to a yelling despot.
23. Jones (1985, 344).
24. It might be significant that the Manhattan Project was carried out during wartime. Many of the scientists who participated claimed to be primarily motivated by the wartime situation and the fear that Nazi Germany might develop atomic weapons ahead of the Allies. It might be difficult for many governments to mobilize a similarly intensive and secretive effort in peacetime. The Apollo program, another iconic science/engineering megaproject, received a strong impetus from the Cold War rivalry.
25. Though even if they *were* looking hard, it is not clear that they would appear (publicly) to be doing so.
26. Cryptographic techniques could enable the collaborating team to be physically dispersed. The only weak link in the communication chain might be the input stage, where the physical act of typing could potentially be observed. But if indoor surveillance became common (by means of microscopic recording devices), those keen on protecting their privacy might develop countermeasures (e.g. special closets that could be sealed off from would-be eavesdropping devices). Whereas physical space might become transparent in a coming surveillance age, cyberspace might possibly become more protected through wider adoption of stronger cryptographic protocols.

27. A totalitarian state might take recourse to even more coercive measures. Scientists in relevant fields might be swept up and put into work camps, akin to the "academic villages" in Stalinist Russia.

28. When the level of public concern is relatively low, some researchers might welcome a little bit of public fear-mongering because it draws attention to their work and makes the area they work in seem important and exciting. When the level of concern becomes greater, the relevant research communities might change their tune as they begin to worry about funding cuts, regulation, and public backlash. Researchers in neighboring disciplines—such as those parts of computer science and robotics that are not very relevant to artificial general intelligence—might resent the drift of funding and attention away from their own research areas. These researchers might also correctly observe that *their* work carries no risk whatever of leading to a dangerous intelligence explosion. (Some historical parallels might be drawn with the career of the idea of nanotechnology; see Drexler [2013].)

29. These have been successful in that they have achieved at least some of what they set out to do. How successful they have been in a broader sense (taking into account cost-effectiveness and so forth) is harder to determine. In the case of the International Space Station, for example, there have been huge cost overruns and delays. For details of the problems encountered by the project, see NASA (2013). The Large Hadron Collider project has had some major setbacks, but this might be due to the inherent difficulty of the task. The Human Genome Project achieved success in the end, but seems to have received a speed boost from being forced to compete with Craig Venter's private corporate effort. Internationally sponsored projects to achieve controlled fusion energy have failed to deliver on expectations, despite massive investment; but again, this might be attributable to the task turning out to be more difficult than anticipated.

30. US Congress, Office of Technology Assessment (1995).

31. Hoffman (2009); Rhodes (2008).

32. Rhodes (1986).

33. The US Navy's code-breaking organization, OP-20-G, apparently ignored an invitation to gain full knowledge of Britain's anti-Enigma methods, and failed to inform higher-level US decision makers of Britain's offer to share its cryptographic secrets (Burke 2001). This gave American leaders the impression that Britain was withholding important information, a cause of friction throughout the war. Britain did share with the Soviet government some of the intelligence they had gleaned from decrypted German communications. In particular, Russia was warned about the German preparations for Operation Barbarossa. But Stalin refused to believe the warning, partly because the British did not disclose how they had obtained the information.

34. For a few years, Russell seems to have advocated the threat of nuclear war to persuade Russia to accept the Baruch plan; later, he was a strong proponent of mutual nuclear disarmament (Russell and Griffin 2001). John von Neumann is reported to have believed that a war between the United States and Russia was inevitable, and to have said, "If you say why not bomb them [the Russians] tomorrow, I say why not bomb them today? If you say today at five o'clock, I say why not one o'clock?" (It is possible that he made this notorious statement to burnish his anti-communist credentials with US Defense hawks in the McCarthy era. Whether von Neumann, had he

been in charge of US policy, would actually have launched a first strike is impossible to ascertain. See Blair [1957, 96].)

35. Baratta (2004).

36. If the AI is controlled by a group of humans, the problem may apply to this human group, though it is possible that new ways of reliably committing to an agreement will be available by this time, in which case even human groups could avoid this problem of potential internal unraveling and overthrow by a sub-coalition.

CHAPTER 6: COGNITIVE SUPERPOWERS

1. In what sense is humanity a dominant species on Earth? Ecologically speaking, humans are the most common large (~50 kg) animal, but the total human dry biomass (~100 billion kg) is not so impressive compared with that of ants, the family Formicidae (300 billion–3,000 billion kg). Humans and human utility organisms form a very small part (<0.001) of total global biomass. However, croplands and pastures are now among the largest ecosystems on the planet, covering about 35% of the ice-free land surface (Foley et al. 2007). And we appropriate nearly a quarter of net primary productivity according to a typical assessment (Haberl et al. 2007), though estimates range from 3% to over 50% depending mainly on varying definitions of the relevant terms (Haberl et al. 2013). Humans also have the largest geographic coverage of any animal species and top the largest number of different food chains.

2. Zalasiewicz et al. (2008).

3. See first note to this chapter.

4. Strictly speaking, this may not be quite correct. Intelligence in the human species ranges all the way down to approximately zero (e.g. in the case of embryos or patients in permanent vegetative state). In qualitative terms, the maximum difference in cognitive ability within the human species is therefore perhaps greater than the difference between any human and a superintelligence. But the point in the text stands if we read "human" as "normally functioning adult."

5. Gottfredson (2002). See also Carroll (1993) and Deary (2001).

6. See Legg (2008). Roughly, Legg proposes to measure a reinforcement-learning agent as its expected performance in all reward-summable environments, where each such environment receives a weight determined by its Kolmogorov complexity. We will explain what is meant by reinforcement learning in Chapter 12. See also Dowe and Hernández-Orallo (2012) and Hibbard (2011).

7. With regard to technology research in areas like biotechnology and nanotechnology, what a superintelligence would excel at is the design and modeling of new structures. To the extent that design ingenuity and modeling cannot substitute for physical experimentation, the superintelligence's performance advantage may be qualified by its level of access to the requisite experimental apparatus.

8. E.g., Drexler (1992, 2013).

9. A narrow-domain AI could of course have significant commercial applications, but this does not mean that it would have the economic productivity superpower. For example, even if a narrow-domain AI earned its owners several billions of dollars a year, this would still be four orders of magnitude less than the rest of the world economy. In order for the system directly and substantially to increase world product, an

AI would need to be able to perform many kinds of work; that is, it would need competence in many domains.

10. The criterion does not rule out all scenarios in which the AI fails. For example, the AI might rationally take a gamble that has a high chance of failing. In this case, however, the criterion could take the form that (a) the AI should make an unbiased estimate of the gamble's low chance of success and (b) there should be no better gamble available to the AI that we present-day humans can think of but that the AI overlooks.

11. Cf. Freitas (2000) and Vassar and Freitas (2006).

12. Yudkowsky (2008a).

13. Freitas (1980); Freitas and Merkle (2004, Chap. 3); Armstrong and Sandberg (2013).

14. See, e.g., Huffman and Pless (2003), Knill et al. (2000), Drexler (1986).

15. This estimate is based on the WMAP estimate of a cosmological baryon density of 9.9×10^{-30} g/cm^3 and assumes that 90% of the mass is intergalactic gas, that some 15% of the galactic mass is stars (about 80% of baryonic matter), and that the average star weighs in at 0.7 solar masses (Read and Trentham 2005; Carroll and Ostlie 2007).

16. Armstrong and Sandberg (2013).

17. Even at 100% of c (which is unattainable for objects with nonzero rest mass) the number of reachable galaxies is only about 6×10^9. (Cf. Gott et al. [2005] and Heyl [2005].) We are assuming that our current understanding of the relevant physics is correct. It is hard to be very confident in any upper bound, since it is at least conceivable that a superintelligent civilization might extend its reach in some way that we take to be physically impossible (for instance, by building time machines, by spawning new inflationary universes, or by some other, as yet unimagined means).

18. The number of habitable planets per star is currently uncertain, so this is merely a crude estimate. Traub (2012) predicts that one-third of stars in spectral classes F, G, or K have at least one terrestrial planet in the habitable zone; see also Clavin (2012). FGK stars form about 22.7% of the stars in the solar neighborhood, suggesting that 7.6% of stars have potentially suitable planets. In addition, there might be habitable planets around the more numerous M stars (Gilster 2012). See also Robles et al. (2008).

It would not be necessary to subject human bodies to the rigors of intergalactic travels. AIs could oversee the colonization process. *Homo sapiens* could be brought along as information, which the AIs could later use to instantiate specimens of our species. For example, genetic information could be synthesized into DNA, and a first generation of humans could be incubated, raised, and educated by AI guardians taking an anthropomorphic guise.

19. O'Neill (1974).

20. Dyson (1960) claims to have gotten the basic idea from science fiction writer Olaf Stapledon (1937), who in turn might have been inspired by similar thoughts by J. D. Bernal (Dyson 1979, 211).

21. Landauer's principle states that there is a minimum amount of energy required to change one bit of information, known as the Landauer limit, equal to $kT \ln 2$, where k is the Boltzmann constant (1.38×10^{-23} J/K) and T is the temperature. If we assume the circuitry is maintained at around 300 K, then 10^{26} watts allows us to erase approximately 10^{47} bits per second. (On the achievable efficiency of nanomechanical computational devices, see Drexler [1992]. See also Bradbury [1999]; Sandberg [1999];

Ćirković [2004]. The foundations of Landauer's principle are still somewhat in dispute; see, e.g., Norton [2011].)

22. Stars vary in their power output, but the Sun is a fairly typical main-sequence star.

23. A more detailed analysis might consider more closely what types of computation we are interested in. The number of *serial* computations that can be performed is quite limited, since a fast serial computer must be small in order to minimize communications lags within the different parts of the computer. There are also limits on the number of bits that can be stored, and, as we saw, on the number of irreversible computational steps (involving the erasure of information) that can be performed.

24. That is to say, the distance would be small on some "natural" metric, such as the logarithm of the size of the population that could be sustainably supported at subsistence level by a given level of capability if all resources were devoted to that end.

25. We are assuming here that there are no extraterrestrial civilizations that might get in the way. We are also assuming that the simulation hypothesis is false. See Bostrom (2003a). If either of these assumptions is incorrect, there may be important non-anthropogenic risks—ones that involve intelligent agency of a nonhuman sort. See also Bostrom (2003b, 2009c).

26. At least a wise singleton that grasped the idea of evolution could, in principle, have embarked on a eugenics program by means of which it could slowly have raised its level of collective intelligence.

27. Tetlock and Belkin (1996).

28. To be clear: colonizing and re-engineering a large part of the accessible universe is not currently within our *direct* reach. Intergalactic colonization is far beyond today's technology. The point is that we could in principle use our present capabilities to develop the additional capabilities that would be needed, thus placing the accomplishment within our *indirect* reach. It is of course also true that humanity is not currently a singleton and that we do not know that we would never face intelligent opposition from some external power if we began to re-engineer the accessible universe. To meet the wise-singleton sustainability threshold, however, it suffices that one possesses a capability set such that if a wise singleton facing no intelligent opposition had possessed this capability set then the colonization and reengineering of a large part of the accessible universe would be within its indirect reach.

29. Sometimes it might be useful to speak of two AIs as each having a given superpower. In an extended sense of the word, one could thus conceive of a superpower as something that an agent has relative to some field of action—in this example, perhaps a field that includes all of human civilization but excludes the other AI.

CHAPTER 7: THE SUPERINTELLIGENT WILL

1. This is of course not to deny that differences that appear small visually can be functionally profound.

2. Yudkowsky (2008a, 310).

3. David Hume, the Scottish Enlightenment philosopher, thought that beliefs alone (say, about what is a good thing to do) cannot motivate action: some desire is required.

This would support the orthogonality thesis by undercutting one possible objection to it, namely that sufficient intelligence might entail the acquisition of certain beliefs which would then necessarily produce certain motivations. However, although the orthogonality thesis can draw support from the Humean theory of motivation, it does not presuppose it. In particular, one need not maintain that beliefs alone can never motivate action. It would suffice to assume, for example, that an agent—be it ever so intelligent—can be motivated to pursue any course of action if the agent happens to have certain desires of some sufficient, overriding strength. Another way in which the orthogonality thesis could be true even if the Humean theory of motivation is false is if arbitrarily high intelligence does not entail the acquisition of any such beliefs as are (putatively) motivating on their own. A third way in which it might be possible for the orthogonality thesis to be true even if the Humean theory were false is if it is possible to build an agent (or more neutrally, an "optimization process") with arbitrarily high intelligence but with constitution so alien as to contain no clear functional analogs to what in humans we call "beliefs" and "desires." (For some recent attempts to defend the Humean theory of motivation see Smith [1987], Lewis [1988], and Sinhababu [2009].)

4. For instance, Derek Parfit has argued that certain basic preferences would be irrational, such as that of an otherwise normal agent who has "Future-Tuesday-Indifference":

> A certain hedonist cares greatly about the quality of his future experiences. With one exception, he cares equally about all the parts of his future. The exception is that he has Future-Tuesday-Indifference. Throughout every Tuesday he cares in the normal way about what is happening to him. But he never cares about possible pains or pleasures on a future Tuesday. . . . This indifference is a bare fact. When he is planning his future, it is simply true that he always prefers the prospect of great suffering on a Tuesday to the mildest pain on any other day. [Parfit (1986, 123–4); see also Parfit (2011)]

For our purposes, we need take no stand on whether Parfit is right that this agent is irrational, so long as we grant that it is not necessarily unintelligent in the instrumental sense explained in the text. Parfit's agent could have impeccable instrumental rationality, and therefore great intelligence, even if he falls short on some kind of sensitivity to "objective reason" that might be required of a fully rational agent. Therefore, this kind of example does not undermine the orthogonality thesis.

5. Even if there are objective moral facts that any fully rational agent would comprehend, and even if these moral facts are somehow intrinsically motivating (such that anybody who fully comprehends them is necessarily motivated to act in accordance with them), this need not undermine the orthogonality thesis. The thesis could still be true if an agent could have impeccable *instrumental* rationality even whilst lacking some other faculty constitutive of rationality proper, or some faculty required for the full comprehension of the objective moral facts. (An agent could also be extremely intelligent, even superintelligent, without having full instrumental rationality in every domain.)

6. For more on the orthogonality thesis, see Bostrom (2012) and Armstrong (2013).

7. Sandberg and Bostrom (2008).

8. Stephen Omohundro has written two pioneering papers on this topic (Omohundro 2007, 2008). Omohundro argues that all advanced AI systems are likely to exhibit a number of "basic drives," by which he means "tendencies which will be present unless

explicitly counteracted." The term "AI drive" has the advantage of being short and evocative, but it has the disadvantage of suggesting that the instrumental goals to which it refers influence the AI's decision-making in the same way as psychological drives influence human decision-making, i.e. via a kind of phenomenological tug on our ego which our willpower may occasionally succeed in resisting. That connotation is unhelpful. One would not normally say that a typical human being has a "drive" to fill out their tax return, even though filing taxes may be a fairly convergent instrumental goal for humans in contemporary societies (a goal whose realization averts trouble that would prevent us from realizing many of our final goals). Our treatment here also differs from that of Omohundro in some other more substantial ways, although the underlying idea is the same. (See also Chalmers [2010] and Omohundro [2012].)

9. Chislenko (1997).

10. See also Shulman (2010b).

11. An agent might also change its goal *representation* if it changes its ontology, in order to transpose its old representation into the new ontology; cf. de Blanc (2011).

    Another type of factor that might make an *evidential decision theorist* undertake various actions, including changing its final goals, is the evidential import of deciding to do so. For example, an agent that follows evidential decision theory might believe that there exist other agents like it in the universe, and that its own actions will provide some evidence about how those other agents will act. The agent might therefore choose to adopt a final goal that is altruistic towards those other evidentially linked agents, on grounds that this will give the agent evidence that those other agents will have chosen to act in like manner. An equivalent outcome might be obtained, however, without changing one's final goals, by choosing in each instant to act *as if* one had those final goals.

12. An extensive psychological literature explores adaptive preference formation. See, e.g., Forgas et al. (2010).

13. In formal models, the value of information is quantified as the difference between the expected value realized by optimal decisions made with that information and the expected value realized by optimal decisions made without it. (See, e.g., Russell and Norvig [2010].) It follows that the value of information is never negative. It also follows that any information you know will never affect any decision you will ever make has zero value for you. However, this kind of model assumes several idealizations which are often invalid in the real world—such as that knowledge has no final value (meaning that knowledge has only instrumental value and is not valuable for its own sake) and that agents are not transparent to other agents.

14. E.g., Hájek (2009).

15. This strategy is exemplified by the sea squirt larva, which swims about until it finds a suitable rock, to which it then permanently affixes itself. Cemented in place, the larva has less need for complex information processing, whence it proceeds to digest part of its own brain (its cerebral ganglion). One can observe the same phenomenon in some academics when they have been granted tenure.

16. Bostrom (2012).

17. Bostrom (2006c).

18. One could reverse the question and look instead at possible reasons for a superintelligent singleton *not* to develop some technological capabilities. These include the following: (a) the singleton foresees that it will have no use for the capability; (b) the development cost is too large relative to its anticipated utility (e.g. if the technology will never be suitable for achieving any of the singleton's ends, or if the singleton has a very high discount rate that strongly discourages investment); (c) the singleton has some final value that requires abstention from particular avenues of technology development; (d) if the singleton is not certain it will remain stable, it might prefer to refrain from developing technologies that could threaten its internal stability or that would make the consequences of dissolution worse (for instance, a world government may not wish to develop technologies that would facilitate rebellion, even if they have some good uses, nor develop technologies for the easy production of weapons of mass destruction which could wreak havoc if the world government were to dissolve); (e) similarly, the singleton might have made some kind of binding strategic commitment not to develop some technology, a commitment that remains operative even if it would now be convenient to develop it. (Note, however, that some *current* reasons for technology development would *not* apply to a singleton: for instance, reasons arising from arms races.)

19. Suppose that an agent discounts resources obtained in the future at an exponential rate, and that because of the light speed limitation the agent can only increase its resource endowment at a polynomial rate. Would this mean that there will be some time after which the agent would not find it worthwhile to continue acquisitive expansion? No, because although the present value of the resources obtained at future times would asymptote to zero the further into the future we look, *so would the present cost of obtaining them.* The present cost of sending out one more von Neumann probe 100 million years from now (possibly using some resource acquired some short time earlier) would be diminished by the same discount factor that would diminish the present value of the future resources that the extra probe would acquire (modulo a constant factor).

20. While the volume reached by colonization probes at a given time might be roughly spherical and expanding with a rate proportional to the square of time elapsed since the first probe was launched ($\sim t^2$), the amount of resources contained within this volume will follow a less regular growth pattern, since the distribution of resources is inhomogeneous and varies over several scales. Initially, the growth rate might be $\sim t^2$ as the home planet is colonized; then the growth rate might become spiky as nearby planets and solar systems are colonized; then, as the roughly disc-shaped volume of the Milky Way gets filled out, the growth rate might even out, to be approximately proportional to t; then the growth rate might again become spiky as nearby galaxies are colonized; then the growth rate might again approximate $\sim t^2$ as expansion proceeds on a scale over which the distribution of galaxies is roughly homogeneous; then another period of spiky growth followed by smooth $\sim t^2$ growth as galactic superclusters are colonized; until ultimately the growth rate starts a final decline, eventually reaching zero as the expansion speed of the universe increases to such an extent as to make further colonization impossible.

21. The simulation argument may be of particular importance in this context. A superintelligent agent may assign a significant probability to hypotheses according to which

it lives in a computer simulation and its percept sequence is generated by another superintelligence, and this might generate various convergent instrumental reasons depending on the agent's guesses about what types of simulations it is most likely to be in. Cf. Bostrom (2003a).

22. Discovering the basic laws of physics and other fundamental facts about the world is a convergent instrumental goal. We may place it under the rubric "cognitive enhancement" here, though it could also be derived from the "technology perfection" goal (since novel physical phenomena might enable novel technologies).

CHAPTER 8: IS THE DEFAULT OUTCOME DOOM?

1. Some additional existential risk resides in scenarios in which humanity survives in some highly suboptimal state or in which a large portion of our potential for desirable development is irreversibly squandered. On top of this, there may be existential risks associated with the lead-up to a potential intelligence explosion, arising, for example, from war between countries competing to develop superintelligence first.

2. There is an important moment of vulnerability when the AI first realizes the need for such concealment (an event which we may term *the conception of deception*). This initial realization would not itself be deliberately concealed when it occurs. But having had this realization, the AI might move swiftly to hide the fact that the realization has occurred, while setting up some covert internal dynamic (perhaps disguised as some innocuous process that blends in with all the other complicated processes taking place in its mind) that will enable it to continue to plan its long-term strategy in privacy.

3. Even human hackers can write small and seemingly innocuous programs that do completely unexpected things. (For examples, see some the winning entries in the International Obfuscated C Code Contest.)

4. The point that some AI control measures could appear to work within a fixed context yet fail catastrophically when the context changes is also emphasized by Eliezer Yudkowsky; see, e.g., Yudkowsky (2008a).

5. The term seems to have been coined by science-fiction writer Larry Niven (1973), but is based on real-world brain stimulation reward experiments; cf. Olds and Milner (1954) and Oshima and Katayama (2010). See also Ring and Orseau (2011).

6. Bostrom (1997).

7. There might be some possible implementations of a reinforcement learning mechanism that would, when the AI discovers the wireheading solution, lead to a safe incapacitation rather than to infrastructure profusion. The point is that this could easily go wrong and fail for unexpected reasons.

8. This was suggested by Marvin Minsky (*vide* Russell and Norvig [2010, 1039]).

9. The issue of which kinds of digital mind would be conscious, in the sense of having subjective phenomenal experience, or "qualia" in philosopher-speak, is important in relation to this point (though it is irrelevant to many other parts of this book). One open question is how hard it would be to accurately estimate how a human-like being would behave in various circumstances without simulating its brain in enough detail that the simulation is conscious. Another question is whether there are generally useful algorithms for a superintelligence, for instance reinforcement-learning techniques, such that the implementation of these algorithms would generate qualia. Even if we

judge the probability that any such subroutines would be conscious to be fairly small, the number of instantiations might be so large that even a small risk that they might experience suffering ought to be accorded significant weight in our moral calculation. See also Metzinger (2003, Chap. 8).

10. Bostrom (2002a, 2003a); Elga (2004).

CHAPTER 9: THE CONTROL PROBLEM

1. E.g., Laffont and Martimort (2002).

2. Suppose a majority of voters want their country to build some particular kind of superintelligence. They elect a candidate who promises to do their bidding, but they might find it difficult to ensure that the candidate, once in power, will follow through on her campaign promise and pursue the project in the way that the voters intended. Supposing she is true to her word, she instructs her government to contract with an academic or industry consortium to carry out the work; but again there are agency problems: the bureaucrats in the government department might have their own views about what should be done and may implement the project in a way that respects the letter but not the spirit of the leader's instructions. Even if the government department does its job faithfully, the contracted scientific partners might have their own separate agendas. The problem recurs on many levels. The director of one of the participating laboratories might lie awake worrying about a technician introducing an unsanctioned element into the design—imagining Dr. T. R. Eason sneaking into his office late one night, logging into the project code base, rewriting a part of the seed AI's goal system. Where it was supposed to say "serve humanity," it now says "serve Dr. T. R. Eason."

3. Even for superintelligence development, though, there could be a role for behavioral testing—as one auxiliary element within a wider battery of safety measures. Should an AI misbehave in its developmental phase, something is clearly awry—though, importantly, the converse does not hold.

4. In a classic exploit from 1975, Steven Dompier wrote a program for the Altair 8800 that took advantage of this effect (and the absence of shielding around the microcomputer's case). Running the program caused the emission of electromagnetic waves that would produce music when one held a transistor radio close to the computer (Driscoll 2012). The young Bill Gates, who attended a demo, reported that he was impressed and mystified by the hack (Gates 1975). There are in any case plans to design future chips with built-in Wi-Fi capabilities (Greene 2012).

5. It is no light matter to have held a conviction, which, had we had an opportunity to act upon it, could have resulted in the ruination of all our cosmic endowment. Perhaps one could argue for the following principle: if somebody has in the past been certain on N occasions that a system has been improved sufficiently to make it safe, and each time it was revealed that they were wrong, then on the next occasion they are not entitled to assign a credence greater than $1/(N + 1)$ to the system being safe.

6. In one informal experiment, the role of the AI was played by an intelligent human. Another individual played the role of gatekeeper and was tasked with not letting the AI out of the box. The AI could communicate with the gatekeeper only by text and was given two hours to persuade the gatekeeper to let it out. In three cases out of five, with

different individuals playing the gatekeeper, the AI escaped (Yudkowsky 2002). What a human can do, a superintelligence can do too. (The reverse, of course, does not hold. Even if the task for a real superintelligence were harder—maybe the gatekeepers would be more strongly motivated to refrain from releasing the AI than the individuals playing gatekeeper in the experiment—the superintelligence might still succeed where a human would fail.)

7. One should not overstate the marginal amount of safety that could be gained in this way. Mental imagery can substitute for graphical display. Consider the impact books can have on people—and books are not even interactive.

8. See also Chalmers (2010). It would be a mistake to infer from this that there is *no* possible use in building a system that will never be observed by any outside entity. One might place a final value on what goes on inside such a system. Also, other people might have preferences about what goes on inside such a system, and might therefore be influenced by its creation or the promise of its creation. Knowledge of the existence of certain kinds of isolated systems (ones containing observers) can also induce anthropic uncertainty in outside observers, which may influence their behavior.

9. One might wonder why social integration is considered a form of capability control. Should it not instead be classified as a motivation selection method on the ground that it involves seeking to influence a system's behavior by means of incentives? We will look closely at motivation selection presently; but, in answer to this question, we are construing motivation selection as a cluster of control methods that work by selecting or shaping a system's final goals—goals sought for their own sakes rather than for instrumental reasons. Social integration does not target a system's final goals, so it is not motivation selection. Rather, social integration aims to limit the system's effective capabilities: it seeks to render the system incapable of achieving a certain set of outcomes—outcomes in which the system attains the benefits of defection without suffering the associated penalties (retribution, and loss of the gains from collaboration). The hope is that by limiting which outcomes the system is able to attain, the system will find that the most effective remaining means of realizing its final goals is to behave cooperatively.

10. This approach may be somewhat more promising in the case of an emulation believed to have anthropomorphic motivations.

11. I owe this idea to Carl Shulman.

12. Creating a cipher certain to withstand a superintelligent code-breaker is a nontrivial challenge. For example, traces of random numbers might be left in some observer's brain or in the microstructure of the random generator, from whence the superintelligence can retrieve them; or, if pseudorandom numbers are used, the superintelligence might guess or discover the seed from which they were generated. Further, the superintelligence could build large quantum computers, or even discover unknown physical phenomena that could be used to construct new kinds of computers.

13. The AI could wire itself to *believe* that it had received a reward tokens, but this should not make it wirehead if it is designed to want the reward tokens (as opposed to wanting to be in a state in which it has certain beliefs about the reward tokens).

14. For the original article, see Bostrom (2003a). See also Elga (2004).

15. Shulman (2010a).

16. Basement-level reality presumably contains more computational resources than simulated reality, since any computational processes occurring in a simulation are also occurring on the computer running the simulation. Basement-level reality might also contain a wealth of other physical resources which could be hard for simulated agents to access—agents that exist only at the indulgence of powerful simulators who may have other uses in mind for those resources. (Of course, the inference here is not strictly deductively valid: in principle, it could be the case that universes in which simulations are run contain so much more resources that simulated civilizations on average have access to more resources than non-simulated civilizations, even though each non-simulated civilization that runs simulations has more resources than all the civilizations it simulates do combined.)

17. There are various further esoteric considerations that might bear on this matter, the implications of which have not yet been fully analyzed. These considerations may ultimately be crucially important in developing an all-things-considered approach to dealing with the prospect of an intelligence explosion. However, it seems unlikely that we will succeed in figuring out the practical import of such esoteric arguments unless we have first made some progress on the more mundane kinds of consideration that are the topic of most of this book.

18. Cf., e.g., Quine and Ullian (1978).

19. Which an AI might investigate by considering the performance characteristics of various basic computational functionalities, such as the size and capacity of various data buses, the time it takes to access different parts of memory, the incidence of random bit flips, and so forth.

20. Perhaps the prior could be (a computable approximation of) the Solomonoff prior, which assigns probability to possible worlds on the basis of their algorithmic complexity. See Li and Vitányi (2008).

21. The moment *after* the conception of deception, the AI might contrive to erase the trace of its mutinous thought. It is therefore important that this tripwire operate continuously. It would also be good practice to use a "flight recorder" that stores a complete trace of all the AI's activity (including exact timing of keyboard input from the programmers), so that its trajectory can be retraced or analyzed following an automatic shutdown. The information could be stored on a write-once-read-many medium.

22. Asimov (1942). To the three laws were later added a "Zeroth Law": "(0) A robot may not harm humanity, or, by inaction, allow humanity to come to harm" (Asimov 1985).

23. Cf. Gunn (1982).

24. Russell (1986, 161f).

25. Similarly, although some philosophers have spent entire careers trying to carefully formulate deontological systems, new cases and consequences occasionally come to light that necessitate revisions. For example, deontological moral philosophy has in recent years been reinvigorated through the discovery of a fertile new class of philosophical thought experiments, "trolley problems," which reveal many subtle interactions among our intuitions about the moral significance of the acts/omissions distinction, the distinction between intended and unintended consequences, and other such matters; see, e.g., Kamm (2007).

26. Armstrong (2010).

27. As a rule of thumb, if one plans to use multiple safety mechanisms to contain an AI, it may be wise to work on each one *as if* it were intended to be the sole safety mechanism and *as if* it were therefore required to be individually sufficient. If one puts a leaky bucket inside another leaky bucket, the water still comes out.

28. A variation of the same idea is to build the AI so that it is continuously motivated to act on its best guesses about what the implicitly defined standard is. In this setup, the AI's final goal is always to act on the implicitly defined standard, and it pursues an investigation into what this standard is only for instrumental reasons.

CHAPTER 10: ORACLES, GENIES, SOVEREIGNS, TOOLS

1. These names are, of course, anthropomorphic and should not be taken seriously as analogies. They are just meant as labels for some prima facie different concepts of possible system types that one might consider trying to build.

2. In response to a question about the outcome of the next election, one would not wish to be served with a comprehensive list of the projected position and momentum vectors of nearby particles.

3. Indexed to a particular instruction set on a particular machine.

4. Kuhn (1962); de Blanc (2011).

5. It would be harder to apply such a "consensus method" to genies or sovereigns, because there may often be numerous sequences of basic actions (such as sending particular patterns of electrical signals to the system's actuators) that would be almost exactly equally effective at achieving a given objective; whence slightly different agents may legitimately choose slightly different actions, resulting in a failure to reach consensus. By contrast, with appropriately formulated questions, there would usually be a small number of suitable answer options (such as "yes" and "no"). (On the concept of a Schelling point, also referred to as a "focal point," see Schelling [1980].)

6. Is not the world economy in some respects analogous to a weak genie, albeit one that charges for its services? A vastly bigger economy, such as might develop in the future, might then approximate a genie with collective superintelligence.

   One important respect in which the current economy is *unlike* a genie is that although I can (for a fee) command the economy to deliver a pizza to my door, I cannot command it to deliver peace. The reason is not that the economy is insufficiently powerful, but that it is insufficiently coordinated. In this respect, the economy resembles an *assembly* of genies serving different masters (with competing agendas) more than it resembles a single genie or any other type of unified agent. Increasing the total power of the economy by making each constituent genie more powerful, or by adding more genies, would not necessarily render the economy more capable of delivering peace. In order to function like a superintelligent genie, the economy would not only need to grow in its ability to inexpensively produce goods and services (including ones that require radically new technology), it would also need to become better able to solve global coordination problems.

7. If the genie were somehow incapable of not obeying a subsequent command—and somehow incapable of reprogramming itself to get rid of this susceptibility—then it could act to prevent any new command from being issued.

8. Even an oracle that is limited to giving yes/no answers could be used to facilitate the search for a genie or sovereign AI, or indeed could be used directly as a component in such an AI. The oracle could also be used to produce the actual code for such an AI if a sufficiently large number of questions can be asked. A series of such questions might take roughly the following form: "In the binary version of the code of the first AI that you thought of that would constitute a genie, is the nth symbol a zero?"

9. One could imagine a slightly more complicated oracle or genie that accepts questions or commands only if they are issued by a designated authority, though this would still leave open the possibility of that authority becoming corrupted or being blackmailed by a third party.

10. John Rawls, a leading political philosopher of the twentieth century, famously employed the expository device of a veil of ignorance as a way of characterizing the kinds of preference that should be taken into account in the formulation of a social contract. Rawls suggested that we should imagine we were choosing a social contract from behind a veil of ignorance that prevents us from knowing which person we will be and which social role we will occupy, the idea being that in such a situation we would have to think about which society would be generally fairest and most desirable without regard to our egoistic interests and self-serving biases that might otherwise make us prefer a social order in which we ourselves enjoy unjust privileges. See Rawls (1971).

11. Karnofsky (2012).

12. A possible exception would be software hooked up to sufficiently powerful actuators, such as software in early warning systems if connected directly to nuclear warheads or to human officers authorized to launch a nuclear strike. Malfunctions in such software can result in high-risk situations. This has happened at least twice within living memory. On November 9, 1979, a computer problem led NORAD (North American Aerospace Defense Command) to make a false report of an incoming full-scale Soviet attack on the United States. The USA made emergency retaliation preparations before data from early-warning radar systems showed that no attack had been launched (McLean and Stewart 1979). On September 26, 1983, the malfunctioning Soviet Oko nuclear early-warning system reported an incoming US missile strike. The report was correctly identified as a false alarm by the duty officer at the command center, Stanislav Petrov: a decision that has been credited with preventing thermonuclear war (Lebedev 2004). It appears that a war would probably have fallen short of causing human extinction, even if it had been fought with the combined arsenals held by all the nuclear powers at the height of the Cold War, though it would have ruined civilization and caused unimaginable death and suffering (Gaddis 1982; Parrington 1997). But bigger stockpiles might be accumulated in future arms races, or even deadlier weapons might be invented, or our models of the impacts of a nuclear Armageddon (particularly of the severity of the consequent nuclear winter) might be wrong.

13. This approach could fit the category of a direct-specification rule-based control method.

14. The situation is essentially the same if the solution criterion specifies a goodness *measure* rather than a sharp cutoff for what counts as a solution.

15. An advocate for the oracle approach could insist that there is at least a possibility that the user would spot the flaw in the proffered solution—recognize that it fails to match the user's intent even while satisfying the formally specified success criteria. The likelihood of catching the error at this stage would depend on various factors, including how humanly understandable the oracle's outputs are and how charitable it is in selecting which features of the potential outcome to bring to the user's attention.

Alternatively, instead of relying on the oracle itself to provide these functionalities, one might try to build a separate tool to do this, a tool that could inspect the pronouncements of the oracle and show us in a helpful way what would happen if we acted upon them. But to do to this in full generality would require another superintelligent oracle whose divinations we would then have to trust; so the reliability problem would not have been solved, only displaced. One might seek to gain an increment of safety through the use of multiple oracles to perform peer review, but this does not protect in cases where all the oracles fail in the same way—as may happen if, for instance, they have all been given the same formal specification of what counts as a satisfactory solution.

16. With sufficiently great—finite but physically implausible—amounts of computing power, it *would* probably be possible to achieve general superintelligence with currently available algorithms. (Cf., e.g., the AIXI*tl* system; Hutter [2001].) But even the continuation of Moore's law for another hundred years would not suffice to attain the required levels of computing power to achieve this.

17. Bird and Layzell (2002) and Thompson (1997); also Yaeger (1994, 13–14).

18. Williams (1966).

19. Leigh (2010).

20. This example is borrowed from Yudkowsky (2011).

21. Wade (1976). Computer experiments have also been conducted with simulated evolution designed to resemble aspects of biological evolution—again with sometimes strange results (see, e.g., Yaeger [1994]).

CHAPTER 11: MULTIPOLAR SCENARIOS

1. Not because this is necessarily the most likely or the most desirable type of scenario, but because it is the one easiest to analyze with the toolkit of standard economic theory, and thus a convenient starting point for our discussion.

2. American Horse Council (2005). See also Salem and Rowan (2001).

3. Acemoglu (2003); Mankiw (2009); Zuleta (2008).

4. Fredriksen (2012, 8); Salverda et al. (2009, 133).

5. It is also essential for at least some of the capital to be invested in assets that rise with the general tide. A diversified asset portfolio, such as shares in an index tracker fund, would increase the chances of not entirely missing out.

6. Many of the European welfare systems are *unfunded*, meaning that pensions are paid from ongoing current workers' contributions and taxes rather than from a pool of savings. Such schemes would not automatically meet the requirement—in case of sudden massive unemployment, the revenues from which the benefits are paid could dry up. However, governments may choose to make up the shortfall from other sources.

7. American Horse Council (2005).

8. Providing 7 billion people an annual pension of $90,000 would cost $630 trillion a year, which is ten times the current world GDP. Over the last hundred years, world GDP has increased about nineteenfold from around $2 trillion in 1900 to $37 trillion in 2000 (in 1990 int. dollars) according to Maddison (2007). So if the growth rates we have seen over the past hundred years continued for the next two hundred years, while population remained constant, then providing everybody with an annual $90,000 pension would cost about 3% of world GDP. An intelligence explosion might make this amount of growth happen in a much shorter time span. See also Hanson (1998a, 1998b, 2008).

9. And perhaps as much as a millionfold over the past 70,000 years if there was a severe population bottleneck around that time, as has been speculated. See Kremer (1993) and Huff et al. (2010) for more data.

10. Cochran and Harpending (2009). See also Clark (2007) and, for a critique, Allen (2008).

11. Kremer (1993).

12. Basten et al. (2013). Scenarios in which there is a continued rise are also possible. In general, the uncertainty of such projections increases greatly beyond one or two generations into the future.

13. Taken globally, the total fertility rate at replacement was 2.33 children per woman in 2003. This number comes from the fact that it takes two children per woman to replace the parents, plus a "third of a child" to make up for (1) the higher probability of boys being born, and (2) early mortality prior to the end of their fertile life. For developed nations, the number is smaller, around 2.1, because of lower mortality rates. (See Espenshade et al. [2003, Introduction, Table 1, 580].) The population in most developed countries would decline if it were not for immigration. A few notable examples of countries with sub-replacement fertility rates are: Singapore at 0.79 (lowest in the world), Japan at 1.39, People's Republic of China at 1.55, European Union at 1.58, Russia at 1.61, Brazil at 1.81, Iran at 1.86, Vietnam at 1.87, and the United Kingdom at 1.90. Even the U.S. population would probably decrease slightly with a fertility rate of 2.05. (See CIA [2013].)

14. The fullness of time might occur many billions of years from now.

15. Carl Shulman points out that if biological humans count on living out their natural lifespans alongside the digital economy, they need to assume not only that the political order in the digital sphere would be protective of human interests but that it would remain so over very long periods of time (Shulman 2012). For example, if events in the digital sphere unfold a thousand times faster than on the outside, then a biological human would have to rely on the digital body politic holding steady for 50,000 years of internal change and churn. Yet if the digital political world were anything like ours, there would be a great many revolutions, wars, and catastrophic upheavals during those millennia that would probably inconvenience biological humans on the outside. Even a 0.01% risk per year of a global thermonuclear war or similar cataclysm would entail a near certain loss for the biological humans living out their lives in slowmo sidereal time. To overcome this problem, a more stable order in the digital realm would be required: perhaps a singleton that gradually improves its own stability.

16. One might think that even if machines were far more efficient than humans, there would still be *some* wage level at which it would be profitable to employ a human worker; say at 1 cent an hour. If this were the only source of income for humans, our species would go extinct since human beings cannot survive on 1 cent an hour. But humans also get income from capital. Now, if we are assuming that population grows until total income is at subsistence level, one might think this would be a state in which humans would be working hard. For example, suppose subsistence level income is $1/ day. Then, it might seem, population would grow until per person capital provided only a 90 cents per day income, which people would have to supplement with ten hours of hard labor to make up the remaining 10 cents. However, this need not be so, because the subsistence level income depends on the amount of work that is done: harder-working humans burn more calories. Suppose that each hour of work increases food costs by 2 cents. We then have a model in which humans are idle in equilibrium.

17. It might be thought that a caucus as enfeebled as this would be unable to vote and to otherwise defend its entitlements. But the pod-dwellers could give power of attorney to AI fiduciaries to manage their affairs and represent their political interests. (This part of the discussion in this section is premised on the assumption that property rights are respected.)

18. It is unclear what is the best term. "Kill" may suggest more active brutality than is warranted. "End" may be too euphemistic. One complication is that there are two potentially separate events: ceasing to actively run a process, and erasing the information template. A human death normally involves both events, but for an emulation they can come apart. That a program *temporarily* ceases to run may be no more consequential than that a human sleeps: but to *permanently* cease running may be the equivalent of entering a permanent coma. Still further complications arise from the fact that emulations can be copied and that they can run at different speeds: possibilities with no direct analogs in human experience. (Cf. Bostrom [2006b]; Bostrom and Yudkowsky [2015].)

19. There will be a tradeoff between total parallel computing power and computational speed, as the highest computational speeds will be attainable only at the expense of a reduction in power efficiency. This will be especially true after one enters the era of reversible computing.

20. An emulation could be tested by leading it into temptation. By repeatedly testing how an emulation started from a certain prepared state reacts to various sequences of stimuli, one could obtain high confidence in the reliability of that emulation. But the further the mental state is subsequently allowed to develop away from its validated starting point, the less certain one could be that it would remain reliable. (In particular, since a clever emulation might surmise it is sometimes in a simulation, one would need to be cautious about extrapolating its behavior into situations where its simulation hypothesis would weigh less heavily in its decision-making.)

21. Some emulations might identify with their clan—i.e. all of their copies and variations derived from the same template—rather with any one particular instantiation. Such an emulation might not regard its own termination as a death event, if it knew that other clan members would survive. Emulations may know that they will get reverted to a particular stored state at the end of the day and lose that day's memories, but be as little

put off by this as the partygoer who knows she will awake the next morning without any recollection of the previous night: regarding this as retrograde amnesia, not death.

22. An ethical evaluation might take into account many other factors as well. Even if all the workers were constantly well pleased with their condition, the outcome might still be deeply morally objectionable on other grounds—though *which* other grounds is a matter of dispute between rival moral theories. But any plausible assessment would consider subjective well-being to be one important factor. See also Bostrom and Yudkowsky (2015).

23. World Values Survey (2008).

24. Helliwell and Sachs (2012).

25. Cf. Bostrom (2004). See also Chislenko (1996) and Moravec (1988).

26. It is hard to say whether the information-processing structures that would emerge in this kind of scenario would be conscious (in the sense of having qualia, phenomenal experience). The reason this is hard is partly our empirical ignorance about which cognitive entities would arise and partly our philosophical ignorance about which types of structure have consciousness. One could try to reframe the question, and instead of asking whether the future entities would be conscious, one could ask whether the future entities would have moral status; or one could ask whether they would be such that we have preferences about their "well-being." But these questions may be no easier to answer than the question about consciousness—in fact, they might require an answer to the consciousness question inasmuch as moral status or our preferences depend on whether the entity in question can subjectively experience its condition.

27. For an argument that both geological and human history manifest such a trend toward greater complexity, see Wright (2001). For an opposing argument (criticized in Chapter 9 of Wright's book), see Gould (1990). See also Pinker (2011) for an argument that we are witnessing a robust long-term trend toward decreasing violence and brutality.

28. For more on observation selection theory, see Bostrom (2002a).

29. Bostrom (2008a). A much more careful examination of the details of our evolutionary history would be needed to circumvent the selection effect. See, e.g., Carter (1983, 1993); Hanson (1998d); Ćirković et al. (2010).

30. Kansa (2003).

31. E.g., Zahavi and Zahavi (1997).

32. See Miller (2000).

33. Kansa (2003). For a provocative take, see also Frank (1999).

34. It is not obvious how best to measure the degree of global political integration. One perspective would be that whereas a hunter–gatherer tribe might have integrated a hundred individuals into a decision-making entity, the largest political entities today contain more than a billion individuals. This would amount to a difference of seven orders of magnitude, with only one additional magnitude to go before the entire world population is contained within a single political entity. However, at the time when the tribe was the largest scale of integration, the world population was much smaller. The tribe might have contained as much as a thousandth of the individuals then living. This would make the increase in the scale of political integration as little as two orders of magnitude. Looking at the fraction of world population that is politically integrated, rather than at absolute numbers, seems appropriate in the present context

(particularly as the transition to machine intelligence may cause a population explosion, of emulations or other digital minds). But there have also been developments in global institutions and networks of collaboration outside of formal state structures, which should also be taken into account.

35. One of the reasons for supposing that the first machine intelligence revolution will be swift—the possible existence of a hardware overhang—does not apply here. However, there could be other sources of rapid gain, such as a dramatic breakthrough in software associated with transitioning from emulation to purely synthetic machine intelligence.

36. Shulman (2010b).

37. How the *pro et contra* would balance out might depend on what kind of work the superorganism is trying to do, and how generally capable the most generally capable available emulation template is. Part of the reason many different types of human beings are needed in large organizations today is that humans who are very talented in many domains are rare.

38. It is of course very easy to make multiple copies of a software agent. But note that copying is not in general sufficient to ensure that the copies have the same final goals. In order for two agents to have the same final goals (in the relevant sense of "same"), the goals must coincide in their *indexical* elements. If Bob is selfish, a copy of Bob will likewise be selfish. Yet their goals do not coincide: Bob cares about Bob whereas Bob-copy cares about Bob-copy.

39. Shulman (2010b, 6).

40. This might be more feasible for biological humans and whole brain emulations than for arbitrary artificial intelligences, which might be constructed so as to have hidden compartments or functional dynamics that may be very hard to discover. On the other hand, *AIs specifically built to be transparent* should allow for more thoroughgoing inspection and verification than is possible with brain-like architectures. Social pressures may encourage AIs to expose their source code, and to modify themselves to render themselves transparent—especially if being transparent is a precondition to being trusted and thus to being given the opportunity to partake in beneficial transactions. Cf. Hall (2007).

41. Some other issues that seem relatively minor, especially in cases where the stakes are enormous (as they are for the key global coordination failures), include the search cost of finding policies that could be of mutual interest, and the possibility that some agents might have a basic preference for "autonomy" in a form that would be reduced by entering into comprehensive global treaties that have monitoring and enforcement mechanisms attached.

42. An AI might perhaps achieve this by modifying itself appropriately and then giving observers read-only access to its source code. A machine intelligence with a more opaque architecture (such as an emulation) might perhaps achieve it by publicly applying to itself some motivation selection method. Alternatively, an external coercive agency, such as a superorganism police force, might perhaps be used not only to enforce the implementation of a treaty reached between different parties, but also internally by a single party to commit itself to a particular course of action.

43. Evolutionary selection might have favored threat-ignorers and even characters visibly so highly strung that they would rather fight to the death than suffer the slightest

discomfiture. Such a disposition might bring its bearer valuable signaling benefits. (Any such instrumental rewards of having the disposition need of course play no part in the agent's conscious motivation: he may value justice or honor as ends in themselves.)

44. A definitive verdict on these matters, however, must await further analysis. There are various other potential complications which we cannot explore here.

CHAPTER 12: ACQUIRING VALUES

1. Various complications and modulations of this basic idea could be introduced. We discussed one variation in Chapter 8—that of a satisficing, as opposed to maximizing, agent—and in the next chapter we briefly touch on the issue of alternative decision theories. However, such issues are not essential to the thrust of this subsection, so we will keep things simple by focusing here on the case of an expected utility-maximizing agent.

2. Assuming the AI is to have a non-trivial utility function. It would be very easy to build an agent that always chooses an action that maximizes expected utility if its utility function is, e.g., the constant function $U(w) = 0$. Every action would equally well maximize expected utility relative to that utility function.

3. Also because we have forgotten the blooming buzzing confusion of our early infancy, a time when we could not yet see very well because our brain had not yet learned to interpret its visual input.

4. See also Yudkowsky (2011) and the review in section 5 of Muehlhauser and Helm (2012).

5. It is perhaps just about conceivable that advances in software engineering could eventually overcome these difficulties. Using modern tools, a single programmer can produce software that would have been beyond the pale of a sizeable team of developers forced to write directly in machine code. Today's AI programmers gain expressiveness from the wide availability of high-quality machine learning and scientific calculation libraries, enabling someone to hack up, for instance, a unique-face-counting webcam application by chaining libraries together that they never could have written on their own. The accumulation of reusable software, produced by specialists but useable by non-specialists, will give future programmers an expressiveness advantage. For example, a future robotics programmer might have ready access to standard facial imprinting libraries, typical-office-building-object collections, specialized trajectory libraries, and many other functionalities that are currently unavailable.

6. Dawkins (1995, 132). The claim here is not necessarily that the amount of suffering in the natural world *outweighs* the amount of positive well-being.

7. Required population sizes might be much larger or much smaller than those that existed in our own ancestry. See Shulman and Bostrom (2012).

8. If it were easy to get an equivalent result without harming large numbers of innocents, it would seem morally better to do so. If, nevertheless, digital persons are created and made to suffer unjust harm, it may be possible to compensate them for their suffering by saving them to file and later (when humanity's future is secured) rerunning them under more favorable conditions. Such restitution could be compared in some ways to religious conceptions of an afterlife in the context of theological attempts to address the evidential problem of evil.

9. One of the field's leading figures, Richard Sutton, defines reinforcement learning not in terms of a learning method but in terms of a learning problem: any method that is well suited to solving that problem is considered a reinforcement learning method (Sutton and Barto 1998, 4). The present discussion, in contrast, pertains to methods where the agent can be conceived of as having the final goal of maximizing (some notion of) cumulative reward. Since an agent with some very different kind of final goal might be skilled at mimicking a reward-seeking agent in a wide range of situations, and could thus be well suited to solving reinforcement learning problems, there could be methods that would count as "reinforcement learning methods" on Sutton's definition that would not result in a wireheading syndrome. The remarks in the text, however, apply to most of the methods actually used in the reinforcement learning community.

10. Even if, somehow, a human-like mechanism could be set up within a human-like machine intellect, the final goals acquired by this intellect need not resemble those of a well-adjusted human, unless the rearing environment for this digital baby also closely matched that of an ordinary child: something that would be difficult to arrange. And even with a human-like rearing environment, a satisfactory result would not be guaranteed, since even a subtle difference in innate dispositions can result in very different reactions to a life event. It may, however, be possible to create a more reliable value-accretion mechanism for human-like minds in the future (perhaps using novel drugs or brain implants, or their digital equivalents).

11. One might wonder why it appears *we humans* are not trying to disable the mechanism that leads us to acquire new final values. Several factors might be at play. First, the human motivation system is poorly described as a coldly calculating utility-maximizing algorithm. Second, we might not have any convenient means of altering the ways we acquire values. Third, we may have instrumental reasons (arising, e.g., from social signaling needs) for sometimes acquiring new final values—instrumental values might not be as useful if our minds are partially transparent to other people, or if the cognitive complexity of pretending to have a different set of final values than we actually do is too taxing. Fourth, there are cases where we *do* actively resist tendencies that produce changes in our final values, for instance when we seek to resist the corrupting influence of bad company. Fifth, there is the interesting possibility that we place some final value on being the kind of agent that can acquire new final values in normal human ways.

12. Or one might try to design the motivation system so that the AI is indifferent to such replacement; see Armstrong (2010).

13. We will here draw on some elucidations made by Daniel Dewey (2011). Other background ideas contributing to this framework have been developed by Marcus Hutter (2005) and Shane Legg (2008), Eliezer Yudkowsky (2001), Nick Hay (2005), Moshe Looks, and Peter de Blanc.

14. To avoid unnecessary complications, we confine our attention to deterministic agents that do not discount future rewards.

15. Mathematically, an agent's behavior can be formalized as an *agent function*, which maps each possible interaction history to an action. Except for the very simplest agents, it is infeasible to represent the agent function explicitly as a lookup table.

Instead, the agent is given some way of computing which action to perform. Since there are many ways of computing the same agent function, this leads to a finer individuation of an agent as an *agent program*. An agent program is a specific program or algorithm that computes an action for any given interaction history. While it is often mathematically convenient and useful to think of an agent program that interacts with some formally specified environment, it is important to remember that this is an idealization. Real agents are physically instantiated. This means not only that the agent interacts with the environment via its sensors and effectors, but also that the agent's "brain" or controller *is itself part of physical reality*. Its operations can therefore in principle be affected by external physical interferences (and not only by receiving percepts from its sensors). At some point, therefore, it becomes necessary to view an agent as an *agent implementation*. An agent implementation is a physical structure that, in the absence of interference from its environment, implements an agent function. (This definition follows Dewey [2011].)

16. Dewey proposes the following optimality notion for a value learning agent:

$$y_k = \arg \max_{y_k} \sum_{x_k y x_{k+1:m}} P_1(yx_{\leq m} \,|\, yx_k y_k) \sum_U U(yx_{\leq m}) P_2(U \,|\, yx_{\leq m}).$$

Here, P_1 and P_2 are two probability functions. The second summation ranges over some suitable class of utility functions over possible interaction histories. In the version presented in the text, we have made explicit some dependencies as well as availed ourselves of the simplifying possible-worlds notation.

17. It should be noted that the set of utility functions $\mathbb{U}$ should be such that utilities can be compared and averaged. In general, this is problematic, and it is not always obvious how to represent different moral theories of the good in terms of cardinal utility functions. See, e.g., MacAskill 2010).

18. Or more generally, since $\mathcal{V}$ might not be such as to directly imply for any given pair of a possible world and a utility function (w, U) whether the proposition $\mathcal{V}(U)$ is true in w, what needs to be done is to give the AI an adequate representation of the conditional probability distribution $P(\mathcal{V}(U) \,|\, w)$.

19. Consider first $\mathbb{Y}$, the class of actions that are possible for an agent. One issue here is what exactly should count as an action: only basic motor commands (e.g. "send an electric pulse along output channel #00101100"), or higher-level actions (e.g. "keep camera centered on face")? Since we are trying to develop an optimality notion rather than a practical implementation plan, we may take the domain to be basic motor commands (and since the set of possible motor commands might change over time, we may need to index $\mathbb{Y}$ to time). However, in order to move toward implementation it will presumably be necessary to introduce some kind of hierarchical planning process, and one may then need to consider how to apply the formula to some class of higher-level actions. Another issue is how to analyze internal actions (such as writing strings to working memory). Since internal actions can have important consequences, one would ideally want $\mathbb{Y}$ to include such basic internal actions as well as motor commands. But there are limits to how far one can go in this direction: the computation of the expected utility of any action in $\mathbb{Y}$ requires multiple computational operations, and

if each such operation were also regarded as an action in $\mathbb{Y}$ that needed to be evaluated according to AI-VL, we would face an infinite regress that would make it impossible to ever get started. To avoid the infinite regress, one must restrict any explicit attempt to estimate the expected utility to a limited number of significant action possibilities. The system will then need some heuristic process that identifies some significant action possibilities for further consideration. (Eventually the system might also get around to making explicit decisions regarding some possible actions to make modifications to this heuristic process, actions that might have been flagged for explicit attention by this self-same process; so that in the long run the system might become increasingly effective at approximating the ideal identified by AI-VL.)

Consider next $\mathbb{W}$, which is a class of possible worlds. One difficulty here is to specify $\mathbb{W}$ so that it is sufficiently inclusive. Failure to include some relevant w in $\mathbb{W}$ could render the AI incapable of representing a situation that actually occurs, resulting in the AI making bad decisions. Suppose, for example, that we use some ontological theory to determine the makeup of $\mathbb{W}$. For instance, we include in $\mathbb{W}$ all possible worlds that consist of a certain kind of spacetime manifold populated by elementary particles found in the standard model in particle physics. This could distort the AI's epistemology if the standard model is incomplete or incorrect. One could try to use a bigger $\mathbb{W}$-class to cover more possibilities; but even if one could ensure that every possible physical universe is included one might still worry that some other possibility would be left out. For example, what about the possibility of dualistic possible worlds in which facts about consciousness do not supervene on facts about physics? What about indexizatics? What about other kinds of fact that we fallible humans might have overlooked but that could turn out to be important to making things go as well as possible? Some people have strong convictions that some particular ontological theory is correct. (Among people writing on the future of AI, a belief in a materialistic ontology, in which the mental supervenes on the physical, is often taken for granted.) Yet a moment's reflection on the history of ideas should help us realize that there is a significant possibility that our favorite ontology is wrong. Had nineteenth-century scientists attempted a physics-inspired definition of $\mathbb{W}$, they would probably have neglected to include the possibility of a non-Euclidian spacetime or an Everettian ("many-worlds") quantum theory or a cosmological multiverse or the simulation hypothesis—possibilities that now appear to have a substantial probability of obtaining in the actual world. It is plausible that there are other possibilities to which we in the present generation are similarly oblivious. (On the other hand, if $\mathbb{W}$ is too big, there arise technical difficulties related to having to assign measures over transfinite sets.) The ideal might be if we could somehow arrange things such that the AI could use some kind of open-ended ontology, one that the AI itself could subsequently extend using the same principles that we would use when deciding whether to recognize a new type of metaphysical possibility.

Consider $P(w|Ey)$. Specifying this conditional probability is not strictly part of the value-loading problem. In order to be intelligent, the AI must already have some way of deriving reasonably accurate probabilities over many relevant factual possibilities. A system that falls too far short on this score will not pose the kind of danger that concerns us here. However, there may be a risk that the AI will end up with an epistemology that is good enough to make the AI instrumentally effective yet not good enough to enable it to think correctly about some possibilities that are of great normative importance. (The problem of specifying $P(w\,|\,Ey)$ is in this way related to the problem of specifying $\mathbb{W}$.) Specifying $P(w\,|\,Ey)$ also requires confronting other issues, such as how to represent uncertainty over logical impossibilities.

The aforementioned issues—how to define a class of possible actions, a class of possible worlds, and a likelihood distribution connecting evidence to classes of possible worlds—are quite generic: similar issues arise for a wide range of formally specified agents. It remains to examine a set of issues more peculiar to the value learning approach; namely, how to define $\mathbb{U}$, $\mathcal{V}(U)$, and $P(\mathcal{V}(U)\,|\,w)$.

$\mathbb{U}$ is a class of utility functions. There is a connection between $\mathbb{U}$ and $\mathbb{W}$ inasmuch as each utility function $U(w)$ in $\mathbb{U}$ should ideally assign utilities to each possible world w in $\mathbb{W}$. But $\mathbb{U}$ also needs to be wide in the sense of containing sufficiently many and diverse utility functions for us to have justified confidence that at least one of them does a good job of representing the intended values.

The reason for writing $P(\mathcal{V}(U)\,|\,w)$ rather than simply $P(U\,|\,w)$ is to emphasize the fact that probabilities are assigned to propositions. A utility function, per se, is not a proposition, but we can transform a utility function into a proposition by making some claim about it. For example, we may claim of a particular utility function $U(.)$ that it describes the preferences of a particular person, or that it represents the prescriptions implied by some ethical theory, or that it is the utility function that the principal would have wished to have implemented if she had thought things through. The "value criterion" $\mathcal{V}(.)$ can thus be construed as a function that takes as its argument a utility function U and gives as its value a proposition to the effect that U satisfies the criterion $\mathcal{V}$. Once we have defined a proposition $\mathcal{V}(U)$, we can hopefully obtain the conditional probability $P(\mathcal{V}(U)\,|\,w)$ from whatever source we used to obtain the other probability distributions in the AI. (If we are certain that all normatively relevant facts are taken into account in individuating the possible worlds $\mathbb{W}$, then $P(\mathcal{V}(U)\,|\,w)$ should equal zero or one in each possible world.) The question remains how to define $\mathcal{V}$. This is discussed further in the text.

20. These are not the only challenges for the value learning approach. Another issue, for instance, is how to get the AI to have sufficiently sensible initial beliefs—at least by the time it becomes strong enough to subvert the programmers' attempts to correct it.

21. Yudkowsky (2001).

22. The term is taken from American football, where a "Hail Mary" is a very long forward pass made in desperation, typically when the time is nearly up, on the off chance that a friendly player might catch the ball near the end zone and score a touchdown.

23. The Hail Mary approach relies on the idea that a superintelligence could articulate its preferences with greater exactitude than we humans can articulate ours. For example, a superintelligence could specify its preference as code. So if our AI is representing other superintelligences as computational processes that are perceiving their environment, then our AI should be able to reason about how those alien superintelligences would respond to some hypothetical stimulus, such as a "window" popping up in their visual field presenting them with the source code of our own AI and asking them to specify their instructions to us in some convenient pre-specified format. Our AI could

then read off these imaginary instructions (from its own model of this counterfactual scenario wherein these alien superintelligences are represented), and we would have built our AI so that it would be motivated to follow those instructions.

24. An alternative would be to create a detector that looks (within our AI's world model) for (representations of) physical structures created by a superintelligent civilization. We could then bypass the step of identifying the hypothesized superintelligences' preference functions, and give our own AI the final value of trying to copy whatever physical structures it believes superintelligent civilizations tend to produce.

There are technical challenges with this version, too, however. For instance, since our own AI, even after it has attained superintelligence, may not be able to know with great precision what physical structures other superintelligences build, our AI may need to resort to trying to approximate those structures. To do this, it would seem our AI would need a similarity metric by which to judge how closely one physical artifact approximates another. But similarity metrics based on crude physical measures may be inadequate—it being no good, for example, to judge that a brain is more similar to a Camembert cheese than to a computer running an emulation.

A more feasible approach might be to look for "beacons": messages about utility functions encoded in some suitable simple format. We would build our AI to want to follow whatever such messages about utility functions it hypothesizes might exist out there in the universe; and we would hope that friendly extraterrestrial AIs would create a variety of beacons of the types that they (with their superintelligence) reckon that simple civilizations like ours are most likely to build our AI to look for.

25. If *every* civilization tried to solve the value-loading problem through a Hail Mary, the pass would fail. Somebody has to do it the hard way.

26. Christiano (2012).

27. The AI we build need not be able to find the model either. Like us, it could reason about what such a complex implicit definition would entail (perhaps by looking at its environment and following much the same kind of reasoning that we would follow).

28. Cf. Chapters 9 and 11.

29. For instance, MDMA may temporarily increase empathy; oxytocin may temporarily increase trust (Vollenweider et al. 1998; Bartz et al. 2011). However, the effects seem quite variable and context dependent.

30. The enhanced agents might be killed off or placed in suspended animation (paused), reset to an earlier state, or disempowered and prevented from receiving any further enhancements, until the overall system has reached a more mature and secure state where these earlier rogue elements no longer pose a system-wide threat.

31. The issue might also be less obvious in a future society of biological humans, one that has access to advanced surveillance or biomedical techniques for psychological manipulation, or that is wealthy enough to afford an extremely high ratio of security professionals to invigilate the regular citizenry (and each other).

32. Cf. Armstrong (2007) and Shulman (2010b).

33. One open question is to what degree a level n supervisor would need to monitor not only their level $(n − 1)$ supervisees, but also *their* level $(n − 2)$ supervisees, in order to know that the level $(n − 1)$ agents are doing their jobs properly. And to know that the level $(n − 1)$ agents have successfully managed the level $(n − 2)$ agents, is it further necessary for the level n agent to also monitor the level $(n − 3)$ agents?

34. This approach straddles the line between motivation selection and capability control. Technically, the part of the arrangement that consists of human beings controlling a set of software supervisors counts as capability control, whereas the part of the arrangement that consists of layers of software agents within the system controlling other layers is motivation selection (insofar as it is an arrangement that shapes the system's motivational tendencies).

35. In fact, many other costs deserve consideration but cannot be given it here. For example, whatever agents are charged with ruling over such a hierarchy might become corrupted or debased by their power.

36. For this guarantee to be effective, it must be implemented in good faith. This would rule out certain kinds of manipulation of the emulation's emotional and decision-making faculties which might otherwise be used (for instance) to install a fear of being halted or to prevent the emulation from rationally considering its options.

37. See, e.g., Brinton (1965); Goldstone (1980, 2001). (Social science progress on these questions could make a nice gift to the world's despots, who might use more accurate predictive models of social unrest to optimize their population control strategies and to gently nip insurgencies in the bud with less-lethal force.)

38. Cf. Bostrom (2011a, 2009b).

39. In the case of an entirely artificial system, it might be possible to obtain some of the advantages of an institutional structure without actually creating distinct subagents. A system might incorporate multiple perspectives into its decision process without endowing each of those perspectives with its own panoply of cognitive faculties required for independent agency. It could be tricky, however, to fully implement the "observe the behavioral consequences of a proposed change, and revert back to an earlier version if the consequences appear undesirable from the *ex ante* standpoint" feature described in the text in a system that is not composed of subagents.

CHAPTER 13: CHOOSING THE CRITERIA FOR CHOOSING

1. A recent canvass of professional philosophers found the percentage of respondents who "accept or lean toward" various positions. On normative ethics, the results were *deontology* 25.9%; *consequentialism* 23.6%; *virtue ethics* 18.2%. On metaethics, results were *moral realism* 56.4%; *moral anti-realism* 27.7%. On moral judgment: *cognitivism* 65.7%; *non-cognitivism* 17.0% (Bourget and Chalmers 2009).

2. Pinker (2011).

3. For a discussion of this issue, see Shulman et al. (2009).

4. Moore (2011).

5. Bostrom (2006b).

6. Bostrom (2009b).

7. Bostrom (2011a).

8. More precisely, we should defer to its opinion except on those topics where we have good reason to suppose that our beliefs are more accurate. For example, we might know more about what we are thinking at a particular moment than the superintelligence does if it is not able to scan our brains. However, we could omit this qualification if we assume that the superintelligence has access to our opinions; we could then also defer to the superintelligence the task of judging when our opinions should be trusted. (There might remain some special cases, involving indexical information, that

need to be handled separately—by, for example, having the superintelligence explain to us what it would be rational to believe from our perspective.) For an entry into the burgeoning philosophical literature on testimony and epistemic authority, see, e.g., Elga (2007).

9. Yudkowsky (2004). See also Mijic (2010).

10. For example, David Lewis proposed a *dispositional theory of value*, which holds, roughly, that some thing X is a value for A if and only if A would want to want X if A were perfectly rational and ideally acquainted with X (Smith et al. 1989). Kindred ideas had been put forward earlier; see, e.g., Sen and Williams (1982), Railton (1986), and Sidgwick and Jones (2010). Along somewhat similar lines, one common account of philosophical justification, the *method of reflective equilibrium*, proposes a process of iterative mutual adjustment between our intuitions about particular cases, the general rules which we think govern these cases, and the principles according to which we think these elements should be revised, to achieve a more coherent system; see, e.g., Rawls (1971) and Goodman (1954).

11. Presumably the intention here is that when the AI acts to prevent such disasters, it should do it with *as light a touch as possible*, i.e. in such a manner that it averts the disaster but without exerting too much influence over how things turn out for humanity in other respects.

12. Yudkowsky (2004).

13. Rebecca Roache, personal communication.

14. The three principles are "Defend humans, the future of humanity, and humane nature" (*humane* here being that which we wish we were, as distinct from *human*, which is what we are); "Humankind should not spend the rest of eternity desperately wishing that the programmers had done something differently"; and "Help people."

15. Some religious groups place a strong emphasis on faith in contradistinction to reason, the latter of which they may regard—even in its hypothetically most idealized form and even after it would have ardently and open-mindedly studied every scripture, revelation, and exegesis—to be insufficient for the attainment of essential spiritual insights. Those holding such views might not regard CEV as an optimal guide to decision-making (though they might still prefer it to various other imperfect guides that might in actuality be followed if the CEV approach were eschewed).

16. An AI acting like a latent force of nature to regulate human interactions has been referred to as a "Sysop," a kind of "operating system" for the matter occupied by human civilization. See Yudkowsky (2001).

17. "*Might*," because *conditional* on humanity's coherent extrapolated volition wishing not to extend moral consideration to these entities, it is perhaps doubtful whether those entities actually have moral status (despite it seeming very plausible now that they do). "*Potentially*," because even if a blocking vote prevents the CEV dynamic from directly protecting these outsiders, there is still a possibility that, within whatever ground rules are left over once the initial dynamic has run, individuals whose wishes were respected and who want some outsiders' welfare to be protected may successfully bargain to attain this outcome (at the expense of giving up some of their own resources). Whether this would be possible might depend on, among other things, whether the outcome of the CEV dynamic is a set of ground rules that makes it feasible to reach

negotiated resolutions to issues of this kind (which might require provisions to overcome strategic bargaining problems).

18. Individuals who contribute positively to realizing a safe and beneficial superintelligence might merit *some* special reward for their labour, albeit something short of a near-exclusive mandate to determine the disposition of humanity's cosmic endowment. However, the notion of everybody getting an equal share in our extrapolation base is such a nice Schelling point that it should not be lightly tossed away. There is, in any case, an indirect way in which virtue could be rewarded: namely, the CEV itself might turn out to specify that good people who exerted themselves on behalf of humanity should be suitably recognized. This could happen without such people being given any special weight in the extrapolation base if—as is easily imaginable—our CEV would endorse (in the sense of giving at least some nonzero weight to) a principle of just desert.

19. Bostrom et al. (forthcoming).

20. To the extent that there is some (sufficiently definite) shared meaning that is being expressed when we make moral assertions, a superintelligence should be able to figure out what that meaning is. And to the extent that moral assertions are "truth-apt" (i.e. have an underlying propositional character that enables them to be true or false), the superintelligence should be able to figure out which assertions of the form "Agent X ought now to Φ" are true. At least, it should outperform us on this task.

An AI that initially lacks such a capacity for moral cognition should be able to acquire it if it has the intelligence amplification superpower. One way the AI could do this is by reverse-engineering the human brain's moral thinking and then implement a similar process but run it faster, feed it more accurate factual information, and so forth.

21. Since we are uncertain about metaethics, there is a question of what the AI is to do if the preconditions for MR fail to obtain. One option is to stipulate that the AI shut itself off if it assigns a sufficiently high probability to moral cognitivism being false or to there being no suitable non-relative moral truths. Alternatively, we could have the AI revert to some alternative approach, such as CEV.

We could refine the MR proposal to make it clearer what is to be done in various ambiguous or degenerate cases. For instance, if error theory is true (and hence all positive moral assertions of the form "I ought now to Φ" are false), then the fallback strategy (e.g. shutting down) would be invoked. We could also specify what should happen if there are multiple feasible actions, each of which would be morally right. For example, we might say that in such cases the AI should perform (one of) the permissible actions that humanity's collective extrapolation would have favored. We might also stipulate what should happen if the true moral theory does not employ terms like "morally right" in its basic vocabulary. For instance, a consequentialist theory might hold that some actions are better than others but that there is no particular threshold corresponding to the notion of an action being "morally right." We could then say that if such a theory is correct, MR should perform one of the morally best feasible actions, if there is one; or, if there is an infinite number of feasible actions such that for any feasible action there is a better one, then maybe MR could pick any that is at least astronomically better than the best action that any human would have selected in a similar situation, if such an action is feasible—or if not, then an action that is at least as good as the best action a human would have performed.

A couple of general points should be borne in mind when thinking about how the MR proposal could be refined. First, we might start conservatively, using the fallback option to cover almost all contingencies and only use the "morally right" option in those that we feel we fully understand. Second, we might add the general modulator to the MR proposal that it is to be "interpreted charitably, and revised as we would have revised it if we had thought more carefully about it before we wrote it down, etc."

22. Of these terms, "knowledge" might seem the one most readily susceptible to a formal analysis (in information-theoretic terms). However, to represent what it is for a human to know something, the AI may need a sophisticated set of representations relating to complex psychological properties. A human being does not "know" all the information that is stored somewhere in her brain.

23. One indicator that the terms in CEV are (marginally) less opaque is that it would count as philosophical progress if we could analyze moral rightness in terms like those used in CEV. In fact, one of the main strands in metaethics—ideal observer theory— purports to do just that. See, e.g., Smith et al. (1989).

24. This requires confronting the problem of fundamental normative uncertainty. It can be shown that it is not always appropriate to act according to the moral theory that has the highest probability of being true. It can also be shown that it is not always appropriate to perform the action that has the highest probability of being right. Some way of trading probabilities against "degrees of wrongness" or severity of issues at stake seems to be needed. For some ideas in this direction, see Bostrom (2009a).

25. It could possibly even be argued that it is an adequacy condition for any explication of the notion of moral rightness that it account for how Joe Sixpack is able to have some idea of right and wrong.

26. It is not obvious that the morally right thing *for us* to do is to build an AI that implements MR, even if we assume that *the AI itself* would always act morally. Perhaps it would be objectionably hubristic or arrogant of us to build such an AI (especially since many people may disapprove of that project). This issue can be partially finessed by tweaking the MR proposal. Suppose that we stipulate that the AI should act (to do what it would be morally right for it to do) only if it was morally right for its creators to have built the AI in the first place; otherwise it should shut itself down. It is hard to see how we would be committing any grave moral wrong in creating *that* kind of AI, since if it were wrong for us to create it, the only consequence would be that an AI was created that immediately shuts itself down, assuming that the AI has committed no mind crime up to that point. (We might nevertheless have acted wrongly—for instance, by having failed to seize the opportunity to build some other AI instead.)

A second issue is supererogation. Suppose there are many actions the AI could take, each of which would be morally right—in the sense of being *morally permissible*—yet some of which are morally better than the others. One option is to have the AI aim to select the morally best action in any such a situation (or one of the best actions, in case there are several that are equally good). Another option is to have the AI select from among the morally permissible actions one that maximally satisfies some other (non-moral) desideratum. For example, the AI could select, from among the actions that are morally permissible, the action that our CEV would prefer it to take. Such an AI, while never doing anything that is morally impermissible, might protect our interests more than an AI that does what is morally best.

27. When the AI evaluates the moral permissibility of our act of creating the AI, it should interpret permissibility in its objective sense. In one ordinary sense of "morally permissible," a doctor acts morally permissibly when she prescribes a drug she believes will cure her patient—even if the patient, unbeknownst to the doctor, is allergic to the drug and dies as a result. Focusing on objective moral permissibility takes advantage of the presumably superior epistemic position of the AI.

28. More directly, it depends on the AI's *beliefs* about which ethical theory is true (or, more precisely, on its probability distribution over ethical theories).

29. It can be difficult to imagine how superlatively wonderful these physically possible lives might be. See Bostrom (2008c) for a poetic attempt to convey some sense of this. See Bostrom (2008b) for an argument that some of these possibilities could be good *for us*, good for existing human beings.

30. It might seem deceptive or manipulative to promote one proposal if one thinks that some other proposal would be better. But one could promote it in ways that avoid insincerity. For example, one could freely acknowledge the superiority of the ideal while still promoting the non-ideal as the best attainable compromise.

31. Or some other positively evaluative term, such as "good," "great," or "wonderful."

32. This echoes a principle in software design known as "Do What I Mean," or DWIM. See Teitelman (1966).

33. Goal content, decision theory, and epistemology are three aspects that should be elucidated; but we do not intend to beg the question of whether there must be a neat decomposition into these three separate components.

34. An ethical project ought presumably to allocate at most a modest portion of the eventual benefits that the superintelligence produces as special rewards to those who contributed in morally permissible ways to the project's success. Allocating a great portion to the incentive wrapping scheme would be unseemly. It would be analogous to a charity that spends 90% of its income on performance bonuses for its fundraisers and on advertising campaigns to increase donations.

35. How could the dead be rewarded? One can think of several possibilities. At the low end, there could be memorial services and monuments, which would be a reward insofar as people desired posthumous fame. The deceased might also have other preferences about the future that could be honored, for instance concerning cultures, arts, buildings, or natural environments. Furthermore, most people care about their descendants, and special privileges could be granted to the children and grandchildren of contributors. More speculatively, the superintelligence might be able to create relatively faithful simulations of some past people—simulations that would be conscious and that would resemble the original sufficiently to count as a form of survival (according to at least some people's criteria). This would presumably be easier for people who have been placed in cryonic suspension; but perhaps for a superintelligence it would not be impossible to recreate something quite similar to the original person from other preserved records such as correspondence, publications, audiovisual

materials and digital records, or the personal memories of other survivors. A superintelligence might also think of some possibilities that do not readily occur to us.

36. On Pascalian mugging, see Bostrom (2009b). For an analysis of issues related to infinite utilities, see Bostrom (2011a). On fundamental normative uncertainty, see, e.g., Bostrom (2009a).

37. E.g., Price (1991); Joyce (1999); Drescher (2006); Yudkowsky (2010); Dai (2009).

38. E.g., Bostrom (2009a).

39. It is also conceivable that using indirect normativity to specify the AI's goal content would mitigate the problems that might arise from an incorrectly specified decision theory. Consider, for example, the CEV approach. If it were implemented well, it might be able to compensate for at least some errors in the specification of the AI's decision theory. The implementation could allow the values that our coherent extrapolated volition would want the AI to pursue to depend on the AI's decision theory. If our idealized selves knew they were making value specifications for an AI that was using a particular kind of decision theory, they could adjust their value specifications such as to make the AI behave benignly despite its warped decision theory—much like one can cancel out the distorting effects of one lens by placing another lens in front of it that distorts oppositely.

40. Some epistemological systems may, in a holistic manner, have no distinct foundation. In that case, the constitutional inheritance is not a distinct set of principles, but rather, as it were, an epistemic starting point that embodies certain propensities to respond to incoming streams of evidence.

41. See, e.g., the problem of distortion discussed in Bostrom (2011a).

42. For instance, one disputed issue in anthropic reasoning is whether the so-called self-indication assumption should be accepted. The self-indication assumption states, roughly, that from the fact that you exist you should infer that hypotheses according to which larger numbers N of observers exist should receive a probability boost proportional to N. For an argument against this principle, see the "Presumptuous Philosopher" gedanken experiment in Bostrom (2002a). For a defense of the principle, see Olum (2002); and for a critique of that defense, see Bostrom and Ćirković (2003). Beliefs about the self-indication assumption might affect various empirical hypotheses of potentially crucial strategic relevance, for example, considerations such as the Carter–Leslie doomsday argument, the simulation argument, and "great filter" arguments. See Bostrom (2002a, 2003a, Bostrom 2008a); Carter (1983); Ćirković et al. (2010); Hanson (1998d); Leslie (1996); Tegmark and Bostrom (2005). A similar point could be made with regard to other fraught issues in observation selection theory, such as whether the choice of reference class can be relativized to observer-moments, and if so how.

43. See, e.g., Howson and Urbach (1993). There are also some interesting results that narrow the range of situations in which two Bayesian agents can rationally disagree when their opinions are common knowledge; see Aumann (1976) and Hanson (2006).

44. Cf. the concept of a "last judge" in Yudkowsky (2004).

45. There are many important issues outstanding in epistemology, some mentioned earlier in the text. The point here is that we may not need to get all the solutions exactly right in order to achieve an outcome that is practically indiscernible from the best outcome. A mixture model (which throws together a wide range of diverse priors) might work.

CHAPTER 14: THE STRATEGIC PICTURE

1. This principle is introduced in Bostrom (2009b, 190), where it is also noted that it is not tautological. For a visual analogy, picture a box with large but finite volume, representing the space of basic capabilities that could be obtained through some possible technology. Imagine sand being poured into this box, representing research effort. How you pour the sand determines where it piles up in the box. But if you keep on pouring, the entire space eventually gets filled.

2. Bostrom (2002b).

3. This is not the perspective from which science policy has traditionally been viewed. Harvey Averch describes science and technology policy in the United States between 1945 and 1984 as having been centered on debates about the optimum level of public investment in the S&T enterprise and on the extent to which the government should attempt to "pick winners" in order to achieve the greatest increase in the nation's economic prosperity and military strength. In these calculations, technological progress is always assumed to be good. But Averch also describes the rise of critical perspectives, which question the "progress is always good" premiss (Averch 1985). See also Graham (1997).

4. Bostrom (2002b).

5. This is of course by no means tautological. One could imagine a case being made for a different order of development. It could be argued that it would be better for humanity to confront some less difficult challenge first, say the development of nanotechnology, on grounds that this would force us to develop better institutions, become more internationally coordinated, and mature in our thinking about global strategy. Perhaps we would be more likely to rise to a challenge that presents a less metaphysically confusing threat than machine superintelligence. Nanotechnology (or synthetic biology, or whatever the lesser challenge we confront first) might then serve as a footstool that would help us ascend to the capability level required to deal with the higher-level challenge of superintelligence.

   Such an argument would have to be assessed on a case-by-case basis. For example, in the case of nanotechnology, one would have to consider various possible consequences such as the boost in hardware performance from nanofabricated computational substrates; the effects of cheap physical capital for manufacturing on economic growth; the proliferation of sophisticated surveillance technology; the possibility that a singleton might emerge though the direct or indirect effects of a nanotechnology breakthrough; and the greater feasibility of neuromorphic and whole brain emulation approaches to machine intelligence. It is beyond the scope of our investigation to consider all these issues (or the parallel issues that might arise for other existential risk-causing technologies). Here we just point out the prima facie case for favoring a superintelligence-first sequence of development—while stressing that there are complications that might alter this preliminary assessment in some cases.

6. Pinker (2011); Wright (2001).

7. It might be tempting to suppose the hypothesis that everything has accelerated to be meaningless on grounds that it does not (at first glance) seem to have any observational consequences; but see, e.g., Shoemaker (1969).

8. The level of preparedness is not measured by the amount of effort expended on preparedness activities, but by how propitiously configured conditions actually are and how well-poised key decision makers are to take appropriate action.

9. The degree of international trust during the lead-up to the intelligence explosion may also be a factor. We consider this in the section "Collaboration" later in the chapter.

10. Anecdotally, it appears those currently seriously interested in the control problem are disproportionately sampled from one extreme end of the intelligence distribution, though there could be alternative explanations for this impression. If the field becomes fashionable, it will undoubtedly be flooded with mediocrities and cranks.

11. I owe this term to Carl Shulman.

12. How similar to a brain does a machine intelligence have to be to count as a whole brain emulation rather than a neuromorphic AI? The relevant determinant might be whether the system reproduces either the values or the full panoply of cognitive and evaluative tendencies of either a particular individual or a generic human being, because this would plausibly make a difference to the control problem. Capturing these properties may require a rather high degree of emulation fidelity.

13. The magnitude of the boost would of course depend on how big the push was, and also where resources for the push came from. There might be no net boost for neuroscience if all the extra resources invested in whole brain emulation research were deducted from regular neuroscience research—unless a keener focus on emulation research just happened to be a more effective way of advancing neuroscience than the default portfolio of neuroscience research.

14. See Drexler (1986, 242). Drexler (private communication) confirms that this reconstruction corresponds to the reasoning he was seeking to present. Obviously, a number of implicit premises would have to be added if one wished to cast the argument in the form of a deductively valid chain of reasoning. (Note that Drexler does not endorse the "related type of argument" discussed below.)

15. Perhaps we ought not to welcome *small* catastrophes in case they increase our vigilance to the point of making us prevent the *medium-scale* catastrophes that would have been needed to make us take the strong precautions necessary to prevent existential catastrophes? (And of course, just as with biological immune systems, we also need to be concerned with over-reactions, analogous to allergies and autoimmune disorders.)

16. Cf. Lenman (2000); Burch-Brown (2014).

17. Cf. Bostrom (2007).

18. Note that this argument focuses on the ordering rather than the timing of the relevant events. Making superintelligence happen earlier would help preempt other existential transition risks only if the intervention changes the sequence of the key developments: for example, by making superintelligence happen before various milestones are reached in nanotechnology or synthetic biology.

19. If solving the control problem is *extremely* difficult compared to solving the performance problem in machine intelligence, and if project ability correlates only weakly with project size, then it is possible that it would be better that a small project gets there first, namely if the variance in capability is greater among smaller projects. In such a situation, even if smaller projects are on average less competent than larger projects, it could be less unlikely that a given small project would happen to have the freakishly high level of competence needed to solve the control problem.

20. This is not to deny that one can imagine tools that could promote global deliberation and which would benefit from, or even require, further progress in hardware—for

example, high-quality translation, better search, ubiquitous access to smart phones, attractive virtual reality environments for social intercourse, and so forth.

21. Investment in emulation technology could speed progress toward whole brain emulation not only directly (through any technical deliverables produced) but also indirectly by creating a constituency that will push for more funding and boost the visibility and credibility of the whole brain emulation (WBE) vision.

22. How much expected value would be lost if the future were shaped by the desires of one random human rather than by (some suitable superposition of) the desires of all of humanity? This might depend sensitively on what evaluation standard we use, and also on whether the desires in question are idealized or raw.

23. For example, whereas human minds communicate slowly via language, AIs can be designed so that instances of the same program are able easily and quickly to transfer both skills and information amongst one another. Machine minds designed *ab initio* could do away with cumbersome legacy systems that helped our ancestors deal with aspects of the natural environment that are unimportant in cyberspace. Digital minds might also be designed to take advantage of fast serial processing unavailable to biological brains, and to make it easy to install new modules with highly optimized functionality (e.g. symbolic processing, pattern recognition, simulators, data mining, and planning). Artificial intelligence might also have significant non-technical advantages, such as being more easily patentable or less entangled in the moral complexities of using human uploads.

24. If p_1 and p_2 are the probabilities of failure at each step, the total probability of failure is $p_1 + (1 - p_1)p_2$ since one can fail terminally only once.

25. It is possible, of course, that the frontrunner will not have such a large lead and will not be able to form a singleton. It is also possible that a singleton would arise before AI even without the intervention of WBE, in which case this reason for favoring a WBE-first scenario falls away.

26. Is there a way for a promoter of WBE to increase the specificity of her support so that it accelerates WBE while minimizing the spillover to AI development? Promoting scanning technology is probably a better bet than promoting neurocomputational modeling. (Promoting computer hardware is unlikely to make much difference one way or the other, given the large commercial interests that are anyway incentivizing progress in that field.)

Promoting scanning technology may increase the likelihood of a multipolar outcome by making scanning less likely to be a bottleneck, thus increasing the chance that the early emulation population will be stamped from many different human templates rather than consisting of gazillions of copies of a tiny number of templates. Progress in scanning technology also makes it more likely that the bottleneck will instead be computing hardware, which would tend to slow the takeoff.

27. Neuromorphic AI may also lack other safety-promoting attributes of whole brain emulation, such as having a profile of cognitive strengths and weaknesses similar to that of a biological human being (which would let us use our experience of humans to form some expectations of the system's capabilities at different stages of its development).

28. If somebody's motive for promoting WBE is to make WBE happen before AI, they should bear in mind that accelerating WBE will alter the order of arrival only if the default timing of the two paths toward machine intelligence is close and with a slight edge to AI. Otherwise, *either* investment in WBE will simply make WBE happen

earlier than it otherwise would (reducing hardware overhang and preparation time) but without affecting the sequence of development; *or else* such investment in WBE will have little effect (other than perhaps making AI happen even sooner by stimulating progress on neuromorphic AI).

29. Comment on Hanson (2009).

30. There would of course be *some* magnitude and imminence of existential risk for which it would be preferable even from the person-affecting perspective to postpone the risk—whether to enable existing people to eke out a bit more life before the curtain drops or to provide more time for mitigation efforts that might reduce the danger.

31. Suppose we could take some action that would bring the intelligence explosion closer by one year. Let us say that the people currently inhabiting the Earth are dying off at a rate of 1% per year, and that the default risk of human extinction from the intelligence explosion is 20% (to pick an arbitrary number for the purposes of illustration only). Then hastening the arrival of the intelligence explosion by 1 year might be worth (from a person-affecting standpoint) an increase in the risk from 20% to 21%, i.e. a 5% increase in risk level. However, the vast majority of people alive one year before the start of the intelligence explosion would at that point have an interest in postponing it if they could thereby reduce the risk of the explosion by one percentage point (since most individuals would reckon their own risk of dying in the next year to be much smaller than 1%—given that most mortality occurs in relatively narrow demographics such as the frail and the elderly). One could thus have a model in which each year the population votes to postpone the intelligence explosion by another year, so that the intelligence explosion never happens, although everybody who ever lives agrees that it would be better if the intelligence explosion happened at some point. In reality, of course, coordination failures, limited predictability, or preferences for things other than personal survival are likely to prevent such an unending pause.

If one uses the standard economic discount factor instead of the person-affecting standard, the magnitude of the potential upside is diminished, since the value of existing people getting to enjoy astronomically long lives is then steeply discounted. This effect is especially strong if the discount factor is applied to each individual's subjective time rather than to sidereal time. If future benefits are discounted at a rate of x% per year, and the background level of existential risk from other sources is y% per year, then the optimum point for the intelligence explosion would be when delaying the explosion for another year would produce less than $x + y$ percentage points of reduction of the existential risk associated with an intelligence explosion.

32. I am indebted to Carl Shulman and Stuart Armstrong for help with this model. See also Shulman (2010a, 3): "Chalmers (2010) reports a consensus among cadets and staff at the U.S. West Point military academy that the U.S. government would not restrain AI research even in the face of potential catastrophe, for fear that rival powers would gain decisive advantage."

33. That is, information in the model is always bad *ex ante*. Of course, depending on what the information actually is, it will in some cases turn out to be good that the information became known, notably if the gap between leader and runner-up is much greater than one would reasonably have guessed in advance.

34. It might even present an existential risk, especially if preceded by the introduction of novel military technologies of destruction or unprecedented arms buildups.

35. A project could have its workers distributed over a large number of locations and collaborating via encrypted communications channels. But this tactic involves a security tradeoff: while geographical dispersion may offer some protection against military attacks, it would impede operational security, since it is harder to prevent personnel from defecting, leaking information, or being abducted by a rival power if they are spread out over many locations.

36. Note that a large temporal discount factor could make a project behave in some ways as though it were in a race, even if it knows it has no real competitor. The large discount factor means it would care little about the far future. Depending on the situation, this would discourage blue-sky R&D, which would tend to delay the machine intelligence revolution (though perhaps making it more abrupt when it does occur, because of hardware overhang). But the large discount factor—or a low level of caring for future generations—would also make existential risks seem to matter less. This would encourage gambles that involve the possibility of an immediate gain at the expense of an increased risk of existential catastrophe, thus disincentivizing safety investment and incentivizing an early launch—mimicking the effects of the race dynamic. By contrast to the race dynamic, however, a large discount factor (or disregard for future generations) would have no particular tendency to incite conflict.

    Reducing the race dynamic is a main benefit of collaboration. That collaboration would facilitate sharing of ideas for how to solve the control problem is also a benefit, although this is to some extent counterbalanced by the fact that collaboration would also facilitate sharing of ideas for how to solve the competence problem. The net effect of this facilitation of idea-sharing may be to slightly increase the collective intelligence of the relevant research community.

37. On the other hand, public oversight by a single government would risk producing an outcome in which one nation monopolizes the gains. This outcome seems inferior to one in which unaccountable altruists ensure that everybody stands to gain. Furthermore, oversight by a national government would not necessarily mean that even all the citizens of that country receive a share of the benefit: depending on the country in question, there is a greater or smaller risk that all the benefits would be captured by a political elite or a few self-serving agency personnel.

38. One qualification is that the use of incentive wrapping (as discussed in Chapter 12) might in some circumstances encourage people to join a project as active collaborators rather than passive free-riders.

39. Diminishing returns would seem to set in at a much smaller scale. Most people would rather have one star than a one-in-a-billion chance of a galaxy with a billion stars. Indeed, most people would rather have a billionth of the resources on Earth than a one-in-a-billion chance of owning the entire planet.

40. Cf. Shulman (2010a).

41. Aggregative ethical theories run into trouble when the idea that the cosmos might be infinite is taken seriously; see Bostrom (2011b). There may also be trouble when the idea of ridiculously large but finite values is taken seriously; see Bostrom (2009b).

42. If one makes a computer larger, one eventually faces relativistic constraints arising from communication latencies between the different parts of the computer—signals do not propagate faster than light. If one shrinks the computer, one encounters quantum limits to miniaturization. If one increases the density of the computer, one slams into the black hole limit. Admittedly, we cannot be completely certain that new physics will not one day be discovered offering some way around these limitations.

43. The number of copies of a person would scale linearly with resources with no upper bound. Yet it is not clear how much the average human being would value having multiple copies of herself. Even those people who would prefer to be multiply instantiated may not have a utility function that is linear with increasing number of copies. Copy numbers, like life years, might have diminishing returns in the typical person's utility function.

44. A singleton is highly internally collaborative at the highest level of decision-making. A singleton *could* have a lot of non-collaboration and conflict at lower levels, if the higher-level agency that constitutes the singleton chooses to have things that way.

45. If each rival AI team is convinced that the other teams are so misguided as to have no chance of producing an intelligence explosion, then one reason for collaboration—avoiding the race dynamic—is obviated: each team should independently choose to go slower in the confident belief that it lacks any serious competition.

46. A PhD student.

47. This formulation is intended to be read so as to include a prescription that the well-being of nonhuman animals and other sentient beings (including digital minds) that exist or may come to exist be given due consideration. It is not meant to be read as a license for one AI developer to substitute his or her own moral intuitions for those of the wider moral community. The principle is consistent with the "coherent extrapolated volition" approach discussed in Chapter 12, with an extrapolation base encompassing all humans.

   A further clarification: The formulation is not intended to necessarily exclude the possibly of post-transition property rights in artificial superintelligences or their constituent algorithms and data structures. The formulation is meant to be agnostic about what legal or political systems would best serve to organize transactions within a hypothetical future posthuman society. What the formulation *is* meant to assert is that the choice of such a system, insofar as its selection is causally determined by how superintelligence is initially developed, should to be made on the basis of the stated criterion; that is, the post-transition constitutional system should be chosen for the benefit of all of humanity and in the service of widely shared ethical ideals—as opposed to, for instance, for the benefit merely of whoever happened to be the first to develop superintelligence.

48. Refinements of the windfall clause are obviously possible. For example, perhaps the threshold should be expressed in *per capita* terms, or maybe the winner should be allowed to keep a somewhat larger than equal share of the overshoot in order to more strongly incentivize further production (some version of Rawls' maximin principle might be attractive here). Other refinements would refocus the clause away from dollar amounts and restate it in terms of "influence on humanity's future" or "degree to which different parties' interests are weighed in a future singleton's utility function" or some such.

CHAPTER 15: CRUNCH TIME

1. Some research is worthwhile not because of what it discovers but for other reasons, such as by entertaining, educating, accrediting, or uplifting those who engage in it.

2. I am not suggesting that *nobody* should work on pure mathematics or philosophy. I am also not suggesting that these endeavors are especially wasteful compared to all the other dissipations of academia or society at large. It is probably very good that some people can devote themselves to the life of the mind and follow their intellectual curiosity wherever it leads, independent of any thought of utility or impact. The suggestion is that at the margin, some of the best minds might, upon realizing that their cognitive performances may become obsolete in the foreseeable future, want to shift their attention to those theoretical problems for which it makes a difference whether we get the solution a little sooner.

3. Though one should be cautious in cases where this uncertainty may be protective—recall, for instance, the risk-race model in Box 13, where we found that additional strategic information could be harmful. More generally, we need to worry about information hazards (see Bostrom [2011b]). It is tempting to say that we need more analysis of information hazards. This is probably true, although we might still worry that such analysis itself may produce dangerous information.

4. Cf. Bostrom (2007).

5. I am grateful to Carl Shulman for emphasizing this point.

BIBLIOGRAPHY

Acemoglu, Daron. 2003. "Labor- and Capital-Augmenting Technical Change." *Journal of the European Economic Association* 1 (1): 1–37.

Albertson, D. G., and Thomson, J. N. 1976. "The Pharynx of *Caenorhabditis Elegans*." *Philosophical Transactions of the Royal Society B: Biological Sciences* 275 (938): 299–325.

Allen, Robert C. 2008. "A Review of Gregory Clark's *A Farewell to Alms: A Brief Economic History of the World*." *Journal of Economic Literature* 46 (4): 946–73.

American Horse Council. 2005. "National Economic Impact of the US Horse Industry." Retrieved July 30, 2013. Available at http://www.horsecouncil.org/national-economic-impact-us-horse-industry.

Anand, Paul, Pattanaik, Prasanta, and Puppe, Clemens, eds. 2009. *The Oxford Handbook of Rational and Social Choice*. New York: Oxford University Press.

Andres, B., Koethe, U., Kroeger, T., Helmstaedter, M., Briggman, K. L., Denk, W., and Hamprecht, F. A. 2012. "3D Segmentation of SBFSEM Images of Neuropil by a Graphical Model over Supervoxel Boundaries." *Medical Image Analysis* 16 (4): 796–805.

Armstrong, Alex. 2012. "Computer Competes in Crossword Tournament." *I Programmer*, March 19.

Armstrong, Stuart. 2007. "Chaining God: A Qualitative Approach to AI, Trust and Moral Systems." Unpublished manuscript, October 20. Retrieved December 31, 2012. Available at http://www.neweuropeancentury.org/GodAI.pdf.

Armstrong, Stuart. 2010. *Utility Indifference*, Technical Report 2010-1. Oxford: Future of Humanity Institute, University of Oxford.

Armstrong, Stuart. 2013. "General Purpose Intelligence: Arguing the Orthogonality Thesis." *Analysis and Metaphysics* 12: 68–84.

Armstrong, Stuart, and Sandberg, Anders. 2013. "Eternity in Six Hours: Intergalactic Spreading of Intelligent Life and Sharpening the Fermi Paradox." *Acta Astronautica* 89: 1–13.

Armstrong, Stuart, and Sotala, Kaj. 2012. "How We're Predicting AI—or Failing To." In *Beyond AI: Artificial Dreams*, edited by Jan Romportl, Pavel Ircing, Eva Zackova, Michal Polak, and Radek Schuster, 52–75. Pilsen: University of West Bohemia. Retrieved February 2, 2013.

Asimov, Isaac. 1942. "Runaround." *Astounding Science Fiction*, March, 94–103.

Asimov, Isaac. 1985. *Robots and Empire*. New York: Doubleday.

Aumann, Robert J. 1976. "Agreeing to Disagree." *Annals of Statistics* 4 (6): 1236–9.

Averch, Harvey Allen. 1985. *A Strategic Analysis of Science and Technology Policy*. Baltimore: Johns Hopkins University Press.

Azevedo, F. A. C., Carvalho, L. R. B., Grinberg, L. T., Farfel, J. M., Ferretti, R. E. L., Leite, R. E. P., Jacob, W., Lent, R., and Herculano-Houzel, S. 2009. "Equal Numbers of Neuronal and Nonneuronal Cells Make the Human Brain an Isometrically Scaled-up Primate Brain." *Journal of Comparative Neurology* 513 (5): 532–41.

Baars, Bernard J. 1997. *In the Theater of Consciousness: The Workspace of the Mind*. New York: Oxford University Press.

Baratta, Joseph Preston. 2004. *The Politics of World Federation: United Nations, UN Reform, Atomic Control*. Westport, CT: Praeger.

Barber, E. J. W. 1991. *Prehistoric Textiles: The Development of Cloth in the Neolithic and Bronze Ages with Special Reference to the Aegean*. Princeton, NJ: Princeton University Press.

Bartels, J., Andreasen, D., Ehirim, P., Mao, H., Seibert, S., Wright, E. J., and Kennedy, P. 2008. "Neurotrophic Electrode: Method of Assembly and Implantation into Human Motor Speech Cortex." *Journal of Neuroscience Methods* 174 (2): 168–76.

Bartz, Jennifer A., Zaki, Jamil, Bolger, Niall, and Ochsner, Kevin N. 2011. "Social Effects of Oxytocin in Humans: Context and Person Matter." *Trends in Cognitive Science* 15 (7): 301–9.

Basten, Stuart, Lutz, Wolfgang, and Scherbov, Sergei. 2013. "Very Long Range Global Population Scenarios to 2300 and the Implications of Sustained Low Fertility." *Demographic Research* 28: 1145–66.

Baum, Eric B. 2004. *What Is Thought?* Bradford Books. Cambridge, MA: MIT Press.

Baum, Seth D., Goertzel, Ben, and Goertzel, Ted G. 2011. "How Long Until Human-Level AI? Results from an Expert Assessment." *Technological Forecasting and Social Change* 78 (1): 185–95.

Beal, J., and Winston, P. 2009. "Guest Editors' Introduction: The New Frontier of Human-Level Artificial Intelligence." *IEEE Intelligent Systems* 24 (4): 21–3.

Bell, C. Gordon, and Gemmell, Jim. 2009. *Total Recall: How the E-Memory Revolution Will Change Everything*. New York: Dutton.

Benyamin, B., St. Pourcain, B., Davis, O. S., Davies, G., Hansell, M. K., Brion, M.-J. A., Kirkpatrick, R. M., et al. 2013. "Childhood Intelligence is Heritable, Highly Polygenic and Associated With FNBP1L." *Molecular Psychiatry* (January 23).

Berg, Joyce E., and Rietz, Thomas A. 2003. "Prediction Markets as Decision Support Systems." *Information Systems Frontiers* 5 (1): 79–93.

Berger, Theodore W., Chapin, J. K., Gerhardt, G. A., Soussou, W. V., Taylor, D. M., and Tresco, P. A., eds. 2008. *Brain–Computer Interfaces: An International Assessment of Research and Development Trends*. Springer.

Berger, T. W., Song, D., Chan, R. H., Marmarelis, V. Z., LaCoss, J., Wills, J., Hampson, R. E., Deadwyler, S. A., and Granacki, J. J. 2012. "A Hippocampal Cognitive Prosthesis: Multi-Input, Multi-Output Nonlinear Modeling and VLSI Implementation." *IEEE Transactions on Neural Systems and Rehabilitation Engineering* 20 (2): 198–211.

Berliner, Hans J. 1980a. "Backgammon Computer-Program Beats World Champion." *Artificial Intelligence* 14 (2): 205–220.

Berliner, Hans J. 1980b. "Backgammon Program Beats World Champ." *SIGART Newsletter* 69: 6–9.

Bernardo, José M., and Smith, Adrian F. M. 1994. *Bayesian Theory*, 1st ed. Wiley Series in Probability & Statistics. New York: Wiley.

Birbaumer, N., Murguialday, A. R., and Cohen, L. 2008. "Brain–Computer Interface in Paralysis." *Current Opinion in Neurology* 21 (6): 634–8.

Bird, Jon, and Layzell, Paul. 2002. "The Evolved Radio and Its Implications for Modelling the Evolution of Novel Sensors." In *Proceedings of the 2002 Congress on Evolutionary Computation*, 2: 1836–41.

Blair, Clay, Jr. 1957. "Passing of a Great Mind: John von Neumann, a Brilliant, Jovial Mathematician, was a Prodigious Servant of Science and His Country." *Life*, February 25, 89–104.

Bobrow, Daniel G. 1968. "Natural Language Input for a Computer Problem Solving System." In *Semantic Information Processing*, edited by Marvin Minsky, 146–227. Cambridge, MA: MIT Press.

Bostrom, Nick. 1997. "Predictions from Philosophy? How Philosophers Could Make Themselves Useful." Unpublished manuscript. Last revised September 19, 1998.

Bostrom, Nick. 2002a. *Anthropic Bias: Observation Selection Effects in Science and Philosophy*. New York: Routledge.

Bostrom, Nick. 2002b. "Existential Risks: Analyzing Human Extinction Scenarios and Related Hazards." *Journal of Evolution and Technology* 9.

Bostrom, Nick. 2003a. "Are We Living in a Computer Simulation?" *Philosophical Quarterly* 53 (211): 243–55.

Bostrom, Nick. 2003b. "Astronomical Waste: The Opportunity Cost of Delayed Technological Development." *Utilitas* 15 (3): 308–314.

Bostrom, Nick. 2003c. "Ethical Issues in Advanced Artificial Intelligence." In *Cognitive, Emotive and Ethical Aspects of Decision Making in Humans and in Artificial Intelligence*, edited by Iva Smit and George E. Lasker, 2: 12–17. Windsor, ON: International Institute for Advanced Studies in Systems Research / Cybernetics.

Bostrom, Nick. 2004. "The Future of Human Evolution." In *Two Hundred Years After Kant, Fifty Years After Turing*, edited by Charles Tandy, 2: 339–371. Death and Anti-Death. Palo Alto, CA: Ria University Press.

Bostrom, Nick. 2006a. "How Long Before Superintelligence?" *Linguistic and Philosophical Investigations* 5(1): 11–30.

Bostrom, Nick. 2006b. "Quantity of Experience: Brain-Duplication and Degrees of Consciousness." *Minds and Machines* 16 (2): 185–200.

Bostrom, Nick. 2006c. "What is a Singleton?" *Linguistic and Philosophical Investigations* 5 (2): 48–54.

Bostrom, Nick. 2007. "Technological Revolutions: Ethics and Policy in the Dark." In *Nanoscale: Issues and Perspectives for the Nano Century*, edited by Nigel M. de S. Cameron and M. Ellen Mitchell, 129–52. Hoboken, NJ: Wiley.

Bostrom, Nick. 2008a. "Where Are They? Why I Hope the Search for Extraterrestrial Life Finds Nothing." *MIT Technology Review*, May/June issue, 72–7.

Bostrom, Nick. 2008b. "Why I Want to Be a Posthuman When I Grow Up." In *Medical Enhancement and Posthumanity*, edited by Bert Gordijn and Ruth Chadwick, 107–37. New York: Springer.

Bostrom, Nick. 2008c. "Letter from Utopia." *Studies in Ethics, Law, and Technology* 2 (1): 1–7.

Bostrom, Nick. 2009a. "Moral Uncertainty – Towards a Solution?" *Overcoming Bias* (blog), January 1.

Bostrom, Nick. 2009b. "Pascal's Mugging." *Analysis* 69 (3): 443–5.

Bostrom, Nick. 2009c. "The Future of Humanity." In *New Waves in Philosophy of Technology*, edited by Jan Kyrre Berg Olsen, Evan Selinger, and Søren Riis, 186–215. New York: Palgrave Macmillan.

Bostrom, Nick. 2011a. "Information Hazards: A Typology of Potential Harms from Knowledge." *Review of Contemporary Philosophy* 10: 44–79.

Bostrom, Nick. 2011b. "Infinite Ethics." *Analysis and Metaphysics* 10: 9–59.

Bostrom, Nick. 2012. "The Superintelligent Will: Motivation and Instrumental Rationality in Advanced Artificial Agents." In "Theory and Philosophy of AI," edited by Vincent C. Müller, special issue, *Minds and Machines* 22 (2): 71–85.

Bostrom, Nick, and Ćirković, Milan M. 2003. "The Doomsday Argument and the Self-Indication Assumption: Reply to Olum." *Philosophical Quarterly* 53 (210): 83–91.

Bostrom, Nick, and Ord, Toby. 2006. "The Reversal Test: Eliminating the Status Quo Bias in Applied Ethics." *Ethics* 116 (4): 656–79.

Bostrom, Nick, and Roache, Rebecca. 2011. "Smart Policy: Cognitive Enhancement and the Public Interest." In *Enhancing Human Capacities*, edited by Julian Savulescu, Ruud ter Meulen, and Guy Kahane, 138–49. Malden, MA: Wiley-Blackwell.

Bostrom, Nick and Sandberg, Anders. 2009a. "Cognitive Enhancement: Methods, Ethics, Regulatory Challenges." *Science and Engineering Ethics* 15 (3): 311–41.

Bostrom, Nick and Sandberg, Anders. 2009b. "The Wisdom of Nature: An Evolutionary Heuristic for Human Enhancement." In *Human Enhancement*, 1st ed., edited by Julian Savulescu and Nick Bostrom, 375–416. New York: Oxford University Press.

Bostrom, Nick, Sandberg, Anders, and Douglas, Tom. Forthcoming. "The Unilateralist's Curse: The Case for a Principle of Conformity." *Social Epistemology*.

Bostrom, Nick, and Yudkowsky, Eliezer. 2015. "The Ethics of Artificial Intelligence." In *Cambridge Handbook of Artificial Intelligence*, edited by Keith Frankish and William M. Ramsey, 315–334. New York: Cambridge University Press.

Boswell, James. 1917. *Boswell's Life of Johnson*. New York: Oxford University Press.

Bouchard, T. J. 2004. "Genetic Influence on Human Psychological Traits: A Survey." *Current Directions in Psychological Science* 13 (4): 148–51.

Bourget, David, and Chalmers, David. 2009. "The PhilPapers Surveys." November. Available at http://philpapers.org/surveys/.

Bradbury, Robert J. 1999. "Matrioshka Brains." Archived version. As revised August 16, 2004. Available at http://web.archive.org/web/20090615040912/http://www.aeiveos.com/~bradbury/MatrioshkaBrains/MatrioshkaBrainsPaper.html.

Brinton, Crane. 1965. *The Anatomy of Revolution*. Revised ed. New York: Vintage Books.

Bryson, Arthur E., Jr., and Ho, Yu-Chi. 1969. *Applied Optimal Control: Optimization, Estimation, and Control*. Waltham, MA: Blaisdell.

Buehler, Martin, Iagnemma, Karl, and Singh, Sanjiv, eds. 2009. *The DARPA Urban Challenge: Autonomous Vehicles in City Traffic*. Springer Tracts in Advanced Robotics 56. Berlin: Springer.

Burch-Brown, J. 2014. "Clues for Consequentialists." *Utilitas* 26 (1): 105–19.

Burke, Colin. 2001. "Agnes Meyer Driscoll vs. the Enigma and the Bombe." Unpublished manuscript. Retrieved February 22, 2013. Available at http://userpages.umbc.edu/~burke/driscoll1-2011.pdf.

Canbäck, S., Samouel, P., and Price, D. 2006. "Do Diseconomies of Scale Impact Firm Size and Performance? A Theoretical and Empirical Overview." *Journal of Managerial Economics* 4 (1): 27–70.

Carmena, J. M., Lebedev, M. A., Crist, R. E., O'Doherty, J. E., Santucci, D. M., Dimitrov, D. F., Patil, P. G., Henriquez, C. S., and Nicolelis, M. A. 2003. "Learning to Control a Brain–Machine Interface for Reaching and Grasping by Primates." *Public Library of Science Biology* 1 (2): 193–208.

Carroll, Bradley W., and Ostlie, Dale A. 2007. An Introduction to Modern Astrophysics. 2nd ed. San Francisco, CA: Pearson Addison Wesley.

Carroll, John B. 1993. *Human Cognitive Abilities: A Survey of Factor-Analytic Studies.* New York: Cambridge University Press.

Carter, Brandon. 1983."The Anthropic Principle and its Implications for Biological Evolution." *Philosophical Transactions of the Royal Society A: Mathematical, Physical and Engineering Sciences* 310 (1512): 347–63.

Carter, Brandon. 1993. "The Anthropic Selection Principle and the Ultra-Darwinian Synthesis." In *The Anthropic Principle: Proceedings of the Second Venice Conference on Cosmology and Philosophy*, edited by F. Bertola and U. Curi, 33–66. Cambridge: Cambridge University Press.

CFTC & SEC (Commodity Futures Trading Commission and Securities & Exchange Commission). 2010. *Findings Regarding the Market Events of May 6, 2010: Report of the Staffs of the CFTC and SEC to the Joint Advisory Committee on Emerging Regulatory Issues.* Washington, DC.

Chalmers, David John. 2010. "The Singularity: A Philosophical Analysis." *Journal of Consciousness Studies* 17 (9–10): 7–65.

Chason, R. J., Csokmay, J., Segars, J. H., DeCherney, A. H., and Armant, D. R. 2011. "Environmental and Epigenetic Effects Upon Preimplantation Embryo Metabolism and Development." *Trends in Endocrinology and Metabolism* 22 (10): 412–20.

Chen, S., and Ravallion, M. 2010. "The Developing World Is Poorer Than We Thought, But No Less Successful in the Fight Against Poverty." *Quarterly Journal of Economics* 125 (4): 1577–1625.

Chislenko, Alexander. 1996. "Networking in the Mind Age: Some Thoughts on Evolution of Robotics and Distributed Systems." Unpublished manuscript.

Chislenko, Alexander. 1997. "Technology as Extension of Human Functional Architecture." *Extropy Online.*

Chorost, Michael. 2005. *Rebuilt: How Becoming Part Computer Made Me More Human.* Boston: Houghton Mifflin.

Christiano, Paul F. 2012. "'Indirect Normativity' Write-up." *Ordinary Ideas* (blog), April 21.

CIA. 2013. *The World Factbook.* Central Intelligence Agency. Retrieved August 3. Available at https://www.cia.gov/library/publications/the-world-factbook/rankorder/2127rank.html?countryname=United%20States&countrycode=us&regionCode=noa&rank=121#us.

Cicero. 1923. "On Divination." In *On Old Age, on Friendship, on Divination*, translated by W. A. Falconer. Loeb Classical Library. Cambridge, MA: Harvard University Press.

Cirasella, Jill, and Kopec, Danny. 2006. "The History of Computer Games." Exhibit at Dartmouth Artificial Intelligence Conference: The Next Fifty Years (AI@50), Dartmouth College, July 13–15.

Ćirković, Milan M. 2004. "Forecast for the Next Eon: Applied Cosmology and the Long-Term Fate of Intelligent Beings." *Foundations of Physics* 34 (2): 239–61.

Ćirković, Milan M., Sandberg, Anders, and Bostrom, Nick. 2010. "Anthropic Shadow: Observation Selection Effects and Human Extinction Risks." *Risk Analysis* 30 (10): 1495–1506.

Clark, Andy, and Chalmers, David J. 1998. "The Extended Mind." *Analysis* 58 (1): 7–19.

Clark, Gregory. 2007. *A Farewell to Alms: A Brief Economic History of the World*. 1st ed. Princeton, NJ: Princeton University Press.

Clavin, Whitney. 2012. "Study Shows Our Galaxy Has at Least 100 Billion Planets." *Jet Propulsion Laboratory*, January 11.

CME Group. 2010. *What Happened on May 6th?* Chicago, May 10.

Coase, R. H. 1937. "The Nature of the Firm." *Economica* 4 (16): 386–405.

Cochran, Gregory, and Harpending, Henry. 2009. *The 10,000 Year Explosion: How Civilization Accelerated Human Evolution*. New York: Basic Books.

Cochran, G., Hardy, J., and Harpending, H. 2006. "Natural History of Ashkenazi Intelligence." *Journal of Biosocial Science* 38 (5): 659–93.

Cook, James Gordon. 1984. *Handbook of Textile Fibres: Natural Fibres*. Cambridge: Woodhead.

Cope, David. 1996. *Experiments in Musical Intelligence*. Computer Music and Digital Audio Series. Madison, WI: A-R Editions.

Cotman, Carl W., and Berchtold, Nicole C. 2002. "Exercise: A Behavioral Intervention to Enhance Brain Health and Plasticity." *Trends in Neurosciences* 25 (6): 295–301.

Cowan, Nelson. 2001. "The Magical Number 4 in Short-Term Memory: A Reconsideration of Mental Storage Capacity." *Behavioral and Brain Sciences* 24 (1): 87–114.

Crabtree, Steve. 1999. "New Poll Gauges Americans' General Knowledge Levels." *Gallup News*, July 6.

Cross, Stephen E., and Walker, Edward. 1994. "Dart: Applying Knowledge Based Planning and Scheduling to Crisis Action Planning." In *Intelligent Scheduling*, edited by Monte Zweben and Mark Fox, 711–29. San Francisco, CA: Morgan Kaufmann.

Crow, James F. 2000. "The Origins, Patterns and Implications of Human Spontaneous Mutation." *Nature Reviews Genetics* 1 (1): 40–7.

Cyranoski, David. 2013. "Stem Cells: Egg Engineers." *Nature* 500 (7463): 392–4.

Dagnelie, Gislin. 2012. "Retinal Implants: Emergence of a Multidisciplinary Field." *Current Opinion in Neurology* 25 (1): 67–75.

Dai, Wei. 2009. "Towards a New Decision Theory." *Less Wrong* (blog), August 13.

Dalrymple, David. 2011. "Comment on Kaufman, J. 'Whole Brain Emulation: Looking at Progress on C. Elegans.'" *Less Wrong* (blog), October 29.

Davies, G., Tenesa, A., Payton, A., Yang, J., Harris, S. E., Liewald, D., Ke, X., et al. 2011. "Genome-Wide Association Studies Establish That Human Intelligence Is Highly Heritable and Polygenic." *Molecular Psychiatry* 16 (10): 996–1005.

Davis, Oliver S. P., Butcher, Lee M., Docherty, Sophia J., Meaburn, Emma L., Curtis, Charles J. C., Simpson, Michael A., Schalkwyk, Leonard C., and Plomin, Robert. 2010. "A Three-Stage Genome-Wide Association Study of General Cognitive Ability: Hunting the Small Effects." *Behavior Genetics* 40 (6): 759–767.

Dawkins, Richard. 1995. *River Out of Eden: A Darwinian View of Life*. Science Masters Series. New York: Basic Books.

De Blanc, Peter. 2011. *Ontological Crises in Artificial Agents' Value Systems*. Berkeley, CA: Machine Intelligence Research Institute, May 19.

De Long, J. Bradford. 1998. "Estimates of World GDP, One Million B.C.–Present." Unpublished manuscript.

De Raedt, Luc, and Flach, Peter, eds. 2001. *Machine Learning: ECML 2001: 12th European Conference on Machine Learning, Freiburg, Germany, September 5–7, 2001. Proceedings*. Lecture Notes in Computer Science 2167. New York: Springer.

Dean, Cornelia. 2005. "Scientific Savvy? In U.S., Not Much." *New York Times*, August 30.

Deary, Ian J. 2001. "Human Intelligence Differences: A Recent History." *Trends in Cognitive Sciences* 5 (3): 127–30.

Deary, Ian J. 2012. "Intelligence." *Annual Review of Psychology* 63: 453–82.

Deary, Ian J., Penke, L., and Johnson, W. 2010. "The Neuroscience of Human Intelligence Differences." *Nature Reviews Neuroscience* 11 (3): 201–11.

Degnan, G. G., Wind, T. C., Jones, E. V., and Edlich, R. F. 2002. "Functional Electrical Stimulation in Tetraplegic Patients to Restore Hand Function." *Journal of Long-Term Effects of Medical Implants* 12 (3): 175–88.

Devlin, B., Daniels, M., and Roeder, K. 1997. "The Heritability of IQ." *Nature* 388 (6641): 468–71.

Dewey, Daniel. 2011. "Learning What to Value." In *Artificial General Intelligence: 4th International Conference, AGI 2011, Mountain View, CA, USA, August 3–6, 2011. Proceedings*, edited by Jürgen Schmidhuber, Kristinn R. Thórisson, and Moshe Looks, 309–14. Lecture Notes in Computer Science 6830. Berlin: Springer.

Dowe, D. L., and Hernández-Orallo, J. 2012. "IQ Tests Are Not for Machines, Yet." *Intelligence* 40 (2): 77–81.

Drescher, Gary L. 2006. *Good and Real: Demystifying Paradoxes from Physics to Ethics*. Bradford Books. Cambridge, MA: MIT Press.

Drexler, K. Eric. 1986. *Engines of Creation*. Garden City, NY: Anchor.

Drexler, K. Eric. 1992. *Nanosystems: Molecular Machinery, Manufacturing, and Computation*. New York: Wiley.

Drexler, K. Eric. 2013. *Radical Abundance: How a Revolution in Nanotechnology Will Change Civilization*. New York: PublicAffairs.

Driscoll, Kevin. 2012. "Code Critique: 'Altair Music of a Sort.' " Paper presented at Critical Code Studies Working Group Online Conference, February 6.

Dyson, Freeman J. 1960. "Search for Artificial Stellar Sources of Infrared Radiation." *Science* 131 (3414): 1667–1668.

Dyson, Freeman J. 1979. *Disturbing the Universe*. 1st ed. Sloan Foundation Science Series. New York: Harper & Row.

Elga, Adam. 2004. "Defeating Dr. Evil with Self-Locating Belief." *Philosophy and Phenomenological Research* 69 (2): 383–96.

Elga, Adam. 2007. "Reflection and Disagreement." *Noûs* 41 (3): 478–502.

Eliasmith, Chris, Stewart, Terrence C., Choo, Xuan, Bekolay, Trevor, DeWolf, Travis, Tang, Yichuan, and Rasmussen, Daniel. 2012. "A Large-Scale Model of the Functioning Brain." *Science* 338(6111): 1202–5.

Ellis, J. H. 1999. "The History of Non-Secret Encryption." *Cryptologia* 23 (3): 267–73.

Elyasaf, Achiya, Hauptmann, Ami, and Sipper, Moche. 2011. "Ga-Freecell: Evolving Solvers for the Game of Freecell." In *Proceedings of the 13th Annual Genetic and Evolutionary Computation Conference*, 1931–1938. GECCO '11. New York: ACM.

Eppig, C., Fincher, C. L., and Thornhill, R. 2010. "Parasite Prevalence and the Worldwide Distribution of Cognitive Ability." *Proceedings of the Royal Society B: Biological Sciences* 277 (1701): 3801–8.

Espenshade, T. J., Guzman, J. C., and Westoff, C. F. 2003. "The Surprising Global Variation in Replacement Fertility." *Population Research and Policy Review* 22 (5–6): 575–83.

Evans, Thomas G. 1964. "A Heuristic Program to Solve Geometric-Analogy Problems." In *Proceedings of the April 21–23, 1964, Spring Joint Computer Conference*, 327–338. AFIPS '64. New York: ACM.

Evans, Thomas G. 1968. "A Program for the Solution of a Class of Geometric-Analogy Intelligence-Test Questions." In *Semantic Information Processing*, edited by Marvin Minsky, 271–353. Cambridge, MA: MIT Press.

Faisal, A. A., Selen, L. P., and Wolpert, D. M. 2008. "Noise in the Nervous System." *Nature Reviews Neuroscience* 9 (4): 292–303.

Faisal, A. A., White, J. A., and Laughlin, S. B. 2005. "Ion-Channel Noise Places Limits on the Miniaturization of the Brain's Wiring." *Current Biology* 15 (12): 1143–9.

Feldman, Jacob. 2000. "Minimization of Boolean Complexity in Human Concept Learning." *Nature* 407 (6804): 630–3.

Feldman, J. A., and Ballard, Dana H. 1982. "Connectionist Models and Their Properties." *Cognitive Science* 6 (3): 205–254.

Foley, J. A., Monfreda, C., Ramankutty, N., and Zaks, D. 2007. "Our Share of the Planetary Pie." *Proceedings of the National Academy of Sciences of the United States of America* 104 (31): 12585–6.

Forgas, Joseph P., Cooper, Joel, and Crano, William D., eds. 2010. *The Psychology of Attitudes and Attitude Change*. Sydney Symposium of Social Psychology. New York: Psychology Press.

Frank, Robert H. 1999. *Luxury Fever: Why Money Fails to Satisfy in an Era of Excess*. New York: Free Press.

Fredriksen, Kaja Bonesmo. 2012. *Less Income Inequality and More Growth – Are They Compatible?: Part 6. The Distribution of Wealth*. Technical report, OECD Economics Department Working Papers 929. OECD Publishing.

Freitas, Robert A., Jr. 1980. "A Self-Replicating Interstellar Probe." *Journal of the British Interplanetary Society* 33: 251–64.

Freitas, Robert A., Jr. 2000. "Some Limits to Global Ecophagy by Biovorous Nanoreplicators, with Public Policy Recommendations." Foresight Institute. April. Retrieved July 28, 2013. Available at http://www.foresight.org/nano/Ecophagy.html.

Freitas, Robert A., Jr., and Merkle, Ralph C. 2004. *Kinematic Self-Replicating Machines*. Georgetown, TX: Landes Bioscience.

Gaddis, John Lewis. 1982. *Strategies of Containment: A Critical Appraisal of Postwar American National Security Policy*. New York: Oxford University Press.

Gammoned.net. 2012. "Snowie." Archived version. Retrieved June 30. Available at http://web.archive.org/web/20070920191840/http://www.gammoned.com/snowie.html.

Gates, Bill. 1975. "Software Contest Winners Announced." *Computer Notes* 1 (2): 1.

Georgieff, Michael K. 2007. "Nutrition and the Developing Brain: Nutrient Priorities and Measurement." *American Journal of Clinical Nutrition* 85 (2): 614S–620S.

Gianaroli, Luca. 2000. "Preimplantation Genetic Diagnosis: Polar Body and Embryo Biopsy." Supplement, *Human Reproduction* 15 (4): 69–75.

Gilovich, Thomas, Griffin, Dale, and Kahneman, Daniel, eds. 2002. *Heuristics and Biases: The Psychology of Intuitive Judgment*. New York: Cambridge University Press.

Gilster, Paul. 2012. "ESO: Habitable Red Dwarf Planets Abundant." *Centauri Dreams* (blog), March 29.

Goldstone, Jack A. 1980. "Theories of Revolution: The Third Generation." *World Politics* 32 (3): 425–53.

Goldstone, Jack A. 2001. "Towards a Fourth Generation of Revolutionary Theory." *Annual Review of Political Science* 4: 139–87.

Good, Irving John. 1965. "Speculations Concerning the First Ultraintelligent Machine." In *Advances in Computers*, edited by Franz L. Alt and Morris Rubinoff, 6: 31–88. New York: Academic Press.

Good, Irving John. 1970. "Some Future Social Repercussions of Computers." *International Journal of Environmental Studies* 1 (1–4): 67–79.

Good, Irving John. 1976. "Book review of 'The Thinking Computer: Mind Inside Matter'" In *International Journal of Man-Machine Studies* 8: 617–20.

Good, Irving John. 1982. "Ethical Machines." In *Intelligent Systems: Practice and Perspective*, edited by J. E. Hayes, Donald Michie, and Y.-H. Pao, 555–60. Machine Intelligence 10. Chichester: Ellis Horwood.

Goodman, Nelson. 1954. *Fact, Fiction, and Forecast*. 1st ed. London: Athlone Press.

Gott, J. R., Juric, M., Schlegel, D., Hoyle, F., Vogeley, M., Tegmark, M., Bahcall, N., and Brinkmann, J. 2005. "A Map of the Universe." *Astrophysical Journal* 624 (2): 463–83.

Gottfredson, Linda S. 2002. "G: Highly General and Highly Practical." In *The General Factor of Intelligence: How General Is It?*, edited by Robert J. Sternberg and Elena L. Grigorenko, 331–80. Mahwah, NJ: Lawrence Erlbaum.

Gould, S. J. 1990. *Wonderful Life: The Burgess Shale and the Nature of History*. New York: Norton.

Graham, Gordon. 1997. *The Shape of the Past: A Philosophical Approach to History*. New York: Oxford University Press.

Gray, C. M., and McCormick, D. A. 1996. "Chattering Cells: Superficial Pyramidal Neurons Contributing to the Generation of Synchronous Oscillations in the Visual Cortex." *Science* 274 (5284): 109–13.

Greene, Kate. 2012. "Intel's Tiny Wi-Fi Chip Could Have a Big Impact." *MIT Technology Review*, September 21.

Guizzo, Erico. 2010. "World Robot Population Reaches 8.6 Million." *IEEE Spectrum*, April 14.

Gunn, James E. 1982. *Isaac Asimov: The Foundations of Science Fiction.* Science-Fiction Writers. New York: Oxford University Press.

Haberl, Helmut, Erb, Karl-Heinz, and Krausmann, Fridolin. 2013. "Global Human Appropriation of Net Primary Production (HANPP)." *Encyclopedia of Earth,* September 3.

Haberl, H., Erb, K. H., Krausmann, F., Gaube, V., Bondeau, A., Plutzar, C., Gingrich, S., Lucht, W., and Fischer-Kowalski, M. 2007. "Quantifying and Mapping the Human Appropriation of Net Primary Production in Earth's Terrestrial Ecosystems." *Proceedings of the National Academy of Sciences of the United States of America* 104 (31): 12942–7.

Hájek, Alan. 2009. "Dutch Book Arguments." In Anand, Pattanaik, and Puppe 2009, 173–95.

Hall, John Storrs. 2007. *Beyond AI: Creating the Conscience of the Machine.* Amherst, NY: Prometheus Books.

Hampson, R. E., Song, D., Chan, R. H., Sweatt, A. J., Riley, M. R., Gerhardt, G. A., Shin, D. C., Marmarelis, V. Z., Berger, T. W., and Deadwyler, S. A. 2012. "A Nonlinear Model for Hippocampal Cognitive Prosthesis: Memory Facilitation by Hippocampal Ensemble Stimulation." *IEEE Transactions on Neural Systems and Rehabilitation Engineering* 20 (2): 184–97.

Hanson, Robin. 1994. "If Uploads Come First: The Crack of a Future Dawn." *Extropy* 6 (2).

Hanson, Robin. 1995. "Could Gambling Save Science? Encouraging an Honest Consensus." *Social Epistemology* 9 (1): 3–33.

Hanson, Robin. 1998a. "Burning the Cosmic Commons: Evolutionary Strategies for Interstellar Colonization." Unpublished manuscript, July 1. Retrieved April 26, 2012. http://hanson.gmu.edu/filluniv.pdf.

Hanson, Robin. 1998b. "Economic Growth Given Machine Intelligence." Unpublished manuscript. Retrieved May 15, 2013. Available at http://hanson.gmu.edu/aigrow.pdf.

Hanson, Robin. 1998c. "Long-Term Growth as a Sequence of Exponential Modes." Unpublished manuscript. Last revised December 2000. Available at http://hanson.gmu.edu/longgrow.pdf.

Hanson, Robin. 1998d. "Must Early Life Be Easy? The Rhythm of Major Evolutionary Transitions." Unpublished manuscript, September 23. Retrieved August 12, 2012. Available at http://hanson.gmu.edu/hardstep.pdf.

Hanson, Robin. 2000. "Shall We Vote on Values, But Bet on Beliefs?" Unpublished manuscript, September. Last revised October 2007. Available at http://hanson.gmu.edu/futarchy.pdf.

Hanson, Robin. 2006. "Uncommon Priors Require Origin Disputes." *Theory and Decision* 61 (4): 319–328.

Hanson, Robin. 2008. "Economics of the Singularity." *IEEE Spectrum* 45 (6): 45–50.

Hanson, Robin. 2009. "Tiptoe or Dash to Future?" *Overcoming Bias* (blog), December 23.

Hanson, Robin. 2012. "Envisioning the Economy, and Society, of Whole Brain Emulations." Paper presented at the AGI Impacts conference, Oxford, December 8–11.

Hart, Oliver. 2008. "Economica Coase Lecture Reference Points and the Theory of the Firm." *Economica* 75 (299): 404–11.

Hay, Nicholas James. 2005. "Optimal Agents." B.Sc. thesis, University of Auckland.

Hedberg, Sara Reese. 2002. "Dart: Revolutionizing Logistics Planning." *IEEE Intelligent Systems* 17 (3): 81–3.

Helliwell, John, Layard, Richard, and Sachs, Jeffrey. 2012. *World Happiness Report*. The Earth Institute.

Helmstaedter, M., Briggman, K. L., and Denk, W. 2011. "High-Accuracy Neurite Reconstruction for High-Throughput Neuroanatomy." *Nature Neuroscience* 14 (8): 1081–8.

Heyl, Jeremy S. 2005. "The Long-Term Future of Space Travel." *Physical Review D* 72 (10): 1–4.

Hibbard, Bill. 2011. "Measuring Agent Intelligence via Hierarchies of Environments." In *Artificial General Intelligence: 4th International Conference, AGI 2011, Mountain View, CA, USA, August 3–6, 2011. Proceedings*, edited by Jürgen Schmidhuber, Kristinn R. Thórisson, and Moshe Looks, 303–8. Lecture Notes in Computer Science 6830. Berlin: Springer.

Hinke, R. M., Hu, X., Stillman, A. E., Herkle, H., Salmi, R., and Ugurbil, K. 1993. "Functional Magnetic Resonance Imaging of Broca's Area During Internal Speech." *Neuroreport* 4 (6): 675–8.

Hinxton Group. 2008. *Consensus Statement: Science, Ethics and Policy Challenges of Pluripotent Stem Cell-Derived Gametes*. Hinxton, Cambridgeshire, UK, April 11. Available at http://www.hinxtongroup.org/Consensus_HG08_FINAL.pdf.

Hoffman, David E. 2009. *The Dead Hand: The Untold Story of the Cold War Arms Race and Its Dangerous Legacy*. New York: Doubleday.

Hofstadter, Douglas R. (1979) 1999. *Gödel, Escher, Bach: An Eternal Golden Braid*. New York: Basic Books.

Holley, Rose. 2009. "How Good Can It Get? Analysing and Improving OCR Accuracy in Large Scale Historic Newspaper Digitisation Programs." *D-Lib Magazine* 15 (3–4).

Horton, Sue, Alderman, Harold, and Rivera, Juan A. 2008. *Copenhagen Consensus 2008 Challenge Paper: Hunger and Malnutrition*. Technical report. Copenhagen Consensus Center, May 11.

Howson, Colin, and Urbach, Peter. 1993. *Scientific Reasoning: The Bayesian Approach*. 2nd ed. Chicago: Open Court.

Hsu, Stephen. 2012. "Investigating the Genetic Basis for Intelligence and Other Quantitative Traits." Lecture given at UC Davis Department of Physics Colloquium, Davis, CA, February 13.

Huebner, Bryce. 2008. "Do You See What We See? An Investigation of an Argument Against Collective Representation." *Philosophical Psychology* 21 (1): 91–112.

Huff, C. D., Xing, J., Rogers, A. R., Witherspoon, D., and Jorde, L. B. 2010. "Mobile Elements Reveal Small Population Size in the Ancient Ancestors of *Homo Sapiens*." *Proceedings of the National Academy of Sciences of the United States of America* 107 (5): 2147–52.

Huffman, W. Cary, and Pless, Vera. 2003. *Fundamentals of Error-Correcting Codes*. New York: Cambridge University Press.

Hunt, Patrick. 2011. "Late Roman Silk: Smuggling and Espionage in the 6th Century CE." *Philolog, Stanford University* (blog), August 2.

Hutter, Marcus. 2001. "Towards a Universal Theory of Artificial Intelligence Based on Algorithmic Probability and Sequential Decisions." In De Raedt and Flach 2001, 226–38.

Hutter, Marcus. 2005. *Universal Artificial Intelligence: Sequential Decisions Based On Algorithmic Probability*. Texts in Theoretical Computer Science. Berlin: Springer.

Iliadou, A. N., Janson, P. C., and Cnattingius, S. 2011. "Epigenetics and Assisted Reproductive Technology." *Journal of Internal Medicine* 270 (5): 414–20.

Isaksson, Anders. 2007. *Productivity and Aggregate Growth: A Global Picture*. Technical report 05/2007. Vienna, Austria: UNIDO (United Nations Industrial Development Organization) Research and Statistics Branch.

Jones, Garret. 2009. "Artificial Intelligence and Economic Growth: A Few Finger-Exercises." Unpublished manuscript, January. Retrieved November 5, 2012. Available at http://mason.gmu.edu/~gjonesb/AIandGrowth.

Jones, Vincent C. 1985. *Manhattan: The Army and the Atomic Bomb*. United States Army in World War II. Washington, DC: Center of Military History.

Joyce, James M. 1999. *The Foundations of Causal Decision Theory*. Cambridge Studies in Probability, Induction and Decision Theory. New York: Cambridge University Press.

Judd, K. L., Schmedders, K., and Yeltekin, S. 2012. "Optimal Rules for Patent Races." *International Economic Review* 53 (1): 23–52.

Kalfoglou, A., Suthers, K., Scott, J., and Hudson, K. 2004. *Reproductive Genetic Testing: What America Thinks*. Genetics and Public Policy Center.

Kamm, Frances M. 2007. *Intricate Ethics: Rights, Responsibilities, and Permissible Harm*. Oxford Ethics Series. New York: Oxford University Press.

Kandel, Eric R., Schwartz, James H., and Jessell, Thomas M., eds. 2000. *Principles of Neural Science*. 4th ed. New York: McGraw-Hill.

Kansa, Eric. 2003. "Social Complexity and Flamboyant Display in Competition: More Thoughts on the Fermi Paradox." Unpublished manuscript, archived version.

Karnofsky, Holden. 2012. "Comment on 'Reply to Holden on Tool AI.' " *Less Wrong* (blog), August 1.

Kasparov, Garry. 1996. "The Day That I Sensed a New Kind of Intelligence." *Time*, March 25, no. 13.

Kaufman, Jeff. 2011. "Whole Brain Emulation and Nematodes." *Jeff Kaufman's Blog* (blog), November 2.

Keim, G. A., Shazeer, N. M., Littman, M. L., Agarwal, S., Cheves, C. M., Fitzgerald, J., Grosland, J., Jiang, F., Pollard, S., and Weinmeister, K. 1999. "Proverb: The Probabilistic Cruciverbalist." In *Proceedings of the Sixteenth National Conference on Artificial Intelligence*, 710–17. Menlo Park, CA: AAAI Press.

Kell, Harrison J., Lubinski, David, and Benbow, Camilla P. 2013. "Who Rises to the Top? Early Indicators." *Psychological Science* 24 (5): 648–59.

Keller, Wolfgang. 2004. "International Technology Diffusion." *Journal of Economic Literature* 42 (3): 752–82.

KGS Go Server. 2012. "KGS Game Archives: Games of KGS player zen19." Retrieved July 22, 2013. Available at http://www.gokgs.com/gameArchives.jsp?user=zen19d&oldAccounts=t&year=2012&month=3.

Knill, Emanuel, Laflamme, Raymond, and Viola, Lorenza. 2000. "Theory of Quantum Error Correction for General Noise." *Physical Review Letters* 84 (11): 2525–8.

Koch, K., McLean, J., Segev, R., Freed, M. A., Berry, M. J., Balasubramanian, V., and Sterling, P. 2006. "How *Much* the Eye Tells the Brain." *Current Biology* 16 (14): 1428–34.

Kong, A., Frigge, M. L., Masson, G., Besenbacher, S., Sulem, P., Magnusson, G., Gudjonsson, S. A., Sigurdsson, A., et al. 2012. "Rate of De Novo Mutations and the Importance of Father's Age to Disease Risk." *Nature* 488: 471–5.

Koomey, Jonathan G. 2011. *Growth in Data Center Electricity Use 2005 to 2010*. Technical report, 08/01/2011. Oakland, CA: Analytics Press.

Koubi, Vally. 1999. "Military Technology Races." *International Organization* 53 (3): 537–65.

Koubi, Vally, and Lalman, David. 2007. "Distribution of Power and Military R&D." *Journal of Theoretical Politics* 19 (2): 133–52.

Koza, J. R., Keane, M. A., Streeter, M. J., Mydlowec, W., Yu, J., and Lanza, G. 2003. *Genetic Programming IV: Routine Human-Competitive Machine Intelligence*. 2nd ed. Genetic Programming. Norwell, MA: Kluwer Academic.

Kremer, Michael. 1993. "Population Growth and Technological Change: One Million B.C. to 1990." *Quarterly Journal of Economics* 108 (3): 681–716.

Kruel, Alexander. 2011. "Interview Series on Risks from AI." *Less Wrong Wiki* (blog). Retrieved Oct 26, 2013. Available at http://wiki.lesswrong.com/wiki/Interview_series_on_risks_from_AI.

Kruel, Alexander. 2012. "Q&A with Experts on Risks From AI #2." *Less Wrong* (blog), January 9.

Krusienski, D. J., and Shih, J. J. 2011. "Control of a Visual Keyboard Using an Electrocorticographic Brain–Computer Interface." *Neurorehabilitation and Neural Repair* 25 (4): 323–31.

Kuhn, Thomas S. 1962. *The Structure of Scientific Revolutions*. 1st ed. Chicago: University of Chicago Press.

Kuipers, Benjamin. 2012. "An Existing, Ecologically-Successful Genus of Collectively Intelligent Artificial Creatures." Paper presented at the 4th International Conference, ICCCI 2012, Ho Chi Minh City, Vietnam, November 28–30.

Kurzweil, Ray. 2001. "Response to Stephen Hawking." Kurzweil Accelerating Intelligence. September 5. Retrieved December 31, 2012. Available at http://www.kurzweilai.net/response-to-stephen-hawking.

Kurzweil, Ray. 2005. *The Singularity Is Near: When Humans Transcend Biology*. New York: Viking.

Laffont, Jean-Jacques, and Martimort, David. 2002. *The Theory of Incentives: The Principal-Agent Model*. Princeton, NJ: Princeton University Press.

Lancet, The. 2008. "Iodine Deficiency—Way to Go Yet." *The Lancet* 372 (9633): 88.

Landauer, Thomas K. 1986. "How Much Do People Remember? Some Estimates of the Quantity of Learned Information in Long-Term Memory." *Cognitive Science* 10 (4): 477–93.

Lebedev, Anastasiya. 2004. "The Man Who Saved the World Finally Recognized." *MosNews*, May 21.

Lebedev, M. A., and Nicolelis, M. A. 2006. "Brain–Machine Interfaces: Past, Present and Future." *Trends in Neuroscience* 29 (9): 536–46.

Legg, Shane. 2008. "Machine Super Intelligence." PhD dissertation, University of Lugano.

Leigh, E. G., Jr. 2010. "The Group Selection Controversy." *Journal of Evolutionary Biology* 23(1): 6–19.

Lenat, Douglas B. 1982. "Learning Program Helps Win National Fleet Wargame Tournament." *SIGART Newsletter* 79: 16–17.

Lenat, Douglas B. 1983. "EURISKO: A Program that Learns New Heuristics and Domain Concepts." *Artificial Intelligence* 21 (1–2): 61–98.

Lenman, James. 2000. "Consequentialism and Cluelessness." *Philosophy & Public Affairs* 29 (4): 342–70.

Lerner, Josh. 1997. "An Empirical Exploration of a Technology Race." *RAND Journal of Economics* 28 (2): 228–47.

Leslie, John. 1996. *The End of the World: The Science and Ethics of Human Extinction*. London: Routledge.

Lewis, David. 1988. "Desire as Belief." *Mind: A Quarterly Review of Philosophy* 97 (387): 323–32.

Li, Ming, and Vitányi, Paul M. B. 2008. *An Introduction to Kolmogorov Complexity and Its Applications*. Texts in Computer Science. New York: Springer.

Lin, Thomas, Mausam, and Etzioni, Oren. 2012. "Entity Linking at Web Scale." In *Proceedings of the Joint Workshop on Automatic Knowledge Base Construction and Web-scale Knowledge Extraction (AKBC-WEKEX '12)*, edited by James Fan, Raphael Hoffman, Aditya Kalyanpur, Sebastian Riedel, Fabian Suchanek, and Partha Pratim Talukdar, 84–88. Madison, WI: Omnipress.

Lloyd, Seth. 2000. "Ultimate Physical Limits to Computation." *Nature* 406 (6799): 1047–54.

Louis Harris & Associates. 1969. "Science, Sex, and Morality Survey, study no. 1927." *Life Magazine* (New York) 4.

Lynch, Michael. 2010. "Rate, Molecular Spectrum, and Consequences of Human Mutation." *Proceedings of the National Academy of Sciences of the United States of America* 107 (3): 961–8.

Lyons, Mark K. 2011. "Deep Brain Stimulation: Current and Future Clinical Applications." *Mayo Clinic Proceedings* 86 (7): 662–72.

MacAskill, William. 2010. "Moral Uncertainty and Intertheoretic Comparisons of Value." BPhil thesis, University of Oxford.

McCarthy, John. 2007. "From Here to Human-Level AI." *Artificial Intelligence* 171 (18): 1174–82.

McCorduck, Pamela. 1979. *Machines Who Think: A Personal Inquiry into the History and Prospects of Artificial Intelligence*. San Francisco: W. H. Freeman.

Mack, C. A. 2011. "Fifty Years of Moore's Law." *IEEE Transactions on Semiconductor Manufacturing* 24 (2): 202–7.

MacKay, David J. C. 2003. *Information Theory, Inference, and Learning Algorithms*. New York: Cambridge University Press.

McLean, George, and Stewart, Brian. 1979. "Norad False Alarm Causes Uproar." *The National*. Aired November 10. Ottawa, ON: CBC, 2012. News Broadcast.

Maddison, Angus. 1999. "Economic Progress: The Last Half Century in Historical Perspective." In *Facts and Fancies of Human Development: Annual Symposium and Cunningham Lecture, 1999*, edited by Ian Castles. Occasional Paper Series, 1/2000. Acton, ACT: Academy of the Social Sciences in Australia.

Maddison, Angus. 2001. *The World Economy: A Millennial Perspective*. Development Centre Studies. Paris: Development Centre of the Organisation for Economic Co-operation and Development.

Maddison, Angus. 2005. *Growth and Interaction in the World Economy: The Roots of Modernity*. Washington, DC: AEI Press.

Maddison, Angus. 2007. *Contours of the World Economy, 1–2030 AD: Essays in Macro-Economic History*. New York: Oxford University Press.

Maddison, Angus. 2010. "Statistics of World Population, GDP and Per Capita GDP 1–2008 AD." Retrieved October 26, 2013. Available at http://www.ggdc.net/maddison/Historical_Statistics/vertical-file_02-2010.xls.

Mai, Q., Yu, Y., Li, T., Wang, L., Chen, M. J., Huang, S. Z., Zhou, C., and Zhou, Q. 2007. "Derivation of Human Embryonic Stem Cell Lines from Parthenogenetic Blastocysts." *Cell Research* 17 (12): 1008–19.

Mak, J. N., and Wolpaw, J. R. 2009. "Clinical Applications of Brain-Computer Interfaces: Current State and Future Prospects." *IEEE Reviews in Biomedical Engineering* 2: 187–99.

Mankiw, N. Gregory. 2009. *Macroeconomics*. 7th ed. New York, NY: Worth.

Mardis, Elaine R. 2011. "A Decade's Perspective on DNA Sequencing Technology." *Nature* 470 (7333): 198–203.

Markoff, John. 2011. "Computer Wins on 'Jeopardy!': Trivial, It's Not." *New York Times*, February 16.

Markram, Henry. 2006. "The Blue Brain Project." *Nature Reviews Neuroscience* 7 (2): 153–160.

Mason, Heather. 2003. "Gallup Brain: The Birth of In Vitro Fertilization." *Gallup*, August 5.

Menzel, Randolf, and Giurfa, Martin. 2001. "Cognitive Architecture of a Mini-Brain: The Honeybee." *Trends in Cognitive Sciences* 5 (2): 62–71.

Metzinger, Thomas. 2003. *Being No One: The Self-Model Theory of Subjectivity*. Cambridge, MA: MIT Press.

Mijic, Roko. 2010. "Bootstrapping Safe AGI Goal Systems." Paper presented at the Roadmaps to AGI and the Future of AGI Workshop, Lugano, Switzerland, March 8.

Mike, Mike. 2013. "Face of Tomorrow." Retrieved June 30, 2012 . Available at http://faceoftomorrow.org.

Milgrom, Paul, and Roberts, John. 1990. "Bargaining Costs, Influence Costs, and the Organization of Economic Activity." In *Perspectives on Positive Political Economy*, edited by James E. Alt and Kenneth A. Shepsle, 57–89. New York: Cambridge University Press.

Miller, George A. 1956. "The Magical Number Seven, Plus or Minus Two: Some Limits on Our Capacity for Processing Information." *Psychological Review* 63 (2): 81–97.

Miller, Geoffrey. 2000. *The Mating Mind: How Sexual Choice Shaped the Evolution of Human Nature*. New York: Doubleday.

Miller, James D. 2012. *Singularity Rising: Surviving and Thriving in a Smarter, Richer, and More Dangerous World*. Dallas, TX: BenBella Books.

Minsky, Marvin. 1967. *Computation: Finite and Infinite Machines*. Englewood Cliffs, NJ: Prentice-Hall.

Minsky, Marvin, ed. 1968. *Semantic Information Processing*. Cambridge, MA: MIT Press.

Minsky, Marvin. 1984. "Afterword to Vernor Vinge's novel, 'True Names.' " Unpublished manuscript, October 1. Retrieved December 31, 2012. Available at http://web.media.mit.edu/~minsky/papers/TrueNames.Afterword.html.

Minsky, Marvin. 2006. *The Emotion Machine: Commonsense Thinking, Artificial Intelligence, and the Future of the Human Mind*. New York: Simon & Schuster.

Minsky, Marvin, and Papert, Seymour. 1969. *Perceptrons: An Introduction to Computational Geometry*. 1st ed. Cambridge, MA: MIT Press.

Moore, Andrew. 2011. "Hedonism." In *The Stanford Encyclopedia of Philosophy*, Winter 2011, edited by Edward N. Zalta. Stanford, CA: Stanford University.

Moravec, Hans P. 1976. "The Role of Raw Power in Intelligence." Unpublished manuscript, May 12. Retrieved August 12, 2012. Available at http://www.frc.ri.cmu.edu/users/hpm/project.archive/general.articles/l975/Raw.Power.html.

Moravec, Hans P. 1980. "Obstacle Avoidance and Navigation in the Real World by a Seeing Robot Rover." PhD dissertation, Stanford University.

Moravec, Hans P. 1988. *Mind Children: The Future of Robot and Human Intelligence.* Cambridge, MA: Harvard University Press.

Moravec, Hans P. 1998. "When Will Computer Hardware Match the Human Brain?" *Journal of Evolution and Technology* 1.

Moravec, Hans P. 1999. "Rise of the Robots." *Scientific American*, December, 124–35.

Muehlhauser, Luke, and Helm, Louie. 2012. "The Singularity and Machine Ethics." In *Singularity Hypotheses: A Scientific and Philosophical Assessment*, edited by Amnon Eden, Johnny Søraker, James H. Moor, and Eric Steinhart. The Frontiers Collection. Berlin: Springer.

Muehlhauser, Luke, and Salamon, Anna. 2012. "Intelligence Explosion: Evidence and Import." In *Singularity Hypotheses: A Scientific and Philosophical Assessment*, edited by Amnon Eden, Johnny Søraker, James H. Moor, and Eric Steinhart. The Frontiers Collection. Berlin: Springer.

Müller, Vincent C., and Bostrom, Nick. 2016. "Future Progress in Artificial Intelligence: A Survey of Expert Opinion." In *Fundamental Issues of Artificial Intelligence*, edited by Vincent C. Müller. Synthese Library; Berlin: Springer.

Murphy, Kevin P. 2012. *Machine Learning: A Probabilistic Perspective.* Adaptive Computation and Machine Learning. Cambridge, MA: MIT Press.

Nachman, Michael W., and Crowell, Susan L. 2000. "Estimate of the Mutation Rate per Nucleotide in Humans." *Genetics* 156 (1): 297–304.

Nagy, Z. P., and Chang, C. C. 2007. "Artificial Gametes." *Theriogenology* 67 (1): 99–104.

Nagy, Z. P., Kerkis, I., and Chang, C. C. 2008. "Development of Artificial Gametes." *Reproductive BioMedicine Online* 16 (4): 539–44.

NASA. 2013. "International Space Station: Facts and Figures." Available at http://www.nasa.gov/worldbook/intspacestation_worldbook.html.

Newborn, Monty. 2011. *Beyond Deep Blue: Chess in the Stratosphere.* New York: Springer.

Newell, Allen, Shaw, J. C., and Simon, Herbert A. 1958. "Chess-Playing Programs and the Problem of Complexity." *IBM Journal of Research and Development* 2 (4): 320–35.

Newell, Allen, Shaw, J. C., and Simon, Herbert A. 1959. "Report on a General Problem-Solving Program: Proceedings of the International Conference on Information Processing." In *Information Processing*, 256–64. Paris: UNESCO.

Nicolelis, Miguel A. L., and Lebedev, Mikhail A. 2009. "Principles of Neural Ensemble Physiology Underlying the Operation of Brain–Machine Interfaces." *Nature Reviews Neuroscience* 10 (7): 530–40.

Nilsson, Nils J. 1984. *Shakey the Robot*, Technical Note 323. Menlo Park, CA: AI Center, SRI International, April.

Nilsson, Nils J. 2009. *The Quest for Artificial Intelligence: A History of Ideas and Achievements.* New York: Cambridge University Press.

Nisbett, R. E., Aronson, J., Blair, C., Dickens, W., Flynn, J., Halpern, D. F., and Turkheimer, E. 2012. "Intelligence: New Findings and Theoretical Developments." *American Psychologist* 67 (2): 130–59.

Niven, Larry. 1973. "The Defenseless Dead." In *Ten Tomorrows*, edited by Roger Elwood, 91–142. New York: Fawcett.

Nordhaus, William D. 2007. "Two Centuries of Productivity Growth in Computing." *Journal of Economic History* 67 (1): 128–59.

Norton, John D. 2011. "Waiting for Landauer." *Studies in History and Philosophy of Science Part B: Studies in History and Philosophy of Modern Physics* 42 (3): 184–98.

Olds, James, and Milner, Peter. 1954. "Positive Reinforcement Produced by Electrical Stimulation of Septal Area and Other Regions of Rat Brain." *Journal of Comparative and Physiological Psychology* 47 (6): 419–27.

Olum, Ken D. 2002. "The Doomsday Argument and the Number of Possible Observers." *Philosophical Quarterly* 52 (207): 164–84.

Omohundro, Stephen M. 2007. "The Nature of Self-Improving Artificial Intelligence." Paper presented at Singularity Summit 2007, San Francisco, CA, September 8–9.

Omohundro, Stephen M. 2008. "The Basic AI Drives." In *Artificial General Intelligence 2008: Proceedings of the First AGI Conference*, edited by Pei Wang, Ben Goertzel, and Stan Franklin, 483–92. Frontiers in Artificial Intelligence and Applications 171. Amsterdam: IOS.

Omohundro, Stephen M. 2012. "Rational Artificial Intelligence for the Greater Good." In *Singularity Hypotheses: A Scientific and Philosophical Assessment*, edited by Amnon Eden, Johnny Søraker, James H. Moor, and Eric Steinhart. The Frontiers Collection. Berlin: Springer.

O'Neill, Gerard K. 1974. "The Colonization of Space." *Physics Today* 27 (9): 32–40.

Oshima, Hideki, and Katayama, Yoichi. 2010. "Neuroethics of Deep Brain Stimulation for Mental Disorders: Brain Stimulation Reward in Humans." *Neurologia medico-chirurgica* 50 (9): 845–52.

Parfit, Derek. 1986. *Reasons and Persons*. New York: Oxford University Press.

Parfit, Derek. 2011. *On What Matters*. 2 vols. The Berkeley Tanner Lectures. New York: Oxford University Press.

Parrington, Alan J. 1997. "Mutually Assured Destruction Revisited." *Airpower Journal* 11 (4).

Pasqualotto, Emanuele, Federici, Stefano, and Belardinelli, Marta Olivetti. 2012. "Toward Functioning and Usable Brain–Computer Interfaces (BCIs): A Literature Review." *Disability and Rehabilitation: Assistive Technology* 7 (2): 89–103.

Pearl, Judea. 2009. *Causality: Models, Reasoning, and Inference*. 2nd ed. New York: Cambridge University Press.

Perlmutter, J. S., and Mink, J. W. 2006. "Deep Brain Stimulation." *Annual Review of Neuroscience* 29: 229–57.

Pinker, Steven. 2011. *The Better Angels of Our Nature: Why Violence Has Declined*. New York: Viking.

Plomin, R., Haworth, C. M., Meaburn, E. L., Price, T. S., Wellcome Trust Case Control Consortium 2, and Davis, O. S. 2013. "Common DNA Markers Can Account for More Than Half of the Genetic Influence on Cognitive Abilities." *Psychological Science* 24 (2): 562–8.

Popper, Nathaniel. 2012. "Flood of Errant Trades Is a Black Eye for Wall Street." *New York Times*, August 1.

Pourret, Olivier, Naim, Patrick, and Marcot, Bruce, eds. 2008. *Bayesian Networks: A Practical Guide to Applications*. Chichester, West Sussex, UK: Wiley.

Powell, A., Shennan, S., and Thomas, M. G. 2009. "Late Pleistocene Demography and the Appearance of Modern Human Behavior." *Science* 324 (5932): 1298–1301.

Price, Huw. 1991. "Agency and Probabilistic Causality." *British Journal for the Philosophy of Science* 42 (2): 157–76.

Qian, M., Wang, D., Watkins, W. E., Gebski, V., Yan, Y. Q., Li, M., and Chen, Z. P. 2005. "The Effects of Iodine on Intelligence in Children: A Meta-Analysis of Studies Conducted in China." *Asia Pacific Journal of Clinical Nutrition* 14 (1): 32–42.

Quine, Willard Van Orman, and Ullian, Joseph Silbert. 1978. *The Web of Belief*, ed. Richard Malin Ohmann, vol. 2. New York: Random House.

Railton, Peter. 1986. "Facts and Values." *Philosophical Topics* 14 (2): 5–31.

Rajab, Moheeb Abu, Zarfoss, Jay, Monrose, Fabian, and Terzis, Andreas. 2006. "A Multifaceted Approach to Understanding the Botnet Phenomenon." In *Proceedings of the 6th ACM SIGCOMM Conference on Internet Measurement*, 41–52. New York: ACM.

Rawls, John. 1971. *A Theory of Justice*. Cambridge, MA: Belknap.

Read, J. I., and Trentham, Neil. 2005. "The Baryonic Mass Function of Galaxies." *Philosophical Transactions of the Royal Society A: Mathematical, Physical and Engineering Sciences* 363 (1837): 2693–710.

Repantis, D., Schlattmann, P., Laisney, O., and Heuser, I. 2010. "Modafinil and Methylphenidate for Neuroenhancement in Healthy Individuals: A Systematic Review." *Pharmacological Research* 62 (3): 187–206.

Rhodes, Richard. 1986. *The Making of the Atomic Bomb*. New York: Simon & Schuster.

Rhodes, Richard. 2008. *Arsenals of Folly: The Making of the Nuclear Arms Race*. New York: Vintage.

Rietveld, Cornelius A., Medland, Sarah E., Derringer, Jaime, Yang, Jian, Esko, Tonu, Martin, Nicolas W., Westra, Harm-Jan, Shakhbazov, Konstantin, Abdellaoui, Abdel, et al. 2013. "GWAS of 126,559 Individuals Identifies Genetic Variants Associated with Educational Attainment." *Science* 340 (6139): 1467–71.

Ring, Mark, and Orseau, Laurent. 2011. "Delusion, Survival, and Intelligent Agents." In *Artificial General Intelligence: 4th International Conference, AGI 2011, Mountain View, CA, USA, August 3–6, 2011. Proceedings*, edited by Jürgen Schmidhuber, Kristinn R. Thórisson, and Moshe Looks, 11–20. Lecture Notes in Computer Science 6830. Berlin: Springer.

Ritchie, Graeme, Manurung, Ruli, and Waller, Annalu. 2007. "A Practical Application of Computational Humour." In *Proceedings of the 4th International Joint Workshop on Computational Creativity*, edited by Amilcar Cardoso and Geraint A. Wiggins, 91–8. London: Goldsmiths, University of London.

Roache, Rebecca. 2008. "Ethics, Speculation, and Values." *NanoEthics* 2 (3): 317–27.

Robles, J. A., Lineweaver, C. H., Grether, D., Flynn, C., Egan, C. A., Pracy, M. B., Holmberg, J., and Gardner, E. 2008. "A Comprehensive Comparison of the Sun to Other Stars: Searching for Self-Selection Effects." *Astrophysical Journal* 684 (1): 691–706.

Roe, Anne. 1953. *The Making of a Scientist*. New York: Dodd, Mead.

Roy, Deb. 2012. "About." Retrieved October 14. Available at http://web.media.mit.edu/~dkroy/.

Rubin, Jonathan, and Watson, Ian. 2011. "Computer Poker: A Review." *Artificial Intelligence* 175 (5–6): 958–87.

Rumelhart, D. E., Hinton, G. E., and Williams, R. J. 1986. "Learning Representations by Back-Propagating Errors." *Nature* 323 (6088): 533–6.

Russell, Bertrand. 1986. "The Philosophy of Logical Atomism." In *The Philosophy of Logical Atomism and Other Essays 1914–1919*, edited by John G. Slater, 8: 157–244. The Collected Papers of Bertrand Russell. Boston: Allen & Unwin.

Russell, Bertrand, and Griffin, Nicholas. 2001. *The Selected Letters of Bertrand Russell: The Public Years, 1914–1970*. New York: Routledge.

Russell, Stuart J., and Norvig, Peter. 2010. *Artificial Intelligence: A Modern Approach*. 3rd ed. Upper Saddle River, NJ: Prentice-Hall.

Sabrosky, Curtis W. 1952. "How Many Insects Are There?" In *Insects*, edited by United States Department of Agriculture, 1–7. Yearbook of Agriculture. Washington, DC: United States Government Printing Office.

Salamon, Anna. 2009. "When Software Goes Mental: Why Artificial Minds Mean Fast Endogenous Growth." Working Paper, December 27.

Salem, D. J., and Rowan, A. N. 2001. *The State of the Animals: 2001*. Public Policy Series. Washington, DC: Humane Society Press.

Salverda, W., Nolan, B., and Smeeding, T. M. 2009. *The Oxford Handbook of Economic Inequality*. Oxford: Oxford University Press.

Samuel, A. L. 1959. "Some Studies in Machine Learning Using the Game of Checkers." *IBM Journal of Research and Development* 3 (3): 210–19.

Sandberg, Anders. 1999. "The Physics of Information Processing Superobjects: Daily Life Among the Jupiter Brains." *Journal of Evolution and Technology* 5.

Sandberg, Anders. 2010. "An Overview of Models of Technological Singularity." Paper presented at the Roadmaps to AGI and the Future of AGI Workshop, Lugano, Switzerland, March 8.

Sandberg, Anders. 2013. "Feasibility of Whole Brain Emulation." In *Philosophy and Theory of Artificial Intelligence*, edited by Vincent C. Müller, 5: 251–64. Studies in Applied Philosophy, Epistemology and Rational Ethics. New York: Springer.

Sandberg, Anders, and Bostrom, Nick. 2006. "Converging Cognitive Enhancements." *Annals of the New York Academy of Sciences* 1093: 201–27.

Sandberg, Anders, and Bostrom, Nick. 2008. *Whole Brain Emulation: A Roadmap*. Technical Report 2008-3. Future of Humanity Institute, University of Oxford.

Sandberg, Anders, and Bostrom, Nick. 2011. *Machine Intelligence Survey*. Technical Report 2011-1. Future of Humanity Institute, University of Oxford.

Sandberg, Anders, and Savulescu, Julian. 2011. "The Social and Economic Impacts of Cognitive Enhancement." In *Enhancing Human Capacities*, edited by Julian Savulescu, Ruud ter Meulen, and Guy Kahane, 92–112. Malden, MA: Wiley-Blackwell.

Schaeffer, Jonathan. 1997. *One Jump Ahead: Challenging Human Supremacy in Checkers*. New York: Springer.

Schaeffer, J., Burch, N., Bjornsson, Y., Kishimoto, A., Muller, M., Lake, R., Lu, P., and Sutphen, S. 2007. "Checkers Is Solved." *Science* 317 (5844): 1518–22.

Schalk, Gerwin. 2008. "Brain–Computer Symbiosis." *Journal of Neural Engineering* 5 (1): P1–P15.

Schelling, Thomas C. 1980. *The Strategy of Conflict*. 2nd ed. Cambridge, MA: Harvard University Press.

Schultz, T. R. 2000. "In Search of Ant Ancestors." *Proceedings of the National Academy of Sciences of the United States of America* 97 (26): 14028–9.

Schultz, W., Dayan, P., and Montague, P. R. 1997. "A Neural Substrate of Prediction and Reward." *Science* 275 (5306): 1593–9.

Schwartz, Jacob T. 1987. "Limits of Artificial Intelligence." In *Encyclopedia of Artificial Intelligence*, edited by Stuart C. Shapiro and David Eckroth, 1: 488–503. New York: Wiley.

Schwitzgebel, Eric. 2013. "If Materialism is True, the United States is Probably Conscious." Working Paper, February 8.

Sen, Amartya, and Williams, Bernard, eds. 1982. *Utilitarianism and Beyond*. New York: Cambridge University Press.

Shanahan, Murray. 2010. *Embodiment and the Inner Life: Cognition and Consciousness in the Space of Possible Minds*. New York: Oxford University Press.

Shannon, Robert V. 2012. "Advances in Auditory Prostheses." *Current Opinion in Neurology* 25 (1): 61–6.

Shapiro, Stuart C. 1992. "Artificial Intelligence." In *Encyclopedia of Artificial Intelligence*, 2nd ed., 1: 54–7. New York: Wiley.

Sheppard, Brian. 2002. "World-Championship-Caliber Scrabble." *Artificial Intelligence* 134 (1–2): 241–75.

Shoemaker, Sydney. 1969. "Time Without Change." *Journal of Philosophy* 66 (12): 363–81.

Shulman, Carl. 2010a. *Omohundro's "Basic AI Drives" and Catastrophic Risks*. Berkeley, CA: Machine Intelligence Research Institute.

Shulman, Carl. 2010b. *Whole Brain Emulation and the Evolution of Superorganisms*. Berkeley, CA: Machine Intelligence Research Institute.

Shulman, Carl. 2012. "Could We Use Untrustworthy Human Brain Emulations to Make Trustworthy Ones?" Paper presented at the AGI Impacts conference, Oxford, December 8–11.

Shulman, Carl, and Bostrom, Nick. 2012. "How Hard is Artificial Intelligence? Evolutionary Arguments and Selection Effects." *Journal of Consciousness Studies* 19 (7–8): 103–30.

Shulman, Carl, and Bostrom, Nick. 2014. "Embryo Selection for Cognitive Enhancement: Curiosity or Game-Changer?" *Global Policy* 5 (1): 85–92.

Shulman, Carl, Jonsson, Henrik, and Tarleton, Nick. 2009. "Which Consequentialism? Machine Ethics and Moral Divergence." In *AP-CAP 2009: The Fifth Asia-Pacific Computing and Philosophy Conference, October 1st-2nd, University of Tokyo, Japan. Proceedings*, edited by Carson Reynolds and Alvaro Cassinelli, 23–25. AP-CAP 2009.

Sidgwick, Henry, and Jones, Emily Elizabeth Constance. 2010. *The Methods of Ethics*. Charleston, SC: Nabu Press.

Silver, Albert. 2006. "How Strong Is GNU Backgammon?" Backgammon Galore! September 16. Retrieved October 26, 2013. Available at http://www.bkgm.com/gnu/AllAboutGNU.html#how_strong_is_gnu.

Simeral, J. D., Kim, S. P., Black, M. J., Donoghue, J. P., and Hochberg, L. R. 2011. "Neural Control of Cursor Trajectory and Click by a Human with Tetraplegia 1000 Days after Implant of an Intracortical Microelectrode Array." *Journal of Neural Engineering* 8 (2): 025027.

Simester, Duncan, and Knez, Marc. 2002. "Direct and Indirect Bargaining Costs and the Scope of the Firm." *Journal of Business* 75 (2): 283–304.

Simon, Herbert Alexander. 1965. *The Shape of Automation for Men and Management*. New York: Harper & Row.

Sinhababu, Neil. 2009. "The Humean Theory of Motivation Reformulated and Defended." *Philosophical Review* 118 (4): 465–500.

Slagle, James R. 1963. "A Heuristic Program That Solves Symbolic Integration Problems in Freshman Calculus." *Journal of the ACM* 10 (4): 507–20.

Smeding, H. M., Speelman, J. D., Koning-Haanstra, M., Schuurman, P. R., Nijssen, P., van Laar, T., and Schmand, B. 2006. "Neuropsychological Effects of Bilateral STN Stimulation in Parkinson Disease: A Controlled Study." *Neurology* 66 (12): 1830–6.

Smith, Michael. 1987. "The Humean Theory of Motivation." *Mind: A Quarterly Review of Philosophy* 96 (381): 36–61.

Smith, Michael, Lewis, David, and Johnston, Mark. 1989. "Dispositional Theories of Value." *Proceedings of the Aristotelian Society* 63: 89–174.

Sparrow, Robert. 2013. "In Vitro Eugenics." *Journal of Medical Ethics*. doi:10.1136/medethics-2012-101200. Published online April 4, 2013. Available at http://jme.bmj.com/content/early/2013/02/13/medethics-2012-101200.full.

Stansberry, Matt, and Kudritzki, Julian. 2012. *Uptime Institute 2012 Data Center Industry Survey*. Uptime Institute.

Stapledon, Olaf. 1937. *Star Maker*. London: Methuen.

Steriade, M., Timofeev, I., Durmuller, N., and Grenier, F. 1998. "Dynamic Properties of Corticothalamic Neurons and Local Cortical Interneurons Generating Fast Rhythmic (30–40 Hz) Spike Bursts." *Journal of Neurophysiology* 79 (1): 483–90.

Stewart, P. W., Lonky, E., Reihman, J., Pagano, J., Gump, B. B., and Darvill, T. 2008. "The Relationship Between Prenatal PCB Exposure and Intelligence (IQ) in 9-Year-Old Children." *Environmental Health Perspectives* 116 (10): 1416–22.

Sun, W., Yu, H., Shen, Y., Banno, Y., Xiang, Z., and Zhang, Z. 2012. "Phylogeny and Evolutionary History of the Silkworm." *Science China Life Sciences* 55 (6): 483–96.

Sundet, J., Barlaug, D., and Torjussen, T. 2004. "The End of the Flynn Effect? A Study of Secular Trends in Mean Intelligence Scores of Norwegian Conscripts During Half a Century." *Intelligence* 32 (4): 349–62.

Sutton, Richard S., and Barto, Andrew G. 1998. *Reinforcement Learning: An Introduction*. Adaptive Computation and Machine Learning. Cambridge, MA: MIT Press.

Talukdar, D., Sudhir, K., and Ainslie, A. 2002. "Investigating New Product Diffusion Across Products and Countries." *Marketing Science* 21 (1): 97–114.

Teasdale, Thomas W., and Owen, David R. 2008. "Secular Declines in Cognitive Test Scores: A Reversal of the Flynn Effect." *Intelligence* 36 (2): 121–6.

Tegmark, Max, and Bostrom, Nick. 2005. "Is a Doomsday Catastrophe Likely?" *Nature* 438: 754.

Teitelman, Warren. 1966. "Pilot: A Step Towards Man–Computer Symbiosis." PhD dissertation, Massachusetts Institute of Technology.

Temple, Robert K. G. 1986. *The Genius of China: 3000 Years of Science, Discovery, and Invention*. 1st ed. New York: Simon & Schuster.

Tesauro, Gerald. 1995. "Temporal Difference Learning and TD-Gammon." *Communications of the ACM* 38 (3): 58–68.

Tetlock, Philip E. 2005. *Expert Political Judgment: How Good is it? How Can We Know?* Princeton, NJ: Princeton University Press.

Tetlock, Philip E., and Belkin, Aaron. 1996. "Counterfactual Thought Experiments in World Politics: Logical, Methodological, and Psychological Perspectives." In *Counterfactual Thought Experiments in World Politics: Logical, Methodological, and Psychological Perspectives*, edited by Philip E. Tetlock and Aaron Belkin, 1–38. Princeton, NJ: Princeton University Press.

Thompson, Adrian. 1997. "Artificial Evolution in the Physical World." In *Evolutionary Robotics: From Intelligent Robots to Artificial Life*, edited by Takashi Gomi, 101–25. ER '97. Carp, ON: Applied AI Systems.

Thrun, S., Montemerlo, M., Dahlkamp, H., Stavens, D., Aron, A., Diebel, J., Fong, P., et al. 2006. "Stanley: The Robot That Won the DARPA Grand Challenge." *Journal of Field Robotics* 23 (9): 661–92.

Trachtenberg, J. T., Chen, B. E., Knott, G. W., Feng, G., Sanes, J. R., Welker, E., and Svoboda, K. 2002. "Long-Term In Vivo Imaging of Experience-Dependent Synaptic Plasticity in Adult Cortex." *Nature* 420 (6917): 788–94.

Traub, Wesley A. 2012. "Terrestrial, Habitable-Zone Exoplanet Frequency from *Kepler*." *Astrophysical Journal* 745 (1): 1–10.

Truman, James W., Taylor, Barbara J., and Awad, Timothy A. 1993. "Formation of the Adult Nervous System." In *The Development of* Drosophila Melanogaster, edited by Michael Bate and Alfonso Martinez Arias. Plainview, NY: Cold Spring Harbor Laboratory.

Tuomi, Ilkka. 2002. "The Lives and the Death of Moore's Law." *First Monday* 7 (11).

Turing, A. M. 1950. "Computing Machinery and Intelligence." *Mind* 59 (236): 433–60.

Turkheimer, Eric, Haley, Andreana, Waldron, Mary, D'Onofrio, Brian, and Gottesman, Irving I. 2003. "Socioeconomic Status Modifies Heritability of IQ in Young Children." *Psychological Science* 14 (6): 623–8.

Uauy, Ricardo, and Dangour, Alan D. 2006. "Nutrition in Brain Development and Aging: Role of Essential Fatty Acids." Supplement, *Nutrition Reviews* 64 (5): S24–S33.

Ulam, Stanislaw M. 1958. "John von Neumann." *Bulletin of the American Mathematical Society* 64 (3): 1–49.

Uncertain Future, The. 2012. "Frequently Asked Questions." The Uncertain Future. Retrieved March 25, 2012. Available at http://www.theuncertainfuture.com/faq.html.

U.S. Congress, Office of Technology Assessment. 1995. *U.S.–Russian Cooperation in Space* ISS-618. Washington, DC: U.S. Government Printing Office, April.

Van Zanden, Jan Luiten. 2003. *On Global Economic History: A Personal View on an Agenda for Future Research*. Amsterdam: International Institute of Social History, July 23.

Vardi, Moshe Y. 2012. "Artificial Intelligence: Past and Future." *Communications of the ACM* 55 (1): 5.

Vassar, Michael, and Freitas, Robert A., Jr. 2006. "Lifeboat Foundation Nanoshield." Lifeboat Foundation. Retrieved May 12, 2012. Available at http://lifeboat.com/ex/nanoshield.

Vinge, Vernor. 1993. "The Coming Technological Singularity: How to Survive in the Post-Human Era." In *Vision-21: Interdisciplinary Science and Engineering in the Era of Cyberspace*, 11–22. NASA Conference Publication 10129. NASA Lewis Research Center.

Visscher, P. M., Hill, W. G., and Wray, N. R. 2008. "Heritability in the Genomics Era: Concepts and Misconceptions." *Nature Reviews Genetics* 9 (4): 255–66.

Vollenweider, Franz, Gamma, Alex, Liechti, Matthias, and Huber, Theo. 1998. "Psychological and Cardiovascular Effects and Short-Term Sequelae of MDMA ('Ecstasy') in MDMA-Naïve Healthy Volunteers." *Neuropsychopharmachology* 19 (4): 241–51.

Wade, Michael J. 1976. "Group Selections Among Laboratory Populations of Tribolium." *Proceedings of the National Academy of Sciences of the United States of America* 73 (12): 4604–7.

Wainwright, Martin J., and Jordan, Michael I. 2008. "Graphical Models, Exponential Families, and Variational Inference." *Foundations and Trends in Machine Learning* 1 (1–2): 1–305.

Walker, Mark. 2002. "Prolegomena to Any Future Philosophy." *Journal of Evolution and Technology* 10 (1).

Walsh, Nick Paton. 2001. "Alter our DNA or robots will take over, warns Hawking." *The Observer*, September 1. http://www.theguardian.com/uk/2001/sep/02/medicalscience.genetics.

Warwick, Kevin. 2002. *I, Cyborg*. London: Century.

Wehner, M., Oliker, L., and Shalf, J. 2008. "Towards Ultra-High Resolution Models of Climate and Weather." *International Journal of High Performance Computing Applications* 22 (2): 149–65.

Weizenbaum, Joseph. 1966. "Eliza: A Computer Program for the Study of Natural Language Communication Between Man and Machine." *Communications of the ACM* 9 (1): 36–45.

Weizenbaum, Joseph. 1976. *Computer Power and Human Reason: From Judgment to Calculation*. San Francisco, CA: W. H. Freeman.

Werbos, Paul John. 1994. *The Roots of Backpropagation: From Ordered Derivatives to Neural Networks and Political Forecasting*. New York: Wiley.

White, J. G., Southgate, E., Thomson, J. N., and Brenner, S. 1986. "The Structure of the Nervous System of the Nematode *Caenorhabditis Elegans*." *Philosophical Transactions of the Royal Society of London. Series B, Biological Sciences* 314 (1165): 1–340.

Whitehead, Hal. 2003. *Sperm Whales: Social Evolution in the Ocean*. Chicago: University of Chicago Press.

Whitman, William B., Coleman, David C., and Wiebe, William J. 1998. "Prokaryotes: The Unseen Majority." *Proceedings of the National Academy of Sciences of the United States of America* 95 (12): 6578–83.

Wiener, Norbert. 1960. "Some Moral and Technical Consequences of Automation." *Science* 131 (3410): 1355–8.

Wikipedia. 2012a, s.v. "Computer Bridge." Retrieved June 30, 2013. Available at http://en.wikipedia.org/wiki/Computer_bridge.

Wikipedia. 2012b, s.v. "Supercomputer." Retrieved June 30, 2013. Available at http://et.wikipedia.org/wiki/Superarvuti.

Williams, George C. 1966. *Adaptation and Natural Selection: A Critique of Some Current Evolutionary Thought*. Princeton Science Library. Princeton, NJ: Princeton University Press.

Winograd, Terry. 1972. *Understanding Natural Language*. New York: Academic Press.

Wood, Nigel. 2007. *Chinese Glazes: Their Origins, Chemistry and Re-creation.* London: A&C Black.

World Bank. 2008. *Global Economic Prospects: Technology Diffusion in the Developing World,* 42097. Washington, DC.

World Robotics. 2011. *Executive Summary of 1. World Robotics 2011 Industrial Robots; 2. World Robotics 2011 Service Robots.* Retrieved June 30, 2012. Available at http://www.bara.org.uk/pdf/2012/world-robotics/Executive_Summary_WR_2012.pdf.

World Values Survey. 2008. *WVS 2005-2008.* Retrieved 29 October, 2013. Available at http://www.wvsevsdb.com/wvs/WVSAnalizeStudy.jsp.

Wright, Robert. 2001. *Nonzero: The Logic of Human Destiny.* New York: Vintage.

Yaeger, Larry. 1994. "Computational Genetics, Physiology, Metabolism, Neural Systems, Learning, Vision, and Behavior or PolyWorld: Life in a New Context." In *Proceedings of the Artificial Life III Conference,* edited by C. G. Langton, 263–98. Santa Fe Institute Studies in the Sciences of Complexity. Reading, MA: Addison-Wesley.

Yudkowsky, Eliezer. 2001. *Creating Friendly AI 1.0: The Analysis and Design of Benevolent Goal Architectures.* Berkeley, CA: Machine Intelligence Research Institute, June 15.

Yudkowsky, Eliezer. 2002. "The AI-Box Experiment." Retrieved January 15, 2012. Available at http://yudkowsky.net/singularity/aibox.

Yudkowsky, Eliezer. 2004. *Coherent Extrapolated Volition.* Berkeley, CA: Machine Intelligence Research Institute, May.

Yudkowsky, Eliezer. 2007. "Levels of Organization in General Intelligence." In *Artificial General Intelligence,* edited by Ben Goertzel and Cassio Pennachin, 389–501. Cognitive Technologies. Berlin: Springer.

Yudkowsky, Eliezer. 2008a. "Artificial Intelligence as a Positive and Negative Factor in Global Risk." In *Global Catastrophic Risks,* edited by Nick Bostrom and Milan M. Ćirković, 308–45. New York: Oxford University Press.

Yudkowsky, Eliezer. 2008b. "Sustained Strong Recursion." *Less Wrong* (blog), December 5.

Yudkowsky, Eliezer. 2010. *Timeless Decision Theory.* Berkeley, CA: Machine Intelligence Research Institute.

Yudkowsky, Eliezer. 2011. *Complex Value Systems are Required to Realize Valuable Futures.* Berkeley, CA: Machine Intelligence Research Institute.

Yudkowsky, Eliezer. 2013. *Intelligence Explosion Microeconomics,* Technical Report 2013–1. Berkeley, CA: Machine Intelligence Research Institute.

Zahavi, Amotz, and Zahavi, Avishag. 1997. *The Handicap Principle: A Missing Piece of Darwin's Puzzle.* Translated by N. Zahavi-Ely and M. P. Ely. New York: Oxford University Press.

Zalasiewicz, J., Williams, M., Smith, A., Barry, T. L., Coe, A. L., Bown, P. R., Brenchley, P., et al. 2008. "Are We Now Living in the Anthropocene?" *GSA Today* 18 (2): 4–8.

Zeira, Joseph. 2011. "Innovations, Patent Races and Endogenous Growth." *Journal of Economic Growth* 16 (2): 135–56.

Zuleta, Hernando. 2008. "An Empirical Note on Factor Shares." *Journal of International Trade and Economic Development* 17 (3): 379–90.

PARTIAL GLOSSARY

Associative value accretion: An approach to value-loading in which a mechanism is specified that leads the AI to adopt new final values over time and in a way that is contingent on its experiences. (Inspired by the way humans appear to acquire values.)

Anthropic capture: A hypothesized phenomenon in which an AI thinks it might be in a simulation, and so tries to behave in ways that will be rewarded by its simulators.

Augmentation: An approach to obtaining a superintelligence with desirable motivations that consists of starting with a system that already has appropriate motivations (e.g. a human being) and making it smarter, instead of attempting to engineer a goal system from scratch.

Boxing: A control method that consists of engineering the AI's environment so as to reduce the AI's ability to interact with the outside world; e.g. running the AI in a carefully isolated virtual reality simulation and with only a restricted channel of communication to its human overseers.

Capability control methods: Strategies for avoiding undesirable outcomes by limiting what an AI can do.

Cognitive enhancement: Improvements to a system's intellectual abilities.

Collective superintelligence: A system composed of a large number of smaller intellects such that the system's overall performance across many very general domains vastly outstrips that of any current cognitive system.

The common good principle: Superintelligence should be developed only for the benefit of all of humanity and in the service of widely shared ethical ideals.

Crucial consideration: An idea or argument that might plausibly reveal the need for not just some minor course adjustment in our practical endeavors but a major change of direction or priority, for example by reversing the sign of the desirability of important interventions.

Decisive strategic advantage: Strategic superiority (by technology or other means) sufficient to enable an agent to achieve complete world dominance.

Direct specification: An approach to the control problem in which the programmers figure out what humans value, and then write code for the AI that explicitly contains the corresponding values or rules.

Domesticity: An approach to the control problem in which the AI's motivation system is designed such as to give the AI very modest ambitions, limiting the range of things it wants to interfere with.

Emulation modulation: Starting with brain emulations with approximately normal human motivations and modifying their motivations using digital drug analogs or other means.

Evolutionary selection approach to value-loading: An approach to the value-loading problem that seeks to obtain an AI with desirable values through a process of iterated selection, analogous to the evolutionary selection process that produced humans.

First principal–agent problem: The well-known problem faced by one human entity ("the principal") that appoints another ("the agent") to act in the former's interest (found, for instance, in the relationship between employer and employee).

Genie: An AI that carries out a high-level command, then waits for another.

Humanity's cosmic endowment: The reservoir of physical resources in the universe that is accessible to technologically mature Earth-originating civilization (starting from present-day Earth).

Human-level AI: An AI that can match the intellectual performance of a typical human being in all practically important domains. (This term has significant ambiguities.)

Human-level hardware: Hardware that matches the information-processing ability of the human brain.

Human-level software: Software that matches the algorithmic efficiency of the human brain, for doing the tasks the human brain does.

Impersonal perspective: The view that one should act in the best interests of everyone, including those who may be brought into existence by one's choices (cf. 'Person-affecting perspective').

Incentive methods: Strategies for controlling an AI that consist of setting up the AI's environment such that the AI has instrumental reasons even if its final goals are not aligned with human values.

Incentive wrapping: Provisions in the goals given to an AI that allocate extra rewards or influence to those who helped bring the AI about.

Indirect normativity: An approach to the value-selection problem in which, instead of directly determining ourselves which values an AI is to promote, we specify a criterion or a method that the AI can follow, using its own intellectual resources to discover the concrete content of a merely implicitly defined normative standard.

Instrumental convergence thesis: We can identify "convergent instrumental values", subgoals that are useful for the attainment of a wide range of possible final goals in a wide range of possible environments—subgoals that are therefore likely to be pursued by a broad class of intelligent agents.

Intelligence explosion: A hypothesized event in which an AI rapidly improves from "relatively modest" to a radically superhuman level of intelligence (in a process that is often imagined to involve recursive self-improvement).

Macrostructural development accelerator: An imaginary lever (used in thought experiments) that would alter the rate at which macro-structural features (such as technology and geopolitical dynamics) develop, while leaving unchanged the rate at which micro-level human affairs unfold.

Mind crime: The mistreatment of morally relevant computational processes (in simulations, or inside an AI, or created in machine substrate for instrumental reasons).

Moral rightness (MR) AI: An AI that seeks to do what is morally right.

Motivational scaffolding: An approach to value-loading in which a seed AI is initially given simple goals that are later replaced with more complex (value-aligned) goals once the AI has developed sufficiently sophisticated representational resources.

Multipolar outcome: A condition after the transition to the machine intelligence era in which there are multiple competing superintelligent agencies.

Optimization power: The amount of quality-adjusted design effort that is being applied to improve a system's intelligence.

Oracle: An AI that only answers questions.

Orthogonality thesis: Intelligence and final goals are orthogonal: more or less any level of intelligence could in principle be combined with more or less any final goal.

Person-affecting perspective: The view that one should act in the best interests of everyone who already exists or who will exist independently of one's choices (cf. 'Impersonal perspective').

Perverse instantiation: An efficient way of satisfying an AI's goal that violates the intentions of the programmers who defined the goal criteria (e.g. achieving the goal "make humans smile" by paralyzing human facial muscles into perpetual grins).

Principle of differential technological development: Retard the development of dangerous and harmful technologies, especially ones that raise the level of existential risk; and accelerate the development of beneficial technologies, especially those that reduce the existential risks posed by nature or by other technologies.

Principle of epistemic deference: A future superintelligence occupies an epistemically superior vantage point: its beliefs are (probably, on most topics) more likely than ours to be true. We should therefore defer to the superintelligence's opinion whenever feasible.

Quality superintelligence: A system that is at least as fast as a human mind and vastly qualitatively smarter.

Recalcitrance: How difficult a system is to improve.

Recursive self-improvement: The process in which an AI (perhaps a seed AI) iteratively improves its own intelligence—using its increasing intelligence to apply increasingly strong optimization power to the task of cognitive self-enhancement.

Reinforcement learning approach to the control problem: An approach in which the AI learns to maximize some notion of cumulative reward (where the reward signal is specified or administered by humans in some way intended to induce appropriate behavior on the part of the AI).

Second principal–agent problem: The principal–agent problem confronting a human "principal" who wishes to design a superintelligent AI ("agent") to work on her behalf. Also referred to as "the control problem".

Seed AI: An AI of initially modest capabilities that can bootstrap into an impressive AI by improving its own architecture.

Singleton: A world order in which there is, at the highest level of decision-making, only one effective agency (though it internally might contain many factions and interests); that is, a condition in which all important global coordination problems are mostly solved. Possible examples include a world democracy, an unchallenged world dictator, or a superintelligent AI powerful enough to suppress any potential rivals.

Sovereign: An AI that acts autonomously in the world in pursuit of broad and possibly very long-range objectives.

Speed superintelligence: A system that can do all that a human intellect can do, but much faster.

State risk: A risk that comes from being in a certain state, such that the amount of risk is a direct function of the time spent there. For example, the state of not having the technology to defend against asteroid impacts carries risk proportional to the time we remain in that state.

Step risk: A risk that comes from making a transition. Here the amount of risk is not a simple function of how long the transition takes. For example, traversing a minefield is not safer if done more quickly.

Stunting: A control method that consists of limiting the AI's internal capabilities, such as by restricting the AI's access to information or engineering limitations to its cognitive faculties.

Superintelligence: Any intellect that greatly exceeds the cognitive performance of humans in virtually all domains of interest.

Takeoff: The transition from a condition in which there is only human-level machine intelligence to one in which there is radical superintelligence. It is often characterized by its speed: a "slow takeoff" takes decades or centuries, a "moderate takeoff" takes months or years, and a "fast takeoff" takes days or less.

Technological completion conjecture: If scientific and technological development efforts do not effectively cease, then all important basic capabilities that could be obtained through some possible technology will be obtained.

Technology coupling: A predictable timing relationship between two technologies, such that developing one of the technologies has a robust tendency to lead to the development of the other, either as a necessary precursor or as an obvious and irresistible application or subsequent step. For example, whole brain emulation is plausibly coupled to neuromorphic AI, because a more primitive version of the technology that would be required for the former might already enable the creation of brain-inspired AI (and there would be strong incentives to use the technology to do that).

Tool AI: An AI that is not "like an agent" but like a more flexible and capable version of contemporary software. In particular, it is not goal-directed.

Value learning: An approach to the value-loading problem in which the AI learns the values that humans want it to pursue.

Value-loading problem: The problem of causing the AI to pursue as final goals the values we want it to pursue.

The wise-singleton sustainability threshold: A capability set exceeds the wise-singleton threshold if and only if a patient and existential risk-savvy system with that capability set would, if it faced no intelligent opposition or competition, be able to colonize and re-engineer a large part of the accessible universe.

Whole brain emulation: Machine intelligence created by copying the computational structure of the human brain.

This glossary is included for convenience, although is neither complete (many distinctive terms and concepts introduced in the book are omitted) nor dispositive (the discussion in the main text should take precedence in cases where it is unclear how some notion is to be understood). (For preparing an earlier version of this, and allowing me to modify it, I'm grateful to Stephanie Zolayvar and Katja Grace of AI Impacts, Machine Intelligence Research Institute. The original version can be found at http://aiimpacts. org/ai-risk-terminology/.)

INDEX